ESCAPE

from

HONG KONG

Royal Asiatic Society Hong Kong Studies Series

Royal Asiatic Society Hong Kong Studies Series is designed to make widely available important contributions on the local history, culture and society of Hong Kong and the surrounding region. Generous support from the Sir Lindsay and Lady May Ride Memorial Fund makes it possible to publish a series of high-quality works that will be of lasting appeal and value to all, both scholars and informed general readers, who share a deeper interest in and enthusiasm for the area.

Other titles in RAS Hong Kong Studies Series:

Hong Kong Internment 1942–1945: Life in the Japanese Civilian Camp at Stanley
Geoffrey Charles Emerson

The Six-Day War of 1899: Hong Kong in the Age of Imperialism
Patrick H. Hase

Watching Over Hong Kong: Private Policing 1841–1941
Sheilah E. Hamilton

The Dragon and the Crown: Hong Kong Memoirs
Stanley S.K. Kwan with Nicole Kwan

East River Column: Hong Kong Guerillas in the Second World War and After
Chan Sui-jeung

Resist to the End: Hong Kong, 1941–1945
Charles Barman, edited by Ray Barman

Forgotten Souls: A Social History of the Hong Kong Cemetery
Patricia Lim

Ancestral Images: A Hong Kong Collection
Hugh Baker

Custom, Land, and Livelihood in Rural South China
Patrick H. Hase

Portugal, China & Macau Negotiations
Carmen Amado Mendes

Scottish Mandarin
Shiona Airlie

ESCAPE

from

HONG KONG

*Admiral Chan Chak's
Christmas Day Dash, 1941*

TIM LUARD

香港大學出版社
HONG KONG UNIVERSITY PRESS

Hong Kong University Press
The University of Hong Kong
Pokfulam Road
Hong Kong
www.hkupress.org

© Hong Kong University Press 2012

First published 2012
Reprinted 2012
First paperback edition 2014

ISBN 978-988-8083-76-3 *(Hardback)*
ISBN 978-988-8083-77-0 *(Paperback)*

British Library Cataloguing-in-Publication Data
A catalogue record for this book is available from the British Library.

10 9 8 7 6 5 4 3

Printed and bound by Liang Yu Printing Factory Ltd. in Hong Kong, China

To Ollie—and to Pop and the other heroes, who 'balanced all the risks against a fighting chance for freedom'.

—James Bertram, *Shadow of a War*

Contents

Illustrations

Photos are used by kind permission of their owners or their families.

Frontispiece (Page xx)
The escape group in Waichow, 30 Dec 1941 (Ted Ross)

Facing Page 160

Facing Page 208

Endpiece (Page 324)

Maps (Pages xxix–xxxii)

(Maps 1, 2, and 3 by Rachel Kesal. Map 4 by Lt Alexander Kennedy.)

Preface and Acknowledgements

On Christmas afternoon, 1941, as the exhausted defenders of Hong Kong surrendered to the Japanese, an unlikely group including China's top representative in the colony (a diminutive one-legged admiral), his aide-de-camp (a towering international athlete), a senior colonial civil servant and several British staff and intelligence officers made a last-minute dash to Aberdeen harbour.

They found an old launch, but came under heavy Japanese fire and threw themselves into the water. Two were killed, several were wounded—among them the admiral. But he and eleven others swam to a nearby island, hiding behind rocks as the shots rained down. On the other side of a hill they linked up with some fifty British sailors manning five small motor torpedo boats—all that remained of the Royal Navy in Hong Kong after eighteen days of fierce battle that had begun within hours of the raid on Pearl Harbor.

They sailed swiftly into the night, heading for the Chinese mainland and landing at dawn at Nanao in Mirs Bay. Guided by Chinese guerrillas, they made their way through Japanese lines. Walking for four days and nights across rough country frequented by bandits and enemy patrols, they arrived to a heroes' welcome in Waichow, held by the Chinese army.

The main naval party continued by river, road and rail all the way to Burma, finally reaching Britain after five months. The officers flew to Chungking to tell the world of the Fall of Hong Kong.

This dramatic break-out laid the foundations of an escape trail used jointly by the British Army Aid Group (BAAG) and Chinese guerrillas such as the East River Column to help inmates of the Japanese prison camps in Hong Kong reach freedom throughout the remaining four years of the war.

More than sixty British members of Chan Chak's escape party survived to pay tribute to the fortitude and leadership of the Admiral and the bravery and selflessness of the Chinese who helped them along their way. Seldom if ever before had the two races joined forces against a common enemy—and certainly not with a Chinese at the helm.

Several members of the escape party were honoured for their roles in both the battle and the escape—most notably, the Admiral himself, who received the rare honour for a Chinese of a British military knighthood. Sir Andrew Chan Chak went on to become Mayor of Canton and helped iron out differences between Britain and China at the time of the Japanese surrender. His friend and fellow escaper, David MacDougall, became Hong Kong's first postwar Colonial Secretary and Acting Governor. He was also awarded one of China's highest medals, the Order of the Brilliant Star.

After the war, two of the party* wrote books about their experiences—largely autobiographical in nature—and a few others wrote magazine articles. But the British servicemen had been warned not to reveal details of the escape, and the exact route was kept secret for many years. While all of those who took part would remember their adventure vividly for the rest of their lives, many preferred not to speak about it, even to their families.

Many of them did, however, leave diaries or letters, some of which only came to light when they died. One case in point is that of my father-in-law, Colin McEwan, who as a Hong Kong resident and member of Britain's Special Operations Executive helped organize and lead the escape. He was a sturdy, delightful man, with a twinkle forever in his eye—and a glass almost forever in his hand (with a pair of chopsticks as likely as not in the other). Sadly, he died soon after his daughter Alison and I were married in 1984. In due course we found his diaries and were intrigued to read about not just his exciting escape but also his later war years with the BAAG, working with Chinese guerrillas behind the Japanese lines.

Somehow, other things such as being a BBC radio journalist got in the way, and it was another twenty years before we managed to get the diaries published. Dr Dan Waters, former president of the Royal Asiatic Society, Hong Kong Branch, proved more than up to the task of editing them, and they duly appeared in the RAS Journal in 2005.

'We landed on a lovely beach and moved off up the valley.' For some reason, that one sentence lingered in my mind long after I read

---

Two of the party: Lt Alexander Kennedy wrote an excellent account of his escape and subsequent return to Hong Kong—'Hong Kong' Full Circle 1939–45—immediately after the war, but was unable to find a publisher. He finally brought it out privately in 1969, printing 500 copies, very few of which remain available. Captain Freddie Guest wrote a highly dramatized bestseller, Escape from the Bloodied Sun, published in 1956.

it. Where was that lovely beach? And where did the valley lead to? Obviously, the spot on the Chinese coast where they landed must have been just a few hours' journey by motor torpedo boat from Hong Kong. But like the others who had written about the escape, Colin was less than specific when it came to details such as Chinese place-names. Although he could get by in spoken Cantonese, there were many possible ways of romanizing Chinese characters. The names given to towns and villages in his and the other English accounts bore little resemblance either to one another or to anything to be found on a present-day map. Since my university degree had been in Chinese and I was by now no longer working full-time, I decided to do some research of my own.

After many a happy hour in the map room of the British Library and the old domed reading room of the Imperial War Museum, deciphering old military maps of China in tandem with assorted diaries and memoirs, I managed to trace more or less the precise route that the escape group had taken on their cross-country march. It was while transcribing her father's diaries that Alison had first had the idea that we should attempt to do the same journey ourselves, and this we now did.

Having no motor torpedo boats, we took a bus from Hong Kong to Nanao and then, just as they had done sixty-seven years earlier, set out up the valley on a bright, crisp Boxing Day morning. What had then been a remote region of paddy fields, rivers and hillside paths was now a booming industrial zone, thick with oil refineries, six-lane flyovers and even a nuclear power station. The wild bandit country the escape party walked through is on the edge of what has become the world's largest mega-city, consisting of Hong Kong, Shenzhen and Guangzhou, with a combined population of more than 120 million. What was surprising was how much of the old had somehow survived.

Nanao itself no longer had that romantic-sounding beach. But behind the reclaimed waterfront with its tall blocks of flats and garish hotels, there was still the original narrow street of simple tile-roofed houses. Further on, we found the temple where the Royal Navy had slept on the floor and the fortress where the guerrillas had their hideout. We were even able to tread the ancient stones of the over-grown smugglers' path over the mountain ridge where one young lieutenant had collapsed from exhaustion.

Accompanied by Francoise la Toison, a friend from our Hong Kong days of the 1970s, and Serene Qiu, our ever-cheerful Hakka-speaking fixer, we succeeded in walking most of the original eighty-mile route to Waichow, taking just the odd motorcycle taxi or bus when there was simply no other way forward across the vast and frenzied building site that is today's China. No one could believe that we actually wanted to walk—pointing us always to a main road in preference to a perfectly good path. One or two older people had heard tell of the one-legged admiral passing through during the war, but the number who could either remember those distant days or showed much interest in them was small.

Back home, however, interest was growing fast among descendants of the original party. Richard Hide, son of Petty Officer Buddy Hide, had set up a website from his Sussex home in 1997, beginning with a single page about his father. Before long he had linked up with Admiral Chan's twin sons, Donald and Duncan, who both lived in Hong Kong, and other families scattered around the world. The website grew apace and plans were made to get together and set up a formal association.

Soon after returning from our walk, in January 2009, we attended the inaugural meeting of what we decided to call the Hong Kong Escape Re-enactment Organisation (HERO). The meeting was held in the Kent home of David MacDougall's second daughter, Sheena, and was attended via Skype by members on three other continents. Just a few weeks later came news of the death in Taiwan of Henry Hsu, the Admiral's former ADC and HERO's honorary president, who at ninety-six is thought to have been the last surviving member of the original escape group. Despite the additional death later that year of Duncan Chan, the new association pressed on with plans to stage a series of commemorative events in Hong Kong and Guangdong Province that December.

Clearly, some form of official backing was going to be needed. Several letters of support were soon obtained from the British side, including one from the Duke of Edinburgh, who recalled his own attendance at the Japanese surrender and described the escape from Hong Kong as 'one of the most remarkable adventures of the war'. Persuading the Chinese to come on board was another matter.

Little has been published in the People's Republic of China about either Chan Chak—who was the Southern President of the ruling Kuomintang or Nationalist party—or his famous escape. In the early years of communist rule, even more than today, the focus was firmly on the future rather than the past. Commemorating the war against Japan was useful only as a means of fostering love for the motherland and the Red Army: it certainly didn't involve hailing the exploits of a Kuomintang admiral, his cooperation with a bunch of imperialist lackeys and the warm reception given to them all by the local peasantry.

But after many months of knocking on official doors, word finally arrived suggesting that this small and forgotten piece of China's long and glorious history had come in for reappraisal. The semi-official China Cultural Development Association received authorization from the Ministry of Foreign Affairs 'to support HERO in their objectives to commemorate the extraordinary episode of Sino-British joint action during World War II'—meaning we were now a recognized organization and could go ahead with our visit.

In the summer of 2009, the Chinese authorities appointed four committees of fifteen members each to research the history of the escape and make arrangements for HERO's proposed major re-enactment by the end of the year. An additional twelve government officials from Beijing were to liaise with the Guangdong provincial government, various mainland departments in Hong Kong and officials of the Chinese Guerrilla Association.

The version of the escape that the Chinese history committee came up with, however, bears little resemblance to the events detailed in the diaries and other first-hand source material. The role of Chan Chak and his Nationalist Party colleagues is mentioned in passing, but is made distinctly subservient to that of the Communists, who at the time were the Kuomintang's uneasy partners in what was supposed to be a united front against the Japanese invaders. The committee's report says instructions for organizing the escape came from none other than Zhou Enlai—already, in 1941, one of the Communist Party's top leaders. The communists are not mentioned at all in most other accounts. The official report says the escape route is 'being preserved' by the present government, although it gives few details of the route itself.

The HERO party which visited China that Christmas consisted of some eighty descendants, from fifteen different families and four generations. We were welcomed with the customary fanfare of speeches, receptions and banquets, though sadly we were not allowed to walk along the escape route for any distance this time, as it was considered 'too dangerous'. The elderly former guerrillas who were brought forward to meet us preferred to talk about the general wartime activities of the communist East River Column rather than the specific role played in this particular escape by the 'pirate-guerrilla' leader, Leung Wingyuen. But we did succeed in recreating the classic group photo taken of the escape party in front of the American Mission hospital—now the People's Hospital—in Waichow. We left with the firm conviction that the great Christmas Day Escape of seventy years ago had now been placed firmly back on the map.

This is the first book to attempt to provide a comprehensive history of the escape. Like the escape itself, its evolution has proved a long journey, with obstacles, meanderings and sudden breakthroughs along the way. Its completion has been made possible only by the kind assistance of a large number of people who have become part of the wider HERO family.

My deepest debt is to the original men of the escape and to their children, grandchildren and other relatives who have so generously shared their personal testimonies, whether in the form of letters, diaries, photographs or spoken reminiscences and anecdotes. My profound thanks to the families of Ronald Ashby, Leslie Barker, Edmund Brazel, Chan Chak, John Collingwood, Leonard Downey, Horace Gandy, Arthur Gee, Freddie Guest, Leslie Gurd, John Holt, Robert Hempenstall, Buddy Hide, Henry Hsu, Alexander Kennedy, David Legge, David MacDougall, Peter Macmillan, Colin McEwan, Chris Meadows, Albert Moore, Harry Owen-Hughes, Max Oxford, Tommy Parsons, Leonard Rann, Ted Ross, Jack Thorpe, Gilbert Thums and Yeung Chuen.

Of those, much extra credit should go specifically to Richard Hide, for putting so many of us in touch in the first place through his pioneering Hong Kong Escape website; to the late Donald Chan, whose death in July 2013 robbed the Hong Kong Escape Re-enactment Organisation of a powerful and charismatic President; Sheena Recaldin, Russell Joyce, Emma Oxford and the other leading lights of HERO for their inspiration and drive in actually bringing everyone together; and to Warwick Ross, Alick Kennedy and Vaughan Ashby for their special help to me with both text and illustrations.

For granting access to their collections and patient assistance in my research, thanks are due to Rod Suddaby and the trustees and staff of the Imperial War Museum; Frances Wood and her colleagues in the Asian and Map sections at the British Library; David Helliwell of the Bodleian Library; Lucy McCann of Rhodes House; and to Howard Davies, Paul Johnson and others at the National Archives at Kew.

In Hong Kong, thanks to Elizabeth Ride and Mo Ching Cheung for showing me the Ride Collection at Hong Kong University Library; to Bernard Hui at the Hong Kong Public Records Office. And to Rosa Yau, NK Wong and Samuel Tse of the Hong Kong Museum of Coastal

Defence, for their cooperation in staging the long-term exhibition, *Escape From Hong Kong*, which Alison and I put together in conjunction with our HERO colleagues in 2009.

For their invaluable assistance with translations, I am indebted to Carmela Wong, Alice Dowling and Yan Wei.

The following kindly sent me material, answered queries, offered introductions or gave other help or inspiration:

Gervais Ange, Wes Anson, Tony Banham, Solomon Bard, Tim Bentinck, Robert Bickers, Ken Borthwick, Bob Callow, SJ Chan, Chan Yinlun, Michael Cheng, Nelson Cheng, Peter Choi, Cong Weidong, Elaine Coyle, Peter Cunich, Rocky Dang, Robert Delaunay, Vaudine England, Paul French, John Gittings, Kieran Godwin, Tom Gorman, Tarquin Hall, Duncan Hewitt, Trevor Hollingsbee, Max Holroyd, Brian Holton, Jack Hughieson, Alf Hunt, Lorraine Jones, Ko Tim Keung, Bill Lake, Lung King Cheung, Pat Luxford, Anne Ozorio, Philip Snow, Peter Stuckey, Steve Tsang, Rusty Tsoi, Lawrence Tsui, Patrick van de Linde, Carola Vecchio, Donald Wagstaff, Dan Waters, Betty Wei, Larry Wong, Michael Wright, Crayon Yao and Kevin Zeng. I am indebted to all of them, though none share any responsibility for what follows.

For this second edition a number of minor amendments have been made. These reflect new information that has come to light since the publication of the original hardback edition two years ago. This has mainly been as a result of new contacts made with the families of the following members of the escape group, some of whom left previously undiscovered material: Bill Dyer, John Forster, William Robinson, Robert Stonell.

I am grateful to Chris Munn, Penny Yeung and their colleagues at Hong Kong University Press for guiding me forward and keeping me to deadlines.

And lastly, thanks to Colin and Betty McEwan's three wonderful daughters: to Meilan, for lending her house on the Isle of Arran; Rachel, for drawing the maps; and Alison, for everything.

The escape group in Waichow, where they were given a heroes' welcome at the end of their four-day march through Japanese lines.

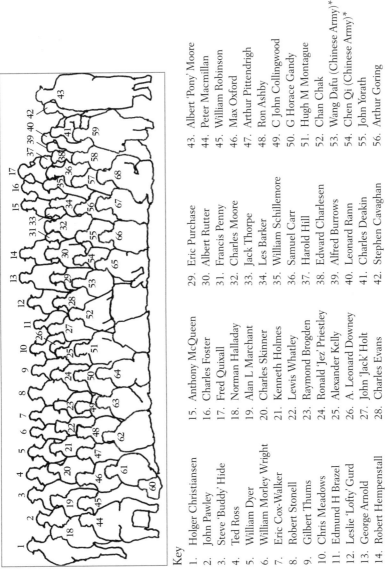

Key

1. Holger Christiansen
2. John Pawley
3. Steve 'Buddy' Hide
4. Ted Ross
5. William Dyer
6. William Morley Wright
7. Eric Cox-Walker
8. Robert Stonell
9. Gilbert Thums
10. Chris Meadows
11. Edmund H Brazel
12. Leslie 'Lofty' Gurd
13. George Arnold
14. Robert Hempenstall
15. Anthony McQueen
16. Charles Foster
17. Fred Quixall
18. Norman Halladay
19. Alan L Marchant
20. Charles Skinner
21. Kenneth Holmes
22. Lewis Whatley
23. Raymond Brogden
24. Ronald 'Jez' Priestley
25. Alexander Kelly
26. A. Leonard Downey
27. John 'Jack' Holt
28. Charles Evans
29. Eric Purchase
30. Albert Rutter
31. Francis Penny
32. Charles Moore
33. Jack Thorpe
34. Les Barker
35. William Schillemore
36. Samuel Carr
37. Harold Hill
38. Edward Charlesen
39. Alfred Burrows
40. Leonard Rann
41. Charles Deakin
42. Stephen Cavaghan
43. Albert 'Pony' Moore
44. Peter Macmillan
45. William Robinson
46. Max Oxford
47. Arthur Pittendrigh
48. Ron Ashby
49. C John Collingwood
50. G Horace Gandy
51. Hugh M Montague
52. Chan Chak
53. Wang Dafu (Chinese Army)*
54. Chen Qi (Chinese Army)*
55. John Yorath
56. Arthur Goring
57. Freddie Guest
58. Thomas Parsons
59. Alexander Kennedy
60. "Bruce"
61. Arthur Gee
62. Fu (Chinese Army)*
63. Au Yeung (?)*
64. Yeung Chuen
65. Hsu Heng 'Henry'
66. Tong (Chinese Army)*
67. David P Legge
68. Tommy Brewer

*Members of welcome party—not on escape.

Note: The following six members of the escape party also reached Waichow but were absent from the group photo: Mike Kendall, David MacDougall, Colin McEwan, Douglas Pethick, John Prest and Monia Talan.

Escape Party

Chinese Liaison Office

Chan Chak, Admiral; Southern President, Kuomintang
Hsu Heng (Henry), Flag Lieutenant Commander; Chan's aide-de-camp
Yeung Chuen, Chan's coxswain/bodyguard
Yee Shiu-Kee, Colonel; Chan's chief of staff (*remained on launch at Aberdeen; escaped separately*)

British Ministry of Information

David **MacDougall**, Head of Hong Kong Office
Ted **Ross**, Chief Assistant to Head

Fortress HQ and Intelligence

Arthur **Goring**, Major; Probyn's Horse (Indian Cavalry)
Freddie **Guest**, Captain; Middlesex Regiment
Peter **Macmillan**, Captain; Royal Artillery
Max **Oxford**, Squadron Leader; Royal Air Force
William **Robinson**, Superintendent; Indian Police

Special Operations Executive

FW (Mike) **Kendall**, Head of Z Force
Colin **McEwan**, Hong Kong Volunteer Defence Corps (Captain)
Monia **Talan**, Hong Kong Volunteer Defence Corps (Captain)

Motor Torpedo Boat Flotilla
MTB 07

Ron **Ashby**, Lieutenant, Hong Kong Royal Naval Volunteer Reserve
Arthur **Gee**, Acting Sub-Lieutenant, Hong Kong Royal Naval Volunteer Reserve
George **Arnold**, Able Seaman, Royal Navy

Charlie **Evans**, Leading Stoker, Royal Navy
Stephen (Buddy) **Hide**, Acting Petty Officer Stoker, Royal Navy
John **Pawley**, Able Seaman, Royal Navy
John (Jix) **Prest**, Petty Officer Coxswain, Royal Navy
Eric **Purchase**, Telegraphist, Royal Navy
Albert **Rutter**, Able Seaman, Royal Navy

MTB 09

Alexander **Kennedy**, Lieutenant, Royal Naval Volunteer Reserve
Tommy **Brewer**, Sub-Lieutenant, Hong Kong Royal Naval Volunteer
    Reserve
Charles **Foster**, Stoker, Royal Navy
Leslie (Lofty) **Gurd**, Able Seaman, Royal Navy
Robert **Hempenstall**, Able Seaman, Royal Navy
Harold **Hill**, Leading Telegraphist, Royal Navy
William **Schillemore**, Coxswain, Royal Navy
Francis **Penny**, Able Seaman, Royal Navy
Ronald (Jez) **Priestley**, Acting Petty Officer Stoker, Royal Navy

MTB 10

G Horace **Gandy**, Lieutenant Commander, Royal Navy (retired); Flotilla
    Senior Officer
Gilbert **Thums**, Chief Petty Officer/Acting First Lieutenant, Royal
    Navy
Raymond **Brogden**, Telegraphist, Royal Navy
Samuel **Carr**, Acting Petty Officer Stoker, Royal Navy
Edward **Charlesen**, Able Seaman, Royal Navy
A Leonard **Downey**, Able Seaman Stoker, Royal Navy
William **Dyer**, Petty Officer Coxswain, Royal Navy
Chris **Meadows**, Telegraphist, Royal Navy
Fred **Quixall**, Stoker, Royal Navy
Lewis **Whatley**, Able Seaman, Royal Navy

MTB 11

C John **Collingwood**, Lieutenant, Royal Navy
David P **Legge**, Acting Sub-Lieutenant, Hong Kong Royal Naval
    Volunteer Reserve
Les **Barker**, Leading Seaman, Royal Navy
Alfred **Burrows**, Acting Petty Officer, Royal Navy

Kenneth **Holmes**, Stoker, Royal Navy
Alexander **Kelly**, Able Seaman, Royal Navy
Anthony **McQueen**, Telegraphist, Royal Navy
Robert **Stonell**, Petty Officer Stoker, Royal Navy
Jack **Thorpe**, Able Seaman, Royal Navy

MTB 27

Thomas **Parsons**, Lieutenant, Hong Kong Royal Naval Volunteer
    Reserve
Charles **Moore**, Petty Officer Stoker, Royal Navy
Charles **Deakin**, Able Seaman, Royal Navy
Stephen **Cavaghan**, Leading Telegraphist, Royal Navy
John (Jack) **Holt**, Able Seaman, Royal Navy
Albert ('Pony') **Moore**, Leading Seaman, Royal Navy
Leonard **Rann**, Stoker, Royal Navy

Other Navy and Merchant Marine

1. Volunteer Crew on *Cornflower*'s launch

William Morley **Wright**, Warrant Officer, Hong Kong Royal Naval
    Volunteer Reserve
Holger **Christiansen**, Cadet/Midshipman, Indo-China Steamship
    Navigation
Alec **Damsgaard**, Captain; Store Nordisk (*remained in Hong Kong
    after being badly injured in attack on launch*)
JJ **Forster**, Sub-Lieutenant; Hong Kong Royal Naval Volunteer
    Reserve/Indo-China Steamship Navigation (*killed in attack on
    launch*)
D **Harley**, Second Engineer, SS *Yatshing* (*killed in attack on launch*)

2. Rowed in skiff to MTBs

Norman **Halladay**, Chief Engineer; Merchant Navy
John **Yorath**, Lieutenant Commander, Royal Navy (retired);
    Commodore's Staff

3. C 410 (Tugboat to Nanao)

Hugh M **Montague**, Commander, Royal Navy (retired); Senior Naval
    Officer, Aberdeen
Edmund H **Brazel**, Second Engineer, Jardines/Hong Kong Royal
    Naval Volunteer Reserve

Eric **Cox-Walker**, Seaman Gunner, Hong Kong Royal Naval Volunteer Reserve

Alan L **Marchant**, Second Officer, Merchant Navy/Hong Kong Volunteer Defence Corps

Douglas Stuart **Pethick**, Lieutenant, Royal Naval Reserve/Jardines Shipping

Arthur **Pittendrigh**, Lieutenant, Royal Naval Reserve/Chinese Maritime Customs

Charles **Skinner**, Chief Officer, Merchant Navy

Abbreviations

ADM	Admiralty
BAAG	British Army Aid Group
BBC	British Broadcasting Corporation
Cdr	Commander
CMG	Companion (of the order of) St Michael and St George
CNAC	China National Aviation Corporation
CO	Colonial Office
CPO	Chief Petty Officer
DSC	Distinguished Service Cross
FO	Foreign Office
GSO	General Staff Officer
HDML	Harbour Defence Motor Launch
HERO	Hong Kong Escape Re-enactment Organization
HKRNVR	Hong Kong Royal Naval Volunteer Reserve
HKVDC	Hong Kong Volunteer Defence Corps
IWM	Imperial War Museum
KMT	Kuomintang (Nationalist Party)
Lt	Lieutenant
ML	Motor Launch
MTB	Motor Torpedo Boat
PO	Petty Officer
PWD	Public Works Department
RA	Royal Artillery
RAF	Royal Air Force
RAS	Royal Asiatic Society
Retd	Retired
RN	Royal Navy
RNR	Royal Naval Reserve
RNVR	Royal Naval Volunteer Reserve
SOE	Special Operations Executive
WO	War Office
WRNS	Women's Royal Naval Service
XDO	Extended Defence Officer

Note on Chinese Names

Names of places in mainland China are generally given in their *putonghua* or Mandarin form, using the standard modern romanization (*pinyin*). Two main exceptions are Huizhou and Shaoguan. These two cities are referred to in almost all the diaries and other documents from the time as Waichow and Kukong, so I have thought it best to keep those names. Likewise, Chungking and Canton are used instead of the modern Chongqing and Guangzhou. Personal names are dealt with in a similar way, with Chiang Kai-shek, for example, being used in preference to Jiang Jieshi.

Hong Kong Chinese names are given in their usual Cantonese form. Where there have been changes over the years in the way a name is written—e.g. Lei Yue Mun for Lyemun—I have gone for the standard form used at the time.

A list of names with their Chinese characters can be found on page 297.

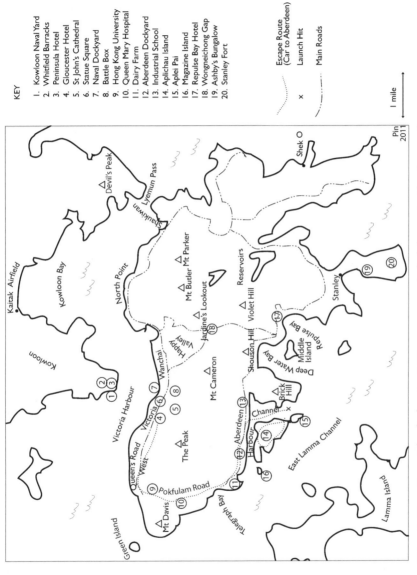

Map 1. Hong Kong Island, showing VIP escape group's dash by car to Aberdeen and brief launch journey

KEY

1. Kowloon Naval Yard
2. Whitfield Barracks
3. Peninsula Hotel
4. Gloucester Hotel
5. St John's Cathedral
6. Statue Square
7. Naval Dockyard
8. Battle Box
9. Hong Kong University
10. Queen Mary Hospital
11. Dairy Farm
12. Aberdeen Dockyard
13. Industrial School
14. Aplichau Island
15. Aplei Pai
16. Magazine Island
17. Repulse Bay Hotel
18. Wongneichong Gap
19. Ashby's Bungalow
20. Stanley Fort

.... Escape Route (Car to Aberdeen)

×   Launch Hit

—··—·· Main Roads

1 mile

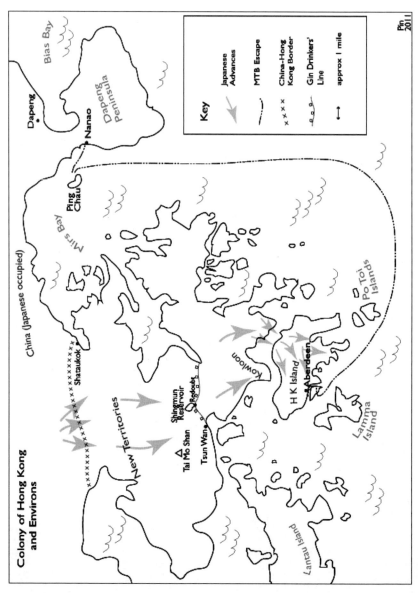

Map 2. Hong Kong and adjoining area of China, showing Japanese advances and route taken to Mirs Bay by the motor torpedo boats

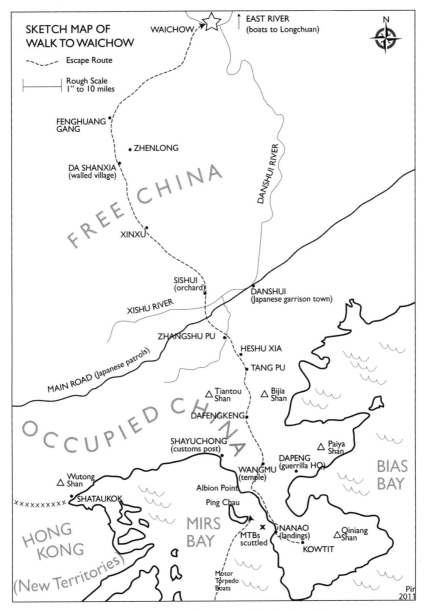

Map 3. March from Nanao to Waichow, 26–29 December 1941

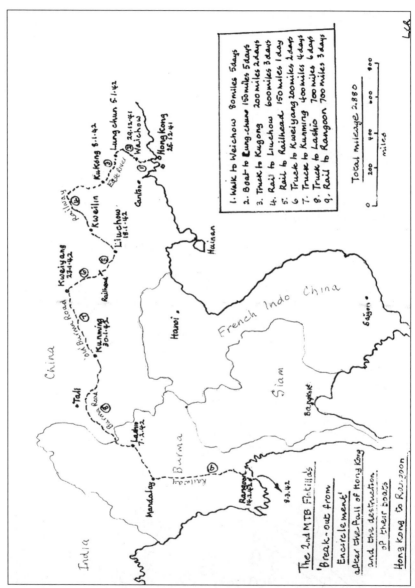

Map 4. Escape party's route from Hong Kong to Rangoon, drawn by Lt Alexander Kennedy, using distances as estimated at the time

Part One
The Invasion

1

Last Ship Out

7 December 1941

Lieutenant Alexander Kennedy drove eastwards along the coast of Hong Kong Island till he had left the city behind. Just before the beacon at Lyemun Pass, he parked his car—a sporty little Standard 9 saloon with sliding sunroof—and stood on the headland, gazing down at the entrance to one of the finest harbours in the world. Across the narrow blue strait, 500 yards away, Devil's Peak reared up from the mainland. Beyond it, a range of higher mountains—the 'nine dragons' that gave the Kowloon peninsula its Chinese name—rose dreamily in a grey-blue mist above the scattered villages and paddy fields of the New Territories. Just behind them, on the Chinese border, 20 miles from where he stood, the Imperial Nipponese Army was readying for attack.

The handsome, red-headed young Scot needed little reminding of just how close the Japanese were. He was commanding officer of a motor torpedo boat—one of a flotilla of MTBs that formed a major part of Hong Kong's token navy. On their patrols around the waters of the British colony, the unit's eight small boats had from time to time come across wrecked fishing junks which had been attacked by Japanese warships. These attacks were apparently meant to discourage Hong Kong people from smuggling war materials or other goods to their compatriots in China, who had been resisting Japanese aggression for years. Kennedy and his crew had also exchanged wary looks with Japanese soldiers stationed along the Chinese coast near Mirs Bay. It was his favourite part of Hong Kong, where the innumerable bays and inlets of crystal-clear water and the surrounding steep green hills reminded him of his sailing days back home.

Kennedy had joined the Clyde Division of the Royal Naval Volunteer Reserve (RNVR) as a midshipman in 1937, while still in his first year of a science tripos at Cambridge. He signed up partly to open an avenue of escape from his family's prosperous laundry and dyeing business in Glasgow, but mainly because of a visit to the 1936 Olympics. His parents—proud of their only child's excellent sporting and academic performance at one of Scotland's finest schools,

Loretto—had taken him to Berlin as a treat before he went up to university. The Games themselves had been well organized and spectacular, he later recalled. But the 'hysterical sieg heils' had come as a shock. As those around them leaped to their feet with right arms extended, the family from Kelvinside remained silently and defiantly seated.

After mobilization in August 1939, Kennedy was promptly dispatched to Hong Kong. Defending a small colony in South China against possible attack from Japan—a country Britain wasn't even at war with—didn't seem the most obvious way to stop Hitler, to either Kennedy himself or the rest of the colony's 10,000-strong British garrison. But his grandmother's parting words remained with him: 'Remember, Alick, always do your duty.'

As well as the regular troops—from Britain, India and Canada—there were locally recruited volunteers. While they may have been less well trained than the professionals, many of these were more motivated, since this was, temporarily at least, their home. Even so, there were few places available among their ranks (and still fewer at officer level) for the ethnic Chinese who formed the overwhelming majority of the population. On land, there was the Volunteer Defence Corps (VDC), up to 2,000 strong; at sea, the HKRNVR, or Hong Kong Royal Naval Volunteer Reserve, whose strength of just 300 at the outbreak of the war in Europe had now been brought up to 800. Almost all the dozen or so young officers in Kennedy's flotilla belonged to this local branch of his own 'Wavy Navy'.

In fact, the only one of them wearing the straight stripes of the regular Royal Navy was Kennedy's flatmate, John Collingwood, who had moved in just last month to share his spacious naval officers' bachelor flat on the upper floor of a two-storey building on the corner of Cameron and Nathan Roads. Aged twenty-eight—four years older than Kennedy—Collingwood was a fellow lieutenant who had come to Hong Kong two years previously as a gunnery officer, and was now second-in-command of the MTB flotilla. Some thought he might even have got the top job when it became available in April, 1941, but instead, the unit was now led by a crusty World War One veteran, Lieutenant Commander GH Gandy, RN (Retd). Fair-minded but set in his ways, Gandy was fond of his men but not afraid to berate them as 'fools and dolts' if they got their splicing or anchor work wrong. Many of the senior officers in Hong Kong's forces were men like him who had been brought out of retirement, since the few younger qualified men were needed in Europe and other parts of the world where their presence was considered more important.

The eight motor torpedo boats each had a lieutenant and a sub-lieutenant, and a crew of between eight and ten Royal Navy ratings. Twice a week, Kennedy and his men carried out dummy attacks on a tame and elderly British destroyer. Firing their 17-foot-long torpedoes from the cramped engine room was not easy. The water had to be the right depth, the MTB had to be accelerating, and to make things even more difficult, the torpedoes came out backwards from the stern of the boat. Hence the warning on the flotilla's flying-fish crest: *Caudae Spiculum Cave* (Beware the Sting in the Tail).

There was a tendency among other sailors to treat the 'glamour boys' of this branch of the navy with good-humoured tolerance: to scoff, for example, at their simple hand signals to turn right. But while they were hardly the most modern or formidable of craft, Hong Kong's MTBs were small and fast, like speedboats. With their 1500-horsepower engines and multiple Lewis machine guns mounted fore and aft, their officers and crews were confident that when the time came, they could at least put up a useful fight. Little did anyone know just how crucially useful these sleek 'Spitfires of the Sea' would soon become.

A steady stream of ships, mainly small merchantmen, was now coming from the harbour to Kennedy's left. A small gunboat towed away the end of the defensive net that had been stretched across the narrow strait to keep out submarines and torpedoes. One by one, the cargo ships passed through the boom and began to steam off into the distance. All of them were heading south—away from China and the approaching Japanese troops.

Japan had invaded the Chinese interior in 1937, after concluding that the puppet state it had previously set up to the north in Manchuria no longer satisfied its needs. Western countries had grabbed colonies and treaty ports from the no-longer-mighty Middle Kingdom, so why not an Asian power? Japanese troops soon captured the capital, Nanking, celebrating their victory by massacring hundreds of thousands of civilians and raping tens of thousands of women. The Nationalist Government of Chiang Kai-shek withdrew a thousand miles farther up the Yangtze to the ramshackle city of Chungking. The war then dragged on, with some five million Chinese soldiers confronting the invaders in a virtual stalemate along a 2,000-mile front. But there was no disputing the fact that the tiny country of Japan now controlled the north and much of the east and south of the world's most populous country—including almost all its key cities, ports and communication lines.

The refugees now slept in tens of thousands on Hong Kong's streets, a daily reminder of what was happening across the border. The population had doubled to 1.5 million since the fall of Canton in 1938. There were calls for Britain to take a tougher line with Japan, but the Foreign Office in London was unwilling to do anything that might increase the chances of a new war on yet another front. In many people's view, Japan would never dare take on Britain, let alone America too.

Kennedy wasn't sure, but he remained upbeat. A few weeks ago, on hearing news of some rare German reverses in Russia and the Middle East, he had written to his parents:

> Recent events should make the little Japs put their thinking caps on again and realise that perhaps after all their waiting . . . they're still in danger of backing the wrong horse. I think they'll hold their hand yet awhile, although after some of their recent belligerent speeches one feels itching to give them a damn good hiding.

The fact was, most of the colony's leading citizens were too preoccupied with money-making, sporting activities and dancing to bother much about any war, be it far away in Europe or on their own doorstep. At thirteen shillings a day, a naval lieutenant such as Kennedy couldn't be said to be making a huge amount of money, but even the most junior officers and the lowest level of white civilians such as clerks lived far better than they would at home. Among the luxuries they came to take for granted was to have at least one Chinese servant, or 'boy', to wait on them in his long white gown and even shave them in the morning. The ordinary British soldier was more likely to have a 'downhomer', or Chinese live-in girl—the going rate for providing all the comforts of home and more being ten shillings a month.

'Some Chinese girls can look remarkably attractive and many a soldier gets married to one,' Kennedy tells his parents in another of his letters, before adding the hasty rejoinder: 'the shortsightedness of such a policy is sometimes quite beyond the powers of their officers to explain to them.' He also admits that prostitution is a problem, complaining that 'one doesn't need to leave the street to be accosted'. He praises sport, on the other hand, because 'it gives men something to do and think about instead of going ashore to the less healthy haunts'. As flotilla sports officer, he not only played rugger himself—for the Navy, against teams such as the Hong Kong Club and, fiercest rival of all, the Army—but also organized everything from athletic leagues to inter-ship swimming relays.

After a morning of work and an afternoon of sport, the typical colonial day ended with cocktails, dinner and dancing. Kennedy himself was more likely to go out to the cinema. But his fellow MTB officer, Ron Ashby, whose wife had been evacuated to England, was a *bon viveur* who had recently helped him celebrate his twenty-fourth birthday at a lively dancing party in a nightclub. And it was noticeable that as war grew closer, some sectors of Hong Kong society had been partying ever more wildly, as in Rome before the Fall.

Kennedy took a letter from his pocket and read it, occasionally looking up to check on the vessels passing below, or simply to gaze into the distance. He would remember the view clearly years later.

It was at the Saint Andrew's Day Ball at the Peninsula Hotel in 1940 that he had danced for the first time with Rachel, a girl he had been introduced to a few months previously. Afterwards they had gone back to the MTB officers' mess, a place he later remembered fondly for its smell of camphor wood and the sounds from next door of clattering mah-jong tiles and high-pitched Chinese singing on the radio. But this was a moment for a tune on the pipes. His late-night bagpipe playing had recently drawn a complaint from a neighbour, the director of the Royal Hong Kong Observatory. But as the smitten Kennedy later recalled:

> Nobody cared that night, least of all myself, and I managed the difficult feat of playing the pipes walking along the mantelpiece without falling off. I saw Rachel home to the lovely house on the Peak where her father, Mr. N.L. Smith, the Colonial Secretary, lived, and this evening turned out to be the first of many wonderfully happy associations and memories shared against the background of Hong Kong.

Rachel was nineteen, small and dark-haired. She had recently returned to Hong Kong from art college in Bournemouth, and was now doing ciphering work for the VAD, or Voluntary Aid Detachment. Over the past twelve months the two of them had spent almost all their free time together. While Britain was enduring the darkest nights of the Blitz and letters from the Kennedy parents spoke of school-friends missing in action, they had lived each moment to the full—exploring the New Territories, swimming off remote beaches, or playing tennis in the garden of the house on Peak Road, against a backdrop of bays and islands stretching to the horizon on a broad expanse of blue. As Alick reflected later, those were happy but hardly carefree days: they could sense what was coming, yet never knew just 'when the balloon was going to go up, as it finally did in December, 1941'.

Rachel's father, Norman Lockhart Smith—or just 'NL'—had served as Acting Governor between the departure of the former Governor, Sir Geoffrey Northcote, and the arrival of the new one, Sir Mark Young.* As Colonial Secretary, he had also received the envoy from Tokyo, Saburo Kurusu, when the senior Japanese official passed through the colony in mid November en route for a final, ill-fated round of peace talks in Washington. But the official policy of getting on with the Japanese had its limits. When the chairman of the Royal Hong Kong Golf Club asked NL whether the club should admit Japan's Consul General as a member, he replied: 'Would *you* want to share *your* changing room with a Jap?'

Rachel's father was now about to retire. His wife (who had over-awed Alick when he first sat next to her at a dinner in Government House) had returned to Britain ahead of him, so his daughter was to accompany him home. Their departure on the Blue Funnel ship *Ulysses* had been put back until the week of Christmas due to damage the ship had suffered in a typhoon. The young couple had been looking forward to having the extra few weeks together, though the gathering war clouds made it an anxious time for all. They were surprised to find that the ship's passenger list was still far from full, which meant many were ignoring the government's advice that anyone able to leave should go.

Alick's letters home, meanwhile, had become increasingly full of Rachel—or Ray, as he called her. He was desperate for his parents to like her, assuring them: 'She's a grand girl with no nonsense about her.' Such a grand girl that on Monday, 24 November 1941, he asked Ray to marry him. His proposal was gladly accepted and the couple celebrated at the Gloucester Hotel with the most expensive cham-pagne they could find. Rachel wrote home to her mother that it would be heartbreaking to leave Alick, but it would be good for her to be able to meet 'his people', and since he had already done two and a half years in Hong Kong he would surely be home soon.

Sir Mark Young: A former governor of Tanganyika, Young was not overimpressed by his deputy in the weeks after arriving in Hong Kong. In a letter to a colleague in London he described NL as 'charming but exasperating' and 'ineffectual'. The word 'flibbertigibbet', he decided, summed him up well. During an earlier period as acting governor in August 1940, Smith was replaced by a general on the advice of local military commanders, who thought he was not decisive or organized enough in the face of a possible military threat from Japan.

A large Blue Funnel passenger ship was now making its way up the harbour towards the boom. Kennedy strained to pick out the figures on deck who were leaning over the railing to get their last look at Hong Kong. He even convinced himself he could see a tiny Ray, waving at him. Farther up the hill behind him, the big guns of the Pak Sha Wan Battery, manned by the 4th Battery of the Hong Kong Volunteer Defence Corps (HKVDC), looked stolidly back across the strait.

The night before—Saturday, 6 December—there had been another dance at The Peninsula, the Tin Hat Ball, to raise funds to build bombers to defend Britain against Germany. There were prizes for 'the most original and humorous costumes'. But the most smartly turned out were the young naval officers, the gold braid on their dress uniforms a perfect complement for the cream and gold lobby with its long line of chandeliers and pillars, palms and ornamental gilt. The 600 guests included the Governor and the man in charge of Hong Kong's defence, Major General CM Maltby. Soon after 11 p.m., the orchestra was halted in mid flow by a man on the balcony waving a megaphone for silence: 'Would all naval personnel, including merchant service personnel, return to their ships immediately,' he announced. Passengers for the *Ulysses* were told they didn't have until Christmas after all—they would be leaving within twelve hours.

Kennedy had offered to see Rachel and her father onto the ship, since he himself was not on duty until later that night. According to his diary, he woke at 5.45 a.m. and made his way across the harbour and up to 297 The Peak. He helped Ray finish her packing, and then accompanied her and her father down to Queen's Pier. At 8.30 a.m., the three of them took a launch out to the ship. The *Ulysses* was just securing to a buoy, her repairs barely complete. On board, NL shuffled his feet as his daughter and prospective son-in-law had a few last precious minutes together. Amid all the leave-taking and raising of anchors, one coaster had just arrived, carrying among its few passengers the Colonial Secretary's successor, FC Gimson. Like almost every other British citizen in Hong Kong, he was about to spend the next three and a half years in an internment camp.

Before driving out to wave his final farewell from the Lyemun headland, Kennedy had returned to Kowloon for a quick lunch at his flat. The radio news was announcing the mobilization of all Volunteers. Regular troops had been on alert for weeks, but this was the most serious sign yet that Hong Kong's war was about to commence. General Maltby had been summoned from the morning's service at St John's Cathedral, where he was reading the lesson from

St Matthew, to be told there were now as many as 20,000 troops from the Japanese 23rd Army moving up to the border. It was just a few months since Maltby—a lightly built man with greying hair and a trim moustache—had arrived in the colony as the new General Officer Commanding, Hong Kong. His thirty years in the Indian Army had taught him plenty, but hadn't prepared him for defending a small, isolated island, with neither armour, sea nor air cover, against a battle-hardened and numerically superior enemy. He gave orders for the entire garrison to stand-to in their battle positions.

The *Ulysses*—the last passenger ship to leave—was now starting to clear the boom defences. 'Read Ray's letter—watched ship' was as much as Kennedy had to say in his diary. But in the book he later wrote about his escape, he admitted he was torn between relief that Rachel had got away, sorrow at losing her and worry that she might still be too late to reach safety. There were reports of a Japanese armada steaming into the Gulf of Siam. The *Ulysses* was bound first for Manila, and would be at risk for several days from bombers in mid ocean. He watched the ship go, trailing a plume of brown smoke and a long white wake like the train of a bride's dress.

Kennedy's engagement to Rachel was still not public knowledge. They had agreed that he would place a notice in the papers the following day. But he had at least managed to write home to Scotland about it. His closely written, 16-page letter would be leaving on tomorrow's flight of the Clipper—the large Pan Am flying boat that was even now sitting by the jetty at Kai Tak Airport, ready for its 8 a.m. take-off.

He drove back into town, past the barbed wire entanglements along the waterfront and the half-frightened faces of bankers and teachers and other Volunteers, heading for the hills in their tin hats and clattering boots. The harbour looked eerily empty, apart from the occasional familiar green-and-white Star Ferry and criss-crossing sampan.

Maybe the announcement—and even the wedding itself—would have to wait a little longer than they had hoped. But at least he had a better reason than ever for ensuring he survived the coming battle—and got away afterwards. If it did come down to making a quick exit, the men in the flotilla knew a motor torpedo boat would be the best thing you could have in a place almost entirely surrounded, as Hong Kong was, by sea.

When he reported in as night duty officer at the MTB base that evening, Kennedy took with him many of his most treasured small possessions, including Rachel's letters, some photos and cufflinks. To his later regret, he left behind his sword and bagpipes.

It was a five-minute walk to the Kowloon Naval Yard along Haiphong Road, full of the usual raucous shouts, overpowering smells and vibrant colours at hawkers' stalls selling everything from cotton shirts to curried squid. Whitfield Barracks lay silent. The Indian troops usually on parade there with their brass bands, turbans and other emblems of imperial glory were now crouching in their darkened dugouts in the New Territories alongside the Royal Scots, who made up the other half of the Mainland Brigade. Hong Kong Island was in the hands of the 1st Middlesex and two battalions of Canadians, last-minute additions to the garrison.

All seemed in order at the naval yard, with the usual boats out on patrol. Each one was known by its number. *MTB 07* had just left its berth (or 'slipped camber' as the skipper, Ron Ashby, wrote in his immaculate logbook) and was heading off to mount overnight guard at the harbour boom. Also not due back till morning were John Collingwood and his crew on *11*, out west patrolling the mouth of the Pearl River, and Tommy Parsons on *27*, up in Mirs Bay. Kennedy did his rounds of the base and turned in well before midnight on his own boat, *MTB 09*. He felt an 'underlying current of restlessness and tension'.

It was still dark, at 5.50 a.m., when his torpedo rating, Bobby Hempenstall, came down the ladder from the wheelhouse with a signal from the Commodore ordering all ships to raise steam. Forty minutes later came another, more explicit order: 'COMMENCE HOSTILITIES AGAINST JAPAN.'

But as the warm glow of dawn turned to a brilliantly clear, cool day, it was Japan that struck first. Just before 8 a.m., more than forty warplanes appeared from over the Kowloon hills and headed for Kai Tak. A few minutes later, the small group of stick-insect-like aircraft lying carelessly dispersed about the aerodrome had gone up in flames. The three obsolete Wildebeeste divebombers and two Walrus amphibians that comprised Hong Kong's entire air force were put out of action with scarcely a shot fired in their defence. Eight civil aircraft were also burnt out—including the graceful Clipper, which had been about to take off with its cargo of mail.

The battle had begun.

2
One-Legged Admiral

8 December

Hong Kong's natural shape—almost like that of a theatre, with the harbour as its stage—ensured that almost everyone could catch at least a glimpse of the war's spectacular opening act. As ever, those in the Mid-Levels and on the Peak had the best seats in the house, gazing over their balcony rails at a sky speckled with swooping warplanes. Many thought it must be a training exercise, till they looked again and saw the coils of smoke rising from the airport. Even then, they couldn't quite believe it was real. Everything else seemed so normal. As one expatriate described the scene, 'sampans and junks crowded the harbour and all around Chinese were about their usual business. Coolies returned from market with their string bundles and I saw amahs hanging out washing in nearby gardens.'

For Admiral Chan Chak, it was more of a ringside view—of a very one-sided fight. He had left his home in a quiet Kowloon suburb soon after 7 a.m. and was crossing over to the island on a ferry as the raid began. From mid harbour, the red discs of the Rising Sun on the wings of the fighters, the roar of their twin cannons, the splashes in the water around him, the angry thuds of the exploding bombs and the desultory crackle of the ineffective anti-aircraft guns were all only too real.

He had seen it all before in China. And he had been expecting it here in Hong Kong, long before being woken by the telephone earlier that morning with the news that Tokyo had announced the start of hostilities against American and British forces. The Japanese-language broadcast had been monitored at 4.45 a.m. by the British Army's chief intelligence officer in the colony, Major Charles Boxer. Further calls told Admiral Chan of bombing raids on Malaya and Manila—and on the US fleet in Pearl Harbor in Hawaii.

He had been on the phone almost ever since, talking both to Fortress HQ and to his own military intelligence colleagues in the Chinese capital, Chungking. He had also been busy contacting some of the many mainland Chinese now based in Hong Kong who would be in grave danger were the Japanese to capture the British colony.

But no one was higher on Japan's blacklist than Chan Chak himself.

'A tough little fellow with a wooden leg and a body that had been battered in every war and dust-up since the Revolution' was how one Old China Hand in Hong Kong at the time described him. The republican revolution of 1911, which Chan had supported as a radical sixteen-year-old naval college student, marked the end of two thousand years of imperial rule. But it also introduced a new period of no rule at all, when the only power was in the hands of city gangsters and provincial warlords, each with his own army roaming the poverty-stricken countryside. It was a time when just to survive—let alone build up a national navy, as Chan was trying to do by the early 1920s—required toughness and even ruthlessness. 'Shoot first, report later' became one of his mottoes.

Soon he was virtually a warlord himself, but one whose army was based on ships rather than on land. He had built up a political base in Canton, while remaining fiercely loyal to his friend and patron, Dr Sun Yat-sen, the father of the revolution and leader of the Nationalist Party, or Kuomintang (KMT). It was Sun who had given Chan his nickname *Chak Suk*, or 'Uncle Chak', using a Chinese character meaning 'strategy' on account of the Admiral's lifelong gift for getting out of tight situations. Chan was credited with having saved the lives of both Sun and his successor, Chiang Kai-shek, in 1922, when he rescued them both by boat from a rival whose troops had hemmed them in.

After Sun Yat-sen's death in 1924, Chiang, having swiftly seized power as President and Generalissimo, rewarded Chan by giving him what amounted to his own fiefdom along the South China coast. It was a loose arrangement involving many well-placed connections and unspecified 'rights'. But the two men were never close, Chan believing Chiang Kai-shek had betrayed Dr Sun's democratic ideals. The Generalissimo switched his attention to fighting the rising Communist movement, while Chan—as head of the Guangdong (Cantonese) Navy in the early 1930s—soon turned to fighting the invading Japanese. He was acclaimed as the 'Hero of the Bocca Tigris' when, as commander of the old Tiger Gate fort at the mouth of the Pearl River, he repelled Japanese advances on Canton in 1937 and 1938. During the siege he received a small wound in his left foot and after this got worse, leading to a blood sclerosis, he was treated at St Theresa's Hospital in Hong Kong, where his leg was amputated. In its place, he received an artificial leg, its lower half made of wood and the upper section hand-made out of a light metal sheet similar to aluminium.

By early 1940, while Chan Chak was still recovering from his operation and learning how to use his new leg (he was already taking his wife to nightclubs by the spring), he had taken up an unprecedented position as the Chinese government's political and military representative in Hong Kong. Since China's ruling party, the Kuomintang, was banned in the British colony, he set up a small stockbroking company as cover for his additional role as head of the party's vast underground network. The firm was called Wah Kee Hong. Its office was on the second floor of the Asiatic Petroleum Company Building, otherwise known as Shell House, in Queen's Road Central. He had an additional, more private office on the fourth floor of Pedder Building, just across the street.

For the past two years Chan had been busy carrying out undercover work against Japan and trying to ensure, through means both legal and illegal, that China remained supplied with fuel and other essential materials despite the Japanese trade embargo. He had also been liaising with colonial police and intelligence officials in a way that the British and Chinese had never been close enough to even attempt to do before.

Now aged forty-six, 'Uncle Chak' was as energetic and forceful a figure as ever, even if he no longer had the ability—or the navy—to go bounding about the decks of battleships. He was short, even for a Chinese, but sturdily built, with a round, youthful face, a defiantly jutting jaw and sparkling eyes that bored into you 'like dark streaks of light'. His enthusiasm, charm and monkey-like sense of mischief won over all who met him. Foreigners became especially endeared to his quaint use of the English language, which included such stirring exhortations as 'Only big storm can test ship' and 'No worry! I tell you how we fix—then we go!'

The Admiral also had a more vulnerable, sensitive streak that was perhaps surprising for one schooled in so rough an environment. One day he was asked by a Hong Kong official: 'If the Pacific War breaks out and Hong Kong is involved, will the Nationalist Government send someone else to be their military representative?' There was probably no bad intention behind the question, according to the noted Chinese historian who related this incident, 'but it made Chan very unhappy because he felt looked down on—due to his qualifications, ability and more especially his disability. So he swore to himself he would make great contributions should there be a war.'

Now the war was here and the Admiral was on his way to see General Maltby. Travelling with him across the harbour were his two chief aides, SK Yee and Henry Hsu. They had picked him up earlier at his home in Prince Edward Road, and he had told them about the raid on Pearl Harbor and the other attacks. As the enemy planes headed back to their bases near Canton, they discussed what it all meant. It was good news, without a doubt, that they would finally have the Americans and British fighting alongside them against those 'piratical dwarfs', as the Chinese liked to call their hated neighbours just across the sea. But Britain and China were more used to fighting against each other than to being allies. As the boat reached the pier, reversing its propellers in a whirling of water and foam, they wondered how the two sides would get on.

Colonel Yee, or just 'SK', was Chan's chief of staff and head of intelligence. He also helped run a network of agents—most of them northern Triad members—for China's notorious grand spymaster, Dai Li, who organized the KMT's terrorist activities against left-wingers and other internal enemies. Dai Li was said to hate the British after being arrested the previous autumn on arrival at Kai Tak Airport. Yee, on the other hand, mixed well in almost any circle. At thirty-seven, he was powerfully built and immaculately dressed, spoke excellent, accentless English and was as good at calligraphy (he had recently lectured on the subject at the Maryknoll Mission) as he was at killing, when he had to, in cold blood. As his cover, he posed as an insurance salesman from Shanghai.

Henry Hsu Heng—or Henry for short—was the Admiral's aide-de-camp. Like Chan, he was a product of the prestigious Whampoa Naval Academy in Canton. As a lieutenant commander, he had an impressive-sounding rank for someone still in his twenties. But just as Chan was now an admiral without a fleet, his ADC was a commander without a ship: there simply weren't enough in the Chinese Navy to go round. At six-foot-three, he could at least claim to be the navy's tallest man (more than a foot taller than his boss). A staunch Christian, Henry was fresh-faced, clean-living and highly competent at everything from running an office to driving a car—not yet a common skill. He had also won gold medals at the Far East Games in Tokyo and Manila for volleyball and football, and was the current Hong Kong freestyle swimming champion.

There was one other member of the party, Yeung Chuen, who always went everywhere that Chan Chak went. He had formerly been a rickshaw puller on the streets of Canton. One day after giving a ride to the Admiral, he noticed his passenger had left behind a briefcase containing a large sum of money and waited patiently for several hours to return it. Impressed by his honesty, Chan engaged him as his own private rickshaw puller. Despite his frail-looking physique, Yeung was a skilled *kungfu* fighter and had now become the Admiral's personal bodyguard and general assistant. His official job title was coxswain.

Once on the island, the Chinese group picked up a very senior army intelligence officer who was visiting from Chungking, General Zheng Jiemin, and drove the short distance up the hill to Fortress HQ. Admiral Chan and General Zheng were escorted past a series of sentries to see the commander of the British forces. General Maltby had taken up his position in the Battle Box—an elaborate, reinforced concrete dugout fifty feet below Victoria Barracks—at five o'clock that morning. He was not unduly worried about the planes lost in the subsequent air raid, since he hadn't in any case planned to use the ancient torpedo bombers against Japan's modern fighters. But he had just heard that thousands of enemy soldiers were now pouring across the border.

The destruction of bridges and other facilities that might help their advance through the New Territories had already begun. The plan was to hold the main line of defence across the middle of the Kowloon peninsula—the 11-mile-long series of pillboxes known as the Gin Drinkers' Line*—for as long as possible and then withdraw to the island. Sufficient rice and other supplies had been stockpiled for 130 days. By that time, or so it was hoped, the besieged garrison would have been relieved by an American or British fleet . . . or even by a Chinese army.

Privately, the General knew the first two of these three possible sources of help had already been made less likely by the latest news from around the region. Much of the US fleet in Pearl Harbor had been destroyed, while the landings in Malaya meant he could expect no help either from Britain's main regional base in Singapore. The Far East Command had now gone so far as to order the withdrawal to Singapore of two of the three destroyers that formed the bulk of his own naval force in Hong Kong. The two ships would sail out this evening, leaving just HMS *Thracian*, four old 'Canton River' gunboats and the 2nd MTB Flotilla.

Winston Churchill himself had said there was 'not the slightest chance of holding Hong Kong or relieving it'. Yet Maltby and his men

---

Gin Drinkers' Line: so called because it began at Gin Drinkers' Bay, a favoured picnic spot for weekend sailing parties. But even along the lightly held defensive line itself, alcohol was very much part of life for the British troops.

were expected to defend it for as long as possible. The colony's many outlying islands and long coastline made it particularly vulnerable to a naval attack, and its defences had been set up with this in mind. The main artillery consisted of huge coastal guns, most of which could only point southwards out to sea. As for land borders, there was just the one, to the north. Hong Kong was hundreds of miles away from everywhere except China—to which it was attached like a flea on the back of a very large and unpredictable elephant.

Now celebrating its 100th year since having been won in a war over the right to sell opium, the colony had from the start been more trading port than military base. It was the China Coast merchants who had always called the shots. But Hong Kong had prospered thanks to not only the efforts of the British *taipans*, but also the enterprise and industry of the Chinese who made up 99 per cent of the population. They had arrived seeking new opportunities or just a haven from hunger, oppression or war. The loyalty of at least the more recent arrivals at a time of war in Hong Kong was an unknown factor, presenting the military planners with a severe problem.

In spite of his many other concerns that morning, General Maltby therefore had good reason to be pleased that China's senior representative in the colony and a top military officer from Chungking had come to see him. Having outlined his battle plan, he was even happier to hear them pledge China's support—and to learn of Chan Chak's determination to stay behind and rally the local community. The Nationalist Government might well have been tempted to withdraw such a senior figure to the safety of Chungking before the colony became cut off—if not for the Admiral's own sake, then to protect his fund of highly sensitive information. Other individuals would surely have taken the chance to get out while they could, and left the British to sink or swim. But the doughty little Admiral seemed positively enthusiastic about the idea of standing and fighting alongside them.

Not that the two Chinese visitors had any illusions about Hong Kong's chances. They had gone to meet the Governor and the General just a week ago and been taken on a tour of the colony's defences. In Zheng's view, Britain's troops in the Far East were militarily mismanaged. After years of colonial garrison duty, they had become soft and had lost 'the willingness to fight'.

Chan Chak, by contrast, had always admired the British and was prepared to give them the benefit of the doubt. As a small child, he had been taken from his home village on the southern Chinese island of Hainan to live in Singapore, which had been under British rule since the 1820s. There, his father had begun his rise from trishaw driver to wealthy merchant. It was another British colony, Hong Kong, that had provided him with a welcome sanctuary a few years later, when the republican revolution faltered in 1912. He had continued to be a frequent visitor to both Hong Kong and the nearby Portuguese colony of Macao, where he kept a residence in Rua S. Lourence and married Leung Shuichi, the daughter of a wealthy Chinese-Filipino, in 1924.

After the seventeen-day battle for Hong Kong was over, the Admiral's verdict would be that the British had fought 'gallantly and steadily against the odds'. But he also made the point that the colony's forces were simply 'not equipped for modern warfare'. As well as lacking an air force and navy, tanks and mortars, they had little or no coordination between different units, he said, and the individual soldiers were hampered by their heavy boots, packs and other old-fashioned gear.

At the same time Chan was only too aware that China's own troops often had to get by with no boots at all, their equipment carried across a coolie's shoulders on either end of a bamboo pole. On a recent visit to the front line in Guangdong, the American writer Ernest Hemingway had found soldiers going barefoot and generals more interested in hosting drunken banquets than fighting the Japanese. The Admiral must have privately doubted if a Chinese army would in fact ever reach Hong Kong. Nevertheless, Chungking had been offering for at least two years to send troops when the time came. The British had been hesitant. Many saw no need for it, so confident were they of Western superiority. Charles Boxer, the intelligence officer, had said it was a 'widespread delusion' that the Chinese could or would be of the slightest assistance against Japan. Others feared the Chinese might just carry on and take the colony back for themselves.

But now Maltby knew he needed all the help he could get. The meeting ended with two agreements: a British liaison officer would go to Chungking immediately to arrange for the sending of a relief army, while Chan himself would remain to play a leading role in Hong Kong's civil defence. He would step up his liaison group's links with the police to help them round up pro-Japanese fifth columnists. At the same time he would mobilize the local population to help maintain order and keep vital services going in the rear 'so that British troops could fight at the front, free from any worry'.

Outside, another bombing raid was going on, this time on the Kowloon dockyard. Fortunately, the motor torpedo boat flotilla had moved to its new base at Aberdeen. But it was now becoming dangerous to go anywhere, and all ferries and other public transport services were about to stop running. With Japanese troops already making rapid progress across the New Territories, Kowloon was not going to be the safest place to be, so Chan decided to move across with his family that same day to stay with Henry Hsu and his wife on Hong Kong Island. The Admiral had nine children, the four eldest of whom (all girls) were away at school in Shanghai—leaving two seven-year-old twin sons and the three youngest daughters with their parents in Hong Kong.

As the fear of entrapment spread, there was a rush to the airport to see if there was any way out before the last line of escape was cut off. The morning's raid had left a mass of craters in the runway as well as destroying the planes parked there. But after dark, a handful of American pilots—accustomed to braving the Japanese blockade of Chungking, the most heavily bombed city in the world to date— somehow landed their China Airlines planes on what was left of Kai Tak's landing strip, offering the chance of a final few flights out to Free China.

Making his way confidently through the throng of desperate passengers in the terminal building was a very tall figure wearing the uniform of a lieutenant colonel in the Hong Kong Volunteer Defence Corps. Harry Owen-Hughes, head of an old family import-export firm and a leading local cricketer, had a specially reserved seat on the last plane that night to Chungking. As someone who knew the Chinese and their language and whose parents had been living in the colony for more than forty years, he had been picked as the man to persuade Chiang Kai-shek and his generals to send an army as soon as possible to save Hong Kong.

'I created quite a stir at Kai Tak which had never before seen a colonel in full warpaint complete with a Battlebowler (steel helmet), Box Respirator (gas mask) and loaded revolver,' Owen-Hughes recalled later. At midnight he received an urgent message from Major Boxer asking that room be found on the plane for General Zheng, who was apparently not as keen as his colleague, the Admiral, to stay and help defend Hong Kong. A wealthy Chinese lady was persuaded to give up her seat for him. General Zheng was dropped off outside the airport by SK Yee. 'He has stuck to me like a leech from moment I brought him into Kai Tak,' wrote Owen-Hughes in his diary. At 2 a.m. the two men boarded CNAC flight no. 47. As their DC-3 turned to the north over an unusually somber Hong Kong harbour and headed for the Chinese interior, they looked down and saw the lights of the Japanese fleet shining bright across Mirs Bay.

3

Men from the Ministry

11 December

Now there were no more flights out: the gates had closed. No more boats out either, the boom firmly locked. But the Japanese didn't need to come in by sea. On land, the lightly equipped soldiers in their rubber-soled, split-toed canvas shoes crossed the New Territories faster than anyone had thought possible. Moving by night on mountain paths, they took the Shingmun Redoubt—the key point in the Gin Drinkers' Line—by catching its few Royal Scots defenders napping inside their pillboxes and dropping hand grenades down the air shafts. Only three days after crossing the border, they were now coming up out of the nullahs*on the edge of urban Kowloon. Plain-clothed Japanese agents mingled on the streets with Chinese rioters armed with staves and axes, as the British Mainland Brigade prepared to beat a retreat across the harbour in a hastily assembled fleet of Star Ferries, sampans and motor torpedo boats.

Nor had there been any let-up in the attack from the air, now focused firmly on Hong Kong Island. The principal targets were the big guns on the commanding heights; the fishing village of Aberdeen, where the motor torpedo boats were now quartered; and a few key military sites along the built-up northern shore, such as the main naval yard (on the site of today's Admiralty). After years of unfettered spying, the Japanese could pinpoint the location of every last pillbox. And they soon proved there was nothing wrong with either their eyesight or their flying skills, whatever the defending troops may have been told beforehand to the contrary.*

David MacDougall left his flat in Barker Road and drove to work, skirting the worst of the shell holes and debris along Magazine Gap

---

nullahs: local name for the storm-water drains that run down from many of Hong Kong's hills.

to the contrary: Senior British officers had assured their men that the Japanese were too short-sighted to make good pilots or to be able to aim their bombs with any accuracy. Soon after the successful airport raid a rumour spread that the planes must have been flown by Germans.

Road. In more peaceful times, he might have taken the Peak Tram, or even walked all the way down to Central along leafy Chatham Path. But he had recently, in his mid thirties, bought his first car—and he had plenty to do before his 9 a.m. appointment with Chan Chak. The Admiral had wasted no time in setting up a daily meeting to exchange information. Apart from Chan himself, these meetings were attended by Charles Boxer, on behalf of the British military, and MacDougall, representing the colonial government.

He and Chan already knew each other. They had met more than ten years previously, when MacDougall was in China for the second half of a two-year Cantonese course. They had played tennis and had later arranged matches between teams from Hong Kong and Canton. Alternating each weekend between the two cities, these were the sort of tennis matches that ended up as drinking parties. The two men had become close friends at a time when relationships between any British and Chinese, let alone senior officials, were rare.

MacDougall also wanted to get a telegram out to his wife, Catherine, while he still could. She and their small daughter Ann were in Vancouver. They had gone there from Scotland, hoping to come on to Hong Kong, but he had insisted it was too dangerous and they should wait. He decided to keep his message short and upbeat. 'All well here,' it read. 'Don't worry. Much love both. MacDougall.'

He and Cathie had met soon after he had first come east in 1928, inspired by the novels of Joseph Conrad. He had joined the colonial service as a cadet and was soon settling rural land cases as District Officer South. It was a job he later recalled in lyrical terms:

> Get up in the morning, not a cloud in sight. Launch waiting for me at Queen's Pier . . . I'd tour the islands on a beautiful blue warm sea . . . They'd meet us at the pier at Lantau . . . whisky and lemonade. I'd say any cases? They'd say a few; to the village hall, settle the case; then off to Cheung Chau . . . Three gorgeous years. It was out of this world; nothing was ever like that again.

In 1939, with Britain at war, MacDougall became Secretary of the Far Eastern Bureau of the Ministry of Information. He found colonial officials harder going than village elders. They were 'pig-headed provincials, with whom intelligent cooperation is impossible,' he told his wife bluntly. 'We cannot combat the Germans, Italians and the Hong Kong Government all at the same time.'

Determined to stand up to the Japanese, he had made several visits to Chungking for talks with Chinese leaders, even though

Britain was desperate not to offend Tokyo. It was a time when any official contact between Hong Kong and China was almost unheard of. On the Nationalist side, he had met both President Chiang Kai-shek and his henchman, Dai Li. (He thought the spymaster 'probably the most powerful man in the world' and 'tremendously impressive' despite his 'women's hands'.) Of the communists, he met Zhou Enlai, whom he found very friendly but with 'not very good English'.

MacDougall parked his car. From just across the harbour came the boom of a last demolition charge going off at an oil depot and the rumble of the big enemy guns in the hills beyond, their shells scream-ing intermittently overhead. He walked briskly across the neatly laid-out lawns of Statue Square, where Queen Victoria gazed placidly out to sea from her domed shrine in front of the Hong Kong Club. A quiet man, who believed absolutely in the rule of law, MacDougall had no time for the trappings of colonialism. Short and wiry, with brown curly hair and dazzling blue eyes, he also had a thinly veiled streak of mischief in him. Amid all the grim reports that would later emerge about the Japanese occupation of Hong Kong, he would find one piece of news to cheer him: that the statues had been removed from Statue Square.

The information bureau had its office on the first floor of the seventeen-storey Hong Kong Bank building, which stood imposingly just across the square, guarded by its two bronze lions. On the ground floor was a plaque saying the Acting Governor, NL Smith, had opened the building in 1935. MacDougall and his staff had spent the first morning of the battle up on the roof, making a burnt offering of code-books and other documents. Afterwards he said he had never known a simple task so difficult: 'I used a tin can and put each paper in sepa-rately, taking great care to see everything was well alight. Yet time and again on turning out the ashes I found sheets untouched by fire, tanta-lizingly legible and had to repeat the process of burning each by itself.'

Since then the bombardment from the mainland had worsened by the day. He and his chief assistant, Ted Ross, were now in the process of moving to another office—a converted hotel room in the labyrin-thine but more sheltered Gloucester Building in Pedder Street. It was on the third floor, with another five floors above them, so they were reasonably safe; and it came complete with its own bathroom and bedding, for when they could no longer go home. It was handy too for the daily meeting with Chan Chak, just across the street.

One of them—either MacDougall or Ross—also had to go up to Command HQ three times a day to find out the latest news of the battle. It could be a lively journey. They started out along Queen's Road, crowded with Chinese families scrambling from one district to the next between raids, then headed up past the cathedral. Dashing across Garden Road, they could feel the hot shrapnel beneath their feet. It was no joke, said Ross later. 'The naval yard was just below and there were gun batteries above, so there was usually quite a hail of fire to go through.'

A lean, fit young Canadian with dark, film-star good looks, a thin moustache and a ready laugh, Ross had dodged Japanese bullets before. Having joined Canadian Pacific Steamships as a ship's purser, he fell in love with Asia, and was working in the company's offices in Shanghai when the Japanese attacked in 1937. He volunteered as a Red Cross ambulance driver, running the gauntlet of enemy soldiers to pick up the wounded. After four years in Shanghai he was posted to Hong Kong, where MacDougall persuaded him to become involved in the war effort on a full-time basis by joining the Ministry of Information.

Now that the war was here, their job was to keep the local population informed of the latest military position through regular press releases issued to the three English and five main Chinese newspapers. Both the General and the Governor had a share in crafting these communiqués, which may explain why they ended up being what one local observer called 'cryptic'. The announcement about the frantic and humiliating retreat from Kowloon on the night of 11 December put a typically brave face on things:

> The mainland was successfully evacuated . . . our position has been stabilized inside the strong defences of the island of Hong Kong and conditions of full siege now exist. The colony is in good heart. There is plenty of food, arms and ammunition and the garrison is confident of the outcome.

It was a confidence no longer widely shared. Some of the other notices they put out appealed to the populace to remain calm and not to listen to scaremongers. Tackling the large fifth column of spies and collaborators was just as important, believed Ross, as the actual fighting:

> They spotted our gun positions and troop concentrations and flashed information across to the Japs, but worse than that they were active disseminating alarmist propaganda and false rumours. We had to combat them by newspaper, radio talks, leaflets, posters and having our own counter-rumourmongerers mingling with the crowds in air-raid tunnels and shelters. It was a great game, and with the valuable

aid of pro-Chungking organizations and volunteer Chinese writers and translators, we definitely won out.

Chan Chak rallied local Chinese in his daily broadcasts and press statements by appealing to their sense of loyalty to China rather than to Britain. But his work went far beyond propaganda. There were serious problems to be dealt with in such vital areas as the monetary situation and rice distribution. On 10 December, Chan brought all the Nationalist organizations in the colony together in one single body, with its own general secretariat, military police, finance, foreign affairs and other departments. It was in effect a shadow government, led by himself. Thousands of volunteers were enlisted to help with food supplies, transport, medical and other services. 'All the central government (KMT) organizations in the colony co-operated to the nth degree,' reported MacDougall.

Chan and his deputy, Colonel SK Yee, were also using their underworld connections to tackle the saboteurs, snipers and other collaborators, to help restore order to the streets. Phyllis Harrop, a spirited young woman from Manchester working at the police headquarters, had just learned she was now attached to the 'Chinese Secret Police'. Her diary entry for 11 December said the phone had been ringing till 5.30 a.m.:

> The Chungking representatives are certainly doing their stuff. SK Yee has never stopped for the past 48 hours. They were ordered to contact all leaders of the triad societies and to persuade them to come over to us on the idea that they are now fighting for their own country and not merely helping us. Propaganda has been put out by the Japanese to kill all Europeans as they are responsible for the war and once they are out of way all fighting will stop. We are afraid to shell Kowloon for fear of frightening Chinese into riots and saying we are killing their own people . . . there are reports of looting and riots, now the police have been taken away . . . SK was told to try to stop the looting and see if he can get the situation in hand.

It was too late to do anything in Kowloon. The civil violence there—much of it organized by triads bought off by the Japanese—would soon end as one set of troops filled the vacuum left by the other. But Chan Chak and his team set to work in their usual robust style to prevent any repetition of the mayhem from happening on the island.

Henry Hsu spent the whole night driving round Wanchai and other parts of town, picking up triad leaders and bringing them back to the office in Shell House. There, Chan and SK used a combination of threats and payoffs to persuade them to abandon any thoughts of massacring Europeans and instead tackle the saboteurs—many of them from rival gangs in the pay of Japan.

An initial force was put together of 2,000 vigilantes (the number soon grew to 15,000). They were paid a small food allowance of HK$2 a day per person to patrol the streets, and to seize suspected troublemakers. Some members wore identifying armbands; others struck gongs. Led by triads from Shanghai and northern China, they adopted the innocuous-sounding name of the Loyal and Righteous Charitable Association.

By the following day Phyllis Harrop was praising the 'wonderful work' done by the Chungking men: 'Arrests are being carried out of 5th columnists. And they are being executed. Several have already been shot. SK reports the situation regarding triads and looters is in hand.'

The Admiral and his chief henchman were almost certainly triad members themselves, as was almost anyone with any pretensions to political power in China. And they were not averse to joining in the action. Several accounts spoke of shoot-outs in which whole roomfuls of men were killed by groups led in person by either Chan Chak or SK Yee. According to Chan's sons, more than a hundred fifth columnists were taken by surprise during a meeting in a cinema when about twenty men led by the Admiral burst in with grenades and killed them all. In a long letter Ted Ross wrote to his mother in January 1942 (published by Maclean's magazine later that year), he said 'rumour had it that, at least three times, those on our side discovered the secret meeting places of the fifth columnists at the eleventh hour, and went in with hand grenades and Tommy guns, mowing down as many as four hundred in one raid.' Ted's son, Warwick, says his father used to recall vividly how 'SK Yee burst into the office with his Tommy gun, looking exhausted and saying: "We got them all!"'

Whoever they got and however they did it, it worked. When David MacDougall listened at the morning meeting first to Boxer's news from the battlefront and then to the latest escapades of Chan Chak and his men, there was no doubt which he found the more inspiring. The energy, determination and bravery of his old Chinese tennis partner became more impressive day by day.

In MacDougall's view, it had always been wrong to even think of defending Hong Kong without accepting China's help. But as he later reported back to London, things would have been a lot worse if the Admiral hadn't insisted on helping anyway. 'Internal order could almost certainly not have been preserved for more than a few days if

Kuomintang influence hadn't been so actively thrown in on our side when the attack came.'

Chan Chak and his Chinese Nationalists had saved the day: now the island could at least await the next Japanese onslaught in something approaching a spirit of calm solidarity.

4
Battle Box

12 December

Hong Kong's defenders never really recovered from the shock of losing the mainland so soon. The days that followed were days of reorganization and battening down of hatches; of artillery duels across the water, aerial blitzes to which they had no reply and invitations to surrender indignantly refused. There was a certain stiffening of resolve as they waited for the Japanese to land. But that early feeling of being pushed back, of withdrawing until there was nowhere left to go—that never went away.

The lucky few who were to find themselves on Christmas Day suddenly breaking out across enemy lines, over blue sea and green hills into Free China, would feel a surge of exhilaration all the more intense for what it was they were escaping from. Not just the grim and uncertain prospect of a prisoner-of-war camp, but even more, the hopeless reality of being under constant siege and of knowing that defeat was just a matter of time. Yet none could have felt a greater sense of release than those who had spent the past seventeen days cooped up inside the Battle Box.

As the bombs and shells began to fall, many people envied those senior or lucky enough to be based inside the thick walls of Fortress HQ. The subterranean nerve centre of China Command, with its own power supply, telephone exchange and ventilation system, had been built to withstand the heaviest of bombardments. Its sunken entrance lay among the sleepy colonnades and sprawling banyans of the colony's original military encampment. Down thirteen flights of steps, steel doors opened onto a catacomb of pipelined passageways, with a series of right-angled turns and small offices leading off on either side.

'It felt so safe and secure down there,' said one of those who dropped by during the battle. They had perhaps gone to report how many of their men they had just seen mown down by machine guns on some bare hillside. But as they saluted and stood awaiting further orders, in a dungeon-like chamber where the air was close and a flickering yellow light cast a lurid glare on pale, harassed faces, many decided they would rather be back on the front line.

Not that those who were based in the Battle Box weren't glad to see them—any news from the real world outside was welcome. One member of the public who called up wanting urgent instructions as to what to do about an approaching enemy soldier got the frank if not very helpful response: 'We're a bit in the dark down here—how many Japs on the island?'

If and when they had time to snatch a few hours' sleep, most of the staff officers preferred, like the General himself, to walk over to Flagstaff House rather than stay below ground. The Battle Box was a 'psychological tomb', said one. 'One could hear and feel the heavy vibrations as shells and bombs landed on top without making any noticeable impression. . . . I felt an unwilling sense of guilty security under all that reinforced concrete.'

Squadron Leader Max Oxford, an intelligence officer attached to the Royal Air Force, found the Battle Box both depressing and demoralizing. He thought the staff remained there for too long: 'One rapidly became a defeatist,' he wrote a few weeks later to his sister in South Africa. 'I preferred the sunlight and perfect winter weather above ground.'

But as their entire fleet of planes had been put out of action before the fighting began, neither Oxford nor any of his Air Force colleagues had been able to get as far above ground as they would have liked. Ever since that initial raid on Kai Tak, the RAF's one hundred or so airmen had been serving as infantry, while he himself had been based along with other intelligence officers in Command HQ. He went out when he could, mainly helping with transport. He and Charles Boxer had visited the Kowloon front just before it collapsed.

There was little air intelligence work to do other than keep an eye on the air raid warning system: it was working well in its 'most beautiful dug-out'. The Air Force were still seething over the fact that the chiefs of staff had refused their request for a fighter squadron. Also that Maltby hadn't let them do anything with the few planes they did have except leave them on the runway. Now Oxford could only watch and take notes as the Zeroes and other Japanese aircraft scattered bombs or leaflets, or simply spotted targets for their artillery.

A dapper, fresh-faced thirty-six-year-old, Max Oxford had left school at seventeen. Breaking away from a strict Methodist upbringing in Dorset, he soon won an RAF commission and trained as a pilot. He was sent to Iraq, and became aide to the British high commissioner, whom he followed to his next diplomatic posting, in Nyasaland. After four years in Africa, Oxford got a job flying for Imperial Airways. He came to Hong Kong in 1938 as assistant manager of the airport.

Living in a new Spanish-style villa near Kai Tak and switching back to RAF uniform with the onset of war, he was soon getting to know people. That was part of his job as an intelligence officer, after all. Hong Kong at the time was a hotbed of spies, intrigue and gossip. Among his friends was the American journalist, Emily 'Mickey' Hahn, who kept a pet gibbon, smoked cigars—and opium—and was having an affair with the senior army intelligence officer, Charles Boxer. 'Max Oxford had a precise drawl that sounded just like his name,' she wrote in her waspish way. She and the married major attended one of Oxford's cocktail parties in 1940, soon after the start of their relationship. 'Everyone in Hong Kong' had been invited, she remembered. 'There were naval officers there and willowy young girls . . . the Empire stood solid and firm.'*

Times had changed. With his white stucco villa now in Japanese hands along with the rest of Kowloon, Oxford had moved into a flat in Robinson Road, which he was sharing with as many as eight lodgers. The building shook from the almost constant Japanese bombardment of the nearby batteries, and at one stage, a shell came through his sitting room ceiling. His car was wrecked by splinters from a bomb that exploded just a few yards away from it. Yet he was still managing to have what he called a 'gentlemanly war, bathing and shaving each day'. After the first two or three days' siege, he wrote later, he lost all fear of being killed. 'But the thought of capture by the Japanese was dreadful to me.'

Arthur Goring was another who was unhappy at the thought of spending the rest of the war caged up in Hong Kong. A large, amiably aristocratic and witty man, he was also a tough, highly respected soldier, and was one of the most senior army officers on the general staff. His official title was GSO II Sec, HQ China Command in Hong Kong.

Solid and firm: Emily Hahn and Charles Boxer further ruffled colonial feathers in the autumn of 1941 when they put a notice in the *South China Morning Post* announcing the birth of their daughter, Carola. Boxer was still married at the time to Ursula Churchill-Dawes, known as 'the most beautiful woman in Hong Kong'. Emily Hahn had earlier been the second wife, or 'concubine', of the Chinese poet, Sinmay Zau, in Shanghai; after the fall of Hong Kong she avoided internment and gave English lessons to Japanese officers in return for food. She and Boxer married after his release from his POW camp in 1945.

If there was ever a moment's lull in the operations room, Goring would wander over to a map on the wall: not one of the rapidly changing ones that tried to keep track of the latest Japanese positions, with scrawled arrows showing the likely next assault, but a substantial, large-scale map of the whole of Asia. His eye followed an imaginary line from the South China Sea on the far right, across a succession of Chinese provinces, then over the Burma Road (now the only way out of Free China) and down to India. 'It seemed a very long way from Hong Kong to Delhi,' he reflected later. 'But that's where I wanted to be.'

The British Raj was as well represented within Fortress HQ as it was outside on the field of battle, where the 2/14 Punjabis and 5/7 Rajputs made up a third of Hong Kong's infantry. There was plenty of material to choose from, after all. The Indian Army List at the time had 2,400 pages of closely typed names—headed by 'King Emperor'. After being commissioned from Sandhurst in 1926, Major Arthur Goring had begun his career by going out east to join the Royal Fusiliers. He had been in India ever since, serving also with the Indian Armoured Corps and Probyn's Horse.

Goring had been brought to Hong Kong four months before the Japanese attack, after strong reports of a planned Sikh mutiny in the army and police force. As many as a third of Hong Kong's policemen were Indian—mostly Sikhs. Their turbans made them tower even more over the average Chinese in the street, with whom they had never been popular. Encouraged by Japanese propaganda, Sikhs had been complaining that the British were ignoring their religious rights by forcing them to wear steel helmets.

The authorities saw the threat of a revolt as serious, and asked Delhi if it could spare some of its top men to come and look into it. As well as Goring, two senior police officers were sent out, including a friend of his from Indian Police Intelligence, Bill Robinson. The three of them took swift and decisive action to resolve the matter. According to a Hong Kong police officer at the time: 'Suddenly a large number of Sikhs disappeared . . . they seemed, literally, to have been spirited away in the night from their barrack rooms, even from their units on exercise . . . All potential mutineers, together with their families, had been shipped back to India.'

Superintendent William Robinson, aged thirty-four, knew a lot about Sikh unrest. His fourteen years in the Indian Police, almost all of them in the Punjab, included a posting to Amritsar, where racial hatred remained strong ten years after the infamous massacre. He had trained as a frontier policeman in a fortress on the Grand Trunk Road near Lahore, where the young officers played polo and chased pigs with sons of the Nawab of Tank and were taught never to go out without a topee.

It was mainly due to Robinson's careful handling that the Sikhs in Hong Kong stopped short of a mutiny and the colony did not have the additional handicap of an Indian fifth column to go with its Chinese one. But the Sikh police remained 'sullen and uncooperative', according to British officers, as the battle started. And they possibly had good reason. 'Indian and Chinese families seem to have had trouble getting food from the officer in charge of Police Food Control,' said the police war diary on 14 December. Luckily Bill Robinson was still on hand, and took over supervision of the feeding of Indians at Central Police Station next day.

Down in the Battle Box, meanwhile, things became ever more fraught as telephones rang and messengers arrived with one piece of alarming news after another: a British ship loaded with ammunition had blown up . . . it turned out to have been fired on by its own side; the Japanese had landed on one of Hong Kong's outlying islands, Lamma, and were now coming over to Aberdeen on junks . . . the MTBs had helped shoot up the junks but they may have been honest fishing folk after all . . . now more Chinese support staff and drivers were going on strike in protest . . .

According to the General's aide-de-camp, Iain MacGregor, the atmosphere in the operations room was like that of an 'animated beehive'. But there were some staff officers, he wrote later, who remained calm at all times. His list of 'unflappables' included the names of Goring and Oxford. It did not include those of the final two men from the Battle Box who ended up on the escape, 'Freddie' Guest and Peter Macmillan.

For such a good bridge player, Captain Reginald Edwin Guest was remarkably good at shooting his mouth off—not to say also putting his foot in it. He had been getting into colourful scrapes of one kind or another for most of his forty-five years. As a cavalry officer in India, he had tried to shoot a cobra, but missed and brought down his bearer's hut instead. On another occasion, he found himself washed up on mud flats and jogged back to base in the nude, sending villagers scattering in alarm. He gave up on India while still a relatively young man and returned to London, where he had originally started out as a post office assistant. The fun had gone out of being a cavalryman, he said, when armoured cars started replacing mules, horses and camels.

With the coming of a new war, Guest rejoined the Army and was put in charge of 800 men bound for the Far East. Leaving his wife and two children in London, he safely delivered his cargo to Shanghai, but then decided to stay on in Hong Kong. With its many clubs, it was a good place to enjoy not just bridge but his other great loves too— polo, horse racing and football (he had once played as an amateur for Chelsea). He also had time to make an accurate appraisal of the military situation. He was said to have stated loudly in the Officers' Club that if Japan attacked 'we would not stand a chance and would be caught like rats in a trap'. Since Air Marshal Sir Robert Brooke-Popham, the visiting British commander in chief for the region, had just been assuring Hong Kong that the Japanese were a 'sub-human species' who posed no threat at all, Guest was duly reprimanded for speaking out of turn.

He and his fellow occupants of 'The Box' were already feeling like rats in a trap, just four days after the Japanese invasion. But he now got himself into even more trouble by making another brash announcement—which again turned out to be only too true. 'Freddie Guest came bursting in one morning and blurted out that he'd just heard the catastrophic news that the Prince of Wales and the Repulse had been sunk by a Japanese air attack off Singapore,' recalled MacGregor, the ADC. 'He was immediately placed under house arrest . . . for spreading false and dangerous rumours likely to affect garrison morale. He was not released till the disaster was at last confirmed by the Commodore's Office.'

In his later writings about his role in the Hong Kong battle, Guest made no mention of being under house arrest. But he did give breathless accounts of various personal missions made beyond the confines of Command HQ, such as the time when he drove Chan Chak up to the Peak to deal with an enemy agent who was flashing signals to gunners across the harbour. The Admiral, he said, hurled a hand grenade tied to a string back down the hill, blowing up the unseen fifth columnist in an almighty explosion.

On many of his other adventures, Guest was accompanied by his good chum Peter Macmillan—who turned to him at one point and said: 'Freddie, you're a tough beggar. I'm glad we're together on this show.' A keen sportsman who went to Eton and rowed for his college at Oxford, Macmillan was big enough to look after himself, but wore an expression of vulnerable, wide-eyed innocence.

He was sent out one night to look into reports that Japanese cavalry were advancing across Happy Valley. As the wraith-like shapes of animals loomed out of the darkness, the sergeant who was with him opened fire, killing or maiming a number of terrified and bewildered racehorses that had broken out of their stables. Macmillan was devastated, but was called away to deal with another emergency before he could put the wounded ponies out of their agony.

'Robust, red-faced, cleanshaven,' wrote Guest, 'he looked more like a junior bishop than an army officer. We always said if he wasn't in uniform he wouldn't need a dog collar for people to mistake him for a parson of some degree.' Peter Macmillan was in fact the son of a bishop. His father was John Victor Macmillan of the publishing and political family, who began his ecclesiastical career as resident chaplain to the Archbishop of Canterbury, and later became Bishop of Guildford.

Peter was a twenty-eight-year-old captain in the Royal Artillery, and was married to the daughter of a vice-admiral. His wife Viola and their baby son Robert had been evacuated from Hong Kong to Australia in 1940. But they were in Manila, hoping to reunite with Macmillan on a Christmas break, when the Japanese attacked the Philippines within hours of invading Hong Kong. In the confusion of recent days there had been no way of finding out if they were safe. One of the few reports to come through about the raids of 8 December had been a radio message from the SS *Ulysses*, saying she was under attack by bombers as she headed for Manila. Again, there were no details. And for most people, that could hardly compare with the devastating news reported by Guest of the loss of the two British capital ships (one a battleship, the other a battlecruiser), which Churchill called the biggest shock of the entire war. They had just arrived in the Far East to spearhead the fleet, and were Hong Kong's last real hope of rescue.

There was always China, of course. The one bit of good news that week was a report Chan Chak had received from Chungking, that a relief army was now well on its way. Some in Command HQ had feared such a force might be a myth. After discussion in the Battle Box, it was decided that here at last was something worth broadcasting. And sure enough, it brought a noticeable lifting of morale. Before it was even officially released, people were ringing up cheerily to ask if they'd heard the news that Harry Owen-Hughes would be riding in at any moment on a white horse at the head of his Chinese army.

5

Cloak and Dagger Boys

14 December

After a week of war, Hong Kong's once-teeming harbour had a desolate air. Junks and other native craft had been herded off into typhoon shelters; freighters and other ships had been bombed or scuttled, and lay keeled over at grotesque angles. The Royal Navy's huge old depot ship, HMS *Tamar*, proved most reluctant of all to sink, even when an MTB fired a torpedo to help. But finally, after forty-four years as home of the Far Eastern Fleet, it too succumbed, settling slowly down into the mud.

At night, where before there had been neon splashes of reds, blues and greens, there were now blackouts on both shores. A pause in the thundering of guns and whining of shells was broken by the sounds of plaintive music, as the Japanese tried another means of softening up the island's defenders. Crackly recordings of 'Swanee River' and 'The Old Folks at Home' wafted across the water from loudspeakers set up along the Kowloon shore and on small boats moving up and down the harbour. The choice of Deanna Durbin, the 'Sensational Canadian Songbird' of the time, to deliver these maudlin offerings was presumably meant to persuade the raw young Canadian troops, in particular, to give up and go home. There were also spoken announcements, exhorting the Chinese and Indians to join Japan's Greater East Asia Co-Prosperity Sphere and turn against the Europeans.

Just to the east, towards the Lyemun Channel, a derelict merchant ship posed a more serious threat. A quarter of a mile out from the Kowloon side, it had been boarded by a Japanese observation team that was now using it as a spotting post to study possible landing points on the shore opposite. The problem was put to Mike Kendall, head of a Secret Services commando unit known as Z Force, on his morning visit to the Battle Box. He offered to sink the boat that night, using some of his 'toys'.

Francis Woodley Kendall, a mining engineer by profession, was a man who 'took booby-traps out of his pocket like a juggler at a children's party'. He was also a tough, charismatic Canadian with red hair and a gift for making decisions and getting things done. At Command HQ, he was sometimes referred to as 'our Canadian Bison' or simply 'our Number One Guerrilla'. But he wasn't one for titles or orders of precedence: he preferred to be known to everyone, including his men, as Mike. Only two members of his squad were with him now—the other seven had taken up position on a rocky mountainside in the New Territories, well behind enemy lines. Colin McEwan and Monia Talan were just the boys, though, for what Kendall had in mind.

McEwan was a strong and fit young teacher with a dry Scottish sense of humour who had been in Hong Kong for the past two and a half years. The son of the Presbyterian headmaster of a village school, he was a qualified instructor in physical education as well as Latin, but also liked his food and drink and kept his colleagues entertained with his poetry. He modestly called himself no more than a 'makee learn' saboteur; but in fact he had not only passed the Chinese language section of the Z Force entry requirements, but had also done his explosives training by the time Kendall picked him earlier that year from the local Volunteer Corps.

His friend Talan had been a lieutenant in the Jewish Company of the Shanghai Volunteers before moving to Hong Kong in 1934. He was a White Russian who had grown up in the Shanghai of the 1920s and early 1930s—a world of big American cars and starving rickshaw boys, girls in high heels and *cheongsams* that flapped open at the thigh, gangsters and kidnappings. Handsome, with a rich head of black hair, Talan was far from being the exotic and excitable adventurer one might have expected. A lifelong friend who went to the same, very English school—an 'Eton in China'—said he was 'quiet, soft-spoken and utterly unflappable'.

Kendall soon had his plan worked out—as McEwan later recalled in his laconic style:

> Like all Mike's plans it was straightforward. We would, during the day, acquire a small boat and prepare delayed action sinking charges. In the evening, once it was dark, we would go out in the boat with Mike rowing, get up tide from the vessel and then drift down on it while Monia Talan would fire bursts of Vickers gun from the roof of the Taikoo sugar refinery to keep heads down on board the ship while he and I got alongside. Monia had been a machine gunner in the Shanghai Defence Force, so that elected him into that job. Mike reckoned that Monia should start firing some forty-five minutes after we had started out. Everything worked as Mike had foreseen. We did get alongside under Monia's fire, Mike held on while indicating to

me where I should stick on the limpets. I slid into the water—after
all as a P.E. teacher surely I was a competent swimmer—fixed the
things on and sure enough, two hours later, when we were safely
ashore again and having a drink with Monia in the refinery area, the
toys exploded and that was one less embarrassment to us.

Kendall had started putting Z Force together more than two years
previously, when Colonel John Newnham—later to be tortured and
beheaded by the Japanese—asked him to form a group to carry out
covert operations behind the lines in the event of an invasion. The
unit would allow itself to be overrun, then use guerrilla tactics to
harass the enemy. Its roles would include blowing up bridges, creat-
ing diversions, gathering intelligence and sending reports back to any
remaining defenders. When the fighting was over, the plan was to
escape into Nationalist China, bringing out as much information as
possible. Madame Chiang Kai-shek came to meet the first members
and gave them special Free China passes from the Generalissimo.
They were told these would enable them to escape, when the time
came, right across China to India.

Kendall already had many contacts in southern China. He had
spent some years there operating his own mining company, until it
collapsed with the arrival of the Japanese in the mid-1930s. He and
his young Chinese wife had then come to Hong Kong, where he had
helped run a refugee camp as cover for his growing activities as a
British military intelligence agent. He set up listening stations and
recruited agents for sabotage work on Hainan and in other places
along the Chinese coast that were under Japanese occupation. He
also formed links with the Chinese guerrilla groups that were spring-
ing up in the no-man's-land between areas held by the Japanese
and by the Nationalist Government. Many of these irregular forces
were pro-Nationalist, acting as a useful buffer for the government
troops. But there was also an increasingly strong communist guerrilla
movement, later to coalesce into the East River Column. It was the
communist groups that were most active against the Japanese, and
therefore, most useful to Kendall.

His wife Betty also mixed in left-wing circles, of a more cultivated
and literary kind. But in the male-dominated British Hong Kong
of the times, she was dismissed by at least one senior officer as no
more than a 'pretty little piece'. In an era when marrying a Chinese—
however well bred or well educated—could mean the end of a colonial career, the plain-speaking Canadian mining engineer was not the

sort of man Hong Kong's military hierarchy would normally have had much time for. Yet in the weeks leading up to the invasion, Kendall made frequent clandestine visits to Flagstaff House, where General Maltby welcomed him in through the French windows to hear the latest reports of Japanese troop movements.

'Mike was endowed with that rare gift of looking at a problem, deciding what to do and then doing it,' recalled a colleague. 'I've seen him handle British Generals, Chinese millionaires, Chinese coolies, Old Etonians, junior clerks . . . and to Mike, all that mattered was whether he reckoned they were good guys or not . . . He was the sort of man who found a natural home on the China Coast.'

Kendall recruited other equally tough foreign adventurers to help keep him supplied with intelligence. Among the most colourful of these was a chunky ex-bodyguard of Sun Yat-sen's, known as Two-Gun Cohen. The son of a Polish Jew, Morris Cohen emigrated in his teens from the East End of London to Canada, where he learnt to ride, shoot and gamble. Having moved on to China, he offered his services to the President, becoming a favoured retainer and acquiring the rank of general in the Chinese Army. He later made a living from arms-dealing and all-night poker sessions at Short-Time Susan's in Shanghai before winding up in Hong Kong, where Kendall hired him at HK$1,000 a month to keep his ears open as he hung around the lounge of the Hong Kong Hotel in his trademark white suit, shoulder holster visible beneath the jacket.

The stay-behind commando group, which Kendall was already working on by 1939, was ahead of its time. It was not until the Fall of France in the autumn of 1940 that the British government realized that behind enemy lines lay potential allies and decided to infiltrate its own agents into occupied countries. The first wireless operator was smuggled into France by air in May 1941, after the failure of two earlier attempts to bring in agents by torpedo boat and parachute. A new department was set up under the Ministry of Economic Warfare, aimed at the 'corrosion of Nazi and Fascist powers from within'. In June 1941 it became known as the Special Operations Executive, or SOE. Its purpose, as Winston Churchill put it, was 'to set Europe ablaze'. Based, like Sherlock Holmes, in Baker Street, it sent out hundreds of agents with code names such as 'Carrot' and 'Kitbag' to carry out sabotage and espionage, and to plot escape networks.

The Southeast Asian branch of the SOE—known in the region as Force 136—had its headquarters in Singapore, where it ran a training camp called Camp 101 outside the city. Its courses included jungle exercises, demolition, night landings, sailing all types of native craft and learning what little was known of Japanese tactics. Senior British army officers in the Far East laughed at the very idea of jungle training: when war came a few months later and the Japanese descended on Singapore through the island city's verdant Malayan hinterland, most of the defending troops had never left a main road. But Mike Kendall was quick to enrol both himself and some of his senior Z Force colleagues for three-week courses. By October, those in charge of Force 136 had been sufficiently impressed by the Hong Kong unit to take it under the wing of the SOE.

Z Force also became known as the Reconnaissance or 'Recce' Unit, since that was its legitimate function for the Hong Kong Volunteers, who provided most of its staff and equipment. But the SOE's Singapore office now also began helping to set up five hideouts in the New Territories which were to house food dumps, weapons caches and sleeping quarters for a stay-behind group when the time came. One of these secret rendezvous was in a disused lead mine on the border near Shataukok. The main hideout consisted of two natural caves 1,800 feet up the southeast face of Hong Kong's tallest mountain, Tai Mo Shan, just below the source of a stream which fed the Shingmun Reservoir. The Royal Engineers had helped camouflage and enlarge the caves to accommodate a total of nine men.

On the first day of the invasion, Kendall, McEwan and the seven other available members of Z Force met up beside the reservoir at a bungalow which the Kendalls had bought for weekends, and which had served as a base for the unit's training. Talan had been left on Hong Kong Island to liaise with the military. The others collected fresh provisions and ammunition, and made their way after dark up the steep, rocky hillside. Range-finding shots fired by their own side whistled over their heads and were soon falling all around them.

McEwan woke up later that night in the smaller of the two caves, wedged between piles of gelignite and Bren ammunition. As the rain fell on the mountain beside him and the guns boomed in the distance, he recorded in his diary how it all suddenly felt a very far cry from Minishant—the small Ayrshire village where he had grown up.

He got up early, washed in the stream and clambered down to the main cave to join the others for breakfast. They soon realized they were now sharing the mountain with the advancing Japanese troops. 'Being a miserable misty morning we could move with freedom, and about tiffin time, we had our first view of the enemy as they came over

Lead Mine Pass to Grassy Hill, and in fact we had our first thrill as one of the shells landed directly among a group of them on the skyline.'

Kendall cranked up the unit's field telephone. But he could only get through to a forward post that had already been abandoned, and he was answered in Japanese. With no wireless sets, they were completely cut off from the rest of the British forces. So Kendall and McEwan had to slip down through the Japanese lines to the Royal Scots' positions at the reservoir to pass on news of the enemy's advance. They had just arrived when the crucial attack was made on the Shingmun Redoubt, whose rapid loss was to prove the biggest setback of the entire battle for Hong Kong.

It was a black night of mist and rain. Dodging between rocks, crawling through the undergrowth and sliding on their fronts across a minefield, the two men from Z Force penetrated the defences of the British front line at Kwai Chung just as easily as the Japanese were doing at the same moment a few hundred yards further east. Having identified themselves as friends, they were duly welcomed by Lieutenant Michael Fenwick of 7 Platoon and persuaded to join him and his two sergeants for a beer, while a runner was sent to take Kendall to the company headquarters within the redoubt, just up the steep, wooded hillside to their right.

Only a few days before, Fenwick had made a dummy attack on the redoubt and found no difficulty getting through. Their best hope, he said, was that reports of the Japanese being unable to operate at night were accurate. But as they were polishing off their drinks, news came through that the scrub-covered warren of concrete bunkers was now under assault by the enemy. Pitch dark or no, the 3rd Battalion of Colonel Doi Teihichi's 228th regiment had swept along Smugglers Ridge and descended from above on 8 Platoon and the company headquarters in their supposed stronghold of machine-gun nests and tunnels. McEwan joined Fenwick and his men as they seized their weapons and raced outside to find a midnight melee in progress farther up the hill:

> Out the platoon tumbled into trenches overlooking the valley in front of the redoubt and anticipating a flanking movement by the Japs covering Bungalow Hill. It was dark and windy and as the battle continued with almost continuous machine-gun fire and explosions of grenades, shouts of men and sharp orders came across. Although only gunfire and torches could be seen one could easily envisage the actual scene. Visible too were the Japanese officers leading up among

the barbed wire entanglements (by the platoon on our right)—using torches and waving swords in feudal manner.

Colonel Doi acknowledged in his diary that the firing from 7 Platoon, to the west of the redoubt, caused his officers some problems after his men had cleared paths through the wire and taken the eastern position by storm:

> Some of the attacking forces threw hand grenades into air vents and went into tunnels; others blocked exits. There was an hour of hand-to-hand fighting. The enemy in the west mounted machine-guns in the open, and harassed the battalion commander and others not in the tunnels; we worked to build cover, while some assaulted the west position and captured it soon after.

One by one each outpost was overrun. Kendall managed to fight his way through to the redoubt by 1 a.m., but by then most of it was firmly in Japanese hands. He and McEwan later took out supplies of booby traps to delay further enemy advances on the left of the Gin Drinkers' Line. As the mainland withdrawal was announced, they helped stop the looting in the streets of Kowloon with Tommy guns.

Back on the island, they picked up Talan. The three 'cloak and dagger boys', as they were known, then joined forces with Chan Chak and his men in tackling the fifth column. As well as blowing up ships in the harbour and patrolling the hills, this involved the grimmer task of punishing offenders with a bullet in the back of the head. The executions were carried out in the city centre in a dead-end lane that came to be known as Blood Alley, where the bodies were left lying in the open, bearing placards as warnings to others. The narrow street ran between the Gloucester Hotel and the colony's smartest department store, Lane Crawford, which, with twelve days to go till Christmas, was still happily urging shoppers to brighten up their homes with 'Aladdin's Lamps' and imported English crystal.

6

Naval Light Brigade

19 December

The Japanese finally made their move on the island on the night of 18 December, crossing the harbour in the same area where the three men from Z Force had blown up the observation ship. There had been several days of increasingly heavy bombardment of the defences around Lyemun and along the island's adjacent northeast coast. The oil and petrol storage tanks at North Point were set on fire and then shelled continuously. The resulting thick black smoke combined with a moonless night, a heavy ground mist and an unusually high tide to provide perfect conditions for a landing.

An advance party of swimmers was followed by other special forces in collapsible boats. They slipped across the narrow strait and established a bridgehead, virtually unobserved. Command HQ had dealt with so many false alarms by now that the first reports of the actual landings were shrugged off with a dismissive: 'windy buggers— at it again'. A venerable group of local businessmen known as the Hugheseliers, none of them less than fifty-five years of age, put up a stout defence of the North Point Power Station. But otherwise, the thin line of defending infantry soon gave way, allowing fresh waves of Japanese soldiers to wade ashore and move swiftly up into the tangled, scrub-covered hills.

The billowing smoke from the oil tanks could still be seen early next morning from as far away as Aberdeen on the other side of the island, where the boats of the 2nd MTB Flotilla were returning from their overnight patrols far to the south and west. But no one here seemed to know what exactly had caused the smoke—still less that there were now enemy troops on the island.

Protected by hills on all sides, Aberdeen's natural harbour had sheltered seagoing craft from Hong Kong's earliest days. It was now home to some 20,000 Hoklo and Tanka *shuishang ren* ('water people'), who lived on board their fishing junks. Stately as galleons when out at sea under sail, the many hundreds of still unmechanized junks were moored together in a forest of masts and banners, their decks stepped up by planked levels to high poops, where whole families squatted under canvas awnings over their breakfast. Long thin sampans wove between their ranks selling vegetables and other supplies, each boat poled with one long oar by a single standing figure in a black shiny tunic and a hat like a huge bamboo lampshade. In peacetime you could almost walk across the mass of junks to the little island opposite, called Aplichau (Duck's Tongue Island). But since the reopening of two small dry docks at the western end of the Aberdeen waterfront, a passage had been closed off to native craft for the use of the Royal Navy, and these days, the stench of cordite had taken over from the more traditional smells of incense, sandalwood and drying salt fish.

Aberdeen was not the most convenient base for motor torpedo boats, whose light wooden build and unconventional design meant they required constant maintenance. (Ashby and his colleagues irreverently referred to their section as the Department of Costly Farces rather than Coastal Forces.) The slipway took only one boat at a time, and the offices and workshops were at the other end of the village, in a high-chimneyed, three-storey building known as the Industrial School. This had formerly been run by the Salesian Fathers as a school for disadvantaged children, but it had been taken over at the start of the battle and turned into a military headquarters. Onshore naval staff and various platoons of soldiers stationed in the southern half of the island were billeted in the dormitories upstairs. The officers and crews of the MTB flotilla lived permanently on their boats—or in the case of the two Thornycroft boats, 26 and 27, which had no accommodation, they slept on board the small China gunboat, HMS *Robin*.

As the boats of the flotilla tied up alongside *Robin* at nine o'clock that morning, orders were received for an urgent new mission: 'proceed into Kowloon Bay . . . and fire at everything in sight'. They were to keep firing until 'nothing remains . . . or your ammunition is expended'. Lieutenant John Collingwood later called it 'the most daring adventure ever carried out in broad daylight by MTBs'. A more modest description appears in the diary of one of his crew, twenty-one-year-old Leading Seaman Les Barker:

> Our flotilla of MTBs was ordered to proceed round the harbour in pairs. This we did and found boat loads of Japs coming over. Under heavy fire from both sides, although we destroyed a large number of them, we could not stop them all.

One of a family of eight from a coal mining community near Nottingham, Barker had lost his father at the age of ten and left school at fourteen to work in a tanning factory. He had joined the Royal Navy aged seventeen and now, after almost four years away, was looking forward to going home to marry his girlfriend, Ida. But like everyone else in the flotilla, he wanted to get a good crack at the enemy first—and here at last was his chance.

Engines roared into life as the flotilla formed into line and headed for a rendezvous behind Green Island, at the western entrance to Hong Kong's main harbour.

The motor torpedo boats had had a busy but frustrating war. Operating from their makeshift base, they had dutifully served as maids of all work—delivering dispatches, ferrying troops, scuttling ships. Their days had been spent dodging the highly accurate artillery and aerial bombardment; their nights out on patrol, looking for non-existent enemy battleships. The only Japanese vessels they had come across to date had been a pair of minesweepers, which they had attacked southwest of Lantau on the night of 15 December with Lewis guns and torpedoes. They had caused some damage and had maybe sunk one of the enemy ships, but they could not be certain in the darkness.

On one occasion they had been called on to help deal with a large group of Chinese junks and sampans which were crossing towards Aberdeen from Lamma Island and were suspected of carrying Japanese soldiers. Chris Meadows, wireless operator on *MTB 10*, described what happened next, in an account that sheds as much light on the British sailors' attitudes towards local fishermen as it does on their lack of shooting practice:

> As we approached them at high speed, gunners were at their guns and every spare man on deck had a rifle or stripped down Lewis gun; I was crouching behind a depth charge with a rifle. As we drew near, order was given to open fire. The lads started blazing away; during the din I realized my rifle wasn't working properly—in the excitement I'd forgotten to take off the safety catch. Luckily there were no Japs on board the sampans (I hadn't handled a rifle for about 2 years).

It was after that incident, in which several of the fishing boats were sunk, that Chinese members of the naval volunteer force who staffed the base at Aberdeen and manned the support vessels began leaving their posts. Their gradual defection continued, until by the time all the auxiliary patrol vessels were scuttled, on the same day as the torpedo boats' raid into Kowloon Bay, there were almost no Chinese RNVR ratings left.

The only time the MTBs had operated in the main harbour before the 19 December raid was when they took part in the Dunkirk-style evacuation from the mainland. This was carried out in two stages: the first on 11 December from Kai Tak; the second late on the following night from Devil's Peak, where hundreds of Rajputs, the last defenders to leave the mainland, calmly lined the waterfront, their mules whinnying in the background as the Japanese fired down at them from the ridge. Although the mules had to be left behind, the flotilla successfully carried out both rescue missions without casualties and won praise from the Commodore in Charge, Captain AC Collinson, RN. But the rocky shoreline and the half-submerged wreckage in the harbour caused further damage to several of the boats.

MTB 08 was lost altogether a few days after the evacuations, when it burnt out on the slipway after a bomb fragment entered its fuel tanks during a raid by twenty-seven heavy bombers on 16 December. The navy's only destroyer, HMS *Thracian*, was fatally hit in the same attack as she lay under repair in the small Aberdeen dry dock. A tug, *Gatling*, was also set on fire and most of her crew killed.

Of the seven motor torpedo boats now remaining, one—*MTB 10*—was unable to take part in today's raid because of a faulty engine. It happened to be the boat captained by the flotilla's senior officer, Lieutenant Commander Gandy, so he stayed behind to direct operations from Aberdeen. He gave orders that MTBs 07 (Ashby) and 09 (Kennedy) were to form the first wave of the attack.

As the six boats lined up in pairs behind Green Island, none of those on board had yet been told the news from the previous night— that the Japanese had already landed on Hong Kong Island, meaning that as soon as the MTBs entered the harbour they would be exposed to enemy fire from all sides. But the flotilla's officers and crews were young, gallant and itching for a fight. Even had they known the full extent of the odds against them it is doubtful they would have given it a second thought. They proceeded to perform, in three magnificent but increasingly tragic acts, what came to be known as the maritime Charge of the Light Brigade.

At 8.45 a.m., their bows lifting proudly, the first two boats roared out to do battle. The oil-slicked harbour at first seemed huge and empty. Puffs of black smoke hung in a clear blue sky. To their left, Japanese flags could be seen all over Kowloon; on their right, the eyes of the Commodore and the entire island were upon them. Ron Ashby led the way:

> Saw nothing, drew no fire until off North Point, when several landing craft, containing about twelve men in each, and in tow from one equipped with an outboard, were sighted. Got to within about 100 yards before opening fire with all five machine guns. Tracer showed bullets spraying targets most effectively. A moment or so later and we ran into a hail of fire from both Kowloon and North Point—rifle, machine-gun and shellfire, while a plane continually dived down on our stern, spraying us with machine-guns and cannon.

Broad-shouldered and rosy-cheeked, with a commanding presence and a carefree laugh, Ashby was a good man to have at the helm at a time of crisis. He had come out east on the Trans-Siberian with his pet rat in his pocket at the age of eighteen after falling out with his father, the owner of a Watford brewery. He had sold trucks for the big trading firm of Dodwells, first in Canton and then in Hong Kong. Here he had settled easily into colonial life, sailing a gaff cutter at the yacht club and becoming one of the first to join the local naval volunteer force, in 1934. At thirty-one, he was young enough to be treated by his men as one of the lads, but old enough to inspire respect.

Signalling by hand to Kennedy to increase speed to full throttle and 'act independently', Ashby swung away to port, swamping two of the shallow-bottomed assault craft in his heavy wash and capsizing them. Able Seaman Albert Rutter—formerly leading seaman but disrated six months previously for drunkenness—made sure with his Lewis gun that there were no survivors.

MTB 09 made for the next group of boats and gave chase as one with a motor tried to flee back to the shelter of junks berthed near the Kowloon shore. It was soon put out of action, thanks to a Bren light automatic operated by the stocky, belligerent figure of Sub-Lieutenant Tommy Brewer. Standing next to his captain on the conning tower and almost maiming him every time he swung his rifle over his head, Kennedy's 'Number-One' was in his element.

As they turned back to the west, enemy fire became ever more intense. Howitzers and mortars joined the attack from either shore. Both boats were hit several times and a shell exploded in *07*'s engine room, killing the leading stoker. The telegraphist was sent to investigate and was killed by machine-gun fire. Two engines were knocked out and the engine room was filling with water, but the second stoker, Acting Petty Officer Stephen 'Buddy' Hide, kept the boat going, even as they came under fresh attack from three aircraft. The first lieutenant, a journalist on the *Hong Kong Mail* called Arthur Gee, noted that the speed had dropped to just eight knots—the 'slowest any of us had ever gone'.

As 07 limped out of the harbour, 09 responded to her call to 'stand by me', and when the third and final engine gave out, took her in tow. Now, at 9.15 a.m., it was the turn of MTBs 11 (Collingwood) and 12 (Colls)* to take up the challenge. As they went in they gave the two departing boats hearty waves, and Kennedy signalled 'God Speed' in return. The Japanese gunners were by now well prepared, and met the new arrivals with a furious barrage of fire. John Collingwood saw that there were still some boats that had failed to reach either shore:

> We went for several parties of Japs who were clinging to and manning wrecks in the harbour, passing fairly close to them and giving them all we could. But we took a lot too. I could feel burst after burst strike the wooden hull, windscreens were smashed, tin hats dented, but not a word from any of the crew except a few smothered oaths as they reloaded or cleared a jammed gun. We turned to come back through the same gauntlet of fire. We were now just a fast-moving target for them. They were giving us everything they had but we were weaving the most fantastic course, we were alive and wriggling, the boat seemed to know and fairly leaped around . . . but oh dear where is MTB 12? She was following just now, but now?

MTB 12, which had disappeared in a cloud of smoke, exploded after being hit in a petrol tank. The details were only learnt much later from two members of the nine-man crew who jumped clear in time. The telegraphist, Alf 'Nobby' Hunt, was wounded in the head and leg, but managed to swim to Kowloon. He was captured by the Japanese, tied up in barbed wire and held prisoner for the rest of the war.* His shipmate, Able Seaman A. Bartlett, swam to Hong Kong Island and was admitted to Queen Mary Hospital, from where he too was transferred to a prisoner-of-war camp after the surrender.

All alone now, *MTB 11* turned and zigzagged back up the harbour. The coxswain was wounded in the throat and a burly stoker,

---

Colls: Lt John Baxter Colls, HKRNVR—a tall, slim, pipe-smoking music lover, who at thirty was one of the older of Gandy's officers.

rest of the war: Hunt not only survived the sinking of *MTB 12* but also that of the Lisbon Maru prison ship in 1942, when more than 800 British POWs died, as he told the author in 2008 at the age of ninety.

Bob Stonell, took over at the wheel. Les Barker, the young leading seaman from Nottingham, and the boat's two able seamen, Alex Kelly and Jack Thorpe, manned the twin Lewis guns mounted forward and aft, firing at anything that moved. One of them broke off to hand fresh pans of ammunition to the first officer, David Legge. He was squatting behind a depth charge outside the conning tower with a stripped Lewis gun in his hands. Legge had joined the naval volunteer reserve in Hong Kong two years before. After enduring six months of 'boring' minefield patrol he had switched to the MTBs, where he was still revelling in having seven Royal Navy ratings for crew instead of 'Cantonese so-called seamen'.

Still in place behind Green Island, ready to go, were the last pair in the flotilla's lineup, MTBs 26 (Wagstaff)* and 27 (Parsons). A message came through at the last moment for them to call off their attack, but 26 failed to receive the signal—or chose to ignore it— and surged ahead on her own. She was last seen drifting helplessly off North Point under heavy fire: 'her motor mechanic rose from the engine room, revolver in hand, loosed it off at the advancing Japs till an enemy bullet found its mark and he fell dying to the deck of the wrecked craft'. None of her seven crew survived.

Waiting back at Aberdeen for the two missing boats, the survivors strained to catch the sound of distant engines, but none came. Instead, as rain clouds gathered, the silence was broken by the sounds of shooting from the hills and mortar shells falling nearby in the dockyard. It was a dark day for the flotilla, reflected Kennedy, and a dark day for the island. As Collingwood saw his badly injured coxswain into an ambulance and wished him luck, he wondered whether the rest of them now stood any more chance of survival than their unlucky colleagues on MTBs 12 and 26.

The gloom deepened. Muffled explosions sent shudders through the water. The minefields defending the southern approaches to Hong Kong had been blown up, their control stations threatened by the enemy's lightning advance across the island. The Japanese now held Mount Parker, Mount Butler and Jardine's Lookout: they had split the island's entire defences in two. As rumours spread that Aberdeen itself was about to fall, preparations were made to evacuate the Industrial School.

Wagstaff: Lt Donald Wagstaff, HKRNVR, whose father, William Wheatley Wagstaff, was the sculptor of the Hong Kong Bank's bronze lions (still there, complete with 1941 bullet holes, in front of today's HSBC headquarters).

That evening, Winston Churchill urged Hong Kong to fight to the last, and a message was sent out from the Battle Box to all forces: 'the time has come to advance against the enemy—the eyes of the empire are upon us.' 'They're not the only ones—there's a heap of bloody Japs with eyes on us here,' was the sour response of the *MTB 10* telegraphist, Chris Meadows.

Churchill's call to advance was hard to reconcile with a stream of other orders that suggested the fight had already been lost. Maintenance staff had only just set about repairing the leaking hulls, smashed fuel tanks and other damage on the five remaining MTBs when orders came through to block the sea approaches to Aberdeen by scuttling 'all ships in the harbour'. HMS *Cornflower*, a 1200-ton sloop built in 1916 and later brought out to the East as a training ship for the HKRNVR, was soon on its way to the seabed, along with one of the three gunboats, HMS *Tern*, and almost all the auxiliary patrol vessels, lighters and other support craft. As their boats were sunk, the crews went off to join the fighting on land.

One group of sailors not yet ready to become soldiers were the surviving members of the motor torpedo boat flotilla. According to Sub-Lieutenant Legge, not only did they believe their boats still had a role to play in Hong Kong's defence, but they also had another use in mind for them:

> Around us was about the most miserable sight that could greet any seaman's eyes: ships in all stages of being sunk, not by enemy action but by our own hands . . . We refused to scuttle because among many reasons we were determined never to give up our boats to the Japs, but to make a break for it at the last moment.

In fact, the MTBs were in any case exempt from the scuttling order, since the higher authorities also had other plans for them. And as it turned out, that evening's panic was premature. When Hong Kong surrendered almost a week later, Aberdeen and the Industrial School were still holding out. But with the Japanese firmly established across much of the island and able to reinforce and resupply at will, the end was only a matter of time. The possibility of eventual escape was now a legitimate topic for discussion. And it soon became clear that the men of the 2nd MTB Flotilla were not alone in planning a getaway.

1. Lyemun Pass. A boom strung across the narrow entrance to Hong Kong's harbour was meant to keep out enemy ships—but instead the Japanese came straight over the hills from China.

2. Lt Alexander Kennedy. The young naval lieuten-ant watched from the hillside as his fiancée sailed out through the pass on the last ship to leave Hong Kong on the eve of the battle.

3. *MTB 09* at speed. Kennedy's was one of eight motor torpedo boats in the flotilla, but the number had been reduced to just five by the time of the surrender.

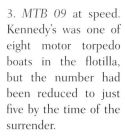

4A. Hong Kong Central waterfront, 1938; photo sent by a Royal Scot back to his mother at Christmas that year.

4B. Hong Kong Harbour; scene of the torpedo boat flotilla's bold raid on Japanese landing craft on 19 December 1941.

6. Lt Cdr GH Gandy, Senior Officer of the flotilla.

5. Lt John Collingwood and his young spaniel, Bruce.

7. Lt Ron Ashby and crew. Note the MTB crest, showing a flying fish, on the front of 07's wheelhouse.

8. Admiral Chan Chak, the Chinese Nationalist Government's representative in Hong Kong in 1941. He is seen here wearing his Chinese Navy cap, but on the escape he wore a borrowed British one.

9. Chan Chak with his wife, Shuichi, and family in Nanjing, 1935.

10. China's One-Legged Admiral. Chan lost his left leg shortly before coming to Hong Kong in 1939, during the Japanese assault on the Bocca Tigris forts near Canton.

11. Henry Hsu, Chan's aide-de-camp. 'The Admiral and his ADC seemed to know all the Chinese guerrillas for miles,' said one of the British sailors.

12. David MacDougall, Hong Kong's Information Chief. An 'anti-colonial' civil servant—or at least, one who saw a need for radical change—he went on to become Hong Kong's Acting Governor.

13. Ted Ross, MacDougall's young Canadian assistant. He had been a volunteer ambulance driver during Japan's attacks on Shanghai, picking up the wounded from the streets. He and MacDougall had plans to escape from Hong Kong in the canoe he kept at Repulse Bay.

14. Mike Kendall, head of the SOE team that arranged the escape. He and his Chinese wife, Betty, met when he was working in southern China in the 1930s as a mining engineer.

15. Colin McEwan, gym teacher and 'makee-learn saboteur', who swam under an enemy-occupied ship in the harbour and blew it up.

16A. Gloucester Hotel, where MacDougall and Ross had their office and where the escape group met up. Photo by Harrison Foreman, 1941.

16B. Fall of Kowloon. Japanese troops advance towards the Star Ferry Pier.

17. Anti-aircraft fire. The tiny naval yard where the flotilla was based at Aberdeen was bombed almost constantly, and like the rest of the colony had no effective defence against enemy aircraft. The MTBs claimed to have brought down at least one Japanese plane, though this was never officially confirmed.

18. *MTB 09* in Aberdeen Channel on 9 December 1941, during a pause in the bombing. From left, Stoker Charles Foster, Coxswain William Schillemore and Able Seaman Robert Hempenstall, RN.

19. Aberdeen from the air. Note the gathering of junks in front of Aplichau Island on the right. The white patch to the left of the town is a big graveyard.

Part Two
The Escape Plan

7

Exit Strategy

20 December 1941

People were sleeping in the Gloucester Hotel a dozen to a room and all along the corridors of the lower floors. The top two storeys, including the eighth-floor restaurant, had been evacuated as the bombing and shelling got worse. The staircases, tea lounge and arcade shops were piled high with sandbags and all the glass was broken. One day, a ten-inch shell crashed through the outer stone wall on the third floor, where David MacDougall and Ted Ross had their office. It penetrated into a couple of rooms but failed to explode. As Ross later recalled, the British Ministry of Information continued working through it all:

> The power station went out on the 18th and we had to carry on by candle light after that. Then the water mains were smashed and the large reservoirs captured, and water became very short and dangerous to drink. We washed and slept in the office. We commandeered a couple of cars to carry on the distribution works—one of them a big new Buick Special. I drove it and boy it was a honey. It broke my heart to have to ruin it driving through streets strewn with glass, bricks and shell holes, but it stood up well and never even got a puncture.

During the first ten days of the battle, Ross had driven out each evening to sleep in his room at the Repulse Bay Hotel. He had begun living there soon after coming to Hong Kong. He kept a small canvas canoe in the bushes by the beach that he used to take out at weekends. On the night after the enemy landings on the island, he arrived at the hotel to find it had become a focal point in the fighting. The Japanese had come down the wooded slope behind and lobbed grenades through the windows at the back. Everything inside his room was wrecked: radio, clothes, photos . . . all he possessed. It all stank of whisky, as they had blown up his drinks cabinet. At dawn when he tried to return to the city over Wongneichong Gap, he ran into a hail of machine-gun and mortar fire. He was forced back, and finally reached the office by taking the coast road via Aberdeen.

The Repulse Bay Hotel held out till 23 December, an unlikely combination of fortress, refuge and hospital. It was defended by a mixed bag of soldiers and naval reserves, a small group of whom had to be rescued after being taken prisoner by the Japanese in a garage. The hotel was sheltering more than 150 women, children and others, mainly elderly civilians. Some of them had adjusted to wartime conditions better than others, who were still indignantly demanding the same sort of standards of service and luxury that had made the Repulse Bay internationally renowned as an oasis of colonial elegance. With no running water and dwindling stocks of caviar, the manageress, Miss Marjorie Matheson, somehow succeeded in holding things together, even as Japanese snipers lurked among the tropical ferns in the manicured gardens and wounded British, Canadian and Indian soldiers staggered in from the hills.

The armed men defending the hotel finally withdrew in the hope of preventing a massacre, but many got no farther than the beach. The Japanese moved in and marched the civilians away after forcing them to watch their erstwhile protectors being tied up, tortured with bayonets and executed. Other atrocities would take place later. The Japanese had been terrorizing China for years, and senior officers habitually allowed their soldiers a day or two after any victory to celebrate in their own way.

The people of Hong Kong, most of them refugees from the mainland, needed no reminding of the dangers they faced once the fighting was over. But some, in both official and non-official circles, had special cause to fear Japanese retribution, on account of their political background. And one name high on the list of those who could expect to be given a 'nasty time' was that of David MacDougall.

From the beginning, the head of the information bureau had been determined to make a break for it if the worst came to the worst. Partly, this was because the thought of being captured and immobilized at such a critical period of history was more than he could bear. But he also knew his own internment was likely to be particularly unpleasant. 'The Japs don't love me,' he acknowledged. MacDougall later denied persistent suggestions that he worked for the secret services, but he did admit he had had to perform 'certain duties' which would have made it very awkward for him if he had been caught:

> I had good reason to know I had been marked down by the Japanese as pro-Chungking (which I was) and as a centre of undercover anti-Japanese intrigue (which I was not). For these and other reasons I decided that the risks of attempting to break out of HK after its fall would be preferable to falling into Japanese hands

as a supposed secret agent in possession of information which I did not in fact have.*

After the siege began, MacDougall asked Hong Kong's Colonial Secretary and Defence Secretary if there would be any official objection to an escape attempt after the cessation of hostilities. Neither saw any problem in principle, and it was agreed that the Colonial Secretary would get back to him should the Governor take exception to the idea. No more was heard of the matter and he therefore began his preparations:

> Ross was keen also and we worked together. First we carefully assembled light packs with concentrated food and vitamins and chocolate sufficient for about six days. Then we tried to bargain with junkmasters. Our plan was vaguely to hide in the hills for 24 hours and then cross to Lantau and thence, travelling by night as opportunity offered, to reach Free China by cautious stages. In the middle of the junk negotiations the Japanese over-ran Kowloon Bay and then occupied Shaukiwan, thus cutting us off from the junk population. Then we planned to cross the harbour by night in Ross's canoe, land at Tsun Wan, cross the Castle Peak Road and travel by night through the hills until we reached the guerilla country over the border. But the enemy captured Repulse Bay and with it Ross's canoe—so we had to begin again. Finally we decided to steal a skiff from the Yacht Club near Deepwater Bay, and in that paddle over the harbour by night and proceed as before.

Just what they would find if and when they did reach the Chinese border was hard to say. As far as Ross was aware, the Japanese had a few troops on nearby islands and held the mainland for a depth of about 25 miles. 'Beyond that were pro-Japanese puppet troops, and scattered here and there were bands of pro-Chungking guerillas, on our side if we could find and convince them we were friends of Free China.'

But there were also other groups roaming the wide stretches of no-man's-land between the two main spheres of China, held by the Japanese on the one hand and the Kuomintang on the other. And the likely attitudes of such groups towards escapers from British Hong

---

did not in fact have: Many of those on the escape always assumed MacDougall's real job was in intelligence, and Ted Ross later stated in one of his recorded interviews that his boss had actually been working for MI6 under the Ministry of Economic Warfare.

Kong were uncertain at best. There were the growing numbers of 'red guerrillas', for instance—some of them tough veterans of ten years' fighting in Mao Zedong's communist armies to the north, others young local recruits, attracted by promises of a less corrupt, less feudal society. There was supposed to be a United Front against the Japanese. But the Nationalist Government tended to put far more effort into hunting down the communists, whom it classified as traitors or bandits, than it did into fighting the Japanese. In truth, both the communist and the KMT guerrillas often doubled as smugglers, pirates or armed guards for hire. Finally, there were plenty of out-and-out bandits who made no pretence at any political allegiance. There was a widespread belief in colonial Hong Kong that anyone bold enough to venture into China's interior was more than likely to get their throat cut by brigands of some description or other.

As far as Captain Freddie Guest was concerned, that risk was still preferable to the prospect of staying behind in captivity. He had made up his mind long ago that he would escape rather than endure the 'slow death' of a prisoner-of-war camp. He would swim across the Lyemun Strait, he decided, walk to the border and trust to luck as he headed deeper inland. He asked Peter Macmillan to join him, and they had a talk with the chief staff officer, Colonel John Newnham, about possible places to head for. They ruled out Canton as it was already occupied by the Japanese, and Macao since they thought it likely to be occupied soon (the nearby Portuguese colony was even less well defended than Hong Kong). Burma was too far away, with too many high mountains to cross. They finally agreed on Chungking. Although it too was remote—1,200 miles away, across some of China's wildest countryside—they believed help would be available once they were in the interior.

Another of the staff officers, Arthur Goring, found Ted Ross peering at the big wall map in the operations room during one of his visits to Command HQ. He sidled up to him. 'What, planning your escape already?' asked the major. 'Yes, I am,' replied Ross. 'When you go, I'll go with you,' said Goring. The young Canadian was unsure how serious he was being.

One night Goring found himself alone with General Maltby and mentioned his intention to escape should the garrison be forced to surrender. The General smiled and told him there was a plan afoot for a small naval party to smuggle out a very important Chinese naval officer, provided there was a suitable boat left unsunk. If he cared to see the organizer there *might* be room for Goring too.

The organizer in question turned out to be Mike Kendall. The SOE commando leader had been summoned to a meeting with Maltby and Newnham on 18 December and asked to prepare an escape plan 'for senior Chinese and British officers'. Kendall later agreed that both Goring and his friend from the Indian police, Bill Robinson, could join the group. He also invited Max Oxford.

One aim of getting such people out was, in Kendall's words, 'so that Hong Kong information could be told'. Somehow, an authoritative account had to be given of what had happened in Hong Kong. Clearly, it was preferable for those in the best position to know such things to report back to Britain and her allies rather than be forced to tell all they knew—about hidden mines, arms dumps and secret agents, for instance—to the enemy. Under prolonged torture, most people had their breaking point.

But the biggest catch of all for the Japanese would have been the redoubtable one-legged Chinese admiral, who had done so much to galvanize resistance and to emasculate their carefully nurtured fifth column. It was made clear to Kendall from the start that the key figures in the escape party were Chan Chak and his two chief aides, Henry Hsu and SK Yee. Chiang Kai-shek would lose trust in Britain if his senior officers in the colony were captured by the enemy. Their torture and death would surely follow.

Kendall and his two Z Force colleagues had therefore been detailed by the British authorities in Hong Kong to make sure these senior Chinese officers got away and to be responsible for their safe delivery. But it's clear that much of the impetus for the escape plan came from China itself. Pressure to keep its top men in Hong Kong out of Japanese hands had been coming from the Kuomintang leadership since early in the battle. Britain's ambassador in Chungking, Sir Archibald Clark Kerr, cabled the Foreign Office in London on 15 December: 'Chinese are still bent on getting some of their people out of Hong Kong. They appreciate that air route is now impossible but they think that enterprising people might now be able to slip out by some other means.'

The message was received in Hong Kong two days later, having been passed on through the War Office with the following Foreign Office note attached: 'We cannot do anything this end but must leave to Governor HK to return such reply as he thinks possible in circumstances . . . the obstacles to success in this are many and obvious.'

Exactly what obstacles it had in mind the Foreign Office did not specify. What was clear was that London did not consider the matter to be of such vital importance that it insisted Hong Kong go ahead and do something about it. After years of failing to give China the support it needed for fear of upsetting Japan, the Foreign Office might have been expected to welcome the chance to make up some lost ground. But the safety of one or two Chinese individuals in a small outpost of empire was not high on its current list of priorities.

In Hong Kong, on the other hand, the value of Chan Chak's role was readily apparent—as was the importance of building bridges with Chungking at a time when the dispatch of a Chinese relief army seemed the colony's best, if not only, hope of survival. The decision to prepare some means of escape for the Admiral was taken 'at the highest level'—in other words, either by the Governor, Sir Mark Young, or by General Maltby. It is possible that during his meeting with Chan Chak on the first day of the battle, Maltby would have recognized the need to do something to help ensure the Admiral's eventual safety. But later, with the General preoccupied with the battle, it is likely to have been the Governor who came to appreciate more fully just how much Chan was doing. Through his various organizations and daily statements to the media, the head of the liaison office was keeping Hong Kong's 1.5 million Chinese fed and sheltered and as loyal and supportive as could be expected. What is certain is that pressure to do the right thing by Chan would have come from people such as David MacDougall and Charles Boxer—people who saw the Admiral every day and who knew China and the Chinese far better than either Young or Maltby.

MacDougall said later that as far as he knew, there was some form of 'gentlemen's understanding' to help Chan escape:

> He condemned himself to a very ugly death if he'd been caught, so that's why he had to be got out one way or another . . . He was most useful to us. I told the Defence Secretary and he said 'yes, get him out whatever you do.'

At this stage MacDougall saw no connection between this and his own planned escape. He assumed Chan would leave just before the end of the battle, whereas he would have to wait till after a ceasefire. But he recognized the special difficulties involved in getting someone as conspicuous as the one-legged admiral through the Japanese lines, and was happy to be able to assure Chan that secret plans for his escape were in hand:

> In general, the best chance of safety for Chinese officials in the event of the Japanese breaking into the colony lay in donning ordinary

"coolie" clothes and mingling with the crowds on the streets. But in view of the fact that he had a wooden leg and that he and his aides were being closely watched by fifth columnists, Chan Chak had little hope of availing himself of this easy disguise. . . . His personal situation was that his departure could not be concealed for long and that once it was known, the encouragement given to the fifth column and the consequent apprehensions inevitable among his own followers would combine to render doubly difficult the task of preventing civil disorder on the scale organized immediately prior to the evacuation of Kowloon. The Admiral accordingly considered it his duty to remain in the besieged city until the last possible moment, although none knew better than he the fate that awaited him if he were to fall into enemy hands. He asked me, as a friend of many years standing, to make myself responsible for informing him when the psychological moment arrived; and this responsibility, being in thrice daily contact with the battle headquarters, I naturally accepted.

The motor torpedo boats, if there were any left, were soon identified as being the best bet for providing a fast and not too conspicuous getaway for the Admiral and his group. FW Kendall and his two SOE colleagues had had a grandstand view of the heroic Kowloon Bay raid from a window at police headquarters. They had also taken the chance to get a close-up look at the MTB flotilla the previous day, when they had gone to Aberdeen in search of a boat for another of their projects—running arms to Mirs Bay for Chinese guerrillas to use to harass Japanese operations near the border. Having got wind of the flotilla's own plans to make a break for it once all was lost, Kendall was now thinking of combining their escape party with his own, and perhaps at the same time linking up with the guerrillas at Shataukok (later to be known as the East River Column).

Lieutenant Commander Horace Gandy was summoned to naval headquarters at 1 p.m. on 20 December. The 2nd MTB Flotilla's forty-five-year-old commanding officer put on his tin hat and rode into town on his motorbike through pouring rain. The streets of Wanchai were full of large craters, with overhead tram cables hanging down and bombed houses spilling debris and dead bodies. The Commodore himself was waiting for him, along with the senior military intelligence officer, Charles Boxer, who told him he had been chosen for an important task.

'I was then given confidential instructions,' recalled Gandy, 'to carry a European guerrilla leader, Mr. F.W.K. and his two assistants in the boats of the flotilla and to land with him north of Hongkong after scuttling, and to endeavour to pass through the Japanese lines with flotilla personnel . . . If it was not possible to pass through the lines I was to operate as a guerilla force against the Japanese with the hope of relief by Chinese forces. I was told that some influential Chinese might also travel with the party and that I was to be guided as far as possible by the advice of Mr. F.W.K. both in preparation for this operation and in the operation itself.'

Gandy was told that Kendall, McEwan and Talan would base themselves on board his boats from the following day. He was to ensure his flotilla was ready to leave on receipt of the word 'GO'. There was to be as little discussion as practicable, even with his own officers. But carrying irregular forces and Chinese passengers, not to mention operating on land as a guerrilla himself, were not the sort of things the young Horace Gandy had been taught back in the days when he was a classmate of the Prince Royal* at Dartmouth Naval College in the first decade of the century. The retired Royal Navy commander confessed later that he found the plan not much clearer than mud:

> The escape was all pretty nebulous to me, barring landing with packs, rifles and revolvers somewhere on the mainland—naturally not too far away, MTB petrol consumption being what it was. A lead-mine in the New Territories was mentioned as a last resort where an armed party with sufficient food might hold out for some time. This led incidentally to having a lot of heavy tinned food (not to be opened without orders) stowed in our knapsacks against emergencies; some tins eventually being landed intact in UK!

After the meeting, Boxer went off in a staff car on a reconnaissance trip to the south of the island. Gandy obtained a map from headquarters—1:250,000 War Office, Hongkong and Canton—showing the area where they were expected to land in China. On his way back he called in to see his wife at their home in Magazine Gap Road. He told her not to worry if she heard nothing from him: that meant he should be safe. Dorothea was a tall Dutch woman whom he had met during his internment in the Hague during the First World War, after his ship, HMS *Aramis* had been sunk by German destroyers. The couple, who had never had children, married first in Holland

---

Prince Royal: Bertie, the stammerer, who would later become King George VI. He and Gandy were both keen yachtsmen and continued to go sailing together after leaving naval college.

and then again in 1920 in England. Dolly and Holly, as they called each other, were very close.

As they prepared for the next day's move out to the boats at Aberdeen, Kendall, McEwan and Talan spent the evening 'in feeding and argument' at the Gloucester. The police had just set up their new headquarters there after being bombed out of the Central Police Station in Hollywood Road, so the hotel now looked likely to become even more of a target than it already was. But still people kept arriving in search of a safe haven. Phyllis Harrop wrote in her diary that she and her two roommates had had dinner with 'Mr Kendall and two of his friends', and that Kendall's wife had now moved in to share their box-room:

> Her house at Shing Mun has been blown up and they have been staying on the Peak, but that house has now been damaged. As her husband is away all day, she is nervous. She is a charming American-born Chinese girl sent to me to look after; what a hope, I can't look after myself, never mind anyone else!

Before working for the police, the blonde and statuesque Ms Harrop had been employed by the government as a 'Lady Commissioner for Chinese Affairs', in charge of rescuing *muizhai*, or slave girls, from brothels and opium dens. Emily Hahn, the writer, couldn't help laughing at her job with wayward girls 'since she looked so wayward herself'. According to Colin McEwan's diary, the evening with Betty's new roommates was a lively one, and culminated in he and Talan finally going to sleep in police quarters after 'heaving our bedding all over the hotel'. The Gloucester's corridors were becoming more crowded than ever, as the net continued to close.

8
Death of a Gunboat

21 December

Next morning, a severely wounded Charles Boxer was brought into Queen Mary Hospital. He had found the road east of Aberdeen blocked by abandoned vehicles below Shouson Hill, and had continued on foot. He was crossing some open ground with Lieutenant TJ Price and Sub-Lieutenant JJ Forster of the HKRNVR when they came under fire from a collection of huts. A bullet entered Boxer's chest close to the lung and came out near the middle of his back. As the shooting intensified and grenades were thrown, the two naval officers carried him to safety, and he was taken to the Aberdeen Industrial School. After a night in the Queen Mary's resuscitation ward, it was decided he would live.

Boxer's place at the daily intelligence meeting in Shell House was taken by Max Oxford. After hearing reports of how local residents had been killed, raped or robbed by the Japanese troops, or kidnapped as porters, Chan Chak said he could no longer tolerate his people's suffering. He was now proposing that his Loyal and Righteous vigilantes should join the fighting on the front line. But he needed the British to provide them with guns and grenades, and this they seemed reluctant to do. He complained later that as soon as he brought up the subject, 'all the British representatives expressed confidence in their ability to defend Hong Kong'. And when the weapons finally did come, it was a matter of too little, too late.

But the Admiral refused to be disheartened. He continued to give hopeful reports about the progress of a 60,000-strong army led by Yu Hanmou. General Yu was commander of China's 7th War Zone, an area that included Guangdong Province. His army's advance guard was now said to be 'on the frontier and about to attack'. Britain's military attaché in Chungking had just sent a telegram saying the main Chinese attack couldn't start for another ten days. But Fortress HQ felt sufficiently emboldened by Chan's optimism to put out a morale-boosting if cautiously worded signal to all units:

There are indications that Chinese forces are advancing towards the frontier to our aid. All forces must therefore hold their positions at all costs and look forward to only a few more days of strain.

There was also another message from Churchill: 'Every day your resistance brings nearer our certain victory.' The Prime Minister seemed to be insisting that lives be sacrificed in Hong Kong to keep the enemy tied down and thus delay its advance elsewhere. But resistance in other parts of Asia was already crumbling. Thailand had succumbed to Japanese occupation within the first few days; in Malaya, Penang had been evacuated; in the Philippines, a large Japanese army had landed and was advancing on Manila.

As enemy soldiers continued to race westwards across Hong Kong Island, the Royal Navy ordered its forces in Aberdeen to fight to the last man. Most of them were now sailors without ships. They were each issued with a rifle and bayonet, a revolver and a bag of grenades, and sent up into the hills in their conspicuous blue uniforms, their bell-bottom trousers tucked into their boots. Those who were still alive after a day or two would wander back into the Industrial School in search of food and shelter. They reported that the enemy seemed to know the lie of the land much better than they did: every Japanese soldier had been equipped with his own pocket-sized map.

The biggest fighting ship still afloat was the 615-ton HMS *Cicala*, with a length of 238 feet and a beam of just 38 feet. The flat-bottomed Insect-class gunboat had first seen action in the 1914–18 War—as had its present captain, Lieutenant Commander John Boldero, as a fifteen-year-old at Jutland. After working between the wars for the Shanghai Waterworks Company, Boldero was recalled to duty in 1939 and appointed commander of the motor torpedo boat flotilla in Hong Kong. He was replaced by Gandy after losing his right arm in a collision on a night exercise in April 1941, but discharged himself from hospital and took over Gandy's earlier command of *Cicala*. He now steered the river gunboat with his left hand—to such good effect that over the previous two weeks she had proved a constant menace to the Japanese and had survived more than sixty bombing attacks. Fitted with triple rudders, she could turn 'almost on a sixpence'. Like the MTBs, *Cicala* had been granted a reprieve from the scuttling; and like them too, she was preparing to stage her own breakout. 'Oil fuel remaining was ample for Singapore and I had acquired the necessary charts,' Boldero recalled later.

But it was not to be. At 10 a.m. on Sunday, 21 December, *Cicala* steamed into Deep Water Bay, battle ensign flying, to help Pillbox 14, which was under assault from Japanese troops advancing towards Brick Hill. The flimsy-looking gunboat saw off the attack for the time being, but came under heavy mortar fire herself. Then six warplanes appeared and took it in turns to unload their bombs upon her. Watching from the hills was James Bertram, a New Zealander who had been one of the first journalists to interview Mao Zedong and who saw this day's Japanese shooting party over the East Lamma Channel as a symptom of the times:

> Insolently the leading bomber went into his shallow dive, and the red flash showed a hit. *Cicala* struggled gamely out into the channel, banging away with her single 3-inch quick-firer. But this British gunboat had been designed, like all her class, to steam up Chinese rivers and settle 'local disorders' with a few well-placed rounds. Now she was meeting Asiatics who had learnt too well the lessons of the gunboat years.

Another New Zealander to witness the scene was Sub-Lieutenant Ralph Goodwin, who was just coming round the headland on *MTB 10*, together with some of the other boats in the flotilla. He counted several more sticks of light bombs before *Cicala* finally succumbed:

> Stick after stick fell about the little ship, but after each salvo, when the columns of spray had slowly fallen, there she was, still afloat and steaming. Fresh waves of planes came over and finally three bombs scored direct hits. *Cicala* was mortally hurt and with her boats holed, steampipes broken and hull shattered, the gunboat was abandoned to the sea. As she slowly sank *MTB 10* went alongside to take off survivors.

The decks were awash with water and the sea thick with oil, but almost all the crew were saved before *MTB 09* hastened the sinking with depth charges. Goodwin's own luck ran out a short while later when his boat came under fire from a field gun just after landing the survivors at Aberdeen, in the next bay. A jagged steel splinter passed through his thigh and dropped on deck. Meadows, the telegraphist, took the wheel while the coxswain, Petty Officer Bill Dyer, attended to the injured first lieutenant. They got him to the crowded clearing station at the Industrial School, but shells from the mainland were bursting all along the road towards the city, so it was almost dark before an ambulance could take him to the Queen Mary. His stretcher stuck out of the open back door as the vehicle clattered and bounced over the broken road surface, past the big cemetery with its solitary palm tree on the hill out of Aberdeen and along the coast towards Mount Davis. The hospital was teeming, the Chinese wards filled to the brim with casualties from the bombing of rice queues in Central Market—one of the few occasions when the Japanese deliberately bombed civilians.

Goodwin's place on *MTB 10* was taken by Chief Petty Officer Gilbert Thums, *Cicala*'s thirty-six-year-old coxswain. The rest of the gunboat's crew were packed off to fight on Bennett's Hill within a few hours of coming onshore. In giving Thums an instant transfer—or 'pierhead jump'—to the role of acting first lieutenant, the flotilla's commanding officer was paying him a rare compliment in an era when officers and other ranks were regarded almost as two separate species. But Gandy knew Thums well from his own days as captain of *Cicala*, when he had found the overweight but hugely popular and competent coxswain 'of great assistance . . . particularly in his cheerful and tactful attitude to officers and ratings'.

As the senior rating on a ship, a chief petty officer was similar to a sergeant major in the army, acting as a bridge between the upper and lower decks. A good CPO tended to be someone who was gregarious and showed initiative: who could be a father figure to the young but could also stretch boundaries and work outside the system.

'Tom' Thums, as his shipmates affectionately knew him, was all these things and more. He had been brought up in Beeston, Nottinghamshire, by his grandparents. He joined the navy in 1920 at the age of fifteen, listing his occupation as butcher's slaughterer. He later met a French girl, Hélène, who had been sent to England by her middle-class family to widen her horizons and was staying with the family of a Captain Ramsey in Devonport. Leading Seaman Gilbert Thums was coxswain of the captain's barge. Hélène became pregnant. Gilbert was the father. They were married in the Devonport Register Office on 2 June 1928. Since then, Thums had made steady progress in the navy, becoming a petty officer after twelve years and a chief petty officer six years later. But his life at sea meant he seldom saw his wife and their two children. He knew they had been having a tough time in Plymouth in the bombing. What he didn't know was that Hélène had started a new life with a French sailor, one of the crew of a submarine that had taken refuge in Plymouth after the Fall of France.

Having just lost his ship, all that mattered to Thums for now was that he was being given the chance to stay afloat, courtesy of the 2nd MTB Flotilla. Tilting back his cap with its gleaming CPO's badge to a more rakish angle than ever, he strode onto the flotilla's lead boat, *MTB 10*, and greeted his new shipmates.

9
Ducking and Diving

21–24 December

The arrival of Gilbert Thums in the flotilla coincided with that of Kendall, McEwan and Talan—or Mike, Mac and John*—as they soon came to be known. The three SOE men heaved their boxes of Bren guns, grenades, guncotton and various 'toys' onto *MTB 10*, where, as McEwan noted in his diary, they were treated to a lively firsthand account of the final attack on *Cicala*:

> The story of how five bombs hit her in line, without completely sinking her, and causing only one death (The Gunner's Mate) changed my idea of the effectiveness of bombs, and told as it was by 'Tom Thumb' [*sic*], later to prove the best of good fellows, gave us a good impression and a lasting one it proved of the Navy in general and also gave us a new phrase for our repertoire, 'Bloody Rubbish', denoting anything unfortunate, unlucky, badly managed, nonsensical, etc.

Although the motor torpedo boats were almost constantly under fire, spirits on board remained high—a welcome change from the tension, gloom and confusion McEwan and his colleagues had come across on land:

> Here was the best morale I had seen, and that too among men who had, in their frailest of craft, no protection against shells or bombs, except wits, courage—and Lewis guns for any low-flying craft. Moored as they were, all one could do was duck and hope—yet the atmosphere was most cheerful, and the relationship between officers and men most pleasant. Everyone realised they were in a tough spot—Aberdeen was no health resort—yet there was not the slightest sign of panic or disorder, and the crews ducked or sat and smoked with an attitude of 'oh well, what a —ing life' that was quite infectious.

The Z Force trio were soon appointed to their various boats. Kendall stayed with Gandy on *MTB 10*, sharing the duties of a first

---

Mike, Mac and John: Talan, for whatever reason, avoided using his usual name, Monia, at this time. His original first name was Moses.

lieutenant with Thums. Talan was on *07* and McEwan on *11*, both of them also taking their turns on watch. The crew's quarters on each boat consisted of a narrow cabin with just enough room for a bench-type seat and a table. This was moved at night to make room for the men to rig their bunks. There was a bucket in the corner for washing. The officers had almost as little space in their wardroom, but they had the luxury of a polished wooden drinks cupboard on the wall and a more comfortable leather berth to sit or sleep on. The fact that most of the men had spent two years or more together in such tiny boats helped explain their strong bonds of comradeship.

After some grim experiences at army and police feeding stations over the past week, the new arrivals were as delighted by the standard of cooking on the MTBs as by the level of camaraderie. They were also happy to make their acquaintance with 'those heavenly twins, Navy Rum and Navy Tobacco', whose praises, declared Mac the poet, 'should be sung in verse and not in mere prose'.

For most of the day, the boats were spread out around the harbour approaches to avoid the worst of the serial bombing and mortar attacks. But towards dusk they came together. The presence of the three heavily armed commandos in their jungle camouflage clothing had already started a round of feverish speculation. Now Kennedy and the other captains received a briefing on who they were and why they were there:

> They had been doing special work during the fighting, sabotage or intelligence, we never knew quite what, as they could all talk fluent Cantonese and had an intimate knowledge of the surrounding country. Apparently if the Chinese Army advanced far enough in time, the flotilla was to be used for landing a British party near the border to link up with the Chinese. There was also the possibility that some of the M.T.B. crews might operate ashore, but nothing had been settled and with events moving fast in Hong Kong the Chinese might well be too late. In this case our alternative would be to land somewhere on the coast and endeavour to break through the Japanese cordon into Free China behind.

Commander Hugh Montague, Senior Naval Officer, Aberdeen, had just sent Gandy a signal saying that in view of the latest enemy advances along the Industrial School road the flotilla should stand by to leave on its special mission with the SOE men immediately. But Kendall insisted they would have to wait for Admiral Chan Chak and his assistant, Colonel Yee. He also said no success could be expected until he had made 'authentic contact with guerilla headquarters in Victoria'.* This was apparently a reference to Liao Chengzhi—who as the senior communist party figure in Hong Kong, operating under the cover of a tea wholesaling business in Queen's Road, was in charge of the three thousand or so East River Column guerillas near the border. Like Chan Chak and his vigilante force of Nationalist agents, 'Fatty' Liao wanted his men to receive British weapons, but a possible deal to supply them involved various conditions, intermediaries and queries over transport, and nothing had yet been finalized.

The news that the MTBs were now under orders to get away at all costs with the official escape party sent a buzz of excitement through the flotilla. 'Were we selfishly pleased!' David Legge later told his brother, a fighter pilot who had recently taken part in the Battle of Britain. 'It was a chance. It was obvious that the island could not hold out very much longer. As, however, we had to keep the whole thing as quiet as possible, we were unable to bring away more people, for whom we had plenty of room. It was rotten to have to leave behind so many of one's pals and slip off in the night as if we were running away at the last moment, even though we realized that that was not the case.'

Meanwhile, the flotilla had to make rapid preparations to operate on land in the very near future. Kendall gave advice on what clothes, footwear, food and weapons they would need. There was no place in guerilla operations for the sick or the wounded, he said—the message was: 'shoot quick and be fit'. Each man was to prepare a pack containing rubber shoes, spare socks, dark sweaters and other personal items. Tinned provisions were divided into small sacks suitable for carrying individually, and ammunition for the Bren guns was distributed likewise. Revolvers were issued on board and rifles drawn from the armoury on shore.

Guerilla kit inspections were carried out on each boat, and as the opportunity arose over the next few days, the clearing station at HQ was visited in search of well-worn walking boots and other items no longer needed by the dead and wounded. The Japanese were now close enough to ensure that any trip to the Industrial School was a lively experience. A blitz of howitzer and mortar fire succeeded in keeping the sailors' heads down as they ran along the half-mile

---

Victoria: the formal name of the main city on Hong Kong Island, though seldom used in practice even then.

stretch of road between the village jetty and the base. Sniping by fifth columnists hiding near the dockyard was an added hazard.

The man in charge of the dockyard was a tall, gaunt figure, with a naval cap firmly pulled down over weathered features and long white hair. Like many other merchant seamen, Lieutenant Pethick, RNR, had joined the Royal Naval Reserve with the coming of war. But he was better known up and down the coast as Captain Pethick of Jardines.

The masters of the shallow-draught, coal-fired vessels of Jardine Matheson, Butterfield & Swire and the other famous China traders were a breed apart. Old salts who in their prime had sailed square-riggers round the Horn, they were rarely questioned by their managers as to what went on between one Chinese port and another. They used their almost unlimited powers at sea to put ashore difficult passengers, tackle pirates as they best saw fit (they often hired White Russian guards, at least when passing Bias Bay) or simply, as in Pethick's case, give full play to their own eccentricities.

Born in southwest England in 1889, Douglas Stuart Pethick was a grandson of one of Plymouth's most famous citizens—the builder, John Pethick. After qualifying as a merchant mariner, he headed for the Far East, joining Jardines' shipping arm, the Indo-China Steamship Navigation Company, and passing his master's certificate in Hong Kong in 1924. The company's schooners and brigs and steamships with their red and black funnels were renowned for setting records, such as being the first to run from Canton to England under sail. Pethick entertained the MTB crews with many a yarn of how he had set new records of his own: the quickest round trip to Shanghai, the shortest steaming route, or the passage using the least coal. According to Kennedy, the old sea captain had now somewhat mellowed from the days when he had been 'liable to knock a man into the scuppers in the traditional manner'. But his earlier fondness for fiery curry tiffins had played havoc with his stomach, and he never ceased to bemoan his fate and curse his ruined digestion.

Pethick played a heroic role in the dockyard during the worst of the bombing raids, and was often to be seen darting about the harbour in a small, flat-bottomed dinghy, driven by a noisy outboard motor. This outfit was affectionately known as the 'Flying Bedpan', Kennedy recalled. 'During one particular raid he was caught in the middle of the channel and apparently enveloped by a rain of bombs. To the anxious onlookers all seemed to be over, when out through a curtain of spray dashed the 'Bedpan', but with no sign of Pethick. He was there, however, his whole length miraculously coiled down in the sternsheets, lying soaked to the skin and expressing his thoughts on the Japanese in the crudest terms.'

Other examples of the lighter side of life under fire included an incident involving 07's stocky coxswain, Petty Officer John 'Jixer' Prest, from West Hartlepool, who 'while climbing out of the conning tower with the rum jar heard a shell coming—ducked—remembered the rum—reappeared, shielding the rum next to his heart—and again carefully ducked to what shelter the thin planking of the vessel could afford'. A further feat of bravado glimpsed by McEwan was performed by 'that gallant sailor Lieut. Ashby who, when a shell burst, instead of going flat, bowed gracefully showing a shiny polished blue serge bottom as his means of all round defence'.

There were also the two small Chinese children whose air raid shelter consisted of a large wicker basket. Each time the shells and bombs descended on Aberdeen, the pair of waifs would dive head-long into the sanctuary of their basket, carefully closing the rattan lid behind them.

As the enemy occupied Violet Hill and moved west with light field guns along the northern slopes of Brick Hill,* new areas came under direct fire. An increasing amount of damage was done among the mass of junks and sampans moored just across Aberdeen Harbour, in front of the old fishermen's temple and boatbuilding yards on the northern shore of Aplichau, also known as Aberdeen Island. The Jesuit Seminary, whose golden Chinese roofs shone out from the headland just across the mouth of Staunton's Creek from the Industrial School, was hit repeatedly—particularly after the Japanese mistook a telescope in the garden for an anti-aircraft gun. A series of shells hit the front of the School itself, badly smashing the hospital area, the MTB office and two dormitories, and cutting off power and phones.

Over the last few days before Christmas, there was little the five remaining MTBs could do other than try to avoid being hit as they waited for the order to go. Their only source of fuel was a lighter moored near Aberdeen that had a defective pump, which meant the petrol had to be transferred by bucket. Since the dockyard had become untenable no new torpedoes could be loaded, and they had no base in which to anchor. To avoid enemy planes they hid behind small islands and in coves and bays just along the coast, tucking themselves in close to the rocks and changing position several times a day.

Brick Hill: near today's Ocean Park.

The flotilla leader, *MTB 10*, stayed in Aberdeen Harbour for as long as possible to keep in touch with the changing situation. At one point the boat was riddled with shellfire while loading ammunition at the T-head pier near the school. Miraculously the only casualty was a duck, which was being kept alive in the semi-flooded after compartment for Christmas dinner and was killed by a splinter earlier than intended. Panic-stricken ducks had been flapping and fluttering all over the boats as the whistling of the shells grew ever louder.

One dilemma for Gandy was what to do with the men from the late *MTB 08*, most of whom were naturally keen to make a bid for freedom along with the rest of the flotilla. The two officers from the destroyed boat, Lieutenant Laurence Kilbee and Sub-Lieutenant Lewis Bush, had been transferred to the flotilla's onshore operations. Bush was sent into town with a petty officer to get provisions for the escape: they filled sacks with torches, batteries and other useful goods after forcing a fearful department store manager to open up at gunpoint. But Gandy was under pressure to have Bush's Japanese wife arrested as a spy, and in the circumstances it seemed wisest not to include her husband in the escape party.* As for Kilbee, Gandy took him onto *MTB 10* for a while as first officer, but finally decided he too should be left behind since he was 'very worried' about his wife and baby daughter in Hong Kong.

The only active use of the MTBs now was as fast ferryboats to Stanley, where the troops of East Brigade were completely cut off. To the north, Hong Kong's main line of defence still held at Happy Valley, thanks to fierce house-to-house resistance by the Middlesex and Royal Marines from HMS *Tamar*. In the southwest, the battle continued to fluctuate just outside Aberdeen, with the Canadians and naval platoons counter-attacking, but then falling back in the face of fresh enemy infiltration.

The Canadians—hailed in the local press on their arrival the previous month as 'tough, bronzed and fit-looking'—were handicapped by their lack of training, equipment and local knowledge. Many of them spoke only French. It was a topic on which the less said the better, in Kendall's view. He considered his fellow countrymen a fine bunch and he knew all their officers, but when it came to fighting it was 'absolute chaos'. 'They didn't have a hope,' he said later. 'The men

---

the escape party: Because of his fluency in Japanese, Bush was later put in charge of surrendering the Aberdeen base. By then the charges against his wife had been dismissed as fabrications.

were ill-equipped and didn't fit in with the garrison troops . . . Most were boys who didn't know one end of a gun from the other.'

If Kendall could be scathing and even brutal at times, he could also be charming and inspirational. According to Gandy, the commando leader was 'an optimistic and encouraging individual' who gave invaluable advice and immediately inspired confidence in all MTBs. McEwan too noticed the intense admiration and interest his boss aroused among the men. 'All of them regular sailors and accustomed to taking orders, they seemed greatly impressed by the appearance of someone who, while obviously in command of things, yet gave the impression of being able to do things and who could be called "Mike" by the very people he was commanding without any loss of face or apparent loss of efficiency.'

Another possible reason for some of the widespread respect for Kendall was that on their first visit to the naval base, the three men from Z Force had been accompanied by his glamorous Chinese wife, Betty, who had waited outside as the talks went on in the office, drawing a crowd of admiring sailors.

Kendall went into Hong Kong Island on an intelligence-gathering trip on 23 December, and again on the following day, when he dropped by to see Betty in her shared room at the Gloucester. According to Phyllis Harrop, he had a rest in the room and then held a conference there with 'the Chungking people', at which they discussed plans for landing a party on the mainland and linking up with Chinese troops. The idea was 'to take MTBs and men and send information back to HQ here'. SK Yee was 'in agreement', and would send signals to Chungking. If such an operation could be done at all, wrote Harrop in her diary, Kendall was the man to do it. She felt sorry, though, for his wife, whose life was 'nothing but intense anxiety. He is always doing some fantastic job or other. However he has already done a fine job and on more than one occasion has destroyed Jap bases by hand grenades. His two able assistants are with him in this crazy plan too.'

Kendall found the situation in the city on Christmas Eve a desperate one. There were fires burning everywhere—the biggest just outside the China Fleet Club. Houses had collapsed and telegraph poles leaned at crazy angles. Streets were pitted with shell holes, which gradually filled with water from broken mains and sewers, drowning any wounded sheltering in them. Small groups of soldiers occupied houses or sheltered in doorways, and these buildings became isolated strongpoints trying to hold back advancing enemy infantry. Artillery and small arms fire came from every direction. It was apparent the defenders could not hold out for much longer.

He returned to Aberdeen, where earlier that day Sir Mark Young and Commodore Collinson had paid an inspection visit. The Governor told the beleaguered occupants of the naval base that he wanted to find out for himself how matters stood instead of depending on the military. It was anticipated the enemy would attack from Shouson Hill and simultaneously along the north slopes of Brick Hill. The Industrial School was a military post of prime importance, he said, and must be held at all costs. Shelling intensified during his visit, with many hits on the building and incendiary bombs starting a large fire on the hill behind. But Sir Mark remained in good spirits. 'He left us with a cheery nod, giving us no indication our position was particularly serious,' reported one of the thousand or more men who were now based at the School.

Kendall told Gandy he had heard a 'splendid rumour' that the advance guard of Yu Hanmou's relief army had reached Shataukok, on the border. Accordingly, plans were discussed to send the fast, silent and low-in-the-water Thornycroft boat, *MTB 27*, with McEwan and Talan, to try and make contact and guide the troops in. The skipper of 27, Lieutenant Tommy Parsons, HKRNVR, happened to be the brother of David Parsons, one of the seven Z Force men still stranded without a radio in their hideout behind the Japanese lines. Their father ran the Hong Kong Hotel garage and was a captain in HKVDC Transport. At the time the Japanese attacked Hong Kong— on his 26th birthday—Tommy had been Naval ADC to the Governor. He was currently not in Gandy's good books, however, since his boat had recently been discovered nearly adrift at the dock entrance while its crew took cover in an air raid shelter.

In the end they decided to wait till morning for firmer news of a Chinese army, which most had by now given up as fictional. Kendall had in any case learnt enough in town to know that by next day— Christmas Day—Chan Chak would be joining them, and it would be time for the whole escape party to leave. Gandy, too, had received a hint that the end was near. He had been handed a private letter addressed to the Commodore's family in Kent and asked to post it if and when he could, since the Commodore himself was not expecting to be in a position to do so for quite some time.

The MTBs slipped their Aberdeen moorings at dusk. They had decided to spread out for the night to the west of Aplichau. They left by the western harbour route, threading through the masts of scuttled ships and attracting some artillery fire from the ridges to the east of the Industrial School. This was preferable, said Gandy, to taking the southern Aberdeen Channel route, which was now open to machine-gun fire from Japanese infantry infiltrating around Brick Hill.

Not a Christmas star was in sight, but there were bright flashes in the sky and a steady roar from the big guns at Stanley. It was to be their last night in Hong Kong.

10
Surrender

25 December

As Christmas Day dawned, some noted ominously that it was another Thursday—the third of the eighteen-day battle. The first had seen the retreat from the mainland; the second the invasion of the island; all that was left was capitulation.

Sir Mark Young had been spending his evenings playing Chopin on the Government House piano, as he wrestled with the agonizing choice of when to admit defeat. No British possession had surrendered itself to the enemy since the American War of Independence some 170 years before.

Churchill's latest message ruled out surrender, calling for vigorous fighting from house to house. But the Governor was the man on the spot, responsible for the lives of 1.5 million people, and his military chiefs were saying further resistance meant pointless slaughter. The key strategic heights had been irretrievably lost and the bulk of the city lay exposed. The water from the reservoirs had been cut off, and government officials had been warning for days that 'the town was now helpless'. But most crucially of all, Hong Kong's defenders had simply run out of energy. On Christmas morning some 8,000 men, utterly exhausted after fighting a rearguard action without air support since day one of the attack, were up against 20,000 fresh troops, confident in the knowledge that there were plenty more behind them.

At 9 a.m. two of the civilians captured at the Repulse Bay Hotel were sent under a white flag to Government House. They handed over a message saying if there was no surrender by three o'clock that afternoon, the entire colony would be blown up and every man, woman and child massacred. Privately, they reported that the scale of the enemy forces they had seen as they were marched across the island led them to believe any further resistance would be suicidal. The Japanese declared a three-hour truce to give the defenders time to reflect. Young still refused to give in, and the attack was resumed at midday with renewed vigour. But as the Governor's consultations with his senior ministers continued into the early hours of the afternoon, one after another of them came to the same reluctant conclusion already reached by General Maltby: surrender was now the only option.

There were no longer even any last rays of hope to be gleaned from reports of approaching Chinese armies. Fortress HQ's sole wireless transmitter had been put out of action by shellfire and the Battle Box was cut off from both London and Chungking. The grenades and revolvers Chan Chak had been requesting for his 'dare-to-die' corps did, finally, arrive . . . after dark on Christmas Eve. But as the Admiral was about to send his men off to fight, he got a message asking him to hold back. Clearly, someone on the British side still had qualms about these 'ruffians and Triad members dashing around in civilian clothes tossing grenades everywhere' (though to be fair, the reason for the concern was said to be less a lack of confidence in the Loyal and Righteous men's fighting ability than fear of Japanese reprisals on the ordinary Chinese population).

According to David MacDougall, if the immediate cause of the fall of Hong Kong was Japan's superior weight and numbers, the ultimate cause was the failure to allow the full and active involvement of either the Chinese government or the local Chinese people. 'What happened can hardly have been duplicated in history since small mercenary armies defended the rich cities of medieval Europe,' he wrote. 'The vast reservoir of manpower within our gates remained largely untapped.' The bold dash for freedom about to be made by a Hong Kong group consisting of both British and Chinese was to become a shining example of what could be achieved when the two sides finally decided to work as a team.

MacDougall had promised to let Chan Chak know when the end of hostilities was at hand, and he was as good as his word. At their last two daily meetings, the British and Chinese sides had agreed on the need to prepare for a 'radical deterioration' and now, at ten o'clock on Christmas morning, the Admiral received due warning of the 'imminent end of resistance'. He and his close colleagues were by this time based full-time in Shell House, sleeping in a bank strongroom in the basement. He ordered his staff to burn their documents and get ready to leave.

On the previous evening, Chan and a few of his family and colleagues had met at the Gloucester Hotel. Among the group was his younger brother, Chan Chi. They listened to the sounds of gunfire coming from Happy Valley. Henry Hsu called it the most disheartening Christmas Eve of his life. Chan finally spoke, raising the subject

of what would happen when Hong Kong fell. Despite the tight blockade by land, sea and air, he would take the risk of trying to 'break
through the encirclement' rather than surrender. He would prefer to
die, he said, than be captured alive by the Japanese:

> I then wrote on my passport 'success or martyrdom'. I quickly wrote
> two letters, one to my parents, the other to my wife. My brother took
> the letters away, tearfully and with bowed head. Having done what I
> needed to do, I was calm and ready for whatever lay ahead.

Chan Chak told his family to leave the city immediately if possible.
But for him it would not be so easy. He was well known to thousands
of fifth columnists and easily identifiable by his physical handicap.
He therefore intended to take up the British authorities' offer of the
use of their last motor torpedo boats, if there were any remaining. His
immediate staff—his number two, SK Yee; his ADC, Henry Hsu; and
his personal bodyguard, Yeung Chuen—would go with him.

Both Chan and his aide-de-camp stated that during the morning
of 25 December they discussed their escape with the Governor
himself. After being informed by Young of his intention to surrender, 'I asked him if he still had a fleet left to hand over to me direct,'
recalled Chan. 'Thereupon the Governor decided to offer me the
only five torpedo boats remaining . . . for a desperate thrust through
the enemy blockading line.' According to Henry Hsu, the Governor
invited them to his office and said that while they were welcome to
use the five boats, he could not tell them exactly where they were. But
their headquarters was at the Industrial School in Aberdeen, and if
they could find just one of the boats, its crew could send a message
to the others.

The arrangement was that the Admiral's party would wait in the
city centre with the various British officers who were to accompany
them. They would be alerted one hour prior to the Governor's actual
surrender and told where and when there would be the best chance
of making contact with the MTBs. No definite rendezvous could be
fixed, as the boats might be forced by bombing and shelling to dodge
continually from one hiding place to another. To make matters even
more uncertain, orders for the MTB flotilla to leave had to be given
before the surrender, since according to military procedure, once the
command was issued for an unconditional surrender, all property
immediately belonged to the victor. Anyone wishing to be on board
the boats when they left therefore needed to move quickly.

Exactly who on the British side was going to accompany Chan and his men was now becoming clearer. Colonel Yee had told David MacDougall, who had been working closely with the Chinese Nationalists, that he was welcome to join the Admiral's party. MacDougall replied that he had already been planning his own escape with his assistant, Ted Ross, and asked if he could come too. SK said: 'Of course, but you've got to help us get out to Aberdeen, to make the rendezvous with the boat.' Ross was only too happy to offer to drive them in the big new Buick Special. He promised to make sure that the car was ready, filled up with petrol and parked in a quiet spot around the back of the Gloucester Building, where the Chinese group were to meet them before leaving. But Ross and MacDougall were still anxious about the actual timing of the departure. They had no wish to make a break before the surrender and be called deserters. If necessary, they would go with the others to Aberdeen, then hide up in the hills and look for a boat of their own later.

The two men from the information bureau spent Christmas morning in the office. They cleared up a few last things and checked that their new knapsacks were ready to go, complete with change of underwear, socks, razor, toothbrush, several bottles of vitamin tablets and as much chocolate as they could cram in. At about noon they said their goodbyes to their few remaining staff (a Chinese assistant, a Portuguese typist and a handful of Chinese messengers), suggesting that they should go home and stay indoors for a few days until things calmed down. Or if they wanted to get away before the Japanese took over, now was the time to change into some 'coolie clothes' and mingle with the crowds.

Over at Command HQ, Arthur Goring was confident that he had now got at least the first stage of the British and Chinese VIPs' escape all fixed up. As agreed earlier with Kendall, he had asked Max Oxford and Bill Robinson to contact Chan Chak's group and to wait with them near a telephone in the Gloucester, with transport available to take them all to the rendezvous when he gave the word. Goring himself would join them as soon as he could get away from his position at the General's side in the Battle Box.

According to Freddie Guest, he and Peter Macmillan had at first been the only ones intending to make the break for freedom, but were then asked to contact Chan Chak and see if they could get him away too. Others maintain that Guest was not a member of the original escape party at all and that he came on board only at the very last moment. Whatever the truth, he clearly knew about the official escape plan by Christmas morning, since by that time he was busy inviting others to join as well. Soon after 9 a.m., Guest was observed outside Fortress HQ, trying to dispose of a pile of books and cipher machines. With him was General Frank 'One-Arm' Sutton, inventor and larger-than-life soldier of fortune. Sutton had lost a limb at Gallipoli but had gone on to become a military adviser to the 'Old Marshal' of Manchuria,* and had continued to play rugby, even in China, fending off tackles with his stump. Having made and lost a fortune from selling stainless steel coffins to the Chinese, he was currently employed as Hong Kong's 'Chief Destroyer of Incriminating Documents'. And according to the one-armed general's biographer, Guest was at this moment in dire need of his help:

> "It's no earthly good just pouring petrol over those papers," Frank told him. "You must crumple up the sheets a bit then soak them properly. As for those cipher machines—well, smash them up if you like but don't forget that the Japs can copy anything and if they find the smallest fragments they'll reconstruct the whole apparatus. Much better to bury them."
>
> "Sutton," said the staff officer when their doleful task had ended, "the Japs haven't much love for you and you won't find a concentration camp too comfortable. There's a good escape party readying up. What about coming with us?"
>
> Frank sat silent a long time. "No, it's no use thinking of it. I'm nearly 60 and, though I put on a good act, I'm not really fit, and you'd find me a bit heavy to carry all the way to Chungking. That's the real reason—I mightn't stand up to it and I can't face the risk of letting your party down. It's a pity but—well, it's just too late."

Guest was right about Sutton not doing well in a prison camp. He died after developing beriberi at Stanley, where a fellow inmate described him, prowling along the wire at the age of sixty, as 'thin, wan, unrecognizable; a lion with a broken heart'.

One of his fellow inmates, George Wright-Nooth, had also rejected an attempt to recruit him into the Chan Chak escape party. This invitation had come from his police colleague, Bill Robinson, who had gone so far as to lend him a large amount of cash for the journey. But Wright-Nooth believed that while soldiers had a duty to escape, the situation was not so clear-cut when it came to police officers. He decided to stay, mainly out of concern about leaving his men.

'Old Marshal' of Manchuria: Zhang Zuolin, a warlord who ruled Manchuria from 1916 to 1928.

General Maltby took a similar view when he too was offered a passage on the MTBs just before the surrender. Goring and Macmillan asked Maltby's aide-de-camp, Iain MacGregor, to try to persuade him to join them. 'I went in to see the very weary and dispirited general and did my best to talk him over,' recalled MacGregor later. "Sorry Iain," he said, "A commander should not desert his men. I must stay with the garrison come what may. The others have my permission and approval to get away as planned. You go with them if you like." Nothing would budge him from that decision. Obviously I would not and could not leave him.'

According to Goring, Commodore AC Collinson, the senior naval officer, had promised to give him an hour's warning of the departure of the motor torpedo boats, to allow the escape party time to reach them. But things worked out differently. At 2.30 p.m. on Christmas Day, the General rang the Commodore and told him that the last line of defence in Wanchai had been broken. He said the Governor had been told further effective resistance was not practicable. Now it was the Commodore's turn to speak to the Governor: 'I told him again I was perfectly prepared to hold on in the dockyard, but we could probably only hold out for 2 hours, by which time it would be getting dark, and the risk of the Japanese then getting out of control and butchering the civilian population, both European and Chinese, did not warrant further resistance. Orders were then given for fighting to cease.'

At 2.45 p.m., Collinson strode into the Operations Room, picked up the phone, called Aberdeen Harbour and gave orders that the MTBs were to sail instantly. In a lively account of the escape published in a men's adventure magazine in 1949, Goring says he looked up from his work and the Commodore gave him an apologetic smile, saying the boats had to leave within the next five minutes.

> Five minutes! Five minutes in which to get the admiral (who had a wooden leg) down three flights of stairs, into a car, and along eight miles of road to Aberdeen! Forthwith I grabbed a 'phone.
>
> "Bill," I said to the Policeman, "Scram like blazes! Get the admiral to Aberdeen in five minutes. And step on it!"
>
> "Right," returned Bill, "and where shall I meet you?"
>
> "Scram!" I roared, and slammed down the 'phone. I wasn't going to meet anyone anywhere; our cherished plan had miscarried.

11
Waiting for the VIPs

25 December

The motor torpedo boats were having their quietest day of the war. Lying in two secluded bays, they were sheltered by hills from both the wind and the enemy's guns, and as they waited for further orders there was nothing to do but sit tight. Hong Kong's weather had been at its winter best for much of the past few weeks, but on Christmas Day it was clearer and crisper than ever, the azure sea and green hillsides bathed in brilliant sunshine.

Three of the MTBs—*10, 11* and *27*—lay just outside Aberdeen Harbour, to the west of Aplichau. The little island—some one and a quarter miles in diameter—had a small fishing village at its northern tip, just across the harbour from the Aberdeen waterfront, but was otherwise uninhabited. It was made up almost entirely of three rugged hills. On top of the middle and smallest of the three was the No. 3 Battery, Hong Kong Volunteer Defence Corps, which early on Christmas morning became the target of an enemy bombardment.

Lieutenant Commander Gandy recorded in his diary that at about 8 a.m. his own boat, *10*, and the two others with it 'received an Xmas present of rubble from the hillside, caused by Japanese bombs aimed at our battery on Aberdeen Island (Aplichau). Berth was shifted and it was found that Jap machine guns on Brick Hill could fire on MTBs if seen through a gap in Aplichau hills and it was concluded that Brick Hill was now completely in Japanese hands, making Aberdeen Channel virtually impassable: the Aberdeen Harbour route commanded by field gun fire would thus be the best.'

MTB 10's radio was defective, so all Gandy's signals had to be passed visually (by lamp or semaphore) to another boat, for onward transmission by radio. This was a considerable handicap on a day when speed was vital. FW Kendall, who was with the flotilla commander on *10*, would have preferred to be moored in Aberdeen where they could keep track of the rapidly deteriorating situation ashore. But the waterfront was under heavy mortar bombardment, and it was thought too dangerous to go in during daylight hours, even by the harbour route.

So they stayed where they were. 'A good breakfast, a good lunch and a double whack of Xmas rum was had by all,' recorded Gandy. 'Dinner consisted of a grand potmess,' Len Rann of *MTB 27* wrote in his diary. 'There was bacon, beans, carrots, peas, turnips, spuds, four sorts of soup, runner beans. All tinned stuff, of course . . . but it tasted good.' According to David Legge, first lieutenant on *11*, the atmosphere was almost that of a launch picnic:

> Except for a distant explosion every now and then you would never have thought that there was a war on. I thought of the Christmas day a year ago with M. and Jens and Kamma* in Shanghai. It seemed ten years ago. Someone managed to get hold of a bottle of champagne somewhere and we had a drink with our not very special Christmas dinner. A few planes were around but didn't seem to notice us or at any rate didn't bother us. Little did we realize the hell that the wretched chaps on the other side of the island were going through.

By the early afternoon it was so warm they even managed a swim—albeit in somewhat oily water. Still, as Chief Petty Officer Thums remarked, it would keep the mosquitoes away. There was a derelict floating barge knocking about against the rocks, and having nothing better to do, the crews started using it as a target for Bren and Tommy gun practice. In the background, mortar fire continued intermittently, each blast sounding, as Lieutenant Collingwood graphically described, 'like a door slamming'.

Since shelter near the MTB base was becoming increasingly hard to find, the other two boats, *07* and *09*, had moved early that morning a little way farther up the west coast of Hong Kong Island to Telegraph Bay.*

'We returned from patrol about dawn and were told to find a secluded spot,' Buddy Hide, stoker on *07*, recalled later. 'My boat went into a very small bay and lay alongside a rather short stone pier. We covered our boats with straw and branches of trees.'

M and Jens and Kamma: 'M' refers to David Pauncefoot Legge's widowed mother, Alice, who taught gymnastics in Shanghai and remarried a Danish sea captain called Jens Elster. Kamma is thought to have been a family retainer. Alice's first husband had been a paper importer who had moved his business from India to China while David was at school in England. He died soon after David arrived in Shanghai at the age of sixteen to work for British American Tobacco.

Telegraph Bay: also known as Tai-ho Wan, and today as Cyberport.

The foliage that was now draped over the two boats' upper decks from stem to stern had a festive look to it—Kennedy had a camera and took a picture—but it was intended as camouflage rather than decoration. And by all accounts it was effective. Aircraft passed over frequently but failed to spot them. Most of the MTBs had been repainted some ten days previously in an attempt to reduce their vulnerability to air attacks, their original blue-grey colour scheme converted to a darker mixture of browns, greens and yellows.

Ashby and Kennedy and their crews had a Christmas tot of rum on the mess deck at midday, just as the others had done. And after a foraging expedition up the hill to the Dairy Farm* there was at least chicken, if not turkey, for lunch—plus plenty of fresh milk and cream. The Italian nuns at the nearby St Teresa's Convent, despite their country's alliance with Germany, were happy to show their support for Hong Kong's defenders by offering them some Christmas Day apple pie. But it was not quite what Alick Kennedy's parents in Glasgow had had in mind a few months earlier when they asked their son to buy a present for his men from them—he had duly promised he would get something special 'to swell their Xmas dinner table'.

As the sound of firing crept closer in the afternoon, they felt the Japanese must surely be in Aberdeen, just a mile or two down the road, if not also in the city itself, about the same distance in the other direction. Wireless reception was poor, but soon after 3 p.m. the telegraphist gave an excited shout. He had just picked up a signal from XDO (the Extended Defence Officer at naval headquarters in Hong Kong) to V2 (the MTB flotilla commander).* It was indistinct, but he thought he heard the word 'Go'.

'Are you sure?' queried Kennedy and Ashby as one. The operator listened intently again.

'Yes, it's just come through again, Sir. One word, "Go".'

As they discussed the implications of the terse signal, someone suddenly exclaimed, 'Look at Mount Davis!'

'We looked,' recalled Kennedy, 'and from different points on the green hillside white flags were fluttering. It was a sad, poignant sight.

Dairy Farm was set up in 1886 on the hillside at Pokfulam with the aim of improving Hong Kong's health by providing its people with non-contaminated milk. Today the company has thousands of outlets worldwide. The old cowsheds are now part of the Hong Kong Academy for Performing Arts Bethanie campus.

V2: The distinguishing signal for the 2nd MTB Flotilla was V and 2 in flags. The flotilla's senior officer was hence known as V2 for short.

So it was true, and this was the end. The time was three-fifteen. Hong Kong had fallen.'

From behind Aplichau, where the other boats were, no white flags could be seen, but Gandy had received the one-word message and knew what it meant. Soon afterwards his telegraphist, Meadows, intercepted another signal, ordering a ceasefire. V2 gathered together the crews of 27, 11 and 10. He told them surrender was about to take place and the flotilla would now carry out its escape instructions. If anyone felt 'unfit or unequal to the difficulties and hardships of guerrilla operations on land' he should say so and be put ashore. There were no takers.

There then arose the vexed question of whether they should set off as ordered despite the lack of any news of their expected passengers. Kendall told Gandy there was a moral obligation to take Chan Chak and SK Yee, after all that they had done during the battle and after Britain's promises to Chiang Kai-shek to ensure their safety. Besides, their own chances of contacting guerrillas in China would be greatly lessened without the local knowledge and guerrilla contacts of the Admiral and his men.

The commando leader wanted to go ashore to see what was happening. Gandy thought it best to wait before going anywhere, since the smallest movement in daylight would be obvious to the enemy. But he agreed they should not leave without the escape group. At 3.30 p.m., he signalled to HQ: 'Propose go after dark. Must pick up two Chinese at Aberdeen dock. Can I enter after dark.' The uncompromising reply came back five minutes later: 'Go all boats.'

Gandy was not the type to look lightly on the disobeying of orders or to put naval lives and property at unnecessary risk. But he had been told by the Commodore to collaborate closely with Kendall. And quite apart from the anxious and persuasive presence of the Canadian at his shoulder and the evident importance of the mysterious Chinese officials, the flotilla commander was convinced that a delayed departure would be best for all.

Four hours of daylight lay ahead, and firing could still be heard to the east. The MTBs had nothing to gain from leaving the sheltered spots where they had been all day. Keeping them where they were would also offer the escape party a choice of possible pick-up points. After further consultation with Kendall, Gandy sent the Commodore the following signal, at 4.45 p.m.: 'Ask Commissioner of Police for Chan and Yee to rendezvous Queen Mary Hospital from 7pm.' The two other boats, 07 and 09, were already in the vicinity of the hospital, in an area that had already been marked down as a final bolt-hole once Aberdeen fell. Gandy had been told several days earlier: 'Should you be forced to withdraw send all you have afloat to Sandy and Telegraph Bays.'

But the main concern now of Commodore Collinson was to get his MTBs safely out of Hong Kong while he still could, before the surrender became effective. In the eyes of the senior naval authorities at the time, 'it was unheard of for a commander to prejudice the safety of his ships to save two Chinese, however distinguished'. Collinson's reply to Gandy's latest suggestion was therefore short and to the point: 'Not approved, proceed immediately with Kendall.' In view of the problems involved in transmitting signals, he had also by now dispatched one of his most senior staff at naval headquarters, Lieutenant Commander JH Yorath, RN, to go in person to find the MTBs and order them to leave.

Yorath ran to his house and drove in his hired car to Aberdeen. He was well acquainted with the set-up there since he had spent the first week of the battle arranging the navy's accommodation in the Industrial School. At the waterfront, he found no MTBs, but guessed they might be sheltering beyond the island. He found a ship's lifeboat alongside a ferry, and persuaded a marine chief engineer, Norman Halladay, to help him row across to Aplichau. A native of North Shields, Halladay had joined Butterfield & Swire in 1919 after serving in the Royal Navy in the World War. He was now forty-eight, overweight and balding. Yorath was only five years younger. The two men manoeuvred the boat out into Aberdeen Harbour, and began threading their way through the assorted wreckage.

Sporadic shelling from four Japanese field guns at first forced them to return to the shore for shelter. They followed the coast to the western end of Aberdeen village. Straining at the oars, they pulled quickly across to the island at the second attempt. Yorath landed and climbed up to a point on the rocks from where he could see the MTBs. They then contacted Gandy and were soon taken on board the flotilla leader's boat.

After delivering the Commodore's orders, the two new arrivals applied to join the escape party. Gandy was glad to have Yorath—a smoothly efficient naval officer of the same rank as himself—but he felt some doubt about accepting Halladay. 'Not only was I unauthorized to take him, he might be letting himself in for more than he realized.' He could only come, insisted Gandy, on the understanding that he would be left behind if found at any time unequal to the job.

Halladay was ready to take his chances 'come what may' and was duly taken on.

But Gandy was now in more of a dilemma than ever. The verbal confirmation of the signal 'Go' made it impossible to continue to ignore it. At around five o'clock, there were heavier-than-usual sounds of shooting, including machine-gun fire, from just over the hill to the east. But there was still no sign of his VIP passengers.

Part Three
The Breakout

12
Getaway Cars

As General Maltby ordered his men to hand in their weapons, the various members of the escape party were still gathering in the centre of town. Chan Chak had received a call at about three o'clock to inform him that the Governor and the General would go to surrender in person to the Japanese in about an hour's time. The Admiral and his three colleagues—Henry, SK and Yeung the bodyguard—made their way across the road to the Gloucester Building, where Bill Robinson was anxiously waiting to accompany them to Aberdeen.

Max Oxford had been up to the Peak to evacuate some women and children from one of the many houses now on fire there. He returned to the Battle Box and when it became clear that it was all over, he, Guest and Macmillan had a final meeting with Maltby. The General said they were free to escape if they could and wished them luck. Goring stayed behind, engrossed in directing the final throes of the battle, but the three other officers hurried down to join the rest of the party at the Gloucester.

According to Guest, Japanese soldiers were by now pouring down Garden Road into the city centre, with more arriving by boat from Kowloon, and he and Macmillan had to take cover in the cathedral grounds before dodging enemy patrols on Queen's Road. Others merely spoke of gunfire from the east sounding ever louder in their ears. Chan Chak said plain-clothed Japanese agents had arrived ahead of the main body of troops and, by the time he left his office, were approaching the British military headquarters, just a few hundred yards away.

MacDougall and Ross were still in their third-floor office in the Gloucester, impatiently waiting for the Colonial Secretary to come and give them the all clear to leave. 'Christ, I wish we could go,' Ross had been saying, as they weighed up the chances of the MTBs ignoring the order to depart and staying on to pick up the Admiral. He calculated that the enemy had by this time reached the cricket ground, just the other side of Statue Square. Finally, at 3.30 p.m., after a ten-minute walk down from Government House, NL Smith's successor, Franklin Gimson, arrived at the Gloucester to confirm that hostilities had ended. MacDougall asked if this meant it was every man for himself. 'Of course,' said Gimson. 'You can do what you want now.' He declined to go with them, saying he would have to stay to take charge in the absence of the Governor, who was about to make his formal surrender.

They joined the others in a private office on the fourth floor. Now there were ten of them. It was time to go. They picked up their things and made for the door. Chan and his staff, who were in ordinary civilian clothes, were each carrying a small hold-all; the two Ministry of Information men had their well-stocked knapsacks; the British military officers, still in their uniforms, had the few items they had been able to lay their hands on before leaving the Battle Box. All ten of them carried revolvers, although MacDougall later admitted he hadn't the faintest idea how to fire one.

They hurried downstairs. The lifts, like the phones, were out of order. It turned out that Goring had worried needlessly about Chan managing the stairs with his wooden leg. Since his operation two years before, the Admiral had put in lots of practice on the staircase at his home in Kowloon, with the help of Yeung and his two other bodyguards.

They darted out of the hotel's side entrance on Pedder Street and dashed around the corner on to Queen's Road, where Ross had parked the Buick in front of the King's Theatre. The heavy, arcaded buildings clustered in the heart of the city provided good protection from the shelling. SK Yee had foreseen that they would be too many for one car and had organized a second—an old four-seater Austin with a canvas roof. Henry Hsu fetched it from the compound at the rear. According to a Chinese biography of Chan Chak, the Admiral now started to take charge as the 'Sino-British commander-in-chief', ordering everyone to get into the two cars. Freddie Guest recalled Chan's actual words as being simply: 'We go now!'

It was shortly after 3.30 p.m. With the rattle of machine-gun fire in their ears as the Japanese approached from the east, they roared off down Queen's Road to the west. Ted Ross led the way with half the party in the Buick, the others following just behind in the Austin, Henry at the wheel.

A glance down Pedder Street towards Queen's Pier, past the neoclassical arches of the ten-storey Pedder Building and the stone columns of the seventy-five-year-old Hong Kong Hotel, showed a clutch of flagpoles jutting out from the offices of the big trading, shipping and insurance firms. Some of them would soon be flying the white flag of surrender or even the red and white flag of Japan.

In an hour or two there would be scenes of panic as news of the capitulation spread and enemy soldiers were seen by many for the first time—until now, objects of ridicule for their pudding-bowl helmets and gold-plated teeth, their split-toe rubber boots and semi-plus-fours that made them look bandy-legged. Frightened figures would be seen emerging from the Club and running frantically along the waterfront, looking in vain for any craft left undamaged by shellfire or bombs. Others would simply tear off their armbands and badges that identified them with the defeated colonial power, throwing them down stairwells or adding them to the piles of debris in the streets.

But for now, here in the heart of the city, an eerie calm reigned between one regime and the next. Apart from a trickle of silent, fearful Chinese refugees from Wanchai, the streets were deserted.

The two cars accelerated past Jimmy's Kitchen on their left and the Queen's Theatre on their right, next to the Grand Dispensary. They had gone only a few hundred yards when a man sprang out from the kerb in front of the leading car. Ross was ready to run him down, but MacDougall cried 'Stop, it's Two-Gun!' and they screeched to a halt. Sure enough, standing in front of the car was the squat, bulging figure of General Morris 'Two-Gun' Cohen. He was even living up to his name by brandishing a revolver in each hand, Ross recalled years later.

> MacDougall quickly said, 'Cohen, if you want to escape come with us. If you don't, get out of the way because there isn't much time.'

Cohen came up and peered in at them, pressing his huge bullet head with its double chin and boxer's nose up against the windscreen. He already knew who they were and where they were going, since after helping Madame Sun Yat-sen onto the last plane out of Hong Kong he had been asked by Kendall to help organize Chan Chak's escape. But like his fellow adventurer and general, 'One-Arm' Sutton, he decided not to take up the invitation to join the escape himself. 'Hell no,' he said, in a rough drawl that was half Cockney, half West Canadian twang. 'I'm staying for the fighting.' The fighting was over, MacDougall assured him. But Two-Gun was adamant. 'No, I'll take my chances,' he said, and walked off down the street.

They continued down Queen's Road as it began to snake through Western. The faded imperial grandeur of the city centre gave way to open-fronted shophouses festooned with signs and hoardings and grimy tenements lined with balconies full of laundry and potted plants. The two drivers each kept one hand firmly pressed on the horn and one foot hard down on the accelerator. Their cars charged on through the winding streets, scattering stallholders and street-sleepers and skinny men in vests carrying huge baskets hanging from bamboo poles. The Admiral was surprised at how normal everything seemed:

> For the local residents and the British sentries along the way, life was seemingly as usual. They apparently were not aware of the Governor's decision to give up on Hong Kong.

They climbed the hill past the University of Hong Kong, the aerial roots of Chinese banyans, or wild fig trees, reaching out across the road above them. Chan's mentor, Sun Yat-sen, had qualified as a medical doctor in 1892 at the college which was the university's forerunner. He had returned as founding father of the Republic in 1923 to tell students to carry Hong Kong's example of good government to every part of China. After his speech, the President had told his bodyguard, Two-Gun Cohen: 'I like the British and I understand them.' But now the British had been humbled and the university reduced to a sorry state of disrepair. More than two weeks of shellfire from across the harbour had removed the roof of the students' union building, damaged the red brick and granite Great Hall, and replaced the clock face at the top of the handsome tower with an ugly, gaping hole.

Then they were out of the town and heading south along the narrow coastal road, past the forts at Belcher's and Mount Davis and an endless array of Chinese graveyards. As they hugged the rocky hillside, there was practically no other traffic, making them a conspicuous target for anyone who might be tempted to try to stop them or stage an ambush along the way. When buildings were approached the danger increased: there had been numerous incidents of sniping from upper windows. But this was one part of the island the Japanese had yet to reach, and if any of Chan Chak's fifth-columnist enemies had spotted him leaving the city centre, they had lost track of him by the time he and his companions were driving along Pokfulam Road.

On their left, at the top of a flight of marble steps, they passed Queen Mary Hospital, where 1,700 wounded civilians had been treated during the battle. The modern, six-storey building had not been spared from enemy fire, probably due to the proximity of the two forts and the guns placed beside its own grounds. Shells and bombs continued to burst nearby throughout most of Christmas Day, their thunderous explosions combining with the crash of the guns to make the building shake continuously. Across the road were the nurses' quarters, with tennis courts and other amenities that members of the MTB flotilla had got to know and appreciate in their leisure hours before the Japanese invasion.*

It was a bright and sunny afternoon, and round by the Dairy Farm all was quiet and peaceful. The officers and crews of MTBs 07 and 09, sheltering in the little bay below, were still puzzling over the 'Go' signal they had just intercepted. They were not to know that the VIP escape party they were waiting for was at that moment driving by, immediately above them. Nor did any of the VIPs notice the two small camouflaged boats tied up to the small stone jetty as their escape cars sped past.

As the cars swept on down towards Aberdeen and the advancing Japanese troops, the road's surface became increasingly studded with craters, caused by the pounding of the enemy guns that were now based on almost every surrounding hillside. The firing was still going on as fiercely as ever. On Christmas afternoon at about this time—soon after 4 p.m.—Aberdeen suffered what one British naval officer called the most intense shelling of the war, with four gun salvoes every five seconds. As well as heavy bursts of artillery, rifle and machine-gun fire, there was also still the occasional plane overhead, dropping bombs. The main road leading in from the west—the one they were travelling on—was a prime target.

George Wright-Nooth, the police officer who had turned down Bill Robinson's offer of a place in the escape party, drove into Aberdeen on 25 December to assess the state of the local police station. It had been hit by at least five shells the previous day, forcing its evacuation. The approach to the village was 'decidedly dangerous', he said, with the final bend, in particular, subject to almost continuous mortar fire: the trick was to keep close in to the side of the road nearest the hill, judge the intervals of fire and then dash through.

It was not a trick that either Ted Ross or Henry Hsu could have been expected to know. But somehow both cars successfully ran the gauntlet of mortar bombs, crashing and bouncing their way around the corner and down onto the waterfront.

---

before the Japanese invasion: One of the nurses at Queen Mary Hospital had become close to Lt John Collingwood. Once he knew he was about to leave on the escape, he threw his treasured photograph album into an ambulance at the Aberdeen dockside, asking the driver to give it to a Miss B. at the Queen Mary. As far as is known, he never saw the nurse again but his family found the album by chance years later in Britain.

Aberdeen presented a sorry sight. The granite dry docks had been bombed to ruins and the nearby fishmarket buildings, the concrete praya and the two-foot harbour wall had all been badly knocked about. 'There were a lot of dead bodies lying along the road, covered in thin straw sleeping mats,' recalled Henry Hsu. Out in the harbour, the water was punctuated with splashes from exploding shells and littered with half-submerged wrecks—the latest being that of the little gunboat, HMS *Robin*, whose scuttling had been ordered within the past hour. A few empty-looking junks and sampans were moored further out towards Aplichau, away from the worst of the bombardment. There was a strong smell of raw sewage, salt and rotting fish.

But there was not an MTB to be seen.

13
Cornflower's Launch

25 December, 4.15 p.m.

As they scoured the Aberdeen waterfront for their promised boats, the escape party spotted some European seamen working on a small launch tied up to a wooden pier. Ross pulled up and ran down to ask if they had seen any MTBs. There had been at least one there late last night, he was told, but they had all taken off again by the morning.

It was now decided that a group of the escapees, led by the Admiral himself (and including David MacDougall, Ted Ross and Henry Hsu), should go and enquire at the Industrial School. This they discovered to be a large, battle-scarred building at the eastern end of the village, covered with camouflage netting and brushwood. There were broken railings and a seven-foot-deep nullah at the front. Inside, chaos reigned, following the news from General HQ that the garrison was to stop returning the enemy's fire. Runners were being sent out to tell all fighting units in the area they must return to the school, hand in their weapons and wait for the Japanese to arrive and take them prisoner. Many were finding this hard to accept. The word 'surrender', they had always been taught, was not in the Royal Navy's vocabulary.

The man in charge at the base, Commander Hugh Montague, was an amiable soul who had spent most of the past decade sheep-farming in New Zealand. He had joined the Royal Navy in 1903 at the age of fifteen, and retired in 1929, aged forty. As well as being Senior Naval Officer, Aberdeen, he had also been commanding officer of the freshly scuttled HMS *Robin*, so was at this moment in even lower spirits than most.

He told Chan and the others he was 'most surprised to see them', as he had passed on orders for the MTBs to leave Hong Kong more than an hour ago. Where they were now, no one knew. In the confusion and speed with which events had proceeded all day, no one had managed to stay in touch with them. He explained that enemy fire was now too heavy to allow the MTBs to come into Aberdeen by day, so they had been hiding out among the islands. 'The boats must be somewhere out there,' he said, pointing across the water towards Aplichau and beyond. Or they might have gone altogether.

MacDougall and Ross asked if there was any chance of using the little motor launch they had seen in the village to help get the Admiral away somewhere. 'That's not much of a boat,' Commander Montague told them. It didn't have the range to get them to the Chinese coast at Mirs Bay and might not be in a fit state to go anywhere at all. But he had another idea. 'If you can wait four or five hours till high tide, we're going to refloat a bigger boat—a diesel tug that we've been using to run supplies into Stanley.'

They couldn't wait that long. They would take a chance on the smaller one. At any moment the Japanese might appear along the road and cut them off, said Ross. MacDougall noted that there were still two hours of daylight left and that the surrounding area was strongly held by the enemy. He had therefore abandoned his earlier idea of hiding out in the hills. But perhaps if they could take the launch, they could go as far as a small island nearby where they could wait till dark and see what happened.

Montague accompanied them back to the pier to find out whether the men working on the boat could get it going for them. All it needed was a battery and some fuel, they said. Ross drove back to the naval stores with one of the men and returned with a battery and four kerosene cans, each containing four gallons of petrol.

Soon they began loading up the little launch with other supplies from the naval depot: rifles, pistols, ammunition, food and water. They took enough tinned food to last them for two days. Freddie Guest was shocked at how much the senior service had hidden away: 'Naval blokes are sly dogs! We had been getting down to rough rationing for the past ten days or so and here was food by the ton practically undisturbed and now ready to fall into Japanese hands *en bloc*.'

While the loading went on, they kept watch for enemy patrols, which according to Guest were 'continually passing to and fro on motor-cycles and forced us to run for cover in a precarious but exciting manner'. To hide their tracks, he said, they got rid of the Austin: 'we simply started it up and sent it off on its own over the harbour wall where it crashed into the water below. That was that!' This was not mentioned by the others, however, and the Buick, at least, survived to live another day: 'We left it standing beside the wharf, intact and full of gas,' said Ross. 'Gosh, it broke my heart.'

As the men on the wharf were fitting the boat's battery, Arthur Goring appeared. He had stayed with General Maltby in the Battle

Box till the very end. When he finally emerged onto Garden Road he had found columns of Japanese coming down from the Peak, 400 yards away from him. He had been lucky enough to find a passing car driven by a young private of the Royal Scots, who had proved happy to take him to Aberdeen . . . but had declined his invitation to join them on the escape.

While dismayed to learn that there were no MTBs, Goring was glad to find that the others had not left without him. And he approved of the decision to commandeer a boat of their own, albeit a small and frail one. He was particularly happy to see Robinson, his old friend from India days, who shook him warmly by the hand and told him he had been 'getting quite worried, because it would have been the first time for eleven years that I had not said "Merry Christmas" to you on Christmas Day!' Guest was growing impatient, however. He was already worried at the size of the party, and could not resist muttering that they had better get started 'before a party of women turn up'.

The group was soon getting even larger, with the recruitment of a five-man volunteer crew that brought their total number to sixteen. Some of the new men were from the party who had been working on the launch; others just happened to be passing—gloomily making their way back from the dockyard to the base after being told of the surrender. They soon perked up when told there might be a chance to get away if they would lend a hand with the boat.

The five fresh recruits included two Danes: a big, older man, Captain Alec Damsgaard, who worked for the Danish cable-laying ship, *Store Nordiske*; and a keen young merchant service cadet called Holger Christiansen. There was also a middle-aged chief engineer, D Harley, who like Christiansen had been serving on the Jardines freighter, SS *Yatshing*, before joining the corps of naval dockyard staff during the battle. And finally, there were two men from the HKRNVR, the naval volunteer reserve: a young warrant officer, William Morley Wright, who had been among the group captured in the hotel garage at Repulse Bay; and a thirty-nine-year-old sub-lieutenant from a merchant navy background in Ulster, John Jacob Forster—one of the two men who had carried the wounded Major Boxer to safety.

It turned out that the 25-foot cabin launch had been the tender to HMS *Cornflower*, the Hong Kong Volunteers' depot and training ship that had been scuttled on 19 December. The *Cornflower II*, as the launch was called, had a small engine capable of a speed of not more than five or six knots, or about seven miles per hour. But they were glad to have found any boat that moved at all. Commander Montague instructed the crew to take the escape party round to Telegraph Bay or just beyond it to Sandy Bay, where he thought the MTBs might still be hiding out. If they found the boats had left, they should wait near the western end of Aplichau, out of sight of the Japanese artillery, until dark. He would check there after the refloating and repair of the diesel tug, called the *C410*, and if necessary, take them to Mirs Bay himself.

At 4.45 p.m. the launch was declared to be in running order and ready to go. They climbed on board. The Chinese and a few others squeezed into the cabin; the rest squatted down outside with the crew. The fierce bombardment that had been going on when they arrived had subsided, leaving a silence broken only by the occasional distant boom of exploding ammunition and oil dumps. They could see smoke rising from countless fires across the island. It was time to leave.

Small as it was, the engine burst into life with a startling roar. They looked at each other and scanned the hills anxiously as the echoes ran around the bay. It was still broad daylight and visibility was perfect. Although it was cool, the sky was brilliantly clear and sunny, the South China Sea shimmering ahead of them. There was a dead calm, which was just as well, they realized, given how low in the water the boat was with the combined weight of passengers and provisions.

Captain Damsgaard, who was one of the men who had got the engine going in the first place, took the helm and began skilfully navigating a path through the upended shipping. Having got clear of the wrecks, he then had to find his way past the mass of moored Chinese junks. The fishermen and their families, keeping their heads down beneath their canvas awnings, stared at them with impassive interest as the launch threaded its way through their floating village and headed down Aberdeen Channel to the east of Aplichau.

Exactly who decided to take this more exposed route is not entirely clear. But it was Major Goring who appears to have assumed charge. As an army staff officer who had only just surfaced from the depths of the Battle Box, he was perhaps not the best person to judge how to take a boat out of Aberdeen. In his magazine article, Goring put much of the blame for taking the ill-fated eastern route on Damsgaard. He said he tried but failed to persuade the Dane to keep well in to the coast of Aplichau:

> We set off down the East channel, giving the West channel as wide
> a berth as possible, for it was not only full of wrecks but was the

beaten zone of the 18-pounder guns which were firing down it.* As commander of the party I told the coxswain to keep to the right of the channel, as close as he could to Aberdeen Island, which I believed to be clear of Japanese. I thought it probable that the left bank of the channel, on the Brick Hill promontory, was in enemy hands. The coxswain, however, insisted on going to the left, because there was said to be another boat down there, the C410, lying somewhere on the rocks, which he said would be a better craft for our purpose if we could get it off. His insistence, poor fellow, cost him his life, and nearly ours as well.

In a few minutes, Damsgaard had taken them clear of the harbour, and they were heading out of the widening channel between Brick Hill Point and the southern tip of Aplichau (Aberdeen Island). All was quiet except for the steady throb of their engine. They were the only boat moving on the water. It was beginning to look as though they might be safe, at least from any land-based attack, and some of those sitting in the cabin were even starting to nod off, when suddenly the early evening calm was shattered by a single rifle shot.

There was a pause. Again they looked at each other. There was another shot. And then another. Within moments they were under fire from as many as forty rifles. Then came the hateful rattle of machine guns. Finally, there was the screech of artillery shells. Water splashed just short of the boat, giving the enemy their range.

The shooting seemed to be coming from all around them. But eventually they traced it to an area some two or three hundred yards away across the bay to their left, near the southwest point of Brick Hill. It had begun from a well-concealed concrete pillbox just above the beach (PB 12) and was soon picked up enthusiastically by an anti-aircraft battery farther up the hill behind it. Both positions had been captured within the past twenty-four hours (the battery only at 7.30 that morning), with much loss of life among their Indian gunners.

For a few minutes, Damsgaard managed to keep the boat going. Chan Chak later paid tribute to him, saying 'thanks to the excellent driving, we were able to speed up towards the exit to the sea.' Describing it as like sailing through a blizzard, Henry Hsu said they would all have died were it not for the helmsman's cool head and quick wit.

---

firing down it: A third possible reason for avoiding it was that the western entrance to the harbour was heavily mined.

Ross, too, remembered 'that wonderful Damsgaard . . . he was a great big fellow, half again my size. Bullets were flying off the boat. Quite consciously I stood beside him away from the line of fire. He was like a wall between me and the machine-guns.'

To David MacDougall, 'it seemed every rifle and machine gun in the Japanese army had opened fire on us. The bullets came through the flimsy wooden hull as if it were paper. . . . We were crouching in the bottom of the boat holding onto our tin hats. Then some immense force struck me a paralyzing blow and for a moment I didn't know what had happened until, rolling over, I saw my own blood trickling down the deck. Before I had quite taken all this in, another bullet went clean through my steel hat, and a third clipped the sole of my shoe.'

At least two of the crew were also hit. Forster, the man who had saved Boxer on the road to Repulse Bay, was now badly wounded himself, after getting a bullet in the stomach. Damsgaard was shot in both legs. Both men collapsed and were assumed to be dead.

Finally a heavy burst of machine-gun fire silenced the engine and the boat stopped. It began gently circling, as if inviting further shots. The hull was soon riddled with bullets all along its side. With petrol spurting everywhere, they were in imminent danger of catching fire from the tracer ammunition the Japanese were using. But since they were also letting in water, it appeared even more likely that they would sink.

There was a shout from Goring to abandon ship, and some men began jumping overboard. These included a third member of the crew, Harley, who drowned soon afterwards. Some accounts suggest he had already been shot before he jumped, but he may have been simply unable to swim. Guest, who was bleeding from a slight wound to his nose after a ricochet off the water, was one of the first to decide swimming was the only means of escape. He threw off his jacket and leaped over the side.

Now was the time for Admiral Chan Chak to come out on deck and take charge—and this he did, in typically forthright fashion. Looking around him, he sized up the situation in a moment. He barked brisk instructions for everyone to swim to the island of Aplichau and meet there on the far side of the hill.

With Henry Hsu's help, Chan then calmly removed his coat, trousers, shoes and socks, and unstrapped his wooden leg. Clad only in his underwear, he told his aide-de-camp to fasten his pistol and passport to his body. Everything else he would leave on the boat—including the artificial leg, which had tens of thousands of dollars hidden inside it.*

'What do you make of our chances?' the Admiral asked his ADC. Henry looked at the island they planned to swim to. Its steep hills looked so close—they were still well within range of the guns, that was for sure—yet at the same time they seemed so far away across the water. He described later how he saw it as a journey to certain death: to escape would be 'harder than climbing to heaven'.

For once at a loss for practical advice, Hsu put one hand on the Bible he always carried with him. He told Chan Chak bluntly that only God could save him and that he should pray for mercy. 'As a Christian,' Hsu recalled, 'I believed Christ would reward me with a miracle . . . At that moment, Admiral Chan raised his left hand and looked at me with curious eyes, saying: "If I get out of this alive, I shall be baptized and become a convert."'

As the shooting went on, Henry Hsu began quickly taking off his own clothes, removing everything except his vest and shorts. He also took off the diamond tiepin his wife had given him as an engagement present, leaving it behind along with other items of jewellery and his Bible. SK Yee, for his part, said he couldn't swim and would therefore remain on the boat.

The Admiral and Henry were about to go over the side when the fourth member of Chan's party—his bodyguard, Yeung—barred their way, saying that it was too dangerous and they would surely die. His boss angrily berated him: how could they even think of giving up when there was still the smallest chance of getting away? It was their only option. Having only one leg didn't mean he had to stay and 'surrender like a slave'.

It turned out that what worried Yeung was not so much Chan Chak's inability to swim but his own: he was terrified of the water. He pleaded with his boss that they should think again and abandon the escape and go back to Hong Kong Island. By this time Chan was furious. 'Any more talk like that and I'll shoot you,' he yelled.

---

hidden inside it: The actual amount of money stuffed inside the wooden leg is usually given as HK$40,000, but in the interview he recorded with Chan's sons shortly before he died in 2009, Henry Hsu gave the figure of HK$200,000 (about US$47,000). The cash is said to have been raised from private individuals and companies in Hong Kong as part of Nationalist Party funds intended for paying the men of the Loyal and Righteous militia their living allowances—or as Hsu put it in his interview, funds for paying off the triads to persuade them to behave.

There was a moment's silence, broken by another burst of gunfire from the shore. The Admiral then assured his bodyguard that anyone could swim if they had to, and reached out with his left hand to pass over a life-ring that was hanging on the side of the boat. As he did so, a bullet smashed into Chan's wrist. With blood pouring from his wound, he threw himself into the water, closely followed by Henry and, last of all, Yeung. SK Yee stayed behind on the boat, together with the prostrate forms of the two crew members who had been hit, Damsgaard and Forster.

The others had already gone overboard by now—including, moments earlier, MacDougall, who was unable to take off any clothes or shoes owing to the wound in his back. The firing into the boat lessened for a moment as the Japanese turned their guns on the men in the water. Ross, one of the last to leave, saw a 'maze of splashes' where the bullets poured around the swimmers. Not many of them were going to make it, he thought, as he threw his clothes onto a seat, careful despite his haste to keep them out of the oil and water in the bottom of the boat:

> The bullets were once again tearing through the boat and believe me, I stripped in nothing flat. The pockets of my jacket were bulging with last minute things I had tried to save, including two thousand Hong Kong dollars I was carrying to see us through if we ever made the guerrilla country. I threw my pistol off—a dandy little 32 Colt automatic given to me by the Assistant Police Chief just at the start of the war. Gosh, it was hard to lose absolutely everything. As I hit the water I can remember feeling my wrist watch and thinking 'That's the last thing I possess, now it's ruined'.

Sure enough, the watch stopped: it was exactly a quarter past five.

14
The Island

After throwing himself into the sea amid a hail of bullets, the Admiral paused, holding on with his right hand to the side of the boat and using it as cover from the gunfire. Henry joined him, half in and half out of the water, and asked how he was doing. 'It's just a small wound,' Chan Chak replied, laughing. 'For me it's nothing.' But as blood 'poured like water' from his left wrist, he had to admit to himself the grimness of his situation. 'Although I was an experienced swimmer, struggling in the cold water under enemy fire, with only one leg and now only one good arm, I realized I might not survive,' Chan wrote later. 'Whatever the hardship and sacrifice, it was my aspiration to follow our forefathers and serve my country by giving all, including my life.'

The two Chinese continued to shelter behind the hull of the gently bobbing launch for about twenty minutes, until the firing slowly eased off. They then called goodbye to their colleague, SK Yee, who was still on board the crippled boat along with the two European crew who had been shot, and finally started swimming towards the nearest point of Aplichau. It was a distance of about 600 yards (just over half a kilometre, or in Chan's traditional Chinese reckoning one *li*). A champion swimmer as well as a Christian, Henry tried to support Chan or at least pull him through the water. But the Admiral told him to go on ahead—it was every man for himself, and he would manage on his own. He had swum in his youth in the Canton and Pearl Rivers and more recently had practised floating for 40 minutes at a time at Repulse Bay and other Hong Kong beaches. He was also very strong and very determined. Although the Japanese guns continued to fire at him, the waves helped to hide him, and by propelling himself with one hand, he made slow but steady progress.

The other swimmers all had their own difficulties, if mostly lesser ones. Bill Robinson 'sank like a stone' when he first jumped in, but while under water, quickly managed to divest himself of his shoes, revolver, tin hat, overcoat and haversack. In due course, he returned to the surface and swam on. Goring continued swimming for three quarters of an hour in full army uniform, complete with pistol and fifty rounds of ammunition. Guest later shuddered with revulsion as he described how he and some others had run into a shoal of giant jellyfish. 'These horrible things measure four and five feet square and can weigh up to 60 pounds each. Hanging down from the centre underneath is a long purple tube and from this it is possible to get a sting which brings out a most unpleasant rash all over the body.' The Portuguese men-of-war would appear to have been a minor hazard in the circumstances, but the former cavalry officer was glad that he was in his clothes on this occasion, as 'these undoubtedly saved me from being stung by the wretched creatures'.

David MacDougall was beyond worrying about things like jellyfish. In a letter to his wife, written three weeks later, he vividly described his desperate struggle through the water with a machine-gun bullet lodged deep in his left shoulder blade:

> I swam first on my face and then, as I tired, on my back . . . I could see the familiar sights, the Peak houses, the Aberdeen Road, the famous fish restaurant on the corner where I had eaten so many lunches: and all the time the Japanese machine gunners on the hillsides 600 yards away went for us hammer and tongs. Bullets fell all around, and I don't know why I was not hit again. I had no serious hope of gaining the island. A little way behind me a man drowned noisily. He took a long time to go down and I could do nothing about it. I had lost some blood and was hard put to it to keep afloat.

He felt he was in a timeless world, and was surprised afterwards to learn that his swim had taken less than 25 minutes:

> I reached the rocks very exhausted and I tore the nails off my right hand trying to get a grip in the swell: my left was of course useless. I saw Ross sheltering on a ledge. I made my way in his direction. He helped me partially out of the water but I hadn't the strength to climb to proper shelter and the snipers kept plugging away at the exposed part of my anatomy. It was bitterly cold and I was without hope and desolate. It seemed merely a question of time until either the snipers found their mark or the Japs came out in a boat to pick us off the rocks like winkles.

Ross had been one of the last off the boat, but was the first to reach Aplichau, swimming as far as he could underwater. Some time after he had helped MacDougall onto the rocks, he heard Chan Chak approaching, with a noise 'like someone putting in an oar: *thwop,*

thwop'. Ross was getting back into the water to help him when Henry Hsu came up and got him out instead. Chan's wound had been well cleansed by the sea but was still bleeding, so his young aide-de-camp ripped off his own vest and wrapped it round the Admiral's wrist.

The Japanese in their battery on Brick Hill were watching them through field glasses, and now began firing incendiary shells. To Chan Chak—already cold, wet and exhausted—this was the last straw: 'No sooner had I and my colleague Henry Hsu Heng climbed onto the land than the enemy's machine guns swept across at us from the opposite shore, and they used firebombs to set the grass on fire. Angry burning flames forced us to hide among the jagged rocks at the foot of a steep hill.'

The Admiral had landed at the southernmost tip of Aplichau on what he described in his memoirs as a separate 'islet'. In fact it was a small extension to the main island, joined by a very thin tongue of land, now known as Ap Lei Pai. He tried to slither over the rough ground to find better cover, but with just a right arm and a right leg, he was seriously unbalanced and could hardly move. His two remaining assistants, Henry Hsu and Yeung Chuen, picked him up, carried him a short way and laid him down behind a big rock in a narrow cleft in the hillside.

As the forlorn party staggered ashore at different points along Aplichau's craggy eastern coastline, they found any effective shelter from the gunfire hard to come by. There was not a tree or a sign of human habitation in sight. They soon realized they would have to use the 700-foot hill that rose sheer from the water as their only protection, by somehow getting over it or around it to the other side of the island.

The Admiral told his two assistants to leave him with a gun and go on without him. They protested strongly, saying if he was going to die, they would die with him. But Chan insisted. He said he had already informed the Central Government that should any accident occur, he had assigned Henry Hsu to report to Chungking on his behalf. He took off his wedding ring, to be given to his wife, Shuichi or 'Auntie Chak', if anything happened to him. He made it clear that he intended to shoot himself rather than be captured. As Henry and Yeung left, they told him not to move and promised to return.

Max Oxford had landed nearby, alone and shoeless. After lying exhausted behind a rock as the occasional shot whistled past him, he set out to tackle the scrub-covered but otherwise bare hillside:

I tried to get over the crest but found the journey too far and exposed so sheltered again. Presently Arthur Goring came up and we made a dash for a low neck of land where we could see some other people and some of us gathered there in the gratefully warm sunshine on the sheltered side from the enemy. There didn't seem much we could do except swim back and surrender!

Goring recounted how he 'came across Max . . . shivering behind his rock, clad only in shorts'. A little earlier he had fallen asleep after watching Henry flit past 'in the most diaphanous pair of silk shorts I have ever seen'. According to Goring, the group that he and Oxford joined up with, which included Robinson, had just had their bare feet badly scorched by the fire that had broken out on the patches of grass at the end of the island where Chan Chak had landed. They said the Admiral had been 'parked behind a big rock with orders to wait there till we came to his rescue after dark'. Guest and Macmillan also joined them. Like Goring, they had been washed up onto the shingle at a tiny beach some 200 yards farther down towards Aberdeen, having jumped off the drifting boat some time before the others.

The group huddled together and considered their situation. It was not good. The winter evening was already drawing in and they had lost all their food, drink and other supplies. They had what they stood up in, which in most cases was very little. The only blessing was that for the moment at least the enemy had stopped shooting at them, possibly thinking they must all by now have been accounted for. They decided to split up again into smaller groups and explore the rest of the island, partly to see if the Japanese were coming after them, partly in search of water, and partly in the faint hope of finding an MTB.

Just before they set out, one of the volunteer crew—the blond-haired cadet, Holger Christiansen—arrived to say he had heard the distant sound of motor boats. Goring told him to 'run like a hare' and see if he could recognize them. The young Dane dashed down to the shoreline and headed over the rocks around the edge of the island.

How many of the original party had survived, no one at this stage could be sure. But some of them—in particular, David MacDougall—did not expect to survive much longer. Still trapped on his tiny ledge of rock, too weak to move, he had been thinking of his wife and daughter with feelings of 'overwhelming desolation' amid visions of his own death announcement:

> 'D.M. MacDougall, aged 37, died Christmas Day, 1941.' I had no expectation that I would live beyond the hour . . . The water lapping

at my feet seemed infinitely friendly and welcoming and I knew that presently when I was shot again I would collapse into its soft oblivion . . . Except that I couldn't fight back, I was in the same position as Hemingway's man at the end of "For Whom the Bell Tolls", and I marvelled at the truth with which he had caught the state of mind of one in that grim situation, where one does not concentrate on anything in particular.* Memories, regrets, apprehensions, and hate succeed each other in one's thoughts—and also inevitably a little self-pity, induced partly by exhaustion and partly by despair . . . Thus I crouched for over an hour while the sun went down in calm beauty.

Ted Ross, described by MacDougall as a model of self-possession throughout, was meanwhile fuming at what he called the 'stupidity and futility of our suicidal attempt at escape'. He cursed the luck that had joined them to this party 'when Mac and I could have hidden in the hills until dark and had a much better chance'. Nevertheless, he set off up the hill to explore the shelter of the far side of the island, telling his boss to hang on somehow until he got back. It was a tough climb but proved worth it, as he later recalled:

My feet soon became cut and bruised climbing through the rocks and undergrowth, but it wasn't very far to the top, and once over the crest I ran into several others of our group who had swum to another more sheltered cove. Suddenly we spotted what looked like three launches tied up in a little cove on the sheltered side of the island and, as we watched, two of them pushed off and out to sea. There was a good chance they were British, as we knew four or five of our torpedo boats had still not been sunk by the Japs. However, there was more than an even chance they were Japanese. The rest of the fellows started making their way down to investigate, and I dashed back to help Mac along.

It was now 6.30 p.m. and the light was starting to fade. The three motor torpedo boats lying just off the west coast of Aplichau—MTBs *10, 11* and *27*—had come together for what they called a

---

anything in particular: An earlier letter from MacDougall to his wife, dated 27 Feb 1941, describes a lunch party he had just given for Hemingway, who spent forty days in Hong Kong during his Asian reporting trip at that time. *For Whom The Bell Tolls* had been published the previous year to much acclaim. The dying character referred to here is Robert Jordan, who has his leg blown off while fighting against Franco. MacDougall described the American novelist as 'the simplest, most direct human being I've met' as well as 'the best drinker I've ever seen'. Hemingway later became godfather to his second daughter, Sheena.

'parley'. Was it finally time to carry out their orders to 'get away at all costs'? Or should they hang on in the hope that their passengers might yet arrive? The Admiral and his party could hardly be expected to show up here in this secluded bay. Commander Gandy had just come to a compromise decision. Since communications via W/T (Wireless Telegraph) were still unsatisfactory, he would send his second-in-command boat, *11*, over to Telegraph Bay to tell the other two MTBs to stand by for further orders.

At that moment Holger Christiansen came rushing down to the water's edge, waving frantically to attract their attention. He had just made his way right round the far edge of the island, alternately swimming and clambering over rocks. On reaching the bay, he had correctly—and delightedly—identified the three boats as British MTBs, and was now desperate to get them to wait for the rest of his party. As he started splashing his way towards them, he shouted in excitement across the water: 'There's lots of chaps behind me coming in a minute!'

In the young cadet's Scandinavian accent, this came across as 'there's lots of *Japs* behind me coming in a minute'—or at least, that's how it was interpreted by the MTB crews. After a long hot Christmas Day in which they had done very little, this put the British sailors into what one described as 'quite a flap'. Anchored as they were near shore, they were an easy target for any machine guns up on the hill. While one boat, *27*, edged in to try to pick up the man who had shouted at them, the others weighed anchor as fast as possible and began to retire to a safe distance, their powerful Lewis guns trained on the island.

The group of men that Ross had sent on ahead were just then emerging through the gap between two peaks and beginning their descent towards the bay. They were still peering at the distant shapes of the camouflaged boats and debating whether they belonged to the enemy or to the Royal Navy. They were about to get an answer; but not quite the one they were hoping for.

David Legge, first lieutenant on *MTB 11*, saw them as they came into view and sprang into action: 'Suddenly over the top of the hill appeared about five heads,' he wrote later. '"The Japs!", we all thought. I happened to be on aircraft watch at the time with a loaded stripped Lewis gun in my hands and without any more ado I let them have the whole pan of tracer. They bobbed down pretty quickly and I fairly sprayed the rocks behind which they were hiding.'

Christiansen danced up and down on the shoreline more frantically than ever, yelling in protest. Goring waved his handkerchief wildly and hugged the steep bare hill as bullets zipped all round him.

Colin McEwan, on the same boat as Legge, was equally trigger-happy . . . if not so well prepared: 'Figures appeared on the skyline and Legge at once grabbed his Lewis and started in. Luckily, as it turned out afterwards, my Bren had no magazine and by the time it was fitted orders not to fire were given. Evidently they were friends, but as to their identity we were to remain in ignorance as we were ordered to Telegraph Bay to contact the other two boats. As fate would have it, this was the very time our engines would not start and only after towing did they roar into life.'

MTB 10 had to lash alongside *11* to 'tow her engines in' at speed, so both boats moved off to the north. They soon came under fire from field guns commanding the approaches to Aberdeen Harbour and were pursued across the gap by 18-pounder shells, the splashes landing all around them. The third boat, *27*, in all the excitement and alarm, pulled back to a position 400 yards from shore.

Although nobody had been hit, the latest turn of events plunged the party on the island into despair. After all they had been through, the disappointment of seeing the boats move off without them was nearly more than they could bear. Guest confessed he was on the verge of tears. They had been approaching the MTBs with rising hopes of rescue only to find themselves once again under machine-gun fire. Some were now convinced the boats must be Japanese after all. 'It was extremely discouraging to find the enemy in possession of our small island,' recalled Oxford. He and Guest had just been investigating another cove where they had found a Carley float, or life raft, with four paddles. But it had proved too heavy for the two of them to operate.

Holger Christiansen had meanwhile succeeded in swimming out to *MTB 27*. Engines were cut back and he was hauled out of the sea with a boat hook. 'Grabbed by many hands,' said one account, 'the swimmer was pulled aboard and floundered helplessly on the deck covered by rifles and a tommy gun.' Weapons were gradually lowered as the crew eventually recognized the young Dane as friend rather than foe, and before too long he was able to tell them his story and so finally establish the identity of the strange-looking group they had seen coming over the hill. They now sent a message to Gandy and prepared to welcome their long-awaited VIP passengers on board.

Henry Hsu was convinced the boats that had fired on them were in fact British, but he thought their crews might have mistaken them for Japanese because they weren't expecting to see British soldiers there. He pointed out that some of their group (Goring and Guest, for instance) were wearing beige or khaki uniforms, similar in colour to the enemy's. 'They might also think we Chinese are Japanese, after seeing Yeung and me through their binoculars,' he reasoned. As they crept nearer the shore, Henry put a suggestion to Warrant Officer Wright—the naval volunteer who had been at Repulse Bay and was now still with them, in his blue and white uniform. Why didn't he try standing up and waving at the remaining MTB, in the hope that the sailors on board would find him more easily recognizable? Wright did so—and sure enough, the British sailors waved back at them cheerily.

The walkers completed the final stretch of their journey with a much lighter step. Since 27 had no dinghy, however, and the bay was too rocky to make a landing, they had no choice but to take to the water again to reach the boat.

As far as Guest was concerned, 'the mere thought of more swimming was a ghastly idea'. This time he decided to go in wearing only his shirt, but soon regretted it: 'All kinds of phosphorescent shapes appeared to be darting hither and thither below me and I began to wish that I had kept to my trousers or, at least, to my short pants.' He later remembered wondering as he swam whether he would ever see England or his family again.

Oxford scrambled and slid over the rocks, in and out of the water, and then swam the last few yards. He only just made it and was very grateful for the rope which dragged him in. Once they reached the boat, they were hoisted up on deck by the strong arms of Able Seaman Jack Holt, a blue-eyed, curly-haired twenty-six-year-old from Burnley; Albert 'Pony' Moore, a dark, six-foot-tall leading seaman from Portsmouth; and their fellow crew members. 'Some angel in naval uniform came up,' Goring recalled fondly, 'stripped me of my clothes, gave me a blanket and thrust a mug of hot tea and rum into my hands. It was Heaven!'

A short while later, all seemed quiet again in the bay as Ross arrived with the wounded MacDougall. They had struggled back over the hill together—one in nothing but his underpants, stained black with oil from the sea; the other almost too weak to move and with the back of his coat drenched in blood. A sniper concealed somewhere on the island had begun shooting at them and they had 'dodged like water-rats from rock to rock'. Then they heard the echoes of the burst of fire from the Lewis guns. They assumed that the boats must have been Japanese after all and that they would soon come across the bodies of the group that Ross had sent on ahead.

Keeping under cover, the two men crawled down towards the shore, examining the single boat in the bay as best they could in the gathering dusk. Finally, MacDougall gave up in despair, past caring. He stood up and made his way forwards in the open, hailing the boat in English as he went. The third hail brought an answer—'It's okay, come on down'—in a voice which Ross later described as the most beautiful and gratifying sound he had ever heard.

Fortunately they did not have to swim, as *MTB 10* arrived back from its towing mission and sent its skiff over to pick them up. Waiting on the shore, MacDougall was still not entirely convinced that all was well. But then, as he described later, the dinghy got nearer and finally revealed itself to be propelled by 'a short, thick-set figure with "Made in England" stamped on every line of his face. He spoke to me and his speech was cockney of transcendental purity. I felt light-headed. We still had to run the Japanese sea-blockade and steal through the Japanese land-lines, but nothing that could happen now could compare with what had happened. Our ordeal was behind us, and cold, weak and destitute as I was, my heart sang.'

15

Finding the Admiral

25 December, 6.30 p.m.

As *MTB 10* turned round after taking *11* halfway to Telegraph Bay and darted back through another barrage of shellfire, Gandy and Kendall were delighted to receive the message that the party they had been waiting for had finally shown up. But when they rejoined 27 at Aplichau and greeted the bedraggled survivors, they were shocked to find that both Admiral Chan Chak and Colonel SK Yee were missing.

Chan's ADC—'call me Henry,' he told Gandy—explained that Colonel Yee was believed to have been killed when their boat was fired on and apparently sunk. Admiral Chan had regrettably been left behind on the island. He was 'hiding in a cave, wounded and without his artificial leg'. But Henry was confident he could find him. He and Yeung, the bodyguard, were sent off forthwith in a skiff rowed by *MTB 10*'s most reliable Able Seaman, a thirty-four-year-old former errand boy called Len Downey with a Devonshire accent and a tattoo of a bird on his left arm.

The other members of the escape party were ushered down into *10*'s cabin and treated to traditional Royal Navy hospitality, including hot rum and cocoa, good solid food and warm dry clothing. Guest was worried about his trousers as he had left them on the shore, but not for the first time that day he found Navy lockers to be well stocked: 'It was astonishing to see what came out of those bunkers: spare shirts, sweaters, boots, shoes, socks and, yes, trousers, for which I was truly thankful.' Someone also handed the soaked and dazed-looking new arrivals a bottle of gin from the drinks cabinet.

The medicine chest was not quite so generously equipped, but MacDougall was grateful for what there was: 'My wound was dressed by the Bo'sun, chiefly by means of a bottle of Dettol which was poured straight into the hole. A rough bandage was affixed and that dressing sufficed without change or care for the next ten days.'

Gandy stayed up on deck while all this was going on, considering the implications of the mislaying of his most important passenger, stuck in a cave somewhere, and the arrival in his stead of a lot of other 'apparently unarmed passengers expecting a ride'. As he wrote later, 'I'm sure my acting first lieutenant, chief petty officer Thums, together with FW Kendall, settled them well on board and that my coxswain Dyer brought out the first aid box for MacDougall's shoulder wound; but uppermost in my mind was naturally the rescue of Chan Chak.'

Without the Admiral and his guerrilla connections, the new party of officials, 'kitless and one wounded', would be no asset, Gandy decided. Although he knew he had to take them all, he wondered about the credentials of some of them. Two were from the Ministry of Information, which struck him as a 'rather low priority Government Department'. He later concluded that this must have been a cover for military intelligence.

Gandy also made clear in his diary what he thought of the decision to take the launch out through Aberdeen Channel. This was an 'unhealthy spot at the best of times', he fumed, and it was 'known surely to military staff' that Brick Hill was occupied. They should have taken the safer route via the harbour—as Yorath and Halladay had done, drawing 'only desultory shellfire'. The letters 'BF' (Bloody Fools) are scrawled in the margin of the commander's notebook.

They all agreed that given the amount of firepower that had been directed at them, it was surprising how few had been hit. A head count revealed that eleven of the original sixteen on the launch had got through, leaving just Chan Chak, SK Yee and three of the volunteer crew still missing.

The latest news of Chan was not encouraging: Henry returned with Downey and Yeung to say the Admiral was no longer in his hiding place. They had rowed around the tip of the island into the enemy field of fire and back to the beach that they had originally swum to, and had searched all around the spot where they had left him. The area was 'still full of gunpowder smoke', they said. But he was nowhere to be found. It was by now getting dark, and they didn't dare use their torches or call out. They feared he must have been killed or captured.

Yorath and Robinson now volunteered to try their luck. For the second time that day, the lieutenant commander from naval headquarters showed excellent oarsmanship under difficult conditions. The police superintendent from India then took the chance to show off his sleuthing skills—whistling loudly as they clambered over the rocks, hoping Chan might be within earshot.

Just as they were despairing of ever finding him, a large stone came rolling past them down the hill. As they made their way up the steep slope to investigate, they called out softly, 'Merry Christmas'. Then an answering 'Merry Christmas'—in Chan's unmistakable English accent—came from just above their heads 'Thank God there was the grand little man, huddled up behind some rocks and clutching his revolver in his good hand,' Robinson wrote later. 'The admiral was practically at the top, although it was a difficult climb,' Yorath remembered. 'I think he must have gone up there to die—Chinese like having their graves on hillsides. We lugged him down and got him in the boat. He must have suffered agonies. As we rowed back, he sat facing me in the stern and crossed himself, which rather surprised me.' Chan had not forgotten his devout promise to Henry of a few hours earlier.

Gandy was later to praise Robinson and Yorath for persevering in this 'very essential and excellent piece of work'. According to Chinese versions of the story, the second search party consisted of at least ten men, including Henry Hsu. Chan is said to have told them when they found him that he had dragged himself farther up the hill to try to find a safer hiding place, having heard more gunfire and assumed the others had run into trouble. An unnamed British officer is mentioned in these accounts as having taken off his jacket to put round Chan's shoulders on the way back in the rowing boat.

It wasn't every day that Gilbert 'Tom' Thums welcomed an admiral on board—let alone a semi-clothed, wounded, one-legged Chinese admiral who had just spent two hours hiding on a bare hillside after swimming through a barrage of cannon and machine-gun fire. But the former butcher's boy with the cultured French wife was more than up to the task. On the return of the dinghy to *MTB 10*, he led his men in a rousing ovation as Chan Chak was lifted aboard in triumph and carried down to the wardroom. Propped up on the settee berth, the Chinese admiral was given his regulation 'tot' to warm him up,* food from the galley (the cupboard next door) and a dressing and bandage for his wound. He had assured Henry that the bullet had merely grazed him, but in fact it was deeply embedded in his wrist— too deeply for it to be taken out there and then or for a long time to

---

'tot' to warm him up: Chan's reaction to Pusser's Rum (the brand name of the fiery West Indian variety that was standard Royal Navy issue) went unrecorded. Henry Hsu said the Admiral was in fact given brandy, which would have been more to the Chinese taste.

come, as was also the case with the bullet lodged in MacDougall's shoulder. Freddie Guest said that it was he himself who dressed the Admiral's wound at this point—and that when asked if he wanted the bullet taken out Chan answered: 'I no mind. You take out, good. You leave in, good. I OK.'

Soon the Admiral's arm was resting in a clean white sling, and he was wearing not just the jacket, but the full uniform of a lieutenant commander of the British navy. He took obvious delight in it— particularly the peaked cap, resplendent with gold braid crown and anchor—even though the two and a half stripes on his shoulder were a lot less than he was entitled to on his own Chinese uniform. It was perhaps not the best fitting of outfits, having originally been made for Gandy, who was tall and thin. But with his left trouser leg folded up anyway above the knee, hiding his stump, it was no problem for Chan to turn up the hem of the right one too.

Gandy took an immediate liking to the Admiral, who he described as radiating 'cheerfulness, pluck and seamanlike confidence'. He was more than happy for him to have his spare uniform (Chan became so fond of it that Gandy ended up presenting it to him), but the British commander may have regretted the loss of his only cap, which left him with a tin helmet or 'battle bowler' as his only headgear for the long journey ahead. This was not only less distinguished-looking than his peaked officer's cap, but also a good deal heavier and less comfortable.

The other three boats had by now joined them from Telegraph Bay. Gandy had sent for them at 8.30 p.m. while the search for the Admiral was still going on. For MTBs 07 and 09 it had been a long, tense day in hiding, with the last few hours dragging by particularly slowly. Tied up as they were at the Dairy Farm pier, they had been that much closer than the other boats to the historic, demoralizing events taking place on Hong Kong Island. Although they had been expecting the inevitable result, no one spoke as they gazed at the white flags on the hillside and the full significance of defeat sank in. Kennedy remembered feeling a 'great pang of despair, and apprehension for Hong Kong which now lay open to the vagaries of a cruel, unscrupulous enemy'.

They were aware that they were among the lucky few who still had the chance to get away and fight their way to freedom—if they could just hold on till nightfall. By 6.30 p.m., although it was still light, it seemed unwise to remain at the jetty any longer. They took off their Christmas greenery and moved out into the middle of the bay. There they were soon joined by *MTB 11*, whose crew had at first failed to spot them in their hiding place, so effective had the camouflage been. The three boats lay alongside each other until the order finally came to 'meet west of Aberdeen Island quietly'.

As they headed for their secret rendezvous, Colin McEwan crouched down behind a depth charge on the deck of *MTB 11*, his Bren 'peeping coyly' over the top. He took a last, lingering look at the familiar hills, now darkening in the wake of a glorious sunset:

> Out we came in one of the most beautiful evenings I have ever seen in Hong Kong. To the west over Lamma there was still a purplish afterglow—the sky was steely clear with odd stars coming out and on the starboard Lantau loomed up a dark purple mass with pinpricks of light at odd intervals. Behind us a building at Pokfulam was madly alight with masses of deep smoke showing up against the sky and beyond farther flames could be seen. There was a curious feeling of tragedy abroad—the setting for some magnificent play was there. Hong Kong had fallen. Only seventeen days, and here we were off on a trip to China—for us at least there was the selfish satisfaction of knowing that there were to be no concentration camps.

They found the other boats on the southwest corner of Aplichau, their decks crowded with an assortment of newcomers dressed in all manner of strange clothing—stokers' overalls, sailors' scarves, bell-bottoms and oilskins. They took two or three on board each boat and fitted them out with other items of warm clothing, including white roll-necked sweaters and even the odd Royal Navy duffel coat.

On *MTB 10*, Kendall and Gandy were conferring with Chan Chak over the urgent issue of where to go now.

Irrepressible, the Admiral had refused to stay below and was sitting up on the bridge in his new uniform, pointing at a coastal map that the others held opened out in front of him. Seeing him for the first time, Kennedy was struck by his bright, alert face and surprisingly cheerful manner despite his wound.

They were now a large and disparate party, and there was much discussion on board the various boats about the best place to head for. In normal circumstances, if the MTBs had gone straight out to sea they could have just reached the northern tip of the Philippines, some 400 miles away, before running out of fuel. But with all the damage done during the battle and their reduced petrol capacity, their only hope now was to follow the coastline. Some of the naval men wondered if they could eventually reach Singapore by creeping down the coasts of China and Indo-China and finding somewhere to refuel on the way. But others knew that the Japanese already occupied a great part of those coasts and that there would be little or no chance of getting through.

Chan, Gandy and Kendall agreed there was nothing for it but to find a point on the coast that was relatively free of Japanese and head inland. Kendall was still thinking of linking up with the newly formed groups of communist partisans near the border at Shataukok. But the Admiral knew of other Chinese irregular forces further along Mirs Bay on the Dapeng peninsula, some 45 miles away from where they were now. It was a wild and mountainous area and he thought it unlikely that there would be any Japanese troops based there—particularly with the danger of being shot in the back by the particular guerrilla group he had in mind. He suggested that the MTBs put in first at a small island just opposite the coast there. It was called Ping Chau, and he knew the village headman.

The Admiral not only radiated confidence, Gandy decided, but also imparted it to others. From this time on there was no doubt—if there ever had been—that it was Chan Chak who was the paramount leader of the expedition, his superior rank and natural air of authority reinforced by his extensive local knowledge and connections. But for now, even he finally admitted he needed to rest, so he was gently helped down the steps to the captain's cabin.

16
Night Voyage

25 December, 9.30 p.m.

'Slip and proceed.'

At 9.30 p.m. on that clear, moonlit Christmas night, the five remaining boats of the 2nd Motor Torpedo Boat Flotilla were ready to leave. With a heart-stopping roar, the centre of the three Napier-Lion aircraft engines that powered each boat broke into life and settled into a steady drone. The passengers who had swum to the MTBs from the *Cornflower*'s launch did their best to keep out of the way (some more successfully than others) as the sailors went to their various stations to secure for sea and prepare for action. Just what sort of action nobody knew.

'Hoist battle ensign sir?'

Able Seaman Robert Hempenstall, the torpedo rating on *09*, would normally have left visual signals to the telegraphist. But Harold Hill was busy fiddling with his radio in the cubbyhole behind the bridge, trying vainly to catch any fresh signals from the now defunct Command HQ or anywhere else in the world.

Kennedy glanced up at *09*'s starboard yardarm, where the White Ensign, with its red St George's Cross and Union Jack in one corner, fluttered in the night breeze. He reminded Hempenstall that they were not going into battle since they were supposed to have laid down their arms. The young North Londoner went below to give a final check, just in case, to the firing mechanism on the boat's single surviving torpedo. One of only three left in the whole flotilla, it was lying on its launching rail in the engine room, where the two stokers, Charlie Foster and Jez Priestley, were adjusting throttles and topping up oil levels.

Alongside Kennedy's boat, on *10*, Acting First Officer Gilbert Thums was in the small wheelhouse just below the bridge, plotting the course. William Dyer was buttoning up his oilskin overalls and eyeing the bottle of gin that the swimming party had left propped up half full just inside the foc'sle. A series of orders rang out around the five boats, just loud enough to be heard above the snarl of the engines, and he hurried off to take his place at the wheel.

'Full ahead,' barked 07's captain, Lieutenant Ron Ashby, down the voicepipe to his leading stoker, Buddy Hide. On 11, Leading Seaman Les Barker took his place in the swivel turret housing one of the two pairs of .303 Lewis guns. Able Seaman Jack Thorpe, a former farm worker from Suffolk, leant over to remove the plaited rope fender that had been hanging between the two boats to protect their paintwork. If they had known that by the end of the night the boats would be lying beneath the sea, they might not have taken such trouble over their appearance.

Like sleek salmon, the five MTBs threaded their way in single file out of the bay and headed down the East Lamma Channel towards the South China Sea. The moon was in its first quarter. As it shone out over the hills of Lamma, it threw a glittering path behind each darkened boat, a crazy paving of sparkles over the calm, silent waters. With a clear sky and a gentle wind, it seemed like a perfect night for a sail—but it was far from ideal for the task in hand. The breaking waves from the bows of each vessel, the white pluming wakes from the stern and the silhouetted black figures standing motionless behind their guns were only too clearly visible from the dark and no longer friendly shores of Hong Kong Island, just a few hundred yards away on their port side.

The throb of the engines beneath them was reassuringly strong and steady but also disconcertingly loud. It was not for nothing that the Chinese for MTB meant 'Fish Thunder Boat'. Sitting with blankets on 07's foredeck, Guest and Macmillan were wondering if it wouldn't have been possible to get through more quietly instead of alerting the enemy with 'all this damned regatta stuff'. As it was, they confided, 'We have certainly told them all about us in a big way.'

But Gandy was keeping to a modest speed of 20–22 knots in order to be as quiet as possible. Standing on the conning tower of MTB 10 at the head of the column, he kept reminding his helmsman, Dyer, to keep well over to the right-hand side of the channel, where a semi-circle of silent junks lay at anchor off Lamma Island.

'Starboard Five.'

'Five of Starboard, wheel on sir.'

Gandy was looking out on the other side at Brick Hill, just across the channel, and hoping the gunners there had had enough sport for one day. He was happy to have offloaded some of the swimming party onto the other boats, achieving what he called 'a more comfortable distribution of passengers'. The ones he still had with him on *10* he could relate to as fellow navy officers—even if it was the Chinese navy rather than his own. He referred to Henry Hsu as Chan's 'flag commander' and Yeung as the Admiral's 'coxswain'. All three might be useful to have around to help while they were still at sea, let alone once they got to the mainland.

As they passed the mouth of Aberdeen Channel they could just make out a distant glow shining out from the Industrial School. The Japanese had yet to arrive there, and the British officer in charge had ordered the lights to be switched on throughout the building to attract the attention of the gunners of the 3rd Battery of the Hong Kong Volunteers, still cut off on the Aplichau hillside and unaware of the surrender.*

Hundreds of dejected British soldiers and sailors who had already handed in their weapons had been disposing of 1,800 gallons of rum (the entire stock of the China Fleet Club and HMS *Tamar*) by smashing bottles against the walls of the Industrial School compound. The Japanese would be there at any moment. 'If they get hold of this lot, God knows what will happen,' said a naval petty officer.

The men on the MTBs could only have guessed at what was happening onshore as they sped past, gazing across the water at the dark, battle-scarred hillsides. But there can have been few of them who didn't wonder at the twist of fate that had left so many others facing captivity, torture or worse, while they disappeared into the night.

Ralph Goodwin, the former first lieutenant on *MTB 10*, was still nursing his wounded leg in hospital. After days of listening to the 'pulsing tumult of battle', on the evening of Christmas Day all suddenly went quiet. But then, as he lay in bed, 'into the silence came a muffled throbbing roar, full of significance for me, for I knew that that came from motors of the five surviving MTBs, tuning up for their

---

unaware of the surrender: In fact the battery's commanding officer was already on his way over in a sampan to find out what was going on, having seen cars driving on the Peak with their headlights on for the first time for eighteen days. After being told the news, he returned to his men and got them to dismantle the big guns and throw what they could into the sea before giving themselves up. A few hours earlier, members of the battery had watched from the top of their hill on the west side of Aplichau as MTBs *10* and *27* took the swimming party on board. One of them, Michael Wright, told the author in 2009 that he had been too far away to see exactly what was going on and when he signalled to the MTBs asking if he could help they failed to respond.

last run. The sound faded and was gone. With it went my last link with the free world; I was a prisoner of the Japanese.'

For Phyllis Harrop, it was a night of fear. The news from her flat in Happy Valley was that her amah had been raped and other servants bayoneted by enemy troops. As she wrote in her diary in the Gloucester Hotel, 'everyone on our floor, including the Chungking people and the Ministry of Information staff, have escaped . . . God help them, I hope they get through. It all seems strangely quiet. There are seven women left and we fear the worst.' The Japanese were already in the hotel. When they later came to search the room, they questioned Betty Kendall, but otherwise left them alone.

As Gandy raised his eyes to the skyline and saw homes on the Peak still ablaze from a final day of bombing raids, he must have thought of his wife Dolly, at 15A, Magazine Gap Road, waiting anxiously for news of her husband and dreading the arrival of the victorious enemy soldiers. She was about to spend the next three and a half years in Stanley internment camp.

'Sir!'

It was the voice of the boat's telegraphist, Chris Meadows. The twenty-two-year-old from Leicester was crouching down by the conning tower with his Aldis lamp. His face was drawn after several days and nights of struggling to stay in touch with fast-moving events with only the most rudimentary of working equipment. But now he was excited:

'Signal by flashing, Sir. From a small island over there. Asking us to take them off.'

Gandy wondered for a moment who it could be. Some of the sailing community kept their yachts on Middle Island. They'd be the sort to know Morse code. But he was not going to start evacuating the whole colony.

'Tell them "Sorry, Impossible".'

Meadows looked crestfallen, but did as he was told.

Soon the line of MTBs had left Deep Water Bay and Repulse Bay behind them. At Stanley they could hear muffled explosions and see bursts of gunfire and the steady glimmer of fires, stretching beyond the village and along the peninsula towards the prison and fort at the southern tip.

As Major Goring had explained to Alexander Kennedy before going below to get his first sleep for three days, communications between Fortress HQ and Stanley had been lost soon after midday. This meant that East Brigade—comprising about half of the remaining British and Canadian forces—were still holding out there, unaware of any ceasefire.

Ron Ashby asked his first lieutenant, Arthur Gee, to take over as he picked up a pair of field glasses and studied the hill just to the right of the village. He was trying to spot his bungalow, where he had spent many happy weekends giving house parties and sailing. It had its own private road and a large garden running down to a little cliff above Stanley Bay, where he kept his gaff-rigged boat. He searched for the distinctive yellow and red tiles of the roof, which was steep and pointed like a Chinese mandarin's hat. But the only yellows and reds he saw came from the flames that were even then, he realized, engulfing his own house. They danced drunkenly in the night, illuminating the ragged, tropical leaves of the banana trees lining the badminton court and the flagpole on the lawn where he had flown the Union Jack every Sunday.

Christmas Day in Stanley had already seen some of the hardest fighting and worst atrocities of the entire battle of Hong Kong. The Japanese had taken the main beach in the early hours of the morning. They met fierce resistance from machine-gunners of the Middlesex Regiment—'The Diehards'—and the Volunteers, many by now armed only with rifles. Both sides suffered heavy casualties. But the enemy then broke through on the east towards the prison. At 6 a.m. Japanese soldiers burst into a casualty hospital in St Stephen's College. Patients were bayoneted in their beds and nurses—British and Chinese—raped and murdered.

At 10 p.m., about the time the MTBs were passing, two officers sent by General Maltby to tell the remaining troops to surrender drew up outside Stanley Fort in a car flying a white flag. But Brigadier Wallis, the monocled First World War veteran who commanded East Brigade, refused to believe it wasn't some ruse and told them to go away again. It was after midnight when Wallis accepted the truth and ordered his own men to surrender, and not till 2 a.m. that fighting in Stanley finally came to a halt, and Hong Kong fell silent.

As he took the wheel back from Gee, Ashby was thankful at least that on his last visit to the house, when it was clear how things would end, he had had the foresight to shoot his dog. He just hoped that the fire would do as good a job of finishing off everything else, including his morning suit and his golf clubs, rather than allow it to be taken over by some self-important Japanese officer. He sensed that it was not just a colony that they were leaving behind, but a whole way of life that would never be the same again.

Their last sight of Hong Kong Island was of a coastal battery searchlight, now in Japanese hands, urgently trying to pick them up. But soon they were too far away. Each man on board the MTBs became lost in his own thoughts as they left the sullen shoreline behind and picked up speed. Some gazed back at the disappearing hills, reliving the battles of the past weeks and thinking of those they would never see again. Others looked ahead into the deepening night and wondered what lay before them. What were the chances of survival in four million square miles of an unknown land called China?

17
Shore Party

25 December, 11.30 p.m.

By degrees it darkened, and in the peculiar half-light, it was difficult to discern the boat ahead apart from its phosphorescent light. As the waters got deeper and blacker, the heavy iron chests containing the flotilla's secret signal books were locked and thrown overboard. The five MTBs passed just to the south of the Potoi island group and continued eastwards past Waglan Lighthouse, on the remote, southeastern fringe of Hong Kong territory. Ten miles on, they turned north and headed towards the wide mouth of Mirs Bay.

Suddenly, out to sea on the starboard bow, the beam of a powerful searchlight swept dramatically across the sky. It was a Japanese warship—a cruiser or destroyer: they were too far away to tell which. It must have heard the roar of the boats and mistaken them for aircraft: they had the same type of engines, and the Japanese had little or no knowledge of motor torpedo boats.

The searchlight again probed the sky, before coming down to the water and reaching out towards them. A red rocket was then fired, lighting up the horizon before fading into tiny specks that came dripping down into the sea like spent fireworks. Gandy wondered if they should cut their engines. Apart from the noise they were making, the wash from an MTB going at speed made it easy to spot from far away at night.

According to Henry Hsu's account of the escape (and other Chinese versions apparently based on his), the British now received some valuable advice. 'Although he was lying on his bed, Admiral Chan was calm enough to come up with a plan,' said Hsu in an English-language report called *The 1941 Battle of Hong Kong*. The gist of the plan was that the MTBs should make not less noise but more. By opening up the throttles and increasing speed, they could fool the enemy into thinking it was dealing with a major force. Even better, get all five boats to come together, side by side, and make a dash towards the warship as though they were making a full-frontal attack—the 'spearhead of an allied offensive', as Chan put it. How were the Japanese to know that it was not for real, and that instead of having two torpedoes each, there were in fact only three left between the whole flotilla?

A biographer of Chan Chak explained that this was a variation of an old Chinese strategy for protecting a defenceless city from an invading army. It was called 'strategy of the empty city' or 'bluffing the enemy with an empty look', and had first been used by a famous adviser to the emperor.

However, none of the British accounts mentioned any Chinese advice on this occasion, and in the event, there was no need to do anything. Having either failed to see them or decided they might be more trouble than they were worth, the warship continued on its course and soon the MTBs were safely out of range.

Speaking much later about the incident, Ted Ross said there was a move on one of the MTBs to stage a genuine attack on the Japanese ship. 'A young, tough Volunteer said, "Sir, can I have a go at them? We've got a torpedo left."' John Collingwood, in his handwritten notes on the escape, also remembered considering the use of a torpedo— but he said no order was given, since the boats were by this time no longer in a suitable fighting condition.

Various members of the party, including both Chan Chak and Ross, later reported that the warship fired four rounds at the MTBs. Others, who gave detailed accounts of the escape as a whole, described the encounter with the enemy ship and its probing search-light but made no mention of any shooting. One explanation may be that by this time the five boats were well spread out from each other.

According to Japanese naval records, two light destroyers, the *Tsuga* and the *Kasasagi*, were patrolling the eastern approaches to Hong Kong when at 23.30 they spotted 'an escaping enemy motor torpedo boat'. At first they took evasive action but soon gave chase and opened fire. They later reported that they had missed their target and that the MTB had disappeared behind the Ninepin Island group.

They sailed on into Mirs Bay. It was now shortly before midnight and the moon had disappeared. Ping Chau lay in the bay's north-east corner, a low, crescent-shaped island some two kilometres long. Although the island and the waters of Mirs Bay were still part of British territory, the white sands and dark mountains looming up just ahead on the mainland belonged to China. But as far as the Japanese were concerned, there was no longer any difference—their troops now con-trolled both sides of the border and were likely to turn up anywhere.

'Make for Ping Chau,' the Admiral had said, 'and you will gain some valuable information.' Chan Chak and Henry Hsu already knew the island. For despite the fact that it was small, remote and uninhabited save for a few fishermen and peanut farmers, it was a key staging post in a thriving smuggling business that they were both involved in.

One of the main tasks of the liaison office in Hong Kong had been to fight the Japanese embargo on trade with Free China. It was an embargo that Britain and other Western countries had taken pains to observe, so anxious were they not to upset Tokyo. Somehow, Chan Chak had had to find a way to get petrol, oil, weapons, medicines and other vital supplies through the Japanese coastal cordon to the Nationalist-held interior.

Less than a mile across the sea from Ping Chau lay the dark and mountainous Dapeng Peninsula—the haunt of bandits and pirates since time began. Some 20 miles long and four wide, it separated Mirs Bay from Bias Bay beyond it. Junks and sampans could be hidden away in its numerous coves and inlets and their cargoes whisked off into the hills. An ancient smuggling route started here, crossing several ridges of mountains before linking up with a network of rivers further inland.

Ping Chau was a perfect offshore base for doing deals and storing goods before sending them along the 70-mile trail to Waichow, the nearest major town currently held by the Chinese Army. The British had stationed a detachment of Marine Police on the island, but they were withdrawn after the war started on 8 December. The question now was whether the Japanese had replaced them or had decided the island was not worth occupying.

Even if enemy troops weren't on Ping Chau, they might well be across the bay along the main stretch of Chinese coast. But they were less likely to have ventured onto the Dapeng Peninsula, with its tricky terrain and its unfriendly pirates. So it was in the 'Ping Chau Roads'—the narrow channel at the eastern end of the island, facing the peninsula—that the five boats now cut their engines. They tied up alongside *MTB 10* at anchor.

There were no lights on the island and no signs of life. After the noise and speed of the past two hours, the sudden silence was overwhelming. Someone closed a hatch on one of the boats. There was a stifled curse. The two sounds rang out in quick succession across the still water.

'We were all armed to the teeth with a variety of weapons given us by the Royal Navy and were prepared to sell our lives dearly,' Goring wrote later. Ross said he had never seen such a well-armed party. 'We had 8 Lewis machine guns, 6 Bren guns, 2 Tommy guns, and almost every man had a rifle and a revolver.'

Chan decided to send Henry and Yeung ashore to make enquiries. They were to be accompanied by Kendall and his two Z Force colleagues, McEwan and Talan—each of them carrying an automatic weapon and grenades. Ross and one or two other volunteers went with them. Two dinghies were lowered, and they were rowed ashore under the cover of manned Lewis guns. There was no pier, but within minutes they had landed on the flat, strangely coloured siltstones on which the island was built. The Chinese called it '10,000-layer cake'.

McEwan had been to Ping Chau before, on sailing weekends. He remembered how he had looked down from his little boat through a sea of peacock blues and greens to the rich pinks and oranges of the stones below. He'd then walked along a narrow beach of smooth white sand, littered with starfish and spiky sea urchins. Now, peering into the eerie blackness and shivering in the cool night breeze, it was hard to believe it was the same place.

The shore party crept over the beach and onto a concrete path, which they followed through small trees and clumps of bushes, cacti and tall grasses. They passed a line of old family tombs, where joss sticks smouldered next to red ancestral shrines, and eventually reached the edge of a small village. The path doubled as the main street. They paused and listened. The squat grey houses sat silently within their thick limestone walls, their tiny windows shuttered and doors barred.

Suddenly a dog went into a frenzy of barking—loud enough for the others to hear out in the bay.

Then silence again.

'Anyone there? Come out, we're friends,' called out Yeung in the local dialect, Hakka.

Kendall and Henry began discussing in lowered voices what to do next. Then they looked up to see two men appear out of the shadows, holding up their hands to show they were unarmed. One was elderly; the other had a pronounced limp.

They greeted Henry in Cantonese. They said the villagers had heard the boats arrive and had hidden, fearing the Japanese had returned. Then they had heard Yeung call out in Hakka and decided the intruders must be thieves or bandits. 'But when we finally heard you speak English, we guessed you were harmless.'

The uninvited midnight visitors must have looked a strange group if not necessarily a harmless one. Two Chinese—one of them six-foot-three, the other smaller but wiry and mean-looking, both dressed in ill-fitting bits and pieces of Royal Navy uniforms; and several hefty Europeans, wearing a mixture of civilian, army and navy clothing—windjammers, jerkins, flannel trousers and boots. All of them bristling with weapons.

'What news from Hong Kong?' the two men asked. 'We've been hearing less firing.'

Henry didn't like to admit the truth—that the battle had been lost and he and his group were now trying to escape. And he didn't even know who these men were. So he lied, saying the fighting had quietened down for the moment but the Chinese and British had now united for an attack on the Japanese rear.

Kendall asked if the 'Japanese dwarfs' had been on the island. They had come two weeks ago, cut the phone lines and gone away again, they were told. And what about on the Chinese coast—were there any Japanese over there?

The two men glanced at each other. However strange looking, their visitors seemed genuine. They decided to help them. It turned out that the older man, who was called Yuen Koonsong, was the village headman. The man with the limp, Wong Manfu, was a middle-ranking officer—a captain, he said—in a big guerrilla band based across the bay on the Chinese mainland. He was in charge of local operations here on the island.

Asked what sort of operations, he admitted he was mainly on the 'business' side. It soon became clear that in keeping with local traditions, the gang was involved in smuggling and even a little light piracy. In fact until recently they had been no more than common brigands. The people they robbed tended to be smugglers themselves. How else were fishermen and peasants round here to survive?

But since the fall of Canton three years ago, the gang had turned their hands increasingly to fighting the Japanese, who had taken over much of the surrounding province of Guangdong. So they now called themselves *youjidui*—guerrillas, or literally 'roving strike force'. The enemy troops usually stayed safe behind the walls of their garrison towns, said Wong. But sometimes they came out in small armoured columns or cavalry patrols—to raid villages, steal rice and animals, rape and burn. Then there might be a good chance to ambush them or cut off stragglers.

In the past week or two, he added, the Japanese had been busy moving troops down to Hong Kong, farther along the coast. Just now, this end of the bay was clear of them, as long as one avoided major roads. The main Japanese line was a couple of days' walk inland, and then it was another day or two to Waichow and Free China.

Kendall and Henry asked for further details about where Wong's group had its headquarters, who its leader was, and whether they were communists or pro-Kuomintang.

Their main stronghold was an old fortress tucked away in the mountains over there, said Wong, pointing into the darkness towards the Dapeng Peninsula just across the water. Being already armed and used to the lifestyle of outlaws had made it easy to take on the Japanese, he boasted. And when a quick getaway was needed, it helped that they already had an intimate knowledge of the paths that led down through the hills to the secluded bays where their boats lay waiting.

Some guerrilla groups reported to Chiang Kai-shek's Nationalist party in faraway Chungking; others to Mao Zedong's communists, even farther away in Yenan. But this band reported only to its own leader, a young man called Leung Wingyuen. And *he* reported to no one, the visitors were assured. But before becoming a gangster and in effect the local warlord, he had served in the marines in Canton under the famous commander, Chan Chak. If there was anyone at all who Leung Wingyuen looked up to, it was Admiral Chan.

The older man, Yuen, revealed that as village headman he had helped the Admiral's people in the past to get supplies for Free China through the Japanese blockade. When told that the man himself was right now on a gunboat here in the bay, the two men were startled and immediately wanted to go and pay their respects. So they all went back to the beach and rowed out to the MTBs, where Chan greeted them warmly.

The Admiral was glad to know that the coast at this point seemed clear of Japanese, and even more delighted to hear the news about his old comrade Leung. He well remembered him as a platoon leader in the marine unit under his command in 1937 during the Japanese blockade of the *Humen*, or Bocca Tigris—the fort at the mouth of the Pearl River. Although lacking any formal education, Leung had been a brave and resourceful young cadet. His unit had been disbanded after being taken over by General Chen Jitang, who as the other main warlord of South China had been a bitter rival of Chan Chak's. So the Admiral had been only too happy to help when Leung got back in touch with him soon afterwards, having left the navy and formed his own armed group.

Old loyalties, networks of influence and 'squeeze' pervaded every aspect of life in China. President Chiang Kai-shek had granted Chan Chak the southern coastal zone as his fiefdom. He in turn allotted areas to certain trusted associates. They were free to make what they could of them, as long as they bore in mind who it was that had given them the chance. As it happened, unlike some of the more flamboyant and militaristic of warlords, Chan was a popular and generous patron—though everyone knew he could be tough enough when necessary. Leung Wingyuen had for some time paid nothing in return for the unofficial remit Chan had given him on this stretch of coastline. True, Leung had loyally allowed safe passage through to Free China of various shipments of military supplies and fuel—but the young guerrilla leader would have taken his own percentage from those, one could be sure. So, the Admiral felt he was owed a favour. Now seemed a good time to call it in.

Without further ado, Chan announced that they would take the MTBs over to the Chinese mainland and make direct contact with the guerrilla chief. They would find him, they were told, at Nanao, a small fishing village lying immediately across the narrow channel from the island, halfway along the Dapeng Peninsula. If he agreed to help them and all looked well, they would sink their boats and make their way on foot across the mountains to the Nationalist-held town of Waichow. After that, who could tell? There would still be a thousand miles of mountains, rivers and jungle to cover before they reached Chungking, but they should at least be relatively safe from capture by the Japanese.

There were murmurs of dismay from some of the naval contingent as they fully realized for the first time what they were being asked to do. For a sailor, sinking your own boat was worse than burning your own home. And then they would have to abandon the sea, their lifeblood, to face the perils of dry land—a strange and most likely wildly inhospitable land, across which they were expected to walk or march (activities heartily detested by sailors) for hundreds of miles.

The seamen received some unexpected support from the senior figure present from the army, Major Goring. As a GHQ staff officer, he knew just how special the motor torpedo boats were, whatever their faults, and he knew what a good job they had done in the Battle of Hong Kong. He pointed out that each MTB was worth at least

£25,000 (equivalent to HK$400,000 at that time). Was there not some alternative to simply destroying them?

Chan insisted that they had no choice. It was precisely because they were so valuable that they could not be left for the enemy. China, sadly, no longer had a navy that could use them. But more important now was the need to remove all sign that the boats ever existed. The Japanese would soon realize, if they hadn't already, that a group of senior Chinese and British officers was missing. Between them, they held a lot of valuable military and political information that the enemy would love to get their hands on. It would also soon be discovered, if the warship hadn't already reported it, that the motor torpedo boats had disappeared. By sunrise there would be naval and air patrols scouring the coast for them. If they caught even a glimpse of an abandoned MTB they would very quickly be in hot pursuit. The boats must therefore be destroyed and everyone got inland under cover, concluded the Admiral, before the light of dawn could reveal their trail.

Part Four
The March

18
Guerrillas

26 December, 2 a.m.

For local boats, the trip across to Nanao was the easiest of sailings. It was little more than half a mile away, after all. But the night was black and the bay was shallow and rocky, so the village headman volunteered two of the island's fishermen as pilots. One of them came on board Gandy's boat and took up position next to him on the bridge. He evidently stood too close for the naval commander's liking, for Gandy later wrote bluntly in his notebook: 'He smelt.'

About ten of the local youths on the island took the chance to go along too, having offered to serve as guards. The five boats moved off slowly, keeping close together. As they approached the bay it suddenly seemed they might need all the guards they could get. Looming up out of the misty darkness ahead of them was a strange-looking craft with a squat, yellow funnel. Of one thing they were sure, it was no ordinary Chinese fishing boat.

'Train the Lewis guns' was the instant reaction. They cut the engines and fingers closed over triggers. Could the Japanese already be out looking for them?

Then over the calm water boomed a distinctly un-Japanese voice: 'A-hoy there!'

Having attracted their attention, the speaker reverted to muttering a stream of very English oaths—with traces of a New Zealand accent.

It was Commander Montague RN, lately senior naval officer in Aberdeen and now most senior naval officer still afloat. Sadly, however, his ship didn't do justice to his rank, and he was barely still afloat at all. His vessel—none other than the *C410*, the little diesel tug from the dockyard that had been used for carrying stores—had arrived about half an hour previously and had run onto the rocks at the entrance to the bay.

It transpired that the Commander had fallen asleep at the wheel. He was now busy describing this in doleful but colourful terms as the worst sin he had committed in his long naval career. They soon recognized another familiar accent—this one hailing from Cornwall.

Lieutenant Pethick—hair white as ever, but now minus false teeth—had been sent below to get some rest when the mishap occurred. He now realized that as a merchant seaman he should never have left the boat in the hands of the Royal Navy. As anyone who had taken a coastal steamer from Canton to Amoy knew full well, Mirs Bay and Bias Bay had the worst reputation for piracy in the whole China Sea. This was no place to run aground. Pethick was thoroughly fed up with the whole affair. But he was determined that the Japanese would never catch him, so he was only too happy, like those with him, to join the already sizeable escape party.

The five other members of Montague's crew were also volunteers from the dockyard, and four of them, like Pethick, were former merchant marine officers. Charles Skinner was a forty-one-year-old from Sunderland who had worked the China Coast for many years and had a taste for both Chinese women and Chinese liquor. Gandy later considered asking the police in China to arrest this 'most plausible individual' owing to the nuisance caused by his overindulgence in rice wine. Eric Cox-Walker's drink of choice was gin. In a few hours time he and *MTB 10*'s coxswain, Bill Dyer, would be reprimanded for being 'drunk while scuttling', having finished off the bottle left out in the forecastle for the swimming party. Edmund Brazel, a bespectacled Jardines engineer, had served on the *Cornflower* as a member of the HKRNVR. And Alan Marchant—another Volunteer, this time HKVDC—was a former 2nd officer in the merchant navy, from Canada.

But if it hadn't been for an ex-member of the Chinese Maritime Customs Service called Arthur Pittendrigh, the *C410* party wouldn't have been there at all. Like Pethick, Pittendrigh was a wartime lieutenant in the Royal Naval Reserve. As a supervisor at the dockyard, he had won praise for his resolution and coolness at the height of the bombing raids on Aberdeen. Soon after 5 p.m. on Christmas Day, he and his dockyard assistants had further impressed Commander Montague by managing to get the stranded *C410* off the rocks near Staunton's Creek, despite coming under heavy fire from Brick Hill.

Montague had told Pittendrigh and his men that he was thinking of using the refloated tug as an escape vessel. They volunteered to act as crew and placed on board rifles, provisions and water. He explained that he had offered to take Chan Chak's group to Mirs Bay, should their motor boat fail to find the MTBs. So at nightfall, at about 7 p.m., they proceeded to the rendezvous near Magazine Island:

'Not finding the motorboat there, we had good hope that the Admiral's party were safely aboard the torpedo boats which we had seen passing near there before sunset,' Montague wrote later in his official report.

They decided to go ahead and try to get away on their own. As a former customs officer, Pittendrigh knew the Mirs Bay area because of its smuggling connections. On the map, he pointed out an old customs station at Shayuchong ('Shark Creek') at the head of the Dapeng Peninsula. He remembered an old white house with a flagpole, overlooking an inlet where junks unloaded at the start of the overland trail to Waichow. He hoped there would be a Chinese customs officer there who could help them. When they got there, they found the place bombed to ruins. But the next village they came to along the coast was Nanao.

Not only had they ended up by chance in the same small bay as the MTBs, but like them, they had also come across a Japanese warship on the way—and had been held in the beam of its searchlight for as long as ten minutes. It happened at about 10.30 p.m., shortly before the other group saw what was presumably the same ship. According to Montague, 'we were greatly alarmed when a searchlight found us. We turned directly away to the South West and presently the light was switched off. It is possible that our yellow funnel looked like a sail and the destroyer thought we were only a sampan. Shortly afterwards the destroyer, which was steaming South Eastward, fired four rounds to the eastward. When she was lost to sight we circled back to the North East.'

Montague's account appears to confirm the reports that the warship fired four rounds at the motor torpedo boats. But this was no time for swapping stories. There was much to be done. The boats had to be stripped of everything movable, unloaded and scuttled by 6 a.m. C410 was not so easily refloated this time, so Montague and his crew were advised to stay where they were till their large store of food and equipment could be landed.

Henry had already gone ahead with a few others to make contact with the guerrillas. Once again, the shore party, carrying a precautionary small white flag, found a deserted beach and then an equally deserted-seeming village. This time, not even a dog or a chicken stirred. A strong smell of dried fish and shrimp paste came from the first row of houses. They faced firmly inland as protection from a sea which in typhoons could turn quickly from provider to destroyer. Judging by the even richer smell of pigs and night soil coming from the other end of the village, that was where the farming section of the community lived. Vegetable plots stretched up towards the dark mountains behind.

Henry saw a movement just above them on the hill and called out: 'We're Chinese and British and we're coming up.' There was a pause. Gradually, dark figures began to emerge from the bushes. Soon the visitors were surrounded by villagers and guerrillas. It was often hard to tell which was which. Most were in any case part-time farmers or fishermen and part-time fighters. All wore loose-fitting, black shiny jackets and trousers, and most held weapons of some description—be they cleavers, farming implements, rifles or pistols.

As on Ping Chau, they had heard the powerful throb of the MTBs and slipped off into the hills. There, expecting a Japanese raiding party, they had trained their machine guns on the approaching boats. Henry asked the guerrillas to send a message to their chief, Leung Wingyuen: 'Tell him the commander's here. He'll know who I mean.'

As soon as word spread that the famous Chan Chak had come to Nanao, there was much excitement and a great show of patriotism. The shore party soon found themselves being eagerly welcomed with hot water, condensed milk and biscuits. The villagers' humble tiled-roofed houses also turned out to be well stocked with the finest British cigarettes, tinned food and blankets. 'They're anti-Japanese but don't let that interfere with their own private looting,' noted Ross. According to one account, the villagers even set up a 'market', so they could trade with their visitors as they waited for Leung to arrive.

When he finally did so, it was in some style, in a smart-looking launch that sailed round the headland accompanied by a phalanx of motorized junks. But for the leader of a gang of pirates turned guerrillas, Leung himself turned out to be a disappointingly small and unromantic-looking figure, with no sign of anything as dashing as a beard or an eyepatch. He was in his late twenties, with a smooth, pale face, large lips, small pointy ears and narrow eyes. He had brought along trusted followers and village elders from the nearby walled town of Dapeng, where he had his headquarters and from where he controlled the whole peninsula. Dozens of local youths—many still in their early teens, with rifles almost as big as they were—had turned out to offer the Admiral their services as an armed escort. And if that wasn't enough to impress Leung's former commander, two large chests full of Chinese money were carried ashore on his men's shoulders and set down on the beach. Word was sent to *MTB 10* that Chan Chak's loyal follower, Leung Wingyuen, was waiting to receive him.

The one-legged admiral was duly brought ashore and carried pig-gyback by Yeung Chuen onto the beach. Any lack of dignity in the manner of his arrival was made up for by the guerrilla leader's formal salute and lavish show of respect. Chan stretched out his good arm and embraced his former subordinate as a long-lost friend.

But there were deals to be made and understandings to be reached. The enemy could arrive at any time. After some discussion, Leung agreed to escort the escape party through the Japanese lines to Free China. To avoid the frequent mounted enemy patrols, he advised that they should stay hidden by day and march by night. He would send scouts on ahead and take care of food and expenses en route.

The Admiral promised that if Leung got them safely to Waichow, he would personally recommend that he be recognized as an official Nationalist Army guerrilla leader. His group was 'keen to fight for the nation but had unfortunately not been recruited by the Government', Chan wrote later. Gaining recognition from the Kuomintang would bring Leung a military rank, as well as a certain amount of moral if not much material support.

At the moment he and his men were more interested in the impressive array of weapons and other items they could see on the British boats. They welcomed Chan's suggestion that they help bring ashore everything that was needed for the journey and divide it up for carrying on the march. They could then strip the motor torpedo boats of anything that was left, he told them, and keep for themselves whatever the British didn't want.

Soon, the five MTBs and *C410* each became the focus of a flurry of activity. Junks and sampans glided alongside them and lithe, black-clad figures slipped on board. They gave cheery Chinese greetings to the surprised Royal Navy crews and began transferring all manner of equipment and stores onto their own vessels.

Most of the British sailors were only too glad of some help as they struggled to dismantle gun mountings and pass each other wireless transmitters and receivers, crates of tinned beef and sausages, cans of oil and petrol and a jumbled assortment of blankets, sweaters and oilskins. As a small mountain of gear built up on the beach, David Legge, who had learnt to speak Mandarin while living in Shanghai, was sent on shore to interpret and sort out what went where. The heavier items, including the Lewis guns and radio sets, were put in separate piles to show they were not needed on the journey. Some were to be left behind on loan, others were offered as gifts. But this didn't deter the guerrillas from having a go at other things too, especially the Thompson sub-machine guns: 'During this period of hurry and rush the most difficult task of all was to prevent the guerrillas, who seemed to have no idea of the old law of mine and thine, from grabbing all and sundry,' noted Colin McEwan.

The villagers would happily have taken over the actual motor torpedo boats too. They hated to see such valuable resources go to waste—the wood alone could have kept their fires alight for the rest of the winter. But they were firmly told that these last remaining vessels from the Royal Navy's Hong Kong fleet had to be sunk without trace. So, at 4.45 a.m., the locals began helping in the cheerless task of scuttling by bringing baskets of big stones to weigh the fragile craft down. Some joined the British sailors in hacking away at the decks with picks and axes.

The MTBs proved harder than expected to sink. Alick Kennedy described how he and his crew struggled desperately to rid themselves of the boat that had been so close a part of their lives for so long: 'With a hatchet we drove holes through the bottom of the boat and slashed the buoyant cushions; we opened the sea-water intakes and did everything possible to hasten the end. At last 09 began to settle as the engine-room filled with water and the weight of the engines took her down. Her bow tilted at an angle as she went, slowly as if reluctant to give up the struggle, and when the decks were awash we left her.'

The 2nd MTB Flotilla was no more. The crews went ashore in sampans in glum silence and mustered on the beach in the cold predawn darkness. In a fever of activity they groped about among the mass of stores that had been landed from the boats. Soon each man had equipped himself with a rifle, revolver, blanket, oilskin and as much ammunition, food, spare clothing and personal kit as he thought he could carry. As they lined up, they cast apprehensive eyes at the dim shapes of the hills that loomed up behind the village. Away to the left, further inland, they could just make out an even more forbidding-looking range of mountains that stretched across the neck of the peninsula.

They were marginally reassured to learn from Mike Kendall that they would not be walking that far immediately—the priority was to get under cover before they could be seen. But they had little time to spare. Dawn in these parts came suddenly. It was now a quarter to six and still pitch dark; by a quarter past it would be broad daylight.

Not everyone was feeling as gloomy as the sailors. The army officers and others who had lost everything when they swam from the

Cornflower II had been enjoying the hot food and drink supplied by the villagers and were now raring to go, decked out in the rich array of oddments they had plundered from the MTBs. Oxford, Goring and Guest were all sporting thick white naval sweaters which they could already tell were going to prove a godsend up in those mountains. MacDougall and Macmillan had camel-coloured duffel coats, Ross a heavy jerkin. Robinson wore a blue sweater and a pair of buttonless trousers six inches too short. Some of them did wonder about the size and suitability of the footwear they had found, ranging from wellington boots to gym shoes. But after what they had been through on Christmas Day, those first rays of light on Chinese soil on Boxing Day morning seemed full of hope.

On their backs each carried a rifle; at their waists, a revolver in a holster. Over their shoulders and across their chests were slung haversacks, pouches and bandoliers containing spare food, water and ammunition. An assortment of headgear would protect against the midday sun. Goring—with jaunty scarf around neck and trusty pistol in low-hanging belt around ample stomach—summed up the mood: 'We had still to make our way through the Japanese army of occupation; but for the moment we were free, and definitely clear of doomed Hong Kong. Our spirits were high.'

Having finally assembled them all on the beach, Kendall addressed the entire British company in stark terms: 'We have a hundred miles to walk through Jap infested territory to Waichow—due north—and I'll see you through if you play the game. I'm boss here now under General Maltby's orders and I'll bump off anyone who argues.' If anyone played the fool, fell out on the march or went sick, Kendall added, he would just shoot—and he'd have done it, Bill Robinson reflected later, 'without turning one of his bright red hairs'.

Henry had lost no time in arranging for a makeshift sedan chair to be prepared for Chan Chak. Consisting of a simple wooden chair strapped to two bamboo poles, each some twelve feet long, it was a far cry from the traditional sedan chairs used for weddings, with their red satin seats and embroidered silk curtains. But it would serve well enough. Two of Leung's men were assigned to carry it, with two more ready to take over when they got tired.

As Southern President of the Kuomintang and a well-known hero of China's fight against the Japanese, Chan Chak was an influential and popular figure throughout the region. His progress from this point onwards was triumphal. Already beaming with pleasure at being safely back on Chinese soil, the returning hero now puffed out his chest and looked proud as a peacock as cheering villagers crowded round to see him off at the head of his colourful cavalcade. It was a memorable scene, captured by Freddie Guest in his book, *Escape from the Bloodied Sun*:

> An interesting crowd we must have looked! There was the Chinese admiral dressed in Naval uniform with cap at a Beatty angle, trouser leg folded up and wounded arm in a white sling, and a pistol round his waist, sitting in a chair carried by . . . Chinese coolies. Yes, and to make it look even more dramatic he was escorted on either side by a bodyguard of the most dreadful-looking bunch of cut-throats one could possibly imagine. I have never, in all my varied career, seen such a bunch of toughs. Bill Robinson came in with one of his wise-cracks. 'What a grand tableau for the Lord Mayor's Show, Freddie!' he observed. 'Yes, Bill, what would you call it?' I asked. 'Chu Chin Chow or Ali Baba and his forty thieves!' he came back and would have burst into song if I hadn't promptly shut him up.

And so, as the day broke, the strange and motley group, laden down with the salvaged gear from the scuttled boats, left the beach behind and headed off in a long, straggling line up the valley.

19
Ready to March

26 December, 6 a.m.

It was just as well that good cover lay only two or three miles from the beach, for they had all misjudged the amount of gear they could carry. The pace was slow and grinding, as they followed the path in single file around narrow rice terraces and small orchards and began to climb ever more steeply into the hills. It was a fine, fresh morning, and as it grew lighter, they paused for a moment to look back past the low, dark shape of Ping Chau across the splendid sweep of Mirs Bay, where a white ribbon of surf separated the blue-green sea from a series of golden beaches.

They kept a sharp ear out for Japanese planes, although if one had come along there was nowhere for their long caravan to hide among the sparse scrub which was often all that surrounded the hillside path. As in many parts of China, most of the trees had been cut down—or at least stripped of their lower branches—by peasants desperate for firewood.

After an hour and a half they reached a cluster of five or six houses in a rare, tree-filled valley that provided perfect cover. They were told to settle down for the day and be ready to move again in the evening. Already, shoulders were aching and feet were sore and it came as a wonderful relief to subside on the grass in the shelter of the surrounding trees. The sacks of food and other supplies from the MTBs were put in the headman's barn, which served as the local grain storehouse. The villagers brought hot green tea and big wooden buckets full of steaming rice. This the men mixed with their 'bully' or 'corned dog', as they called their tinned beef, for a hearty breakfast. The meal was topped off by some of them with deliciously sweet tangerines plucked straight from the tree.

The hamlet appeared on the map as Kowtit—a name that inevitably invited ribald jokes. The War Office map that Gandy had managed to obtain before leaving turned out to be the only map of any kind they had between them. Henry frequently borrowed it over subsequent days as he and the guerrillas plotted their route to Waichow on paths and tracks that as far as possible avoided enemy positions. Two major ridges and several rivers had to be crossed in haste before the Japanese had time to work out where they had landed and stop them from crossing over into Free China.

For the first time, they were now able to look around and see who was who. Again, it was Gandy who was the most organized, drawing up a list of names and ranks. The total party, not counting the dozen or so Chinese guerrillas who had escorted them from Nanao, now numbered sixty-eight. 'Excluding Admiral Chan Chak, his flag commander and coxswain and excluding the European guerrillas FW Kendall, McEwan and Tallon (*sic*), the rest of the party numbers 62,' wrote the retired naval lieutenant commander—known to all as V2— in his diary.

'The 62 is formed of two distinct groups. The first or MTB group numbers 44, is well armed and well supplied and consists of 8 MTB officers and the 36 active service naval ratings from MTB's whom I organize into sections and messes according to their boats so that in case of separation officers will be with their men. The second or miscellaneous group consists of the remainder, mostly RNR, merchant service and military staff officers and officials, all very much less well equipped as to food, clothing or arms.

'This also means that they have very much less to carry when on the march,' Gandy pointed out, before adding meaningfully: 'The food is of course pooled equally between all.'

The ever-efficient senior officer of the no-longer-floating flotilla proceeded to designate leaders and roles for the different groups. Montague, as the senior British officer, was in general charge; Gandy himself remained head of the MTB group; and Yorath was to be responsible for the miscellaneous group—also known in V2's diary as the 'Odds and Sods'. Messes would be formed accordingly and sentries provided by the MTBs—with Gandy's own boat, *10*, appointed duty section this first day to provide camp guards. 'The officer of the duty boat should see camp sanitary arrangements are made for any long stay,' he decided.

If Gandy thought he was being more than generous, others had their doubts. Freddie Guest was already worrying about the sheer size of the naval contingent: 'Knowing that they would consider themselves a self-contained body, I could see there would be trouble ahead. . . . I knew perfectly well the first problem to come up would be connected with food. It always is on shows like this one.'*

They all seem to have agreed that the man actually running this particular show was Mike Kendall—who fortunately was on neither one side nor the other of the army-navy divide. Chan Chak, it's true, was the undisputed *star* of the show and ultimate authority on all matters—especially those concerning China. But after consulting either the Admiral, Henry or the guerrillas, it was the SOE leader who from now on gave the orders, whether directly to the men or through one of the senior British naval officers. In his official report, Montague simply noted that 'Mr. Kendall of the Special Service then took charge of the whole party'. Gandy tells the Commodore: 'I cannot speak too highly of Mr. FW Kendall's service and advice to the party.' And even Goring, who had earlier seen himself as in charge, now thought Kendall was the natural leader: 'After we had landed on the China coast, because he knew the country and spoke the language, we unanimously agreed to follow him,' he wrote later.

Such overwhelming support for Kendall is perhaps surprising in view of what was said later about some of his post-escape activities. In months to come, he would be forced to leave Nationalist China after being accused of getting too close to the communist guerrillas. This 'Canadian with a various past' would then be cold-shouldered by British officials as 'continually obstructive . . . autocratic', 'totally unreliable' and 'a complete failure'. Unlike other members of the escape party, Kendall never received any official British decoration. When a possible honour for him was being discussed, Macmillan and Goring—both by then back in India—were asked for their opinions of him. Their letters of reply are broadly positive, but with decided reservations. Macmillan described him as a 'brave and tough adven-turer with very few scruples. He . . . will not always do exactly what is expected of him and I would not trust him any farther than I could throw him.' Goring said 'there are opportunities for service for which Kendall is admirably fitted; there are others for which in my opinion

---

shows like this one: Some idea of the mutual wariness between the army and the navy can be gleaned from a small incident at this time described by Gandy: 'While I'm brushing my teeth by the side of the ditch today I'm joined by one of the staff officers who says: "You are V2 aren't you," to which I reply "Yes and you are one of the staff." "The bloody staff," he rejoins with a humorous lift of the eyebrow, being quite a good fellow with a sense of humour. I keep silence.'

he most definitely is not. He undoubtedly has the quality of being able to lead a gang of "tough guys" in difficult circumstances, but I am inclined to think that a good deal of his success is due to the fact that those same tough guys know he would have no hesitation whatever in pulling his gun on them.'

As they all sat around weighing each other up and calculating their chances of success, it was clear that guns were one thing there was no lack of. One of them described the escape party as an 'army'. Another admitted: 'we could not help but feel that it would be a fairly unlucky patrol which came across us.' Their Brens and Thompson sub-machine guns continued to attract intense interest from their guerrilla escorts: 'Our Tommies were demonstrated and compared with theirs,' recalled McEwan later, 'and the speed with which they learned the mechanism would have been an eye-opener to any British army instructor. Their own guns varied from Mausers to old Japanese rifles, but all had one common feature—absolute spotlessness.' Each guerrilla carried a toothbrush, which dangled along with a mug and other odds and ends from his harness of straps, bandoliers and cartridge belts. It soon became clear that this was not, after all, a personal hygiene measure, but a brush for cleaning his gun.

Having spent much of the day resting, eating and freshening up in the nearby stream, the British began rearranging their kit in readiness for the evening's march. The guerrillas were keen to help. 'They're experts at the game of slinging impedimenta and try to show us how to do it,' said Gandy. 'They consider us over-burdened—we're not yet used to living on Chinese resources and can't risk discarding. But they're biased as we know they'd like our rifles and pistols.'

After a long sleep in the paddy field, David MacDougall woke up to find the large pistol that he had managed to keep strapped to him during the previous day's swim had gone missing. Many days later, when they were saying their goodbyes at the end of the march, he saw it among the various guns and daggers being worn by one of the guerrillas. But he was delighted it had found such a good home—he knew as well as anyone that it was of more use in the hands of its new owner than it would have been had it stayed with him.

Being a Cantonese-speaker, MacDougall soon got to know some of the guerrillas. He later wrote an article about them:

> Mostly they were village lads and their families were securely hidden in the neighbourhood. The prime aim in life was to spot a Japanese

detachment far from its base at nightfall. . . . The guerrilla at whose side I mostly marched was a lad of sixteen . . . who had left school when he was thirteen because he thought it dull and there were Japanese to fight. He had been with the Kwangtung guerrillas for nearly a year and claimed nine Japanese victims. 'Do you know what the Japanese fear more than anything else in the world?' he asked me. He patted his Mauser pistol affectionately, 'They fear the voice of this by night.' He told me few prisoners were taken on either side. 'When the Japanese catch one of our men, do you know what they do? They press lighted cigarettes all over his face and kill him slowly. When we take one of them we cut off his head immediately.'

As for their appearance, MacDougall wrote:

The average guerrilla is a well set up youth, lithe and lean, dressed in black clothes, a felt hat of dark colour and light rubber shoes. Over his shoulder he slings his blanket. Around his waist is strapped his Mauser pistol, which is his most prized possession. He seems to carry no food with him and to live off the country. Wherever he goes it is noticeable even to the stranger that he has the sole confidence of the country folk, who welcome him and feed him.

At 5 p.m. the British produced a meal of their own, thanks to the efforts of the two men appointed by Gandy as 'commissariat officer and assistant'— Sub-Lieutenant Brewer of *MTB 09* and Stoker Petty Officer Stonell of *MTB 11*. The meal consisted of bread, tinned meat, tinned vegetables, tinned fruit, cheese and tea or cocoa. Freddie Guest feared it would be a long time before they ate in such style again. This was the last of their bread, and they would need to find 'a devil of a lot of rice' to make up for it.

It was during this final Boxing Day feast that they first heard the 'dreaded hum of a Jap plane', Guest recalled. 'It came over from the direction of Hong Kong and appeared to be following the coastline. It did not alter course or circle around so we felt that there was no immediate cause for alarm.' Japanese ships and planes were by no means uncommon in the area. Mirs Bay and Bias Bay, on either side of the Dapeng peninsula, had been in regular use over the previous few weeks for landing troops and supplies. Enemy ships had also favoured Mirs Bay as a base from which to bombard Hong Kong's defences. Less recently, Bias Bay had been where Japan's main invasion force landed in 1938 before capturing Canton.

At 5.30 p.m., Kendall advised the party to get going by throwing blanket and oilskin across one shoulder, rifle and haversack across the other, and delivering the first, ear-splitting rendition of what would become a familiar battle cry: 'Ready to march!' Further gingering-up followed in the form of a short pep talk. There was to be a ten-minute stop every hour but no smoking and as little talking as possible. 'You'll need all your breath,' they were told. They formed up and trooped off in single file, with guerrilla scouts ahead and astern. The Admiral's sedan-chair bearers set a lively pace for the main party. Kendall led the way with the staff officers; his two SOE colleagues, Talan and McEwan, brought up the rear with the navy.

They retraced their steps to Nanao and halted there just before dark. According to Gandy, this allowed them to see that there was no obvious trace of the scuttled motor torpedo boats remaining above water. Others have disputed this, maintaining that the upper parts of the boats were in fact all too visible. The navy was better at sailing its ships than sinking them, muttered the staff officers to each other. Gandy was perhaps unwilling to admit in his diary entry that he had allowed his boats to be sunk in water too shallow to hide them. Although parts of Nanao Bay had a depth of as much as seven fathoms, there hadn't been enough time to move the boats out into these deeper areas. As a result they were scuttled in only two fathoms— barely sufficient to cover the top of an MTB's bridge, let alone its mast. The water was in any case so clear that even when submerged, the boats could be seen from above. Over the coming days, the villagers would do their best to hide the evidence by hacking off any parts that were still visible. They also used explosives—which had the benefit of bringing an unusually good haul of fish to the surface. The villagers were well aware that if the enemy saw the wrecks they would face brutal retribution for having helped the escape party, in which case all those surplus naval stores would be little compensation.

Kennedy was now carrying a special memento of his own from *MTB 09*. During the scuttling earlier that day, his Number One, Tommy Brewer, had wrenched off the painted crest from the front of the wheelhouse, remarking that he might as well take a souvenir from the boat before she sank. The boat's captain wished he had thought of this himself and later in the day, when they were rearranging their packs, he asked Brewer if he could have it instead. 'It's yours, old boy, with pleasure,' came the swift response. 'Feel the damn thing.' Kennedy then lifted the crest up and half regretted the impulse. It turned out to be made of solid bronze, weighing almost four pounds.

It was too late to back out, so padding it carefully with a spare sweater he squeezed it into his pack. It had a long journey ahead of it.*

As they headed north from Nanao and wound onwards along the coast of the peninsula, even those who had succeeded in lightening their earlier loads found they were still carrying too much for comfort. All too soon, straps began to cut, clothes to chafe, and neat bundles to unroll. The pace slackened a little, but Kendall strode on relentlessly. His two SOE colleagues at the back were disconcerted to find packets of ammunition and other unwanted items lying beside the path where they had been thrown away. The root of the problem, according to Sub-Lieutenant Legge, was that cross-country hiking simply wasn't the sort of thing sailors were trained or equipped to do:

> In all, the pack of each person weighed a good sixty pounds. Some wore gym shoes split down the middle because they were too small. Some had boots, some shoes, some socks, some none. The worst thing was that there was no proper equipment for carrying things, like shoulder straps, haversacks, water bottles, etc. It would have made the load much lighter in each case but the navy was not meant to make route marches.

At hourly intervals the eagerly awaited order to halt came down the line and the long column disintegrated into untidy heaps on the ground. But just as stragglers caught up, the rest of them pressed on again, in a long, ghostly procession, as described by Gandy in his diary:

> From Albion Point we strike inland across level padi fields in bright moonlight and a line of seventy writhes snakelike and silent along the curves and reverse curves of the padi bunds: absolute silence is the rule and the clink of a boot or a water bottle brings vigorous hushings and shushings to the clumsy delinquent.

One name not included in the lists drawn up by Gandy or anyone else that day was Bruce. The escape party in fact consisted of sixty-eight men and one dog. Bruce was a large and affectionate spaniel who had been given to John Collingwood as a puppy and had subsequently accompanied him and his fellow officers on weekend

---

journey ahead of it: Kennedy later told his family that he finally managed to persuade one of his men to carry the crest in return for a supply of cigarettes. After travelling all the way across China and back to Scotland, it ended up on the wall of the downstairs toilet in his son Alick's home near Stirling. It went on display in December 2009 as part of a long-term exhibition, *Escape From Hong Kong*, in the Hong Kong Coastal Defence Museum.

duck-shooting expeditions in the New Territories. The soft-hearted captain of *MTB 11* had smuggled the animal onto his boat during the siege. He had been secretly relieved just before the escape when his proposal to shoot it had been met with outrage by his men. 'But Brucie's a member of the crew,' they'd protested.

David Legge, Collingwood's first lieutenant, must have looked on the dog with mixed emotions. He had a spaniel of his own in Hong Kong called Wendy. He had left her in the care of his landlady at the start of the battle. Somehow he knew he would see neither Wendy nor his landlady again.

Another first officer with a dog—Lewis Bush of the stricken *MTB 08*—later vividly described how he had witnessed its death outside the Industrial School shortly before the escape began:

> Shells from the mountain guns screamed into and around the building. Some soldiers were burying the dead and as I looked into Joan's trusting and enquiring brown eyes I knew we had to say goodbye. A chief petty officer took her to the back of the building and put a .45 bullet into her head. It was the only way. The Chinese would have eaten her. I dug her grave, my face streaming with tears, wrapped her in a small naval ensign, put her in a beer crate and heaped a mound of stones over her, and at that moment I hated the Japanese more I think than at any time during the war.

One might have expected the meticulous Gandy to have objected to the presence of a dog on the escape. But he himself had often gone along on his colleagues' duck-shooting parties, together with Legge and Ashby, so he may well have formed his own attachment to Bruce and appreciated the field spaniel's abilities as a silent and obedient companion on the very kind of terrain they were now travelling on. Goring, however, was less appreciative, recording how as they marched along goat tracks in the dark they kept tripping over a 'most tiresome mongrel which someone had brought along'.

The barking of local village dogs welcomed them to the small settlement of Wangmu, enclosed in a dark clump of trees. It was by now after 10 p.m., and although the map showed that the evening's march had brought them just five miles, they all agreed the distance they had actually walked was more than twice that. Hot water and green tea were brought out into the square for them, and there was a welcome surprise: it had been decided that the next 20 miles over narrow hill paths could be safely and more easily covered in daylight, so they would spend the night here.

The village was a stronghold of the anti-Japanese resistance. Wangmu's Dragon Stone Temple, built into the side of the Guanyin (Goddess of Mercy) Hill beneath a huge rock, also served as a guerrilla training centre. It had a schoolhouse and a kitchen attached to it, and a courtyard in front with a deep well. Leung's gang had its headquarters just a mile or two down the hill towards Bias Bay, in a group of teahouses in Da Ma Lu, the single wide street running through the old fortress town of Dapeng. The Japanese had raided the town on a number of occasions and had occupied it for six months following the capture of Canton.

Preparations had already been made for their arrival, and Kendall directed them to the various billets suggested by the guerrillas. The Admiral was to be the guest of the village elder, the VIP or miscellaneous group were assigned to another house and the sailors were given the temple, or 'Joss House' as they called it. Its floor had been specially laid with rice straw. Kennedy's diary records that it still felt very hard to sleep on, but Gandy thought the MTBs had done well. Chinese temples were 'matey places', he noted happily, where non-believers such as themselves were welcome but pigs and chickens weren't, making the earth floor cleaner than that of the normal hut or small house. He posted a sentry just in case and billeted himself near the door, where in spite of clothes, oilskin and blanket he found the draught 'most penetrating'.

20
Through Japanese Lines

27 December, 6 a.m.

Reveille was called with a shiny, curved ship's whistle, or 'bosun's pipe', that Les Barker wore on a lanyard around his neck next to his .455 Webley revolver. Small and slight as he was, the cheery young leading seaman was taking turns with David Legge in carrying their section's heavy and cumbersome Bren gun, complete with bipod mounting and ammunition. The march facing them today was a challenge for anyone, even without any extra load. The plan was to get over the mountains by dusk in order to get past the main Japanese-held town of Danshui under cover of darkness that same night. There must be no appreciable pause on the way that would allow news or rumours of their approach to get through ahead of them.

The men tumbled out of the temple for an orgy of washing and tooth-brushing round the well. A few even attempted a shave, having packed razors in their gas-mask bags. But most were by now growing unruly beards, of the sort that helped make foreigners appear even more fearsome to the average Chinese than they did already. These particular barbarians were considered worst of all. After all, it was the British, and specifically the British navy, who had waged the Opium War one hundred years before, seizing Hong Kong and beginning an era of decline and humiliation for China that had yet to end.

Apart from the inevitable staring crowd, however, it was almost as if the presence of fifty-odd British sailors in the village temple was an everyday occurrence. More buckets of rice and tea were brought to go with their tinned sausages for breakfast, and by 8 a.m. they were on their way. Admiral Chan had procured a second sedan chair for his injured friend, MacDougall, who had so far struggled along gamely on foot. The villagers had also made a pair of rustic crutches for the times when Chan insisted on walking. There was a reinforced escort of some thirty guerrillas, most of whom went on ahead as scouts. And a number of villagers, both male and female, were employed to carry provisions and kitbags. This they did in the traditional manner, in two baskets hanging from either end of a pole across the carrier's shoulders.

The weather was still sunny and spirits were high as they strung out along the raised paths through the paddy fields. It was beautiful walking country, the surrounding hillsides dotted with clumps of bamboo along the streams, lychee orchards and pink and red clusters of oleander and hibiscus. A shiny, blue-black water buffalo stood and stared at them, a small boy in a pointed bamboo hat perched on its massive neck. An old woman jog-trotted past beneath a towering burden of firewood.

The rice paddies—flooded in summer for the harvest—were now dry, but they noticed that many fields had been left uncultivated. The war that had been going on for so long in China was never far away. In some villages, they were welcomed by women and children and were told the men were all off fighting the Japanese—either with the guerrillas or the Kuomintang army. In others, rows of houses lay in charred ruins, showing what happened when the enemy came to visit. Generally, they were told, the Japanese stayed on the other side of the mountains, content to hold onto the main roads and other communication lines—the very ones the escape party hoped to cross that night. Round here, as in most of China, the only communication lines were the ribbon-like footways they were now walking on, made of low walls of mud running from one rice field to the next. Perhaps that was why Japan was finding this such a difficult country to conquer.

A few hours' steady going saw them well into the hills, a twisting trail visible ahead of them as it wound over the first range. They were soon pouring with sweat—'like a team of hard-driven dray horses', groaned Kennedy. 'However, any inclination to take extra stops was dispelled by the sight of Lieutenant Pethick with a growth of white stubble showing up on his bright red face, or Commander Montague, over sixty, purple but plodding grimly on.'

Once again, packs that had earlier been carefully rearranged became too heavy. Something had to be done to speed up progress, so Henry—who was already playing an invaluable role as an all-purpose 'Mr Fix-it'—recruited more porters at the next village. 'Our following train of coolies grew still larger,' recorded McEwan, 'as overcoats, blankets and odds and ends proved to belong to the class of "not wanted on voyage".' The Chinese carriers, some of them only teen-aged girls, soon put the British men to shame, skipping up the mountain passes with both their baskets weighed down with naval stores and making nothing of it.

As the sailors fell further behind, Guest noticed that some of them were even adding their rifles and ammunition to the coolies' loads. 'The rarefied air began to fray the tempers of the more unfit . . . (and) the Naval officers had to speak rather sharply to some of their men.' Various members of the party simply threw away their rifles and had to be ordered by their commander to go back down to find them, said Ross later. Gandy himself did not mention this, and his diary suggested his tone was more one of stern encouragement than rebuke. 'This march is all a matter of willpower,' he told a burly stoker petty officer, hobbling uphill. 'But willpower doesn't cure blisters and corns,' came the plaintive reply.

In the end it was one of the young officers who was the first to collapse. Tommy Parsons, captain of *MTB 27*, keeled over at the top of the first ridge, complaining of heart trouble. 'The only thing he could ask for,' recalled a colleague later, 'was hot rum and water.' Several others passed out too, according to Kennedy's diary, but it was only Lieutenant Parsons who was deemed worthy of a place in the growing sedan chair party, once a third chair could be found. Not that this was an experience for the faint-hearted, given the speed at which the chair carriers waltzed and whirled along the narrow and often highly precipitous path.

Even if few were in a state to appreciate it, the view from the top of the pass was magnificent. As they looked back, Bias Bay with its craggy islets and crystal coves lay below them to the east, the head of Mirs Bay to the west, and between them stretched the peninsula where they had landed at Nanao. Just off to the left was the jagged peak of Paiya Shan—'Hanging Tooth Mountain'—and away to the right, Wutong Shan—'Parasol Tree Mountain'—where a tiger was said to live in a cave near the summit.

They descended along a narrow valley to the pleasant village of Dafengkeng, cupped in the hills. At 1.30 p.m., said Gandy, they halted here 'in a meadow for tiffin . . . a hearty meal of tinned stuff (and) the usual rice and tea from the villagers.' After lunch they made for the second ridge, between the twin peaks of Tiantou Shan—'Head in Heaven' Mountain—and Bijia Shan—'Pen Rest' Mountain, shaped liked the stand for a scholar's writing brush. Each was about 2,000 feet high. Reaching this latest pass proved less arduous than expected. It was a short but steep climb up a series of wide stone steps, con-cealed under a canopy of overhanging trees and shrubs. This was a key section of the famous smugglers' route. They could see where the great flat stones had been worn smooth by the passage of thou-sands of padding feet, as merchandise unloaded from junks on the coast was conveyed by a chain of human carriers across this rough, bandit-infested country for sale in the interior. Badly needed supplies still came this way through the Japanese blockade, which explained why those now acting as their guards and porters knew these paths so well.

When they rested at the top they had their last view of Hong Kong territory—a distant peak on the west coast of Mirs Bay. Thoughts flashed back to those they had left behind and their uncertain fate in enemy hands. Heading on down the hill on the other side, their attention turned to the more immediate prospect of meeting Japanese troops here in China.

Most of the guerrillas were rarely in sight, having gone ahead to check for any sign of the enemy. 'The guerrillas knew the exact strength and positions of the Japanese for miles around,' Ross told his mother. 'Their intelligence work was perfect, and occasionally we would spot one or two away off on some hilltop, threading along on our flanks to prevent any surprise attack.' In his official report, Montague also praised the guerrillas for their 'masterly scouting and screening', while David Legge wrote to his brother: 'Those guerrillas were incredible . . . We passed within a few miles of (the Japanese) several times without their being aware of the fact.' Chinese guerrilla bands often relied on children as young as seven or eight, known as *xiaoguei* ('little devils'), to work as couriers and sentinels, roaming the hills and keeping the rest of the group informed.

As they descended through rolling hills to the enemy-occupied plain below, some of the sailors fell even farther behind and the column became increasingly extended. Eventually, as much as two miles separated one end from the other. Those at the front waited for the others at Tangpu, in the next valley, where a few white stone houses faced a threshing ground and a duck pond. They had gone almost as far as they dared in daylight. At 5 p.m. they reached the next village, Heshuxia, where they had a hasty meal to fortify them-selves for the dangerous section ahead. Despite the closeness of the Japanese, the villagers once again seemed happy to see the large party of Hong Kong escapees, offering them not just tea, but also turnips, cabbages and bananas.

The Admiral was in good spirits and was standing up to the journey well. He was clearly someone who enjoyed mixing with the ordinary people of the villages. Yet here in Japanese-occupied terri-tory there was a large reward on his head—on all of their heads, for that matter—and they were well aware of the danger that someone might be tempted to betray them. It would not have been hard for a villager to pass on word of their whereabouts—either to the Japanese themselves or to members of the puppet Wang Jingwei regime, which administered the occupied zone. Chan Chak noted that 'pro-enemy agencies' had been set up in the villages they passed in this area. 'Nevertheless,' he said, 'along the journey we were met by the locals with nothing but sincere welcome.' He used some of the funds given him by the guerrilla chief, Leung, to help smooth the way and build up the villagers' support for the Kuomintang: 'I organized meetings to pass on messages of care from the government, encouraging them to hold on for our victory, and gave out money as awards,' he wrote later. But according to Ted Ross, other forms of persuasion were also used. 'The guerrillas went ahead and terrified villagers, threatening them if they told the Japanese about us,' he said years later in an interview.

At dusk they moved off again, with the large naval body now split into three sections. Kendall led a mixed group at the front, McEwan took two boat crews in the middle and another two went with Talan at the rear. For the first time, arms were carried at the ready. The knowledge that they were now in Japanese territory gave them a second wind and they moved swiftly over what seemed an endless plain, where sugar cane grew alongside the inevitable rice fields.

At Zhangshu Pu, they came to the first of the rivers they had to ford. The guerrillas told them there might well be Japanese lurking there, so they approached with great caution. Taking off boots and shoes and hanging them round their necks, they waded across in small groups, holding their rifles over their heads. Those behind and in front stood ready to give covering fire. The water proved to be shallow but ice cold. It was difficult in the half-light to avoid making noisy splashes, so their guides tried to cover up for them. 'The guerrillas keep up a continuous Chinese chatter to give the effect of home-going villagers after the pubs are closed,' wrote Gandy in his diary. 'Or at least that seems to me the nearest equivalent.' He had visions of disaster. 'What a mix-up, if there had been Japs, guerrillas and sailors firing all over the place in the dark.' The anticlimax as they all finally got across without incident came as a huge relief.

Soon they could see before them the dimly winking lights of the town of Danshui, which had been occupied by the Japanese for the past few months. The normal population of 25,000 had been supplemented by an enemy garrison of 4,000 troops, including 500 cavalrymen. Barbed wire and loopholes—narrow slits for firing through—had been added to the old city walls and gates. The open country here was criss-crossed by a maze of paths and tracks, and the guerrillas planned to avoid the town by veering to the left of it. But they would still have to cross the busy main road, regularly patrolled and used by the Japanese. This passed straight through Danshui, running east and west across the plain. They knew it would take a large and well-armed force to bar their way, and as Les Barker pointed out, they were all 'prepared to put up a good fight for freedom, tired as we were'. It would still be preferable, however, to slip by undetected, avoiding the hue and cry that would follow an alarm.

After a short break under trees, when some took the chance to change their socks, they set off again, in single file and as quietly as possible. Towards the back of the long column, Kennedy realized they had reached a crucial moment in their journey:

> It was again a clear night and the moon enabled us to pick out the paths, even narrower than before, which meandered between the paddyfields. Scouting ahead the guerillas led us by devious ways, skirting farm-buildings and avoiding the broader tracks. The air was still and the silence was broken only by occasional barking in the distance. From the rear the column looked like a long black serpent in the dim light as it wound slowly along. It will always remain a vivid picture in my memory.

Suddenly a rifle shot cracked through the silence. Everyone stopped. According to Goring, the man at the front halted so abruptly that 'we all crashed into him and fell in ignominious confusion into the ditch'. Tension mounted as they peered into the shadows, watching for any sign of movement. They then heard the guerrillas arguing fiercely with someone. Who it was exactly, they never found out. Some said it was one of the guerrillas' own sentries whose gun had gone off accidentally. According to others, a man in the remote village they were passing had heard his dog bark and had taken a nervous shot at them. 'However, our guerrilla escort got hold of the villager and scared the wits out of him,' wrote Ross, 'and we crept away with the nearby Japs apparently quite unaware.'

In later years, Ted Ross spoke of another incident near Danshui that night, this time involving Japanese cavalry. They were walking along the raised path through the paddy fields, he said, when guerrillas hurried along the line telling everybody to get down. As they lay hidden between the furrows, they heard the approaching sounds of the 'clippety-clop' of horses and the jingling of harnesses, and a column of about twenty or thirty mounted Japanese cavalrymen rode by. 'You could almost reach out and touch the horses' hooves,' Ross told his family in a recorded interview. Bill Robinson, he added, tried to grab his rifle away from him at this point, apparently because he thought that as a policeman he could put it to better use. But having had it for several days by now, Ross had grown fond of his gun and succeeded in hanging on to it.

Then came the long-awaited crossing of the main road. Shortly before 10 p.m., about half a mile short of the highway, they were told to wait in strict silence while scouts went ahead to monitor the movements of Japanese motorcycles, trucks and other vehicles. After a while, the signal was given for them to advance. 'Ready to march' came down the line—this time in a whisper, instead of Kendall's usual harsh bark. As the column drew nearer, the scouts waved them across in small groups. Kennedy and his colleagues watched anxiously from the back, seeing the Danshui-Pingshan Highway as the last barrier to freedom. Finally it was their turn to go: 'The road stretched silent and deserted. All was well.' Each step now made success more sure, and their spirits rose.

'Once again we were free men,' wrote Eddie Brazel, one of the crew of *C410*, about the moment when they crossed that Japanese patrol line. 'What a feeling! No one who has ever been a captive or nearly so can know just how it feels.'

Freddie Guest's version of the crossing of the road featured a little more drama as well as the usual more prominent role for Captain Guest. He said he and Peter Macmillan went forward to a spot only a few yards from the road, and watched as a convoy of Japanese in trucks with field guns went by. He then lay there, watching the road, while Macmillan went back to fetch the others. But sixty to seventy men moving along in the dark did not prove to be as quiet as he had hoped:

> My heart would pound away like the devil for fear things would go wrong. Then, when our party seemed to be making the most noise, a motor-cycle and sidecar came along and stopped almost opposite to where I was lying. A Jap officer got out and looked up and down the road. Thoughts went through my head as to what I would do if they got suspicious of the noise. Could I get them both with my pistol? My hand went down to the holster and the feel of it made me easier. Just then another motor-cyclist arrived from the other direction and, after a few quick words, they all went on their way. The noise of their engines fading in the distance was one of the sweetest sounds I ever heard.

Arthur Goring also had his own take on the crossing of the road. He described how he and his colleagues were confronted not by Japanese but by a group of Chinese 'Watch and Ward' guards—community police—who were determined to extort a large fee for letting them pass. Chan Chak himself dealt with the matter:

> To our astonishment, the little Admiral—sitting erect in his chair—insisted on being placed in the middle of the road to argue with the ruffians, although at any moment a Japanese patrol might come cycling round the corner. Those grasping villagers demanded twenty-five thousand dollars; all the indignant admiral would offer was a hundred . . . After what seemed an interminable delay, the argument ended in the Admiral paying over a thousand Chinese National dollars—which put our price at 2s 9d each!

They were certainly worth more than a few pence by the time the journey was over, for other accounts hinted at similar scenes elsewhere along their route—if not necessarily at such a crucial point as the Japanese patrol line. Local bandits levied tolls both on the district itself and on those they conveyed or allowed to pass through it. The historian, Jen Yu-wen, who knew Chan Chak personally, said Leung Wingyuen bought peaceful transit for the Admiral's group by 'negotiating with local powers' or simply 'by means of sumptuous gifts'. Colin McEwan said he saw money being handed over whenever a change of guard occurred. On more than one occasion, there appeared to be an argument as to the amount of money to be paid.

They strode on across open moorland. When they came to a second river, many favoured stopping for a rest and something to eat before getting wet again. But Chan Chak said they were not yet clear of danger and insisted that they cross the river first. They would be safer from any pursuing troops on the other side, he pointed out. So once again they waded through water, numbing their blistered feet. They then began looking for a place to sleep, but local farmers begged them not to stop, saying their homes would be destroyed if the Japanese discovered they had stayed there. Just before midnight, near Sishui ('Four Waters'), they found a farmer who said they could rest in his orchard. But they were warned that Japanese patrols had already visited the farm three times that day.

'Apparently acting on the gaming principle of a limit to repetitions', wrote Gandy, 'it is considered safe to bed down in the orchard for the night. The farmer cannot house us for fear of Japanese reprisals but he allows us to take straw for protection against the truly biting East wind.'

Since 8 a.m., Gandy calculated, they had marched 31 miles. 'Not bad for flat-footed sailors,' he boasted. They were all so tired and sore, wrote another diarist, Les Barker, that they were glad of the chance of a couple of hours' sleep with just 'the moon for a blanket'. But most found it too cold to sleep for more than a few minutes at a time, even by wrapping themselves in the rather damp straw and lying close together under the trees. At least there was no rain. And, with dark figures continually getting up during the night to stamp and swing their arms, for once there was no need to post a sentry.

20. Queen's Road, where the two escape cars set off after the fighting ended on Christmas afternoon, almost running down the famous adventurer, 'Two-Gun' Cohen, as they accelerated down the otherwise-deserted street.

21. Telegraph Bay, where two of the motor torpedo boats (below) were waiting. The cars sped by on the road that is visible top left on their way to Aberdeen.

22. *MTBS 07* and *09* in Christmas camouflage, Dairy Farm jetty, 25 December 1941.

23. Aberdeen harbour, showing the pier where the escapers found the *Cornflower*'s launch.

could not venture into open water in daylight because of the bombing.

At half-past nine that night we sailed, heading North; and I, for one, having had no sleep for three days and nights except for the half-hour on the beach, curled up thankfully on a bunk, willing to sleep for a week. Our memorable Christmas Day was over!

THE LANDING

It was half-past three in the morning when we nosed our way into the sand of the Chinese mainland. Engines had been shut off, and every ear was strained to catch the slightest sound from the shore. We were all armed to the teeth with a variety of weapons given to us by the Royal Navy, and were prepared to sell our lives dearly.

Suddenly a voice was raised from the darkness ahead of us. "A - h o y there!".

Believe it or not, it was that incredible N e w Zealander w h o had given us the b a t t e r y at Aberdeen!

After he had rendered us this signal service he had gone off, although we pressed him to come with us, and had scuttled his own boat, the *Robin*. Then, wandering along the shore, he picked up a seventy - year - old merchant seaman, and between them they got the stranded *C.410* off the rocks. The New Zealander then decided to try to overtake our little motor-boat party—what we had over-looked—that we only had enough petrol for fifteen miles. But he missed us, for after we abandoned her our little craft had drifted away with the tide.

Once out to sea our friend evidently saw no reason for going back to captivity. Sending the old merchant seaman below to

get some rest, he took the wheel himself. It was then, he told us, that he committed the gravest crime of his Naval career. He had fallen asleep! He awoke with a start to find his boat aground—where he didn't know. Half an hour later we arrived at the very same place!

This was no time for swapping stories, however; there was much to be done. Those five M.T.B.s and the *C.410* had to be stripped of everything movable before daylight. We busied ourselves carrying ashore arms, ammunition, wireless sets, cushions, blankets, food—everything. And then, to prevent the Japanese from discovering them and using them against us elsewhere, those precious little M.T.B.s, which had done such grand service, and cost £25,000 apiece, had to be scuttled. A most melancholy business, but absolutely necessary.

Our entire "army," now some sixty strong, made off towards a small village in the hills, the Admiral's gunman carrying his crippled chief pick-a-back. We had still to make our way through the

"The Admiral calmly took to the waves."

24. 'Abandon Ship!' illustration accompanying Goring's magazine article.

25. Aplichau, from Aberdeen Reservoir. Note the steep hills the escapers climbed under continuing fire after their swim. Lamma is in the distance. This photo was taken in the 1940s, before Aplichau's development into one of the most densely populated areas in the world.

26. 'The Swimming Party'. The twelve survivors from the launch, photographed later in Waichow. Back row: Robinson, Wright, Macmillan, Guest, Yeung, Ross. Front row: Christiansen, MacDougall, Chan, Goring, Oxford, Hsu.

27. Swift dash into the night. *MTB 11* at speed, Hong Kong Island behind. Prewar.

28. Ashby's bungalow. The escapers saw the house in flames as they sailed past Stanley, where the defending troops, out of touch with HQ, were still staging a heroic last stand.

29. 'Snakelike and silent': Marching across the paddy fields. Guerrillas of the Hong Kong and Kowloon Independent Brigade in North Sai Kung, 1943.

30. Chinese soldiers near the walled village of Dashanxia, 28 December 1941. They were a welcome sight for the escape group, who knew they were now out of the Japanese occupied zone.

31. Waichow's West Lake. The escape party staged a triumphal march past the ancient pagoda—one of the few buildings to have survived the bombing. Photo taken in 1942.

32. The American Mission hospital, Waichow, where beds and hot baths awaited—and where the men took cover among the bushes when an enemy plane came over. Photo taken in 1984.

33. Nurses and officers pose together after the big group photo at the mission on 30 December 1941. Back row: Kennedy, Hsu, Gandy, Yorath, Halladay, Parsons, Ashby, Collingwood; front: Gee, Brewer, Legge; nurses' names unknown.

34. *MTB 09* crew, Waichow, 30 December 1941. Rear: Penny, Gurd, Hill, Hempenstall, Foster, Schillemore, Priestley; front: Brewer, Kennedy.

35. Kennedy and Chinese Army girls on their sightseeing trip, 30 December 1941. Behind them is Waichow's main bridge, damaged by bombs.

21
Into Free China

28 December, 5.30 a.m.

When the signal to move came at dawn, they were only too glad to get going. Kendall led off at a cracking pace, saying they could have breakfast at their first stop in unoccupied China: a village called Xinxu, where the Nationalist Army had a small forward post. But that was still almost ten miles away. By the time the sun came up and the warmth began to seep into their bones, many of them were already beginning to fall behind again. Henry went on ahead with an advance party of guerrillas to make arrangements for the promised meal and to plan their onward journey.

Soon the orchards and sugar cane groves began to look more fertile and better cultivated, and there were fewer signs of Japanese influence. They walked along a ten-foot-wide dyke through the paddy fields and crossed yet another river, this time by a bridge. The countryside seemed to run with rivers, irrigation ditches and canals. Then they joined a rough road where the Chinese had dug tank traps to stop Japanese motorized patrols moving any further inland. The large square holes had straight, deep sides and were dug alternately on each side of the road so no vehicle could pass.

They headed further northwest through open country consisting of low, rolling hills with occasional clumps of bushes. They felt they must surely now be almost beyond the enemy's reach. Although the going was far less arduous than on the previous day, there was less incentive to make haste and less immediate danger to keep them on their toes.

Len Rann, a tall, dark stoker in a belted black oilskin, was smiling more broadly than ever: today, he suddenly remembered, was his twenty-first birthday. But for many of his shipmates, the initial thrill of the escape and the unexpected joy of finding themselves alive and free were starting to wear off. Instead, thoughts were turning to aches and pains and the distance to Waichow . . . or even further, all the way back to Britain.

'Just a rough track leading over plains and hills,' wrote Les Barker in his diary, 'through isolated villages with the inhabitants sometimes all turning out to see us all file past. Very monotonous, hour after hour. A lot of suffering from blisters and sore feet . . . All the paths are terrible but we keep trekking along, hoping that the end means England.'

Buddy Hide, the youngest of seventeen children, was another sailor with a girl he was waiting to marry as soon as he got home. His nine years in the navy had taken him to exotic locations throughout the Middle East, and on leave he was ever the centre of attention back home in Sussex with tales of his travels. But this time he felt it was only the prospect of getting home that was keeping him going. He was one of those suffering from 'Hong Kong foot'—the local name for athlete's foot—which made every step a painful experience.

Others with sore feet included those with the most body weight to carry. Sammy Carr, *MTB 10*'s hefty leading stoker, was one. His even bigger shipmate, Chief Petty Officer Gilbert Thums, was another. Thums had told his half-brother Eric before the war that he hadn't been able to see his feet for years. But now they were giving him hell. Like many of the others, he was wearing a pair of 'dead man's boots' salvaged from the clearing station at Aberdeen. The problem was that the Canadian who had owned them before him must have had much smaller feet than he had. Thums told his family later that during one of their stops he was given a Chinese remedy of 'herbs, roots, leaves and mud' to put in the toes of his offending boots. How effective this proved is not known.

In the meantime, unlike some of his colleagues, the former Beeston pig slaughterer made light of his suffering. During each ten-minute rest stop, Kendall would walk among them and ask each man with a laugh: 'Ready to march? Ready to march?' . . . words some of them were growing to dread. At the end of the break Thums would put away his pipe—a much-loved object with a dip in it where the flame had burnt away the wood—and get the men to fall in, reporting to Kendall with a brisk: 'Ready to march, Sir.' On this occasion he reported wearily: 'Ready to fall over, Sir.'

During one of these brief halts, Gandy chatted in pidgin English to half a dozen guerrillas, one of them a girl. She was armed with the usual pistol and dressed like many of the others in faded blue, with a rolled blanket over her shoulder. He asked her what her parents thought about her present role. 'I belong to the New China, but they do not,' she said.

Her reply, simple as it was, suggests that some of those escorting the escape party belonged to the category of 'red' rather than 'merchant' guerrilla. Or at least that they were more ideologically motivated than their leader, Leung Wingyuen, and his gold-toothed, homburg-hatted smuggler accomplices, who spent much of their spare time gambling. From his own chats with the guerrillas along the road, David MacDougall was left in no doubt that Leung's guerrilla group as a whole were pro-Nationalist. But the Kuomintang had never had a strong grip over this traditionally wild and lawless Hakka region, and it would be surprising if at least some of the recruits had not been caught up in the growing trend among the nation's youth towards the new, revolutionary doctrines of Mao Zedong. He and his followers had ended up at Yenan in the north of China after their famous Long March in the mid-1930s. Their Communist Party now had some 700,000 members, over 90 per cent of whom had joined since the start of the war against Japan.

In the region adjoining Hong Kong, the East River Column of the Guangdong People's Anti-Japanese Guerrillas had direct links to the Communist Party in the north. Under the leadership of the staunchly anti-Kuomintang Zeng Sheng, the group enjoyed a growing local reputation for treating the peasants sympathetically and fighting the Japanese zealously. It was also busy organizing what was to become a highly successful 'escape corridor' for hundreds of prominent left-wing Chinese trapped in Japanese-occupied Hong Kong. Many non-Chinese who later escaped from the internment camps used the same route. According to Zeng's son, it was an early version of this communist escape network that was now helping to smooth the way for Chan Chak's party. 'The East River Column arranged for villagers to feed and look after the group along their route to Waichow,' Zeng Deping told the author in 2009.

But the guerrillas now talking to Gandy were less interested in politics than guns—in particular, his light-calibre Mauser. Their own pistols were all of heavy calibre, with notches cut into the handles to keep a tally of the Japanese they had killed. The naval commander told them proudly that his gun 'was sighted up to 500 yards when mounted on its wooden holster as a rifle stock'. They asked for a demonstration. A crow perched on a tree 200 yards away was indicated as a target. Everyone gathered round. 'I took aim very very carefully and squeezed the trigger,' recalled Gandy. 'Puff! No explosion, but laughter from the guerrillas. My ammunition was faulty, deteriorated with age. Mortifying, of course, but just as well because there would be no more hints that Chinese forces needed modern arms.'

As the walkers finally reached the approaches to Xinxu, they were cheered by the sight of the greenish-yellow cotton uniforms and padded jackets of the regular troops of Free China. The Spandau machine guns cradled by the Kuomintang soldiers were a reminder that Germany had until a few years ago been China's main arms supplier. Hitler had decided in 1938 that Japan was a more promising Far Eastern ally, leaving the Chinese with only Red Russia to help them. But all that had changed in the three weeks since Pearl Harbor. Now Chiang Kai-shek could have almost anything he wanted from both the Americans and the British. His new allies' performance against Japan so far had been less than impressive, however, and some of the escape party were a little nervous about how to explain Hong Kong's rapid capitulation to their Chinese hosts, who had held out on their own for so many years.

But their welcome in this first outpost of Free China was as warm and unquestioning as it had been in the occupied zone and in the no-man's-land in between. Commander Montague, for one, was delighted: 'Here we were within the lines of the Chinese Regular Forces, and owing to their kindness, were generously fed and comfortably housed.' Xinxu had a population of only 100, and had nothing to offer by way of accommodation—its only eating place a temporary matshed—but it did boast its own school, and this was handed over to the escape party as their quarters for the day. They were invited to make themselves at home on a bed of straw in primitive but picturesque grey stone outhouses, while the Admiral sat in a small courtyard with a non-playing fountain in the middle and exchanged courtesies with an official reception committee. This consisted of some village elders, the captain of the garrison and some 'smart, pleasant-looking' officers who had rushed down from the next town to meet him after word had been sent on ahead of their arrival.

Still smarting from the episode with the guerrillas, Gandy vented his frustration on his own men. First, he seized the chance to give them a little homily as to the necessity for 'cooks of messes getting busy immediately on arrival instead of flopping down exhausted as soon as a halt is called'. His diary for the day also records crossly that 'messes no. 1 and 2 swiped all the cocoa, rest got none'—but as the guilty parties in this case were the non-MTB 'odds and sods', there was little he could do. Finally, when his men fell in, he insisted they did so in a more orderly fashion than had become their wont, 'now that the eyes of the Chinese army might be upon us'.

But the flotilla commander faced further discomfort when at 1 p.m. they eventually had their first food of the day. The villagers brought them an elaborate meal of rice and pork with boiled turnip tops, water chestnuts and other vegetables. Some of these, Gandy noted, had bits of mud adhering to them. He tried them anyway as he thought they would be nourishing, but promptly withdrew, feeling sick. 'I made the mistake of dipping into a dish of water lily roots and felt extremely sorry for myself for two hours afterwards.'

Others fared better out in the street, where it turned out that the villagers were happy to accept Hong Kong dollars. They were aware that there had been 'big trouble Hongkong-side', but evidently they thought the British colony's currency would outlive Japanese rule. The locals suggested a not-too-unreasonable rate of 5 to 1 (five Chinese dollars for one Hong Kong dollar) and were soon doing brisk business. Even at HK$1 each, the local oranges were good enough to persuade Ron Ashby to part with his cash. And John Collingwood earned the undying gratitude of Colin McEwan by presenting him with two 'great fresh duck eggs'.

After a sound sleep they took to the road again at about 4.30 on a fine afternoon. Half an hour's walk saw them through a narrow pass guarded by more Nationalist soldiers. The military post, marked by a tattered flag on a stick beside a derelict hut, doubled as a toll station. The soldiers at such posts searched passers-by for contraband and seized hens and rice destined for occupied areas—this policy being aimed more at the communists than the Japanese. Here, mention of Chan Chak's name was enough to assure the escape party's smooth progress. The descent on the other side brought them through lovely, wooded scenery down to a large plain plentifully scattered with villages. The combination of relief at really being in Free China and the beautiful evening had its effect, and this time there were few laggards.

Just before nightfall, they reached the Chinese garrison town of Zhenlong. A mile to the southeast of it, in front of a steep hill, lay the old Hakka walled village of Dashanxia. They entered through one of three gates. The sign above it contained three painted characters— meaning, they were told, 'Charity brings Happiness'. Within the walls lay a mandarin's *yamen*—the residence and offices of the district magistrate. This was where they were to spend the night. A series of courtyards, archways and passages led to black-tiled ancestral halls, scholars' retreats and family shrines. Deep blue pillars flanked a flight of steps up to a traditional Hakka 'sky well'—a small pond where raindrops fell through a hole in the roof. Ceilings were hung with lanterns and glazed ceramic figures paraded along eaves that curved gracefully upwards at either end. Few of them had ever seen anything like it.

The whole compound had been taken over as a temporary military headquarters and barracks. They were told that General Yu Hanmou's reinforcements for Hong Kong had managed to reach this point, only to learn that the colony had just surrendered. They had turned round and headed back towards Waichow the previous day. So, the famous relief army was real after all. What a pity, wrote Chan Chak later, that the defence of the colony hadn't lasted a little longer.

One story has it that British officers on the escape told Chan Chak that Hong Kong might have sustained its resistance for longer if not for a secret order from Winston Churchill. According to this account, which has appeared in various Chinese histories, the Governor telegraphed Churchill in the last desperate hours of the siege to say that with the help of the Admiral and the approaching Chinese army it was possible the defending troops could still hold out. But the Prime Minister is said to have replied that it would be better to surrender: for if the colony fell to Japan, Britain could reclaim it in due course, but once the Chinese were allowed to get their foot in the door, Hong Kong might be lost forever.

By the same reasoning, some say the Nationalists were never too worried whether or not their relief army arrived in time, since rather than help Britain hang onto its colony, they hoped to arrange for Japan to return Hong Kong directly to China, after the war. It seems both sides may have wanted Hong Kong too much for themselves— and if that meant letting Japan have it in the short term, then so be it.

However good the décor at the escape party's latest lodging place, dining and accommodation facilities received mixed reports. Dinner—hosted by the Chinese military—included meat and fish as well as vegetables and 'a certain but not excessive amount of rice wine'. Ron Ashby, for one, was impressed: 'Really good Chinese food provided by our kindly hosts,' he wrote in *MTB 07*'s logbook. 'Plenty of variety, very hot.' For others, a shortage of chairs, tables and Western-style cutlery proved more of a problem. 'Dinner was a fairly hilarious affair,' according to Colin McEwan, 'with the General Staff proving a very poor second at lying on their bellies and grabbing at food with chopsticks.'

The staff officers did better when it came to sleeping arrangements. After drawing wooden buckets of water at the pool in the central court and bathing their feet, they slept on straw in what appeared to be the magistrate's family temple. It was all spotlessly clean and, according to Goring, 'extremely comfortable'.

But for Gandy, who had already had a bad day and was in need of a good night's rest, it was another story. His MTB group had been allotted the mess hall as their dormitory. There were no beds to be seen, and up on a stage at one end of the room, Kendall and various Chinese generals continued eating and drinking late into the night. Finally deciding to try to sleep anyway, Gandy claimed his right to a plank and trestle rather than lie on the mud floor. The results were disastrous: 'My recollection before closing eyes was to see FW Kendall playing the finger guessing game* with the generals for "yum sing" (bottoms up drinks) . . . My next impression was a rude awakening when I fell off my bench.' There followed what his diary describes as some 'v. sulphuric language'. Gandy's crew from *MTB 10*, whose usual nickname for him was Mahatma, told him later that from that moment they christened themselves 'Gandy's Guerrillas'.

---

finger guessing game: How to play this common drinking game is explained by McEwan in his diary: 'you faced your opponent with the right hand outstretched. Then, at speed and calling in Chinese, you opened so many fingers, your opponent doing the same and you guessed aloud at the total number of fingers displayed'.

22
Welcome to Waichow

29 December

Their goal today was Waichow, now only 14 miles away. Here they were told they would find a British military representative and an American mission, as well as a medical post, shops and other amenities. On a beautiful, sunny morning they were washed and ready to leave by eight o'clock. About forty 'bicycle-taxis' had been sent from Waichow to meet them, in case the older or more footsore members of the group weren't up to any more walking. This seemed a splendid idea, they thought—until they saw the bicycles and learned that this particular form of travel could be as slow and certainly as painful as walking. While the Chinese cyclist did the pedalling, the passenger perched on the pillion seat—a threadbare cushion on an iron frame over the mudguard—with his large, blistered feet sticking out in ungainly fashion on either side. Most of those who tried it found there were too many rocks, chasms, water buffalo and other obstacles to allow anything but a succession of spills and walks interspersed with the briefest and bumpiest of rides.

But for Goring, any transport was better than none:

> My particular host was very small indeed, while I am no pigmy; so I proposed I should ride the cycle while *he* sat on the carrier. But this he would not hear of. Indeed he became quite cross about it. So with my two blankets, rifle and all, I bestrode the carrier; he mounted the diminutive bicycle and we wobbled off . . .
>
> Presently we came to some enormous cavities extending right across the road—tank traps some 15 feet deep and half-filled with water. As we approached the first, I was horrified to observe that my cyclist did not slacken speed; he obviously intended to pedal across the narrow plank which spanned the gap! I protested violently but he rode doggedly on . . .
>
> I shut my eyes; I honestly believe my cyclist did the same. We sailed across that plank in a manner which would have turned Blondin green with envy. Yet, the moment we reached *terra firma* on the far side, the Chinese wobbled worse than ever!

Ted Ross, who was carrying the injured David MacDougall on the back of his bicycle, was not so lucky. He lost control as they were crossing one of the tank traps and they both fell into the bottom of the trench below. 'I was worried about Mac because he wasn't in very good shape,' said Ross. 'But somehow we both got out all right. The bike's front wheel was a bit bent but we kicked it straight and went on.'

Commander Montague was happy enough for his bicycle and its rider to be 'borrowed' from time to time by one of the few guerrillas who were still accompanying them. 'No hardship to discard my machine on loan,' he said cheerily when Gandy found him walking. Others walked all morning and only accepted the offer of a lift for the last few miles. About half the total party insisted on doing the whole day's journey on foot, deciding that having come this far, they would not be beaten on the last lap—although many of them did agree to allow their packs to be carried for them.

Those who walked split up into four separate groups, to make smaller targets in the event of air raids. MTBs 07 and 09 formed one group, now consisting of just six men (three officers: Ashby, Kennedy and Brewer; and three ratings: Rutter, Gurd and Hempenstall). With Parsons still unwell, McEwan was acting as commander of *MTB 27*. Aided by some musical accompaniment from one of the crew, he soon had his men moving along at what he called a good 'heel and toe' pace: 'Spirits were high,' he noted, 'and the mouth organ suddenly produced by Pony Moore lifted our feet along the moorland road.'

After a couple of hours, a *pailou*, or decorative archway, announced that they were approaching the village of Fenghuang Gang ('Phoenix Ridge'). Alongside the usual semi-circular duck pond, there was a teahouse and a temple with a Hakka-style gabled roof that looked almost more Dutch than Chinese. Here they halted for some 'chow', says Kennedy. Barker suggests they were now on strict rations—and were more interested in reaching their first big stop later in the day than in local village architecture: 'At about 1200 we stopped and were each given a half of one tinned sausage each. We were that eager to arrive in Waichow we were all for pushing on again.'

Later, two patrolling Japanese aircraft came into sight and everyone took cover. Montague, Gandy and others in the bicycle party dismounted and hid in a field near a crossroads. The planes passed over without incident. The cyclists eventually caught up with the walkers at about 1.30 p.m. on the outskirts of Waichow, where Chinese civic officials and army officers met them at a military rest house. There was also a small force of soldiers, who drew up to attention to salute them as they came within sight of the ornamented gates in the town's massive walls, 30 feet high and 50 thick. There was to be a formal entry into the town, to give the local population its first ever look at the Royal Navy.

But the start of their parade was delayed by an air raid alert. Japanese bombers staged raids on Waichow so frequently that hardly anyone worked there any more in the daytime. Instead, the towns-people spent their days sheltering out in the countryside, returning before dark to do their shopping and conduct their business. Most of what was worth bombing in the town had by this time already been destroyed; the main aims of the continuing air raids were to disrupt normal activity and remind people of the close Japanese presence.

While they waited for the all clear, the members of the escape party were treated to tea and Chinese cakes. These were typically peanut, lotus or sesame flavoured buns, steamed and wrapped in a green banana leaf. For the next hour, they watched column after column of Chinese soldiers pass by—part of the army that would have relieved Hong Kong, they were told, if the British had held out for two more days. After marching south for almost a month, the troops had now been ordered to turn round and march north to Changsha, 300 miles away, where the Japanese had mounted another major assault.

The Kuomintang Government had millions of soldiers like these all over China, many of them forcibly conscripted and roped together like slaves. Poorly equipped and undernourished (some spent their spare time hunting rats and snakes to augment their rations), they sloped along in their thin cotton uniforms and straw sandals, chant-ing numbers mechanically to help them keep up the required pace. Separate groups of coolies carried cooking pots and sometimes bundles of rifles, dangling from poles slung over their shoulders. Others pulled big sacks of rice on three-wheeled carts or led mules with panniers slung on either side. Occasionally an officer would come by on horseback, brandishing a pistol.

Now it was the turn of the British to try to smarten up and march in time as they showed themselves off to Waichow. Unshaven, unkempt and with no two men dressed alike, they formed up three abreast, shouldered their various weapons and paraded past the chief magistrate (the equivalent of a sheriff or mayor). He and other local luminaries then led them in ceremonial style through the bombed streets, setting a low-geared pace, which according to Gandy, was almost impossible for Europeans to keep in step with.

At the head of the Hong Kong party, Admiral Chan Chak, still dressed in his British naval commander's uniform, sat smiling in his sedan chair. Flanking him as standard-bearers were Alex Kelly and Eric Purchase—the only two sailors still aged less than twenty—one holding aloft China's scarlet and blue national flag and the other the Royal Navy's White Ensign. Commander Montague and Lieutenant Commander Gandy came next, followed by the five sections of the flotilla, the officers of each boat marching beside their crews and trying manfully to keep them in step. The military staff and the other naval officers and seamen brought up the rear.

Things started quietly enough. But soon the mouth organ came out, the singing started and word spread that the one-legged admiral and his foreign friends were coming up the road. Before the centre of town was reached, Kennedy reckoned the procession a confirmed success: 'A host of dogs and small boys appeared from nowhere and kept pace beside us. The crowd increased, cheering as we went by, and firecrackers cascaded on to the street. This barrage exploding under our feet made it hard to preserve any semblance of military order, but who cared? It was an excellent party and a fine welcome.'

Lively a spectacle as it was, the impression Colin McEwan was left with as he trailed along at the back was that of a drunken Salvation Army Saturday night route march: 'I felt an irresistible urge to giggle and in this was not helped by the fact that the mouth organ band was playing the Beer Barrel Polka followed by Macmillan's rendering of "I don't want to be a soldier" while striding along with a definitely martial air.'

Some of them did wonder later if it might have been wiser to enter the town less conspicuously, for there were still enemy aircraft about. And it seems the unusual happenings in the streets below did not go unnoticed. Waichow, the headquarters of a Nationalist front-line division, had already changed hands several times and was liable to be overrun again at any time.* Japanese troops were based nearby, as were Japanese planes. The fact that most of the buildings in the town centre were in ruins was due not so much to the frequent but small-scale bombing as to fires started by the Japanese each time they

---

overrun again at any time: this in fact happened the following month, the Japanese burning and looting the city with particular venom—perhaps because of the sanctuary given to the escape party—before withdrawing and allowing the Chinese to recapture it in early February, 1942.

withdrew. The few bridges over Waichow's two rivers, the Danshui and the mighty East River, had also been blown up and were in various states of disrepair.

Spread out around the confluence of the two rivers, some 70 miles east of Canton, Waichow was the centre of a brisk trade among the *shuishang ren*, or water people, of southern China, plying their sampans and barges to and from Danshui and the towns further upriver. It lay in a rich, fertile valley where the way of life had scarcely altered for centuries. Nine hundred years ago it had been a fine and prosperous city, home to the great Song Dynasty poet and statesman, Su Dongpo.

They were now marching alongside Waichow's beautiful West Lake, leaving a red trail of firecracker paper along their route. A seven-storey, thousand-year-old pagoda stood on one of the lake's many tree-covered islands, linked to the shore by a delicate, hump-backed stone bridge—this one, too, damaged by bombs.

They turned off to the right, down a cobbled road filled with a 'milling conglomerate of humans, dogs, chickens, pigs and even rats'. At the far end they crossed a newer, concrete bridge connecting Waichow's two twin townships. This bridge was only partially down and what remained was being used by a steady flow of pedestrians, bicycles, rickshaws, handcarts and mule-carts.

Out in the eastern suburbs, at the end of a narrow lane lined with dilapidated old stone houses, they finally reached the haven of the Wai On Hospital, part of an American Seventh-Day Adventist mission. Walled compounds housing Christian missions—generally centred round a hospital—could be found in towns and cities throughout the province of Guangdong. They typically contained a small church and a few Western-designed houses for the foreign missionary couples who ran them, scattered among large, well laid-out gardens. This one, looking over the East River and the mountains beyond, was no exception. The main hospital building had tiled roofs, white wooden shutters and meshed windows that kept out the flies; there was a well at the front with a small windmill pump; and a line of Flame of the Forest trees screened three attractive two-storey staff houses from a small church set in the middle of an open grassy space. Ralph Goodwin, the torpedo boat sub-lieutenant who had remained in Hong Kong after being injured, later stayed here during his own escape, describing it as 'a most delightful place, with lawns shaded by huge old trees, with flower gardens and a lake on which ducks swam in leisurely contentment. The whole atmosphere of the garden was one of peace and repose.'

Until just three weeks before the group's arrival, the hospital had flown an American flag. The Stars and Stripes had also been painted onto the roofs of the three staff houses to warn Japanese planes against bombing them. But since the raid on Pearl Harbor, the roofs had been overpainted with black. Although founded by Americans and apparently still funded by them, the mission and its hospital were now staffed entirely by Chinese. The pastor was called Li Mingdao; a Dr Su Huiqiang and his wife ran the hospital.

Inside, there were whoops of joy at the prospect of being able to bathe in hot water—even if only in a wooden bucket—and to sleep in real beds with real spring mattresses. Best of all was to be pampered by the hospital's small team of professionally trained nurses. According to Barker, 'the Chinese nurses were very kind to us indeed. We were each shown to a bed and were able to wash and shave etc, for which we were very thankful. The nurses treated our wounds and blisters etc, and made us really feel at home.'

The simplest of comforts seemed like the ultimate in luxury and sophistication. Kennedy found it 'a great treat to have a wash-down and exchange a thick jersey for a rather soiled shirt out of my pack'. Ashby did even better, 'by some form of magic appearing in collar and tie and looking like a very senior Rear Admiral'. It all helped to imbue the right spirit, for they had been invited to dine that evening at Chinese Army Headquarters as guests of Lieutenant-Generals Wang Dafu and Chen Qi, the two senior commanders in the area.

The main government and military compounds were about a mile away, between the junction of the two rivers and West Lake. Washed, refreshed and with appetites duly whetted, they were escorted there by an armed patrol in the cool of the early evening along the grassy bank of the East River, past venerable banyan trees and clumps of giant bamboo. The garrison had its headquarters in a grand and elaborate mansion with an ancestral hall at the centre. The banquet, held in honour of Chan Chak, was attended by as many as 3,000 people, Henry Hsu said later—though it is hard to believe this can't have been an exaggeration. Proceedings started at 6.30 p.m. and finished, twenty courses and many toasts later, at 9 p.m. Government rules banning drinking and limiting the number of dishes at official dinners were evidently overlooked (a frequent occurrence both then and now). The escape party only learnt later that the local population had given up a week's meat ration to feed them.

Among the 'unlimited delicacies' placed before them, pigeon's eggs, bamboo shoots and suckling pig are the ones picked out by Kennedy as worthy of mention. He thought fondly of the many Chinese meals he and Rachel had shared on their evenings out together in Hong Kong. Most of the other men were less accustomed to Chinese food. 'None of us sailors could use chopsticks at first which is very funny to watch,' confided Barker. Lieutenant Commander Yorath made use of a small china spoon he had brought with him as a souvenir from the Hong Kong Club. Many of the group, as they had been doing at other meals, resorted to their fingers. Their hosts were understanding and reached over with their chopsticks to put morsels in their bowls for them from the dishes at the centre of each big round table. According to Buddy Hide, they would all become very adept with chopsticks by the end of their journey, since it was a case of either that or starve. On his return to England, he told his local newspaper in Sussex that wherever they went in China, the people had given them the best they could: 'Of course it was all Chinese chow, poor class Chinese chow, which is all rice boiled dry, no milk or sugar, and sufficient meat for one Englishman was shared amongst ten of us; the same with the greens which was nearly all garlic.'

Stomach problems were about to replace sore feet as the naval party's most common ailment. But the Waichow banquet wasn't just about eating. As well as offering a series of toasts to Chan Chak, they drank to the MTBs and also to the final victory of the 'ABCDs'. This was an acronym the Chinese had enthusiastically adopted for the new alliance between the Americans, British, Chinese and Dutch (whose colonies in the East Indies were already under serious threat). The British sailors were quick to learn to respond to the toastmaster's *yumsing* (cheers) with the required cry of *ganbei* (literally, 'dry cup'). The Chinese, for their part, were taught that use of the expression 'bottoms up' was only allowed when the toast was to the Japanese navy. It struck Collingwood that the Chinese officers were 'very keen to make friends'. Even Gandy seems to have had a good time, writing later: 'I don't remember it very well, but the note I have reads: "very good food and much *yum sing*".'

23
Photos and Shopping

30 December

Orders came to assemble at 8 a.m. for an official photograph, but most made as much as they could of their unaccustomed beds by having as long a lie-in as possible. While the officers were sleeping two to a room, the ratings—or 'troops' as they were known—were packed into dormitories, just like in the old days in Hong Kong. From now on, ranks were being re-established in strict Royal Navy tradition. On the march through dangerous territory over the past four days and nights, the captain and first lieutenant of each boat had lived and travelled together with their eight or nine crew as a single, integrated unit. But Lieutenant Commander Gandy had decided that it was time to end such 'close-packed organization', and that he and his fellow officers would once again live separately from their crews. Whether this decision had anything to do with falling off his bench in front of his men the night before is not known.

Many saw the reintroduction of the old system of segregation as a step to be regretted—among them McEwan and his SOE colleagues: 'It did seem a pity and wholly unnecessary that after days such as they had been through where officers walked, ate and slept with their men that, on return to a more or less normal living, there came the definite split. Requests for a separate officers' mess—the request, it must be admitted, coming from a few only—was refused tactfully but firmly and in our position of "superior civilians" we had the opportunity and pleasure of watching all the sideplay.'

Those keen to pull rank had a good chance to do so as they lined up for the formal group photo outside on the lawn, where chairs from the mission schoolroom had been laid out in front of the main hospital building. The British naval and army officers sat in order of precedence on either side of Chan Chak and the two Chinese generals who had hosted the previous night's banquet. The White Ensign and the Chinese flag were draped over the knees of the Admiral and the men on either side of him—Commander Montague on his right, and General Wang on his left. Other ranks were ranged in two or three uneven lines behind them, with the back row standing on chairs. Sitting cross-legged on the grass at the front were Henry and Yeung Chuen with three more of the group's Waichow hosts and three of the junior MTB officers—not forgetting Bruce, who, like the well-trained gun dog that he was, 'had not made a sound the whole way'.

The local photographer had only one glass plate left, so was particularly anxious to get everything right. The resulting black-and-white image captures the swashbuckling if endearingly ramshackle and bedraggled nature of the escape group—despite Gandy's appeal for everyone to look 'as spick and span as possible'. It also happens to be the only record we have of what most of its members looked like at the time. The Admiral gave each man his own print of the photo when they were in Kukong the following week. A large caption written in Chinese and English at the top says: 'Admiral Chen* Chak with British officers and men whom His Excellency led through the Japanese lines after the Fall of Hong Kong and arrived safely at Waichow.'

Today, the Waichow photo has taken on an almost iconic status among anyone interested in or connected with the escape. Among a number of original copies known to survive is one belonging to the family of Les Barker, who told his local newspaper after he got home: 'I shall always keep this photograph as a souvenir. There are 65 of us pictured—a motley company, wearing all kind of clothing and uniforms. Quite a lot had steel helmets. But throughout the march I wore a sweater (originally white), blue trousers and a couple of shirts. I had no hat.'

Six members of the party are absent from the group. Two of them were sick—Pethick had stomach problems and Prest had suspected dysentery. Kendall, McEwan and Talan were part of the Secret Service, and so had to remain incognito (especially as they were due to stay on in Waichow for further undercover operations). MacDougall also chose not to take part—either because of his own role in intelligence, or due to his injury. But he did pose for a smaller group photo called 'The Swimming Party' with the eleven other men who had swum from the launch at Aberdeen. Kennedy took the chance to get two more shots taken with his camera of smaller groups: one of himself and his crew from *MTB 09*, and another of officers and nurses.

Admiral Chen: the spelling of his name as pronounced in Mandarin or standard Chinese (today's *putonghua*). The original caption also gives a date—29 December 1941—which is that of their arrival rather than of the photograph itself.

After the photo session, hot water was soon in high demand for baths and laundry. It was proposed to stay a second night in Waichow, and Goring was among those only too glad of a chance to take it easy:

> It was a warm, sunny day, so we washed our clothes and hung them on the bushes in the mission garden to dry, meanwhile lying about on the lawn, sunbathing. It seemed good to be alive, but presently the air-raid gongs sounded and a large Japanese bomber circled low over the hospital three times. We scrambled to cover. What the pilot made of the scene I do not know; but there were the tell-tale clothes lying all about, with an occasional naked form wriggling to conceal itself in a bush.

At this point the hospital administrator, Dr Su, is said to have grown 'very agitated', imploring everyone to disperse quickly and keep out of sight—though whether he was more worried about protecting his mission from Japanese bombs or his nurses from the sight of sunbathing British sailors is hard to say. In the event, no bombs were dropped and the plane flew off towards Canton Bay. But the close interest shown in them suggested the previous day's parade had indeed been noticed, and it might be as well to stay no longer than necessary in Waichow.

Some of the Hong Kong party were beginning to get the impression that their arrival had complicated the position of the local Chinese commander with his Japanese counterpart. A cosy agreement had apparently been reached whereby neither side took aggressive action against the other, and it looked as if this had now been disturbed. The Japanese commander had lost face as a result of the mass escape through his lines and would now feel obliged to launch an attack, they were told. According to Kendall, the Nationalist Chinese generals were also concerned by the involvement of communist guerrillas during the escape. They considered the Reds to be public enemy number one; the Japanese came a poor second. They apparently accepted, however, that Leung Wingyuen himself was no communist, and as long as the other guerrilla escorts now filtered back to the coast, they agreed to allow Leung and a few others to go on with the escape party as far as the provincial capital, Kukong, some 200 miles further inland. There, at the headquarters of the 7th War Zone, General Yu Hanmou could consider Chan Chak's recommendation that the former bandit be given an army rank and his group formally recognized as official Kuomintang guerrillas.

They had a late and leisurely breakfast of duck eggs, ham and rice in the hospital dining room—though some were already starting to tire of Chinese food. 'A good meal, I thought,' concluded Gandy, 'but inevitably one heard remarks like, "Don't they ever serve bread in China?"' The cooking was done by 'a dear old Chinese dame'— and far from insisting on having separate officers' eating arrangements, Goring, Oxford, Parsons and Ross helped to serve the food and wash up.

The entire group then reassembled outside and paraded across the compound to attend a civic reception at the mission church. On the crenellated tower above the doorway of the small, ex-German Protestant chapel were three Chinese characters reading 'Fuyintang', or Gospel Hall (literally, 'Happy Sounds Hall'). Inside, the tiny wooden pews to the right of the nave were neatly filled by Chinese—for whom they had been built—with the Europeans squeezing into those on the left. From the pulpit, the chief magistrate and another local dignitary gave welcoming speeches, unintelligible to most of them but still conveying a spirit of friendliness and comradeship. Chan Chak now rose to thank his British comrades for saving his life by bringing him away from the clutches of the Japanese. He went on, to the sound of rousing cheers, to call for a new onslaught by the ABCD allies against their common enemy. As a Chinese major prepared to follow this with another speech, it became clear that the British contingent would have to come up with a suitably powerful response of their own. Whether their leaders had sufficient theatrical flair, McEwan, for one, had his doubts:

> Up rose the Major and in a flow of impassioned oratory informed all and sundry that ABCD was the stuff, that Japan's days were numbered and that soon under the Generalissimo etc etc. The toast was replied to by Commander Montague who was jolly glad to be there, appreciated their hospitality and informed them they had been decent to us. The buck having again been passed to the Chinese they piled on more points by giving us an elaborate choral rendering of the first four letters of the alphabet—extolling each in turn with the responses being given by the Hoi Polloi in the rear. Having the game well in hand now they proceed to sweep us off the court by a series of well organised cheers which would have done credit to any American college. Service came back to us but we double faulted badly with feeble hurrahs for each letter in turn and lost the second set. The final game was played at speed and with fury, the Chinese

sweeping all before them with '*Che Lai*',* although we were saved from total collapse by Mike's prompting, in an unreachable falsetto, of "God Save the King". This made us 15–40 but our slight hopes were blasted with the presentation of huge baskets of fruit, cigarettes, towels, etc. Game, set and match for our Chinese allies.

According to Gandy, the British side of the church came in lustily in support of Montague at the first 'God Save', with musical accompaniment provided by naval ratings blowing through combs wrapped in toilet paper. He admitted that they managed only one verse, 'our memories not being up to oriental standard'. But the performance must have been satisfactory, his diary entry concludes, 'because our hosts seemed pleased and chattered cheerfully as they left the church'.

After the ceremonies were over, Montague told Gandy that a British military intelligence officer who happened to be in Waichow, a Colonel Chauvin, had made arrangements for the Chinese Army to take over the flotilla's rifles next day since the group were now under the jurisdiction of the Kuomintang Government. The two commanders agreed that 'for the honour of the gunnery branch of the Royal Navy' some part of the afternoon must therefore be devoted to rifle cleaning. They had earlier planned to give everyone time off (or 'shore leave' as they still called it) from 1 to 5 p.m., to give them all a chance to look round Waichow and do some shopping. But it soon became apparent that the prices were far too high for most of them to be able to afford anything—and in any case, Hong Kong dollars were no longer accepted here. 'No point giving more than an hour or two's leave,' Gandy decided, 'to roam moneyless about the town.'

Henry Hsu then arrived to tell Montague and Gandy that Chan Chak would like to see them at the house where he was staying in the centre of Waichow. The three of them walked up there together. They found the Admiral in cheerful mood, with plans to move the whole party up the East River by motor barge the following day. There was a telegram for Montague from Colonel Harry Owen-Hughes, the liaison officer who had left Hong Kong on the last plane to Chungking on the night of the invasion. The first reports of the escape had just been passed on to him by the Chinese military in Kukong, where

---

Che Lai: or *qilai*, meaning 'arise'—was the first line of the March of the Volunteers, a patriotic song written in 1934 to stir up resistance against the Japanese. It was adopted as China's national anthem by the Communists after they came to power in 1949.

he had been staying while trying to hasten the sending of General Yu's relief army. He was now proposing to meet the Hong Kong party off the boats at Longchuan, some 150 miles upriver from Waichow, before taking them on to Kukong by road. He was anxious in the meantime to know more details: 'How many are you. Do you require clothing. State names principal officers,' his message read. There were no telephones in Waichow (nor electric lights, for that matter) but Montague dictated a reply for Henry to take to the telegraph office, listing the names of senior officers and giving the total number of men in the British party as 62. He confirmed that warm clothing would be required by all and added: 'surgical aid required for one casualty—bullet in shoulder'.

The outside world knew from Japanese broadcasts that Hong Kong had fallen, but it still had no idea of the true details. Nor was anything known of what had become of the colony's defenders—for now, they were reported merely as 'missing'. The bare facts of the escape as they filtered through from Waichow were relayed by Owen-Hughes in Kukong to the British Embassy in Chungking and then on to London, though it would still be many days, weeks or in some cases even months before the families of those who had got away received word that their loved ones were safe.

It was now, however, that the first, dramatic reports about the escape began to appear in the world's press. These were based initially on the sketchy and garbled versions of events passed on by the Chinese Army before the party had even arrived in Waichow. In London, *The Times* of 30 December, quoting Chungking Radio, said a group of eighty-three people had escaped, of whom sixteen had died. There had been a 'running fight' in which three motor torpedo boats and several enemy vessels had been sunk. Chan Chak gave a more accurate account when he spoke to the local Chinese press on 31 December, making clear that just four of the original party were missing, including SK Yee. The Admiral also took the chance to send a report to the Central Government.

Meanwhile, Chan told Montague and Gandy that the British naval contingent deserved some spending money. He handed over enough to give each MTB officer a hundred Chinese dollars (about US$5), with some left over for what was described as a 'flotilla canteen fund'. While the British felt embarrassed by Chan's continued generosity, Gandy was at least able to reassure himself that the little admiral could afford it. Kendall had told him that Chan Chak had been 'virtually a guerrilla paymaster for years'.

Walking back through town, Gandy and Montague made some initial purchases of cigarettes and toothpaste. The main shopping thoroughfare, Shui Dong Jie ('East of the Water Street') was lined with grey-brick, tiled-roofed buildings housing open-fronted stores, both wholesale and retail, selling food, hardware, furniture, clothes and stationery. But peering into the dark interiors of the shops, the two British naval commanders and their colleagues soon discovered there was precious little to choose from. All imported goods came from Hong Kong and now even that source of supply had gone. According to Ashby, the 'fantastic' prices being asked for what few items were available precluded much buying. 'Pirate' brand cigarettes were selling at $1.40 for ten, Lifebuoy soap at $1.70 per tablet and sweatshirts at $32 each.

One man more in need of supplies than most was David Legge. On the last leg of their journey the previous day, when the bicycle-taxis had been engaged, the unfortunate first lieutenant from *MTB 11* had lost everything he owned except what he stood up in: a tattered uniform and a pair of half-wellington boots. As he told his brother Brian shortly afterwards, he had rashly accepted an offer to carry his bag—a gas-mask container in which he had packed whatever valuables he had managed to rescue from his boat: 'My camera, about 300 postcard enlargements (the result of a year's work in Hong Kong), my fountain pen, diary, passport, the photos of all the family, and some spare socks and cigarettes and matches. I never saw them again nor could I trace them at all. Of course I was a fool to trust such things to coolies, but if the truth be known I was past caring what happened to me that morning provided I got to somewhere where I could rest up for a day or so.'

Ted Ross was rueing the loss of the HK$2,000 he had left on the *Cornflower*'s launch. He and MacDougall had now borrowed money from the Admiral, however, so they were able to buy a few things, including a razor each at $15 and blades at $3 a piece. Although there were no leather shoes or boots to be had, they managed to find some rubber tennis shoes, and Ross bought himself a cotton singlet for $26. But most of their time in Waichow was spent trying to do something about the bullet still in MacDougall's back. Since the Wai On Hospital had been partially evacuated, it was unable to offer treatment for such serious injuries. But they were directed downtown to a Chinese doctor's consulting room. Ross later described how the doctor laid MacDougall out on a table, face down, and with no anaesthetic 'took out a great long thing that looked like an ice-pick and started poking it into Mac's wound. Finally I had to grab his arm and stop him. He nearly killed him. He didn't even know where the bullet was.' The instrument made such a mess, said Ross, that the wound soon began to fester.

Years afterwards, MacDougall attributed his survival to a curious chance, stemming from when he went out shopping—apparently later that same day—with his old friend Max Oxford. He had to take care in the crowded early evening streets for fear of being jostled, and they were taking refuge inside a junk shop when Oxford spotted a bottle of the antibacterial drug, sulphanilamide. It had presumably found its way there along the same smuggling route from Hong Kong that the escape party had just taken. 'It was very new at the time and was regarded as a wonder drug,' MacDougall recalled. 'We poured that in and when we finally got to Chengdu the thing was clean as a whistle.'

Kennedy and Brewer were being shown round town by two Chinese Army girls, and ended up taking them both to tea. Many of the British men only knew by hearsay of the women's branch even of their own navy—the Wrens. This was certainly their first sight of the Chinese military's new corps of females, whose job it was to write letters for the troops, do propaganda work among the villages . . . and now to act as tourist guides to visiting foreign sailors. Apart from saying how helpful they were, Kennedy gives us few details about the girls: 'One could speak a little English and was called Chuck Fung Ying, or Edna Chuck,' he wrote. 'But with her companion we could get no further than Miss Wong!' On the back cover of his brand new black pocket diary, however, he persuaded Miss Wong to write her full name—Huang Yu, or 'Yellow Jewel'—in Chinese characters.

Kennedy was conscious that there was still a long way to go before he would have any chance of seeing or even hearing from Rachel again—assuming, that is, she had survived her own journey on the *Ulysses*. Though he was not to know it at the time, the next 3,000 miles of the naval party's trip across China to Rangoon, and their subsequent voyage home after a further confrontation with the enemy, would end up taking another five months to complete. But that was all far ahead. For the moment, he and his fellow sailors were just happy to be in Free China, with their 70-mile walk behind them. For now, interest centred on the immediate future . . . and the welcome prospect on the following day, the last of 1941, of returning to the water.

Part Five
The Way Home

24
River Boats

31 December . . .

Next day, the early morning sounds of soldiers' bugles and peddlers' street cries were once again interrupted by the thudding gongs of the air raid alarm, as the Japanese bomber returned for another look at the mission. The airbase was so close that there was never time for adequate warning. But if the pilots saw people scattering they were apparently satisfied, and no bombs were dropped. Even so, the Admiral was anxious to save the people of Waichow from reprisals, and it was clear that today's planned departure was not before time.

Colonel Hector Chauvin, the man supervising the handing over of rifles, was a staff intelligence officer who had worked with Boxer in Hong Kong and with Kendall in China. He was now part of the British Military mission based at the embassy in Chungking. He had lived for some years in Canton, where he had driven a Rolls Royce and become something of a local celebrity. Variously described as a charming snob and an overweight charlatan, Chauvin made no secret of his preference for the company of Chinese to Europeans and of males to females. He spoke fluent Cantonese with a distinctive local accent picked up from his Chinese manservant. He was currently travelling with a Count Bentinck, a member of the Coldstream Guards and formerly of the Imperial Camel Corps, whose retinue of eighteen servants—including a batman to lay out his manicure set—was reminiscent of the Arabian Nights.

Perhaps not surprisingly, Chauvin had a slight falling-out with the strait-laced commander of the 2nd MTB Flotilla. Gandy was already less than impressed at the amount of effort the colonel had put into welcoming his fellow countrymen to Waichow—and was by no means convinced he was really a colonel at all.* After taking over the

---

really a colonel at all: Gandy's doubts may have been justified. Chauvin was no more than a captain when he left Hong Kong on 19 November 1941—the higher rank was doubtless intended to give him more influence with the Chinese. He was soon to revert to captain (and even be labelled 'unsuitable for future employment') after incurring the wrath of British embassy officials in Chungking in early 1942. But he went on to do wartime work in India and later became an official in the Hong Kong Labour Department.

sailors' newly gleaming rifles on behalf of the Chinese Army, Chauvin demanded that they surrender their pistols too. This was 'for some purpose of his own', according to Gandy, who refused to comply. Describing this attitude as 'unnecessary', Chauvin remarked that some people 'didn't know there was a war on'. V2 recorded crossly in his diary that he had missed an opportunity—he should have replied that 'it didn't take the army to tell the navy there was a war on'. In the end, Gandy collected as many of the flotilla's pistols as he could from staff officers and others who had been carrying them and handed them for safekeeping to Chan Chak. The Admiral asked if he could have one for himself, and Montague gave him his.

One section of the escape party not continuing beyond Waichow was the SOE contingent, whose three members were to stay behind in South China. Kendall was mulling over a plan to stage undercover raids into Hong Kong and bring out more groups along the same escape corridor, using his connections with both the communist guerrillas and groups such as Leung Wingyuen's. He had already agreed with Leung to have his own wife, Betty, smuggled out of Hong Kong and brought to Waichow for the 'usual fee' of HK$2,000.

To seal their relationship as fellow guerrilla leaders, Kendall and Leung spent part of the morning taking part in a triad-style blood ritual. According to secret society tradition, they should have sworn thirty-six oaths in front of an altar while the blood of a freshly killed cockerel dripped into a bowl of wine. But this particular ceremony—witnessed by Kendall's colleague, McEwan—was rather more clinical: 'Instead of the story book atmosphere of cutting open the arm and mixing the blood by use of a cock's feather by the light of a glittering candle, here we had a qualified practitioner scraping the arms with a scalpel after disinfecting the skin—a slight graze—the two arms pressed together—application of iodine and here the ceremony was completed and over . . . unless, as Mike suggested later, some syphilitic blood had been transferred to him.'

New bonds of various kinds had been formed by all of them. During the exciting days that were just over, they had not only broken out through the various encirclements of the enemy blockade, but had also crossed other, less tangible lines. After a hundred years of suspicion and war, British and Chinese were finally operating together as equals in a single entity, fighting side by side against a common enemy.

One of the great novels of Chinese literature, *Shuihu Juan*, or *Water Margin*, tells of the exploits of a group of Song Dynasty outlaws known as the 108 *lo-hon*, or heroes. When Chan Chak and Henry

Hsu saw the first copy of the Waichow group photograph, the Admiral said, 'I see 108 *Lo-Hon*.' His ADC agreed that the number of men in their party seemed to have grown wondrously from the original sixty-eight. Having started out as hard-drinking rogues and rebels, the heroes of the fourteenth-century novel ended up fighting for the emperor (just as Robin Hood and his Merry Men loyally supported King Richard the Lionheart). In a sense, Chan was now following in the same tradition by taking the former bandit and gangster, Leung Wingyuen, on to the provincial capital and making him an officially recognized Chinese army guerrilla. Rebelling and changing sides are both considered perfectly excusable in Chinese chivalric code, as long as they are done for honourable motives.

After high tea at 3.30 p.m., they gathered their gear and headed down to the river. The boats were waiting at a floating pontoon five minutes' walk away, near the St Joseph's Catholic Mission. This was set in the former Italian legation, a fine building with long verandahs facing a church across a courtyard. Some of the men had already been made welcome there by the smiling, brown-robed Father Ma— all big ears and spectacles—and by the little Chinese nuns in their headdresses and long white habits. The three SOE men who were now seeing off the rest of the party would soon be renting one of the buildings in the compound from Father Ma and turning it into the first Advance HQ of Lindsay Ride's newly-formed escape and intelligence organization, the British Army Aid Group.

The five-day journey to Longchuan was to be made in four flat-bottomed river barges or 'long boats', the native craft of the East River. They were each of similar basic build, about 15 feet across and 70 in length. Two of them were essentially large, unmotorized sampans intended for carrying rice, their only covering an open-ended, semi-circular canopy made of rattan and bamboo. Each of these was towed by a propeller-driven barge with an antiquated engine and a flimsy deckhouse amidships, barely high enough to stand up in. Chan Chak's group, Montague and the military staff went in the first of these motorized boats, towing the officers and crew of MTBs 07 and 09 in one of the sampans. The men from *MTB10* and *C410* went in the other motor boat, towing the men of *11* and *27*. A group of about twenty Chinese soldiers and guerrillas accompanied the Admiral in his boat as guards. In unoccupied or semi-occupied parts of the country such as this one, there was often still a danger of Japanese raiding parties. There were also pirates on the river, they were told, and robbers lurking in the villages where they would be stopping along the way.

They set off at 6.15 p.m., leaving Mike, Mac and John standing on the riverbank in the twilight. 'A grander trio of reliable crooks I never expect to meet,' was how Bill Robinson summed up the general sense of regret at losing them. The SOE men were about to head downtown in search of a friendly bar in which to bring in the New Year (they ended up doing so three times, owing to a mix-up over Chungking, Waichow and Hong Kong time zones, which led to the weaving of a very erratic homeward path and to McEwan almost shooting Kendall in the foot).

Other Scots such as Kennedy and MacDougall soon found themselves celebrating Hogmanay lying in sardine-like rows on the decks of dark and draughty riverboats. The engines broke down or blew up repeatedly, and first one boat then the other had to tie up to the bank.

All in all, declared Kennedy in his new diary, it was 'b. cold' and a 'v. unpleasant night'. Screens of straw matting rigged up in the bows of the sampans did nothing to prevent the wind from sweeping along the bare boards on which they lay, envious of those in the motor boats who at least derived warmth from the engines. Ashby—again part of the same group, the one which had been at the back with Mac on the march—pointed out that while the motor boats were enclosed and comfortable, the sampans were 'open fore and aft' and lacked 'appointments'. It was almost as cold as the night in the orchard, he decided. David Legge, in the other unmotorized boat, was one of the lucky few who had a blanket as well as a raincoat. Even so, he wrote later, 'the wind whistled through that junk like nobody's business . . . when morning came it was a great effort to try and eat the bowl of rice and dish of cabbage with chopsticks, our fingers were nearly numb.'

They were going northeast, against the current, at a speed of less than two miles per hour. For most of the time the only sound was the steady chug of the motor boats' engines, which had been taken from old Ford V8 cars and converted to using charcoal gas. The *lowdah*, or captain, signalled to the engineer in the stern by pulling one of two strings. These either rang a bell, to stop, or agitated a bunch of rushes, to go on again; the number of swishing, rustling noises indicated the power required. When the supply of gas faltered, a small boy known as a *cheesai* fed the primitive boiler with a basket of charcoal.

Since the East River was shallow in winter, with shifting sandbanks, navigation was difficult and the boats frequently ran aground. When this happened, other members of the crew, dressed in ragged black fishermen's pyjama suits, sprang into action, armed with long bamboo poles. For a while there would be much shouting, running, pushing and heaving until they were clear again. To those who wondered if they might not be better off using some other form of transport, it was pointed out that owing to the destruction of railways, roads and bridges in the wide area between occupied and unoccupied Guangdong, rivers formed the only existing through routes to the interior.

Even so, the river—at this point some 100 yards wide—was largely empty save for the odd rusty mine, hulk of a crippled steamer or some other relic of war. What other traffic there was consisted mainly of flimsy sampans, bobbing gently downstream. Occasionally there was a large junk, either gliding moth-like under dark parchment sails or hauled from the towpath by lines of coolies, wearing little but their broad shoulder-bands and intoning a slow, rhythmic song as they strained against the current.

Collingwood mentions passing a 'pretty gorge', but for the most part, the banks were lined with giant pampas grass and bamboo and all they could see over the top was a long thin scroll of mountains unfolding in the distance. China was beautiful and endlessly fascinating, but they were beginning to realize just how wretched it was too. Now and then a village drifted by, screens of mangrove falling away to reveal picturesque scenes which turned out to consist of decaying houses and filthy streets full of squealing pigs, screaming children with holes cut in the rear of their trousers and shabby figures bent double beneath shoulder-poles, carrying buckets of night soil off to the fields.

The river served as bathroom and rubbish tip for all—including those on the boats, where the latrines consisted of two planks over the water. For many of the British sailors, this was no great hardship. At his small terraced house in Hucknall, Nottinghamshire, Les Barker shared an outside toilet with half the street. 'They'd all look out of the windows to see who was going, so they could know when was a good time to get in and have their go,' he would later tell his grandson, Russell.

There was more time now for writing diaries, and from Barker's entry for New Year's Day we learn that he was sharing a junk with fifteen others, with just enough room to sleep on straw: 'The scenery is very good on both sides. Stopped because Japanese aircraft were sighted and proved hostile, but passed out of sight and so we took this opportunity to stretch our legs for half an hour. We embarked again, and this was after a farmer chased us away for stealing his sugar cane. This was very refreshing. We have one petty officer on the boat which is towing us who is ill with dysentery, hope he soon recovers as we have no official doctor on board.'

According to V2's diary, Prest's dysentery had improved after the cold night and 'Old Pethick' was also perking up. 'Our boat passed the admiral's in the night,' adds Gandy, competitive as ever. Chan Chak was developing stomach problems of his own and his wrist wound was becoming inflamed. He spent most of the time trying to sleep, but the single large room on his boat was 'much overcrowded', according to Max Oxford, with Chinese troops and guerrillas at one end, the Admiral's group in the middle and the British officers at the other. Chan had told everyone to stay under cover at all times to avoid being seen by the Japanese planes.

The only person who seems to have taken this warning seriously was Freddie Guest. He was horrified to see that items of white washing had been hung up on one of the other boats and yelled at the navy to 'take the damned stuff down'. At another point the river went alongside a road on which Guest says he saw many Japanese patrols: he told the others they should make sure not even to look out of a window. In his autobiography, Guest recalls that both sides of the East River were occupied by Japanese soldiers in great numbers, making it a thoroughly nerve-wracking five-day journey: 'To think that fifty to sixty British Naval officers and men and our own party of three Army officers, together with our beloved one-legged admiral and his escort of armed guerrillas, were for the best part of a week right in their midst without their knowing it was almost unbelievable.'

But apart from the odd air patrol, no one else even mentioned the Japanese in their various accounts of the endless-seeming river trip. The talk on Gandy's boat was more of Chinese bandits. The ship's master, who had already been paid an advance by Chan Chak, began demanding an extra $300 for food and protection against robbery.

Gandy's first stalling tactic was to say the Admiral would sort matters out when he caught up with them. By next day this still hadn't happened, the other boat's engine being in such a bad state that they had had to send back to Waichow for another motor boat. The *lowdah* (literally, 'old and great') was meanwhile insisting he could go no further without payment. Gandy went ashore and reported the matter to a local police officer. The boat's skipper finally relented after being assured that a senior British army officer was waiting to meet them at Longchuan, presumably well supplied with funds.

Any bandits who did happen to stage an ambush would doubtless have got a shock to find that the boats contained dozens of well-armed soldiers, guerrillas and British sailors instead of the expected cargo of rice. The reasons why banditry was flourishing—and rice becoming even more precious than usual in China—were many. Hard times were the result not just of war and ever-worsening Kuomintang corruption and mismanagement, but also of drought. Successive years of bad harvests were to culminate in a great famine in Guangdong Province in 1943–44 in which an estimated 1.5 million people would perish.

While this was hardly something the men from Hong Kong could have known about, it does help put into perspective their preoccupation over food. Apart from a supply of buns and oranges brought on board with them, their daily ration was two small bowls of rice, cooked by the crew on a small charcoal stove out on deck. The river-boat journey was the only time when getting enough to eat was difficult, Kennedy recalls in his book, *Full Circle*. But that was a small price to pay for having escaped imprisonment, he points out.

Guest had all along believed food was their main problem. He describes how he and the guerrillas on his boat ended up drawing pistols on each other in a dispute over a plate of rice and a tin of bully beef. Relations improved after he went ashore and killed some chickens he found on a farm, bringing them back to be shared by everyone on his boat, including the guerrillas.

Apart from stealing sugar cane, the sailors were making ends meet by using the Admiral's funds to buy sweet potatoes, oranges and toffee during stops at small towns along the way. They all went ashore for lunch on 2 January at Guanyinge, a 'small dirty village' where Ross bought green bananas and eggs. Kennedy and a group of others went to a chow shop with Henry, watching a Japanese plane pass over as they tucked into their noodles.

The engines had finally given up the struggle of hauling the sampans, so these were cast off and their occupants squeezed into the motor boats. Ashby and Kennedy's group found this both warmer and pleasanter, though Goring grumbled that there was 'very little room left to lie down'. Even those who managed to sleep did not do so for long. The captains of both 07 and 09 complained that when V2's boat came alongside theirs at 3.30 a.m. on 3 January, Gandy woke everyone up with his shouting. He then carried on upriver, leaving them in peace.

The flotilla commander had earlier caused a different kind of disruption when he went ashore and joined a crowd that had gathered round a street entertainer: 'I got considerable amusement watching a pea and thimble juggler trying to entice his audience to try their luck,'

Gandy wrote in his diary, 'until I realized I must move on because his non-success was due to me the foreign devil as the centre of attraction.'

While many of the locals just stared, others were actively keen to make friends. In Heyuan, Kennedy went ashore with Montague, Yorath and others for a breakfast of soup, noodles and duck eggs. They were embarrassed to be told at the end of the meal that it was all on the house. The proprietor, a Mr Deng Yingyuan, would not listen to their protests, asking only that they exchange autographs and visiting cards.

Although some of the travellers were growing impatient with their slow progress, many were starting to overcome the European urge to press on, and were gradually acquiring a more fatalistic, Eastern approach. Barker's diary entry for 3 January makes it clear that spirits among the sailors were high—being back on the water for a few days had doubtless helped:

> Under way again at 5 a.m. and left the admiral's boat behind again. Lovely weather today now that the sun is up. It's 12 noon now and we've been aground eight times this morning on the sand. This river is very shallow and sandy and we have to steer a very erratic course. You can tell how fast we are going as there is a coolie woman on the bank who has been keeping up with us all morning and is now passing us. All the boys are cheerful and are lying about this small space which we have in the bows, smoking and talking about home and the Burma road. (The thing that I would like most now is a nice T-bone steak with all the trimmings)! Have just been informed that the spuds are on again so must shake a leg and get my share.

A 20-pound 'barbel-like fish' purchased from a passing fisherman near Yi He provided those on Gandy's boat with a satisfying meal to round off what proved to be their last day on the river. The new boat had by now arrived from Waichow, so they were able to spread themselves more comfortably between three craft, all with motors. They proceeded upriver in convoy through the night, headed by the Admiral. On a promontory high above the right-hand bank stood a tall, resplendent pagoda, with upturned gables like the rim of a mandarin's hat.

25

'Bow, You Buggers, Bow'

4 January 1942 . . .

Next morning, the passengers had to make their own way on foot along the riverbank, while their lightened boats were poled and even bodily lifted over the biggest sandbanks yet. By 1 p.m., the men from MTBs *07, 09, 11* and *27* were at least an hour ahead of everyone else, since their boat had found the best route through the shallows. As the leading group walked round the final bend in the river before Longchuan, they were hailed by a small party that had come out from the town to meet them.

Towering over the Chinese officials around him was the unmistakable figure of Lieutenant Colonel Harry Owen-Hughes. There was no sign of his famous white steed (in days to come he was often asked, 'Where the hell were you and your bloody white horse?'). Nor of the battle bowler and gas mask he had worn as he strode through the crowds at Kai Tak. 'What surprised us,' recalled Gandy, 'was to see him dressed in a Chinese merchant's silken gown and skull cap.'

Whatever he was wearing, the sight of the six-foot-three-inch British military liaison officer excitedly spreading his arms to greet his travel-weary compatriots like long-lost friends was a very welcome one. He became an instant source of badly needed funds, making them less dependent on Chinese hospitality. And he had already managed to procure them each a *meenlap*, or padded jacket—though these turned out to be on the small side for many, being standard Chinese Army issue. He had also been busy planning their onward travel: they were to set off next day in hired lorries for Kukong.

Owen-Hughes had driven down from Guangdong's wartime capital with two Chinese major generals, representing the provincial governor, General Li Hanhun, and the regional commander, General Yu Hanmou. They had got in the previous evening and begun making hasty arrangements to ensure that Longchuan laid on a suitably grand reception for the returning hero, Admiral Chan Chak, and his escape party.

The only problem was that the Admiral himself had not yet arrived, since his boat had got stuck on a sandbank. The men of the MTB flotilla thus found themselves receiving his welcome for him. Drawn up along the riverbank were massed ranks of boy scouts, girl guides and soldiers with coloured paper flags on bamboo sticks stuck down the barrels of their rifles. Ordinary citizens armed with firecrackers lined the surrounding streets. The boats had been expected since early that morning, so the assembled crowds had already been waiting in the blazing sun for some hours and were more than ready to let off steam, irrespective of whose arrival it was they were celebrating. The British sailors did their best to rise to the occasion, but it wasn't easy, as David Legge explained:

> We had to make a sort of triumphal march through the town. A more down at heel set of toughs you never saw before. The firecrackers were more of a trial than any of the bombardments in Hong Kong, especially when they kept landing down our necks, setting our bedding alight and generally deafening us . . . You would have thought that we had won the war, instead of being the fleeing remnant of a beaten army.

Luckily they did not have far to go. The naval ratings were being put up in a middle school near the centre of town where the headmaster, a Mr Chan Fong, had made 'excellent preparations' for them. The school was for children who had been evacuated from occupied Canton. The students had moved out of their dormitories and given up their bedding 'for our comfort', noted Barker appreciatively. The officers were assigned to two hotels. Goring described these as primitive, but according to Ashby, the one the MTB officers were in was very comfortable. Gandy merely noted its paper windows. After leaving their gear, they repaired to a large open space in the centre of town where a civic reception was to be held at 5 p.m.

Chan Chak's boat had by this time finally arrived. Owen-Hughes and the Chinese generals had gone downriver in the first of the motor boats to meet it. There was supposed to be a formal greeting ceremony at the jetty, with the British lining up with their Chinese counterparts to salute the Admiral as he came on shore, but again things didn't turn out quite as planned. Chan was bundled into a chair and was being borne off down the street before the first introduction had been made or the rest of his party had even alighted.

The town's entire population of some 3,000 people had by now gathered in the square, which also served as a sports ground. A wooden platform had been erected for the occasion, with life-size pictures of Chiang Kai-shek and Sun Yat-sen standing behind it. Commander Montague and the staff officers sat alongside Chinese dignitaries on the raised dais, while the MTB party sat on rows of rickety chairs facing them. The townspeople pressed in behind the sailors to get a closer look.

There were long speeches from the district magistrate (a Mr Tang), a local general (Cheung Kwong Chin) and Chan Chak, who told the story of the fall of Hong Kong and the escape and praised the new alliance. Commander Montague made a brief speech of thanks and Owen-Hughes delivered a message in Cantonese on behalf of the ambassador. This 'went down very well' but was 'perforce very short', he wrote later. It's not known if his words were any easier to follow than those of the Chinese interpreter, who evidently had problems with the English letter 'r'. According to both Collingwood and Kennedy, each time he referred to 'you heroes' it was pronounced as 'you heels'.

National anthems, first Chinese and then British, were sung enthusiastically and respects paid by all to the portraits of the two leaders of the Republic, past and present. Montague then turned to Chan Chak and told him the sailors wished to thank the local people for their kindness and hospitality. Would it be best to give three hearty cheers, he wondered? This might cause the locals to run away in alarm, said Chan. He suggested that the British mariners should instead make two or three low bows, with arms in their sleeves in Chinese fashion.

The senior naval officer turned 'a deep shade of pink', according to one of those sitting nearby, but marched over to his men and explained what was to happen. He stood them to attention and in his best parade-ground voice bellowed out: 'British Party will turn about and bow three times to their Chinese allies . . . Ships' Company about turn!' As they faced the townspeople, with eyes firmly to the front and chins held high, they received their next order. 'Prepare to bow to the populace of Longchuan . . . Ship's Company, bow!' There was a moment's pause, then, realizing more encouragement was needed, Commander Montague added in an undertone that could be heard by all:

'Come on! Bow you buggers, bow!'

And bow they did, to the delight of the crowd, who bowed back . . . and of the rest of the party, who struggled to suppress their laughter. Goring's verdict was that 'Never before, surely, in the long history of the Royal Navy has such an order been given, or so magnificently carried out!'

A ten-course banquet was arranged that evening to celebrate the escape. The men were to eat at the school and the officers separately in a hotel's VIP room with Chan Chak. But the Admiral would not hear of it and they all ended up dining together at the school. 'Where his troops ate there ate he,' commented Owen-Hughes approvingly. 'That is the sort of man he is, a splendid 5 foot 2 worth of guts.' The party was told later that the meal had been donated by the towns-people, who, knowing of the British fondness for beef, had obtained special dispensation to slaughter a bullock for the occasion.

After dinner and the distribution of the padded coats, Owen-Hughes had a long chat with Oxford and Macmillan about the war. They told him Hong Kong had been overwhelmed by numbers and by its incompatible roles as refuge and fortress. In Oxford's view, the fall was 'the inevitable result of badly conceived defence plans, lack of fighting spirit in the troops, no air support and a million civil population who if not against us were largely indifferent'.

Explaining his own role, Owen-Hughes said he had been cordially received in the Chinese capital by Chiang Kai-shek and other leaders, but after nine days of fruitless meetings had come south with ever-fainter hopes that any relief army would reach the colony in time. 'It did seem that Chungking's control over distant War Zones might not be complete,' he wrote in his official report. 'And was it not a fact that General Yu Hon Mow (Yu Hanmou) who commanded 7th War Zone was the man who gave up Canton when the Japanese attacked in 1938 with little indications of a fight?' He concluded that the Zone commanders were in a sense still warlords, with considerable independence. He had even struggled to get his own people in Chungking to take him seriously. 'The personnel at that time in the Embassy were attuned to the Foreign Office attitude towards Peking and Shanghai while the significance of Hong Kong, which turned to the Colonial Office in London, seemed to need serious emphasis.'

After reaching Kukong on 18 December, Owen-Hughes had been in daily contact with the senior Chinese officers based there at the regional military headquarters, but his requests for more action continued to meet 'excuses of one sort or another'. Some generals, he learned, wanted to recapture Canton before moving on to help the British. Coupled with the lack of communications—at no time was he able to speak to Hong Kong—the sheer size of the Chinese forces made progress difficult. 'A study of my diary makes it clear that our 7th War Zone was not going to move,' he wrote later. 'Together with Central Government troops our strength was 219,000. The Japanese had some 80,000 in Kwangtung (Guangdong) of whom 38,000 were employed in the attack on Hong Kong, while the colony was struggling with 12,500.'

None of the Hong Kong party was able to give Owen-Hughes news of his elderly parents, although his father—an air raid patrol officer—had been seen at his post at Hillcrest some days before the end, 'striding along as erect as ever'. During the long, unoccupied hours on the riverboats, there had been time to go over the events of the previous month more fully, and to speculate on the likely fate of the vast majority who had failed to get away. Most of the party had heard rumours of Japanese beatings, rapes and bayonettings of unarmed prisoners just before the surrender, which gave little grounds for optimism about what might happen later. There was also the odd firsthand report. William Wright, the young naval warrant officer who had swum from the *Cornflower's* launch, had seen clear evidence of atrocities carried out during and after the siege of the Repulse Bay Hotel. The guerrilla leader, Leung Wingyuen, had also told them of an incident witnessed by villagers in the New Territories in which captured British soldiers had been tied to trees, stripped to the waist and 'carved up with knives'.

At 6 a.m. on Monday, 5 January, the five Dodge trucks hired for the journey to Kukong picked up their passengers outside the Canton Middle School and rumbled out of Longchuan. They crossed the town's bomb-damaged bridge over the East River and headed northwest past stubbly, red-earthed paddy fields towards the mountains. A private car led the way, containing the Admiral, his staff and MacDougall. Two of the naval party were sick and were left behind to catch up later: Cox-Walker, in hospital with possible pneumonia, and Pethick, whose latest affliction was piles. 'The latter is well over 60 and marched with the best of them,' noted Owen-Hughes admiringly.

The others sat as best they could on wooden benches fitted in the back of the trucks, which were semi-closed, with narrow slits along the top of each side for windows. The road was unsurfaced and full of potholes. Each bump raised a cloud of dust from the straw on the floor. Soon they began to climb steeply into the hills, the continual hairpin bends throwing everyone against each other until their combined weight became more than the corner victim could bear and they all had to shift back again. This at least helped to warm them up, for even in their new padded jackets the air felt chilly. The mountains they had to cross were the highest in Guangdong. The road wound its way up through groves of fresh-smelling pine trees to an eventual height of 5,000 feet.

Sitting up at the front of his truck with the driver, Kennedy had the benefit of seeing the scenery but the disadvantage of seeing the operational side of things too. 'Our Chinese hosts had warned us cheerfully the night before that enemy planes often machine-gunned the road at its higher stretches', he wrote later, 'but we were much more concerned about the wire and string that held the truck together, and the completely nonchalant way in which the Chinese driver took the sharpest bends and steepest inclines without change of speed or alteration of technique.'

Apart from ox and horse carts, trucks and buses were almost the only vehicles in use in wartime China. The severe shortage of petrol meant most of them were converted to run on charcoal or at best used a mixture of petrol and alcohol. Other fuels pressed into service were camphor oil, rice wine and buffalo buttermilk. Drivers often economized by switching off the engine when going downhill, oblivious to oncoming bends and traffic and the sheer drop on one side. A road journey, particularly in the mountains, was a dangerous experience—as members of the escape party would later learn to their cost.

The first of several minor breakdowns came when the truck carrying the non-naval contingent broke two front springs after crossing the first range (few of its occupants were aware till then that it had any springs to break). It caught up with the others at 11.30 a.m. at Chenxin, where they stopped at a restaurant for a good Chinese meal. Afterwards they were treated to some 'excellent' coffee, tea and biscuits by an American Roman Catholic missionary, Father William M O'Brien. The forty-year-old Maryknoll priest had been working in the area for the past twelve years under Bishop Francis Xavier Ford, who was later to suffer at the hands of the communists and be hailed by the church as a martyr.* O'Brien—like Ford, the sort of missionary who was interested in more than just saving souls—briefed his visitors on the local political, economic and military situation, while at the same time plying them with American cigarettes. 'As these came out of his meagre year's supply, and there was no prospect of his receiving any more for an indefinite period, this was hospitality indeed,' reflected Goring. He also gave them some detective and Wild West magazines, which were appreciated almost as much as the coffee and tobacco.

---

as a martyr: The Bishop was placed under house arrest in December 1950 and later publicly beaten and degraded. He died in prison in Canton in 1952.

They moved on at half past one, crossing a second range of mountains known as the Nine Peaks. Each of them was of the conical limestone or 'sugar loaf' variety, completely sheer with quaint trees in the most unlikely places. They would find plenty more when they got to Guilin, but most had only ever seen such fantastically shaped mountains painted on Chinese scrolls and had never believed they could be based on reality.

By 3 p.m. they had reached Lianping, a 'pleasant little town' which had grown out of an old walled village. Here they broke their journey for the night. There was another civic welcome, with a large meal provided by the local bank, but to their relief no speeches. They were put up at two Chinese inns, rated as very comfortable by Barker and Collingwood, 'tolerable' by Gandy and 'simple' by Goring—who did, however, enjoy the local rose petal wine.

They were on the road again at 4 a.m. next morning. The headlights soon failed on one truck, but the driver continued to wind his way through mountain gorges in the dark. Shortly after sunrise, they overtook more of the Chinese troops originally bound for Hong Kong. They were moving from the southern part of the province towards Kukong 'in two long lines that stretched on either side of the road for miles'. Ashby estimated the total number of soldiers and camp followers at 10,000. Although not first-line troops, they were well equipped with Brens and trench mortars, he noted. MacDougall thought they 'looked as if they meant business'.

They stopped at the village of Longxian for breakfast and were told they had missed hostile aircraft by an hour. The road presently descended into a fertile plain, where water lilies grew in ponds along the roadside. Kennedy's truck had already fallen behind the others after bursting a tyre; it now ran out of petrol and had to wait until a few gallons could be purchased from a passing lorry. As a result, he and his fellow passengers missed a visit to the imposing temple and monastery at Nanhua, some 20 miles outside Kukong.

The others had been making better progress than expected, and had halted at the temple so as to reach their destination at the prearranged time of 3 p.m. With aching buttocks and beards thick with straw dust, the men clambered out of their lorries and wandered in a daze through a carved wooden gateway guarded by two huge gilded Buddhas. They skirted the Pond for Released Fishes, drummed their fingers on an enormous bronze bell and entered the Hall of Heavenly Kings, where row upon row of coloured porcelain figures gazed down at them. Some looked fierce, others smug. A series of five terraces led on up the slopes of the Bao Lin mountain, each level containing a cluster of buildings whose yellow and vermilion eaves and green-tiled roofs merged into a sea of maple trees and Chinese cypresses.

The Nanhua Temple was founded after a Buddhist master from India stopped there in the year 502. Ashby noted in his log that this was the oldest and most famous temple in South China and contained three mummies, 'one some 1,200 years old, of Loktsu, the sixth reincarnation of Buddha, the other two being lesser fry of only 400 years' vintage—all very well preserved.' The three figures sat in glass cases wearing faded robes, their mahogany-coloured features disfigured by innumerable layers of varnish applied over the years.

On what had turned into a beautiful, sunny afternoon, saffron-robed, shaven-headed monks padded silently between the wooden-beamed meditation halls and pavilions, clutching their prayer beads. Others tended the surrounding orchards or were busy renovating the pagoda and other buildings under the energetic direction of their ninety-three-year-old abbot. The provincial governor, Li Hanhun, was personally sponsoring the work, which had been going on since 1933.

Harry Owen-Hughes described the two-hour stopover as remarkable. 'I do not imagine any in that party will forget the peace and restfulness in that ancient Buddhist monastery,' he wrote. Afterwards, he and Montague joined the Admiral in his car for the final stage of the journey, past fields of rice and sugar cane and flocks of black goats, to the dusty outskirts of Kukong.

26
Kukong Comforts

6 January . . .

The lorries halted near the customs gate on the edge of the city. A large crowd had gathered there and banners prepared by the army's political department had been hung across the road. 'Hearty welcome to General Chen Chak and the Hong Kong defenders,' read one in English. 'Welcome to heroic, outstanding Chan Chak,' said another in Chinese.

No sooner had he been helped from his car than Chan was besieged by a throng of admirers, who surged forward to give him his most rapturous reception yet. A large bouquet of flowers was thrust towards him as excited townspeople pressed in behind beaming military officers and government officials. There were press photographers too, making this the best documented episode in the entire journey. The story of the escape was already attracting huge interest, and the one-legged admiral—still dressed in the somewhat lopsided cap and uniform of a British lieutenant commander—was rapidly turning from local hero to national and international celebrity.

The rest of the party was by no means ignored. Montague found himself clutching a second bunch of flowers as he was warmly greeted by Mrs Muriel Jones, wife of a member of the local Methodist mission, Constance Green, matron at the mission hospital, and other representatives of the local foreign community. As another fusillade of firecrackers went off, MacDougall—still in his naval duffel coat—dealt in his quietly competent way with a spate of questions from an eager Chinese reporter in a trilby. And from all sides, girl guides ran up to pin on each man's lapel a favour in the form of a small red and yellow rosette, the ribbon printed with the characters *zhong yong sha di*, meaning 'loyal and bold in slaughtering the foe'. According to Goring, the rosettes given out by this 'choir of maidens' must have given them freedom of the city, for in subsequent days 'even the smallest shop at the sight of this talisman would give us what we'd chosen to buy as a present'.

The British sailors grinned at all the fuss as they emerged from the trucks in their grey padded jackets, naval caps, tin hats and assorted scraps of uniform, lighting up cigarettes (or in Thums's case, his pipe) and posing obligingly for photos. Hide and Rutter slung comradely arms around the shoulders of Leung Wingyuen, whose semi-military clothing and Sam Browne belt reflected his soon-to-be-official guerrilla status. Collingwood took the chance to give Bruce some badly needed exercise on the end of an improvised lead.

Gandy, deciding that a more formal display of Royal Navy vigour was called for, ordered another parade. The men duly formed up into three ragged columns under the White Ensign and performed a token march for a few hundred yards up the road between the lines of Chinese spectators. They then ambled back to the lorries, earning themselves another black mark in their commander's notebook. But Gandy soon turned his attention to an American called Lockwood—head of the local YMCA—who was busy telling him about Kukong. It had 'good public parks, commercial banks and excellent communications,' he learned. It was on the main Canton-Hankow railway line, but was now the most southerly station, the Chinese having raided the metal tracks between Kukong and Canton for use elsewhere.

Although commonly known as Kukong ('Bend in the River'), the city was officially called Shaoguan.* It had expanded rapidly since replacing Canton as provincial capital the previous year. By early 1942, more than half the population were in uniform—either the greenish-yellow of the military or the dark blue of the civilian government.

The Japanese had been bombing Kukong heavily since the start of the war. The area around the railway station which the lorries now drove through as they set off again past more lines of welcoming streamers and marching troops had caught fire in an attack by thirteen planes just a week before. Three months earlier, a single raid had killed as many as a hundred people, many of them women and children sheltering in a temple.

The heart of the city lay on a peninsula between two tributaries, the Wu and the Zhen, which joined here to form the Bei Jiang, or North River. This in turn flowed on down to Canton, where it became the Pearl River. The southern end of the peninsula jutted out into the main stream like the prow of a mighty ship. To reach it, they drove over an attractive stone bridge which had somehow survived the bombing and was lined with shops and stalls, reminding them

---

Shaoguan: The name Kukong was dropped after the war, and today Shaoguan is the city's standard name.

of pictures of the old London Bridge. After passing through the city centre, they drove up the east bank of the Wu River for a mile until at 4 p.m. they reached a quiet riverside spot called Wuliting, where several houseboats were moored.

A large blue and white boat called the Hoi Kok ('Sea Palace') had been hired by Owen-Hughes to serve as the party's accommodation during its stay in Kukong. It normally operated as a 'flower boat'—a floating brothel—but for now, at least, it had been emptied of its flowers. It proved tolerably clean and comfortable, despite the nocturnal activities of rats and the cold wind that whistled through the large cracks in the wood. Much of the space inside was divided into small 'entertainment' cubicles. These were shared by the officers, two to a cabin (Guest and Oxford twinned up in one, Gandy and Yorath in another). The ratings made do with floor space on the upper deck, the petty officers got the verandah and the merchant service had a dormitory in a sampan moored alongside. A sleeping mat and two *meentoi* quilts, or padded cotton covers, had been provided from army stores for each man, and these became their portable bedding from now on. The houseboat also had lots of 'rather primitive' mattresses lying about but little by way of other furnishings except for 'one or two English pictures' hanging in several rooms. There were separate mess rooms for officers and men and a basic kitchen service that the naval party helped keep going for the rest of their ten-day stay.

They were still settling in when cars arrived to take the officers to a 5.30 p.m. dinner engagement in the city centre. The venue was Bun's Place (*Bun Lo*), an exclusive dining and drinking establishment in a colonnaded two-storey building that formed part of the Provincial Government Headquarters. Balconies overlooked Minsheng Street at the front and the Zhen River at the rear. War Area Command was close at hand, making this a regular after-hours meeting place for top military men and civilian officials—including the two men hosting tonight's dinner, Yu Hanmou and Li Hanhun.

General Yu and Governor Li—the two most powerful figures in South China—were often at loggerheads. But for now they were united in having had their respective stars eclipsed by that of Chan Chak, who was the man of the moment in the eyes of both Chungking and the general public. By staging a lavish welcome for the Admiral, they may have been hoping some of his glory would rub off on themselves.

General Yu was in any case fond of banquets—the more celebratory, the better. He had arranged one to welcome Ernest Hemingway the previous year, at which the two men had engaged in a drinking contest: the famously hardheaded writer found that even he had almost met his match. For this latest dinner, according to Gandy, the general was wearing a black patch over one eye. Kennedy merely describes him as looking fat and prosperous—surprisingly so, he says, for a man who was supposed to have fallen out of favour over the loss of Canton.

In contrast to the bull-necked and pleasure loving general, Governor Li was a small, serious man—a passionate idealist, prone to giving long speeches. At dinner, Kennedy sat next to his private secretary, who turned out to be a fellow graduate of Cambridge and acted as his interpreter during speeches by the governor, the general and the Admiral. The visitors had a useful interpreter of their own in the Mandarin-speaking Legge, who later expressed wonder at the high circles they were moving in. Of the thirty Chinese officers present, he could find only one below the rank of general. Most had trained with European armies—several in Germany—though they had little experience of actual battle and tended to owe their positions more to political connections than military capabilities. They gleamed and bristled with medals, canes, leather straps and silk scarves.

While doing their best not to let the disparity in rank overawe them, the British officers were a scruffy-looking bunch in comparison (and beards were in any case poorly regarded by the Chinese Army). They also committed at least one cultural faux pas. A long series of dishes ended with the customary plate of fried rice, which one is supposed to toy with and set aside, to show one's host that what has gone before has been plenty. In this case, the guests were guided less by etiquette than by their ravenous appetites, and within minutes the *chow fan* had completely disappeared.

By 9 p.m. they were back at the Sea Palace and tucked up in bed, listening to the sound of the water lapping at the hull. Owen-Hughes took MacDougall back to the Methodist mission, to share the room where he had been staying for the past two weeks in the home of the medical superintendant, Dr Moore. It was the first time Mac had had the luxury of a proper bath or even taken his clothes off since the twelfth of December. Chan Chak wanted to join the rest of the men on the houseboat but was told it was too crowded; so for the next couple of nights he slept elsewhere, till he too moved to the mission to have his wound treated by Dr Moore.

Next day, the men mustered at 2 p.m. and marched across town for a grand reception. This provided the best chance yet to appreciate the love of mass meetings which was as much part of Chiang Kai-shek's China as it would later be part of Mao Zedong's.* Rousing music from a band and cheers from a packed audience greeted the entry of the Hong Kong party into a large hall, the *Wu Lai She*, bedecked with banners and placards. These declared dramatically: 'Welcome glorious warriors', 'Smash the Axis alliance—restore world peace', 'Democracies Unite, wipe out aggression' and 'Hail to ABCD Powers! All Hail!' Yu Hanmou presided over the enthusiastic shouting of slogans and singing of anthems. A shield was presented to Chan and there were more flowers for him and Montague. Both gave speeches, as did General Yu and Governor Li.

The governor's speech was so interminable that one of the British 'matelots', according to Owen-Hughes, leant across to the man from the mission sitting next to him and said: 'He spouts like a ruddy Priest, don't he!' The Reverend Peredur Jones readily agreed. The troops by all accounts enjoyed the tea provided afterwards, complete with large quantities of rice cakes, buns, dough balls and peanut biscuits. 'No fancy foreign stuff,' one of the men told Gandy approvingly. Polite conversation was difficult as the band played on with gusto throughout the afternoon, ending with 'God Save the King' and 'Anchors Aweigh'.

Earlier in the day, senior members of the British party had got in touch with their embassy in Chungking, making use of a military telephone line Owen-Hughes had had installed in his room. MacDougall had asked Ross to pass on various messages, so the young Canadian joined Montague, Gandy and the staff officers as they made their way down to the mission from the houseboat. It was a gentle half-hour walk beside the banks of the Wu River, where tall bamboo grew in graceful, feathery tufts. There was a pleasant scent on the breeze and just enough warmth in the winter sunshine to ease the effects of the previous evening's banquet. After heading south along the towpath, they crossed the wide river on a bridge of boats linked together and continued along the west bank, past wooden shacks built on stilts resting on the river bed. Against the sun-splashed hills they could see a Japanese reconnaissance plane cruising past, some two miles away.

A flight of granite steps shaded by a great banyan tree led up from the river to the walled mission compound, with its hospital, nurses' home, boys' school and library. The Hosai Hospital had been treating

---

Mao Zedong's: It was easy to forget, given its hatred of the Chinese Communist Party, that the Kuomintang had been founded on Leninist lines and had employed senior Soviet advisers.

the people of Kukong for forty years and was as busy as ever—some said it was the only dependable hospital in South China. The man who ran it, Dr Samuel Moore, was an Irishman, known by his Chinese name of *Mooi* (meaning 'plum'). He lived with his wife Jean and small daughter Margaret in one of the four large two-storey houses that lay spread out among the compound's neat lawns, flower beds and low hedges. There was a wooden bridge over a stream and a tennis court, which until 8 December had been painted over with a big British flag.

The Moores' house had old English fireplaces, varnished wooden floors, Chinese rugs, rattan furniture and French windows leading onto a wide verandah. Jean Moore, a New Zealander whose parents had been Presbyterian missionaries in Canton, had told Owen-Hughes to bring his colleagues for lunch before making their call, and she came out and greeted them warmly when they arrived. She was always glad to see visitors, and over the next ten days—despite being heavily pregnant with her second child—spared no effort in making the entire escape party feel at home. As well as church services and tennis matches, there were high teas and evening parties at which communal songs were sung, parlour games played and large quantities of hearty British fare consumed. The Moores' cook, Chung Mo, who was 'very short and had an alarming sniff, especially when serving at table', was famous for his lemon meringue pies. According to Jean Moore's autobiography, the one thing he served that the British sailors did not care for was 'the peanut butter which we ground from peanuts and used as a butter substitute. One even said to me, "Ma'am, give me dry bread if you like, but don't give me that stuff!".'

After lunch, Owen-Hughes took his colleagues up to his room, which doubled as an office. Their call to Chungking lasted almost an hour and a half, and the operator had to be frequently asked for more time. They read out a list of names, addresses and service numbers of the entire party, carefully drawn up by Gandy. They had to shout over the heavy static on the line, but even so, many of the names turned out later to have been misheard. There was also much news to exchange. Ross found himself talking to an old friend, Colin MacDonald of *The Times*,[*] who wrote a piece for the next day's edition about this 'first direct contact . . . with survivors of the thrilling Christmas Day dash

---

Colin MacDonald of *The Times*: As well as being the British newspaper's Far East correspondent, MacDonald was apparently also helping out at the embassy. He had left Hong Kong less than a month before on board one of the two British destroyers which sailed for Singapore on the day of the Japanese attack.

from Hong Kong'. It said the 'intrepid escapees' were looking forward to coming to grips with the enemy again after their gruelling ordeal.

The latest international news was hardly encouraging. Manila had already fallen, the Japanese were making rapid advances in Malaya and their planes were now attacking the Burmese capital, Rangoon, from their new bases in Thailand. The propagandist broadcasts of Tokyo Rose had meanwhile announced that the authorities were aware of the flight from Hong Kong of a group from the Royal Navy and were about to seize the members of the escape party. According to other Japanese radio reports, they were already dead, having all drowned before even reaching China. This conclusion was apparently based on the discovery of a jacket discarded during the Aberdeen swim, bearing a label with the name of a Captain Guest and the address of his London tailor.

The main message from the embassy in Chungking was that Montague, MacDougall and Ross and the five military and intelligence officers were to be flown up to the Chinese capital as soon as possible. They would then be able to tell the world what had happened in Hong Kong, and help to assess any lessons to be learned. The rest of the party, under Gandy, were to continue by road and rail across the southwest of China—a part of the country not yet occupied by the Japanese—towards Rangoon. The fall of such a major outpost of empire as Burma still seemed almost inconceivable—and besides, not only were American fighter planes already shooting down many of the enemy bombers over Rangoon, but the Chinese had promised to send an army across the Burmese border to help.*

The various onward arrangements would take time to sort out, as it was hard to find seats on planes to Chungking and there were few overland transport links to the west. Having the embassy in charge meant things no longer worked so smoothly, mused one member of the party. At any rate, it meant that for most of them the days that followed were restful ones, spent at leisure on the houseboat, at the mission or wandering around town.

Several men took the chance to send cables home individually, in case the official list of names hadn't got through. Kennedy's telegram

---

the Burmese border to help: The promise of Chinese troops sounded an all-too familiar one to some of the more jaded Hong Kong escapees. But in fact Chungking's offer to help in Burma had once again been accepted by Britain's high command with less than immediate enthusiasm, which may have had something to do with the slowness of this latest Chinese army to arrive.

to his parents read 'SAFE WELL FREECHINA'. He sent it on the tenth of January and it arrived in Glasgow four days later. He started several letters to Rachel but laid them aside, his mind full of wild forebodings as to what might have become of her. There had still been no word since the message more than a month ago saying the *Ulysses* was being bombed by Japanese aircraft.

There was an air raid alarm in Kukong almost every morning— part of a warning system involving an army of spotters on hilltops for hundreds of miles around. At the second alert they were supposed to leave the Sea Palace and join others in their trenches and dugouts. But after they had done this once and had sat out in the cold for what seemed like hours without even hearing the drone of a plane, they decided to wait in future for the final warning—a rapid beating of the gong and a warden singing down a megaphone to announce where the aircraft were heading.

The weather had turned decidedly wintry, with a morning frost settling on the houseboat. The result was 'feverish buying of warm underwear' by those who still had a supply of Hong Kong banknotes. These, they found to their surprise, could still be exchanged at the Central Trust Bank at the rate of 4.7 Chinese dollars for one Hong Kong dollar. MacDougall still had a whole bundle of Hong Kong notes, soaked with salt water but otherwise none the worse for wear. Owen-Hughes distributed more spending money from the embassy in Chinese dollars, or National Currency (NC). He made special payments totalling NC$268 (about US$14) for those who wished to get their hair cut or their shoes mended, assuring his superiors on his claim form that 'the ministration of the barber and cobbler were most necessary'.

Owen-Hughes also gave Gandy a package containing NC$14,000 for the onward journey. With a Sterling value of 3d (three pennies) per Chinese dollar, this was more bulky than valuable, but the MTB commander wrapped it in a towel and slept with it at night. Gandy's diary goes on to say he and his naval colleagues discussed the 'iniquity of Max Oxford drawing thousands of dollars from Colonel Chauvin at Waichow, and now from Owen Hughes at Kukong'.

If Oxford did indeed have such sums of money, he was finding it hard to spend them. On 8 January, he wrote to his sister:

> Shopping is difficult for there is little to buy and that of poor quality and very expensive. A pair of H.K. shoes costs Ch.N. $350 (about 70/-), a razor blade 1/-. My total worldly possessions are a pair of

36. On the East River. Two of the four river barges that took the party on from Waichow, seen here on 3 January 1942 near Yi He.

37. Riverbank group: Ashby, Kennedy and Chinese soldiers take a break during the five-day river journey, at Guanyinge on 2 January 1942.

38. Arrival at Lian Ping, 5 January 1942. The five trucks—'held together with wire and string'—had frequent breakdowns on the rough mountain roads. Chan's bodyguard, Yeung Chuen, stands behind him, with Gandy to the left.

39. Chan Chak steps from his car to be greeted by officials on the outskirts of Kukong. 6 January 1942.

40. Returning hero. Cheering crowds line the roadside as the Admiral slowly makes his way forward, bouquet in hand. Yeung Chuen is on Chan Chak's right, Henry Hsu on extreme left.

41. Sweet smell of freedom. Commander Hugh Montague and other officers line up for the cameramen with Muriel Jones of the Methodist mission. From left: (Macmillan), Yorath, Goring, Mrs Jones, Robinson, Montague, Hsu.

42. Leung Wingyuen, the guerrilla leader, with newfound Royal Navy friends, Stoker Petty Officer Buddy Hide (right) and Able Seaman Albert Rutter.

43. Lt Cdr Gandy marshalls his 'troops' as Leading Seaman Les Barker and the rest of the men stretch their legs after the journey. The favours that local girls have just pinned onto their Chinese Army padded jackets say 'loyal and bold in slaughtering the foe'.

44. David MacDougall, one of the few Chinese speakers in the British party, tells reporters about the escape.

45. Chief Petty Officer Gilbert Thums.

46. Captain Freddie Guest.

47. Captain Peter Macmillan.

歡迎會之中中英級高將領

蔣副司令長官　情報部長麥道高　海軍中校文地高　余司令長官　陸軍中校曉士　王參謀長俊

48. Page from Chan Chak's album showing senior members of the escape party meeting the head of the Seventh War Zone, Yu Hanmou, and other generals in Kukong; from left: Jiang Guangnai, David MacDougall, Hugh Montague, Yu Hanmou, Chan Chak, Harry Owen-Hughes, Wang Zhun.

49. Alexander Kennedy at the 'Sea Palace', the floating brothel where the men were billeted during their ten-day stay in Kukong.

50. Dr Moore's house at the Methodist mission in Kukong, where Chan Chak had his bullet removed. Jean Moore can be seen on the verandah.

51. Mountain scenery near Guilin. 17 January 1942.

52. Group photo in Guiyang with the Provincial Governor, General Wu, in front of the Chinese Nationalist flag. Douglas Pethick, 52 years old at the time, had been too ill to be in the main Waichow photo but can be seen here, front row, second from right.

53. Horace Gandy speaking at a reception in Guiyang. Looking on are Dr Lim, their host and head of China's Red Cross, and lieutenants Arthur Pittendrigh and Tommy Brewer.

54. The naval party's day-trip to Huachi (above) included a chance for lieutenants Collingwood and Parsons to take Dr Lim's daughter, Effie, out boating at the water mill (Photo 55). She and a friend, one of the visiting Chen sisters from Shanghai, are also seen (Photo 56) chatting to sub-lieutenants Arthur Gee and David Legge, who had been injured when one of the lorries crashed a few days earlier.

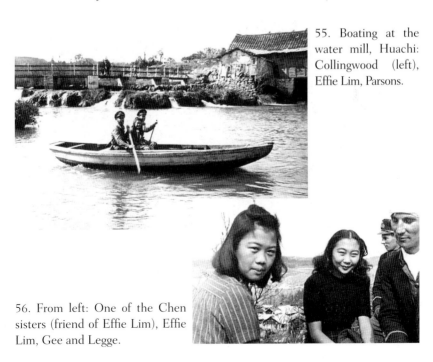

55. Boating at the water mill, Huachi: Collingwood (left), Effie Lim, Parsons.

56. From left: One of the Chen sisters (friend of Effie Lim), Effie Lim, Gee and Legge.

57. Kunming city gate, 31 January 1942.

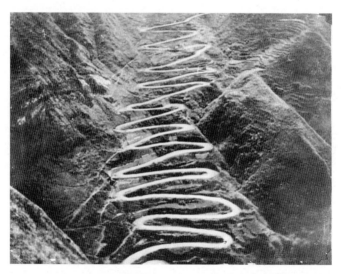

58. Hairpin bends on the old Burma Road, seen from the air.

59. Traffic jam, 5,000 feet above the Salween River, 5 February.

60. Burma border: Ashby and British soldiers from the Frontier Force oversee the transfer from Red Cross to Dodwell trucks, 7 February 1942.

flannels, too long and with holes in the seat, 2 prs of socks, 1 shirt (no collar), a submarine sweater and 1 Chinese vest and a pair of Chinese slippers. Rather different from a month ago with car, flat, radio, gramophone, saddling, golf clubs and masses of clothes! But a cheap price for liberty.

Pittendrigh, Collingwood, Brewer and Legge were among a group who took rickshaws one afternoon across the stone bridge and along the railway track to visit the YMCA's Mr Lockwood and his wife. Their house, complete with piano and gramophone, was described by one guest as 'very homey', with 'piles of tea and cakes and card games afterwards' and lots of tips about making European dishes from Chinese food. The Lockwoods also kindly sent a collection of books over to the houseboat, from which Kennedy selected a Sherlock Holmes. Gandy had already borrowed a Georgette Heyer from Mrs Moore. But he was anxious for the rest of his men to be as active as possible to keep up morale, so was glad to learn that the YMCA were challenging the flotilla to a game of seven-a-side football.

The match was played on a dusty pitch in the Zhongshan Park in front of an enthusiastic crowd of as many as 3,000 spectators. The MTB team was captained by *11*'s chunky and cheerful stoker petty officer, Bob Stonell, whose other duties included being 'custodian of chow and cigarettes'. It ended up losing by eight goals to two. Excuses, according to Gandy, were: 'ground too small, ball too small, opponents too small and agile'. Ashby reckoned the outcome not too bad, considering the British sailors were out of practice and were new to this particular variety of the game ('small football', played in gym shoes). Perhaps things would have been different if Henry Hsu—a soccer gold-medallist at the Far East Games in 1934—had turned up as promised to play in goal.

Despite the odd bout of exercise, the slackening of pace in Kukong after the rigours and excitements of the previous few weeks brought a turn for the worse in the men's general state of health. On 8 January, two days after their arrival, Christiansen and Halladay had been sent downriver to the mission hospital in a sampan, one with a high fever, the other with dysentery. At least four others were admitted with influenza, and many more had colds, stomach pains and diarrhoea. As well as attending to all these and dealing with continuing problems with feet, the mission's medical staff vaccinated everyone against typhoid.

Pethick and Cox-Walker, the two men who had been left behind at Longchuan, arrived on 12 January in good shape. MacDougall began to feel sprightlier too, after a few days in bed. As the hospital had no X-ray machine, they had decided to leave his bullet where it was till he got up to Chungking. He 'must have been in considerable pain,' recalled Jean Moore, 'but was invariably cheerful and courteous and brought back from a shopping expedition in the city some tins of IXL jam as a gift for my small daughter.'

Chan Chak's bullet had become embedded in the bone and he was told he needed an operation right away. He was worried that if this was unsuccessful he might lose his left arm altogether, leaving him with just one arm and one leg. But an old friend persuaded him to go ahead, and the bullet was successfully removed by Dr Moore on 8 January.

After the operation, Chan was advised to stay in hospital to recover, but the Chinese top brass decided a private ward was not good enough for him and insisted the Moores give him a room in their home. Margaret duly moved in with her parents, leaving the Admiral her bed in the nursery. He made good progress there for a while, but after three days, had a severe haemorrhage due to a gastric ulcer. He had been getting treatment for this in Hong Kong, but it had flared up again as a result of all the celebratory wining and dining since reaching China.

Dr Moore decided on a direct blood transfusion. Out of many volunteer donors, the twenty-nine-year-old Welsh missionary, Peredur Jones, was selected as having the most compatible blood. In the event, it clotted badly—making this a much lengthier performance than Leung and Kendall's rather different kind of blood-sharing twelve days earlier. But all turned out well and Chan presented his donor with a bottle of whisky in gratitude. As a good Methodist minister, Jones had no use for it, but his wife Muriel decided to exchange it with some European friends for a tin of paraffin.

Dr Moore told Chan he was still a sick man and must have no visitors while he recuperated. But gradually, with British blood in his veins, 'Uncle Chak' recovered his old vitality. Before long he was sitting propped up in bed, wearing a spotless white sling and surrounded by pictures of Mother Goose, graciously receiving a stream of generals and other well-wishers, many bearing gifts. According to the doctor's wife, the constant tread of feet up to the nursery door left the stairs quite 'bereft of paint', so great was the Admiral's popularity.

27
Parting of the Ways

10 January . . .

Among the many visitors to the one-legged admiral's bedside at the mission was the guerrilla leader, Leung Wingyuen, who came to bid an emotional farewell to his former marine commander. As promised, Chan had put in a good word for him with the Chinese Army, recommending him to no less a figure than Yu Hanmou as a 'bold and patriotic' fighter. General Yu responded by formally appointing the ex-bandit as a guerrilla captain under the Waichow area army command. As well as giving his whole group and its various activities the official seal of approval, this meant Leung was entitled, at least in theory, to funding and weapons from the government. Chan thanked him for all he had done, and urged him to go back and tell his men to work for the good of the country.

Leung's triumphant return a few days later to his base on the Dapeng peninsula was witnessed by an American banker, J Arthur Duff, who had slipped out of occupied Hong Kong on 8 January. He had been rescued by Leung's band after being captured by pirates in Bias Bay. He later described how the guerrilla chief—wearing a Chinese Army uniform and looking like a 'typical Cantonese officer'— was escorted into Dapeng by a long column of armed men who had gone out to meet him: 'In the evening he came to see me, accompanied by his young Cantonese wife (a gardenia in her hair, dressed in a new gown which he had brought back from the interior).' Leung scolded his second-in-command, who was also his uncle, for not giving their guest better quarters. He then offered a sum of money to Duff for his onward journey, telling him: 'It is the business of all of us to aid and assist foreigners at the present time. We are allies in a great cause and property is common between us.' He was evidently a changed man.

It was also time to bid farewell to Yeung Chuen. Wearing the rattan hat and loose blue clothing of a peasant and carrying a concealed gun, the Admiral's bodyguard was being sent back to Hong Kong on a special mission to rescue his boss's wife and children.

He later told his family that he reached the captured British colony after walking for five days and was stopped on the way by 'two secret service agents' who pulled off his hat, exchanged flashes of acknowledgement, then let him go. Having tracked down Mrs Chan, who had been hiding in the Gloucester Hotel, he learned that Leung's guerrilla group had already made arrangements for her escape. In the event, she and one of her daughters were caught by the Japanese, placed under house arrest and questioned about her husband's escape, but she later managed to get away. As soon as they heard the Admiral had arrived safely in Free China, another daughter and one of the seven-year-old sons, Donald, escaped with Henry's wife. The other son, Duncan, went separately with his aunt and grandmother. (He had until then been dressed as a girl as it was feared the twin sons would attract attention and recognition.) They all met up in Macao and the whole family was finally reunited in Guilin. As for Yeung, he returned, at the Admiral's suggestion, to his home village near Longchuan, where his first, or 'country' wife lived. Soon afterwards, he made another trip to Hong Kong to bring out his second wife, who had been working there for Chan Chak.

Reports reaching Kukong of conditions in Hong Kong spoke of food shortages and brutal controls after an initial period of looting and chaos. Europeans, it was said, were being forced to do menial jobs such as sweeping streets and pulling rickshaws, with the object of making them a laughingstock in the eyes of Asians. In fact there was no need for such stunts: it was already becoming clear that Britain's standing among the Chinese had sunk to a new low. Despite the official welcome for the escape party as heroes, many people in China are said to have 'flatly despised' the British for capitulating to the Japanese so quickly. The British hadn't even fought, a Chinese reporter from Hong Kong told Owen-Hughes. He replied that they had, but out of sight of civilians.

Goring and Macmillan visited the 7th War Zone HQ on 10 January to give a briefing to the Chinese Army on what had gone wrong. The two staff officers believed the colony's easy defeat could be blamed on various factors: poor intelligence and a failure to take prior security measures; a lack of training in night-work and in bush and mountain warfare; a dependence on fixed positions—or as they put it, 'concrete and concrete-mindedness'; and, above all, a tendency to underestimate the enemy. In their view the Japanese were a formidable fighting force, whose soldiers had at times shown 'fanatical bravery'. But they were confident that Japan could be beaten by suitably equipped and well-led troops.

Two days later, on 12 January, Goring became the latest member of the party to fall sick. He was carried through the gateway of the mission hospital in a 'raging fever' and diagnosed as having a severe attack of malaria. He spent the next ten days and nights laid up in considerable pain, and as a result was unable to join his fellow officers when they finally left for Chungking.

It was late on the night of 13 January when Owen-Hughes heard from the Chinese military that there would be seats available on a small aircraft the following day. The seven men who were to be spared the arduous overland journey—Montague, Guest, Macmillan, Oxford, Robinson, MacDougall and Ross—packed their things next morning and said their goodbyes. The normally bright and breezy Freddie Guest had a lump in his throat as he stood by the Admiral's bed and held out his hand: 'I had come almost to love this quiet, courageous and stricken figure of a different race,' he declared later. 'I was leaving behind a great man and a great friend.' He was apparently less sorry to be saying farewell to some of his fellow countrymen. He confessed that he and his army colleagues found it a 'great relief' that the navy party, who were going to be leaving in two days' time, had decided to make their way separately to Rangoon and contact 'their own people' there.

After lunch, the Chungking group were taken by truck to the old walled town of Nanxiong and then on to its airport, a bumpy grass field with one bamboo matshed. Later that evening they finally climbed aboard their plane, a 14-seat Douglas DC-2. It was flown by a highly experienced American pilot known as 'Pop' Schwey—one of those pilots who, in the words of Ted Ross, 'flew by the seat of their pants'. They took off in pitch darkness at 9.15 p.m., had a one-hour stop in Guilin, and landed in equally pitch darkness at 3.40 a.m. in Chungking, coming down sharply from high up to avoid bombers. 'My gosh,' Ross enthused, 'when it became light and we saw where we had landed in the dead of night we were almost bowled over. Towering cliffs on both sides, with high-tension wires strung across the top, and we had slid right under the wires and between the cliffs and landed on a sand bank in the middle of a river.'

The rugged mountains that cut off the province of Sichuan from the rest of the country—making it 'harder to get to than Heaven', according to the poet, Li Po—had helped protect Chungking from Japan's armies but not from its aircraft. Crammed onto a great boulder at the junction of the Yangtze and Jialing rivers, the city had been bombed into a state of semi-ruin over its four years as the nation's temporary capital. But with their usual doggedness and resilience, the Chinese had burrowed into the riverbanks to create air raid shelters, emerging between raids to rebuild and carry on as best they could.

As foghorns sounded from the pale green river, the new arrivals crossed a wobbly pontoon and climbed up to the makeshift customs house. Endless flights of wet stone steps stretched skywards past black houses that clung to the cliff, propped up by wooden struts and poles that jutted out at every angle. They were met by staff from the embassy, who had arranged accommodation for them with the local offices of Shell Oil, Butterfield & Swire and other companies closely linked to Hong Kong. Later in the day they went to see the ambassador, Sir Archibald Clark Kerr—a 'charming and highly intelligent person', according to one recent visitor, whose wife, 'a Chilean beauty, was called The Pocket Venus because she was only five feet tall'.

The embassy was in a bomb-damaged but still grandly porticoed European mansion, with high-backed chairs in ornate rooms overlooking the river. Drinks were served, congratulations offered on the escape and the first of countless questions asked about how they had got away, what had happened to others and, most urgently, what lessons could be learned that might help stop the relentless Japanese advance across the rest of Asia.

Montague and his six colleagues were fully debriefed by members of the military mission and other sections of the British embassy, before moving on for further interviews over the following days at the embassies of the United States and other friendly foreign powers. They also did the rounds of Chinese government and military agencies, press offices, newspapers and broadcasting stations. Guest was sent to talk to the Russians; Robinson gave a speech defending the fighting record of Hong Kong's Indian troops; Oxford briefed the US Air Force; MacDougall and Ross dealt with press attachés and journalists. In the evenings, there were plenty of others keen to wine and dine these first few survivors to emerge from Britain's captured colony. Their presence added further glamour to what was already an almost festive atmosphere in the Chinese capital in the wake of Pearl Harbor. American, British and other foreign offers of aid were flooding in as never before, as China eagerly pulled up its seat at the world table as an equal ally of the Great Powers.

As soon as he could, MacDougall sat down to write to Cathie in Canada. He began his letter:

Here I am in Chungking sitting before a good fire, fully clothed, reasonably well and lunch just coming up. I mention these things because since I last wrote I have faced the probability of never again experiencing them . . .

In the last week of January, the ambassador arranged for a car to take MacDougall on a two-day drive to Chengdu for the latest examination of his shoulder wound. The chief surgeon in the hospital attached to the city's West China Canadian Mission found that the bullet had passed right through the bone, leaving a small hole, and had lodged almost up against the heart. The extensive operation needed to remove it could wait a little longer, he decided. But MacDougall's nervous system was deemed 'rather unsatisfactory' owing to the experience of the past few weeks, and it was recommended that he leave China as soon as possible.

By the time he got back to Chungking, the other members of the group had already gone. British officials had given Ross a new job as transport manager and he had left on 28 January on a DC-3 bound for Calcutta, flying over the Hump via Kunming and Lashio. Montague and Macmillan went with him—the former going for now just as far as Burma, where he was to report to the Royal Navy in Rangoon, and the latter to see about a new staff job in Delhi, where his uncle was a top general. Guest, Robinson and Oxford flew to India three days later. Guest found it grand to be back in what he called 'the East' after the insecurity of China, and headed straight for the still undisturbed colonial splendours of the Bengal Club. Oxford soon returned to Chungking to take up a job as assistant air attaché at the British embassy.

On 19 February, MacDougall became the first member of the escape party to return to Britain. According to Owen-Hughes, who had joined him in Chungking a few days earlier, he was hurrying back partly to have his bullet removed, but more importantly, 'to talk about Hong Kong with the Colonial Office before NL gets home!'*

MacDougall may not have known that NL Smith was the prospective father-in-law of Alexander Kennedy. But he did know from personal experience that the former Colonial Secretary was unlikely

---

NL gets home: Although NL Smith had retired from his post in Hong Kong, MacDougall was right in thinking he did not regard his career as over. In the event he became head of the Hong Kong Planning Unit in London in 1943 until succeeded by MacDougall the following year.

to favour the sort of drastic political change he himself believed was essential if Hong Kong was to have a future as a British colony. They had met no one in China who believed the humiliated British could ever rule Hong Kong again. Instead, it was assumed that a defeated Japan would hand the place back to the Chinese (also the outcome favoured by Washington). But MacDougall was convinced that Hong Kong would benefit from a further period of British rule—just as long as it was a new kind of rule that gave local people equal rights and a genuine say in how they were governed.

That was the basis of proposals he put forward in Whitehall before finally having his bullet removed and going up to Perth to see his parents. While there, he contacted a Mrs Kennedy from Glasgow, who had seen his name in the papers and had written to ask if he had any news of her naval lieutenant son. He was able to confirm to her that Alick had escaped and to tell her he had been 'fit and cheerful' when he had last seen him in South China. He added that her son had been on the point of going west by road with the rest of his flotilla 'for orders in Burma or India'.

An account of the naval party's overland journey follows in the final chapters. But for now we return to Kukong, where Chan Chak was continuing to recuperate at the Methodist mission. For it was here, shortly after almost all the others had moved on, that certain unresolved strands of the story of his escape finally came together.

By the end of January, Kukong had begun to take on the air of a refugee camp, as more and more people began to turn up from Hong Kong. Most were Chinese, able to leave the captured colony relatively easily, but they also included the first Europeans to escape from the newly established prisoner-of-war camps and the civilian internment camp at Stanley. They arrived without money or possessions and dressed in a fantastic assortment of clothes—one Englishman was in rags and a monocle. Most of them had been robbed at least once while crossing the no-man's-land on the Chinese side of the border, but once they fell into the hands of genuine guerrillas, all was usually well.

Colonel Lindsay Ride, a member of the Hong Kong Volunteer Defence Corps and in peacetime a professor of physiology at the University of Hong Kong, escaped from the Shamshuipo prison camp on 9 January. Accompanied by three others—DW Morley, DF Davies and Francis Lee Yiu Piu—he chose a similar route to the one used by Chan Chak, receiving help from communist guerrillas along the way and reaching Kukong after three weeks. Accepting an invitation from Owen-Hughes to install himself on his verandah, 'Doc' Ride, as he was known to all, was soon holding long talks at the Admiral's bedside. And it was here at the mission over the following days that the idea for the British Army Aid Group was born (at much the same time as Jean Moore's son). Initially set up to help prisoners from Hong Kong reach freedom, the BAAG developed into the main British undercover organization in South China, becoming a key source of military intelligence for the Allies.

Two men from the flotilla, Penny and Quixall, who like Goring had been too ill to travel with the others, joined Ride's escape companions, Morley and Davies (both also naval men, from the HKRNVR) when they left Kukong on 4 February to travel by rail and road to Burma. Goring himself had already left by then, going by train to Guilin on 24 January and on by air to Chungking.

Ride didn't have to look far for men to staff his new group. Kendall, McEwan and Talan—'the three musketeers', as they had become known—had arrived from Waichow with Chauvin on 20 January. They were now living on one of the houseboats and looking for something to do. Not that they had been idle since seeing off the others on the East River. On the morning after their New Year's Eve tour of the bars, McEwan and Talan had set off briskly back to Nanao to try to recover some of the equipment the escape party had left behind with the guerrillas. They got there on 3 January to find that most of the weapons, radios and 'toys' had disappeared. They were proudly given MTB beds to sleep on, however, and Royal Navy tinned salmon to eat. The boats themselves they found to be still only half-submerged. '09 still had her bows above water,' McEwan told Kennedy years later, 'but the Nips came over and bombed her about the 3rd/4th and that finally settled her.' The villagers left their homes and sought cover in the hills when they saw the Japanese aircraft approaching. But the SOE men on the spot could not confirm reports received in Kukong on 14 January that Nanao itself had been bombed and its people 'made to pay hell'. Nor was there any truth to another report that the Japanese had raised the boats soon afterwards.*

Kendall's hopes that his group could continue to operate in China as an anti-Japanese sabotage unit soon foundered when it became clear that there was no chance of getting Kuomintang

---

soon afterwards: The sunken MTBs ended up being salvaged for scrap by the Chinese in the 1950s.

permission—particularly in view of his own communist guerrilla links. Instead, the three SOE men agreed to become founding
members of the BAAG, which had similar though more cautious
aims. The Chinese Army's suspicions of Kendall and his own clashes
with Ride meant he did not stay a member for long, leaving for India
with Talan in August. McEwan, however, remained in China with the
BAAG until the end of the war—as did another SOE man, Ronald
Holmes, one of the seven-strong group who had been trapped in the
hills behind enemy lines. When they realized the fighting was over,
he and two others* made their way across the border and on up to
Kukong, leaving their four junior colleagues—including Tom Parsons'
brother, David—to give themselves up to the Japanese.

The most unexpected new arrival in Kukong was Colonel SK Yee.
Last seen on the stricken launch saying he couldn't swim, and pre-
sumed to have died soon afterwards, the Admiral's chief of staff suddenly appeared on 5 February looking none the worse for wear. He
was not happy, however, at having been left behind.

His partial account of what happened after the others jumped
into the sea is contained in a letter to be found in Britain's national
archives, dated 3 March 1942, and addressed to a 'Betty' in Shanghai.
It is signed by someone called 'Suyamu', who was staying at the
YMCA in Kukong and 'doing some practice in the clinic of the
Methodist mission hospital'. She had already heard from others in
the party that one of the casualties during the escape had been the
Danish coxswain, Alec Damsgaard, whose wife she and Betty knew
well in Shanghai. She was therefore delighted to meet Yee and eagerly
pressed him on the chances of there being any other survivors. He
told her the boat had finally drifted ashore on Aplichau, with himself
and two wounded crew, Damsgaard and Forster, still on board. Later
on, the Dane recovered sufficiently to be able to speak, and SK soon
got to know all about him. The letter continued:

> During their terrible night together, when they were expecting at any
> moment to be killed, Alec told of his two sons in the States and his
> wife in Shanghai.

---

he and two others: Eddie Teesdale, who like Ronnie Holmes would later become
a very senior Hong Kong civil servant; and Robert Thompson, who went on to
join Wingate in Burma, achieving fame after the Malayan emergency as one of
the world's leading experts on subversive warfare.

In the morning, said Yee, he had put the two others on a junk, asking the fishermen to take them across to a hospital on Hong Kong Island. Suyamu's letter goes on to say that an escaped doctor who had just reached Kukong had told her he had seen the wounded men being brought in and had assured her that Damsgaard's leg wounds were 'now healing well'. It later emerged that the second man, Forster, had soon died from his injuries.*

SK Yee had lain low for several days on Aplichau, sheltering in the Harbour Mission Church, tucked away behind the waterfront in the village. According to Henry Hsu, it was thanks to having Henry's Bible on him that he was able to gain sanctuary in the church. Other reports say that after sneaking back onto Hong Kong Island, SK disguised himself as a coolie and was conscripted by the Japanese as a labourer, before losing himself in the stream of refugees crossing into China.

Two days after his dramatic reappearance in Kukong, SK equally dramatically disappeared again, amid reports of a major rift with Chan Chak. 'The next startling piece of news is that Yee is in "durance vile" for usurpation of power by order of the admiral,' wrote Harry Owen-Hughes in his diary on 7 February. He had already noticed a lack of 'perfect harmony' between the two men but wasn't clear as to the reason. When Ted Ross later told his family that the Admiral had had his chief of staff 'seized and thrown into the locker,' he said it was because Chan thought SK was trying to upstage him and steal his glory. Mike Kendall insisted there was more to it than that, alleging that Yee was 'a worthless man' who was jailed after being 'discredited'.

The row seems to have been connected with the disappearance of the large sum of money said to have been hidden by the Admiral in his false leg before leaving Hong Kong. Some have suspected that by refusing to jump overboard like the others and escaping alone with whatever was left on the boat, SK Yee made himself a rich man. Both he and Chan had been telling anyone who asked that it was the other one who had last been seen with the money. Since each of them assumed the other had been killed, this had seemed a safe thing to say. But now here they were, both very much alive. Henry Hsu said Yee gave back some of the other things left on the boat, including his Bible and his

from his injuries: Forster's wife and two small children were interned in Hong Kong for the rest of the war, unaware of what had happened to him. He is commemorated with a plaque at Plymouth reading 'Remembered with honour.'

shoes—which he had noticed SK was wearing when he reappeared—but never returned his jacket, his diamond tiepin or the money.*

Yee remained under armed guard for four days. 'I was lucky not to be strung up,' he told Ted Ross later, adding that he was only saved in the end after he got a message through to his patron, Dai Li. The sinister head of China's Gestapo promptly intervened to get him released. It is perhaps no coincidence that it was about now that Chan Chak's political star began to wane. 'Unhappily, by this time Chinese intrigue had come into play and the Admiral had fallen from favour,' wrote Owen-Hughes. 'I never found out why, but suggest he had achieved too much popularity.'

Chiang Kai-shek, who had earlier sent a congratulatory message to Chan, had still not sent the plane he had been asked for. He may have feared that Guangdong was once again looking to its own local heroes rather than to himself, in faraway Chungking. The Generalissimo knew from having done his own military and political training in Canton that the south had a dangerous tendency to go its own way. It's also possible that Chan Chak may have just become too close to the British, who had never been popular with either Chiang or Dai Lee.

In that case, the British were hardly doing the Admiral any favours as they lined up to shower him with praise. Owen-Hughes himself had become one of Chan's biggest fans. 'He is a very loyal friend of England and unshaken even by what I gather was an exasperating lack of cooperation with Hong Kong of late,' he wrote in his diary. In his official reports, the liaison officer called on Britain to 'foster and return this friendship to the best of our ability'. As a small first step, he wrote to his opposite number at Chinese military HQ, imploring him to let the British pay for the Admiral's medical treatment at the mission: 'In appreciation of his distinguished service to our cause and his gallant leadership during the epic escape from Hongkong, the British People would deem it an honour to be allowed to consider the Admiral as their guest during his stay in this Hospital.'

Britain's diplomats in Chungking wondered if Chan Chak could be the key to future cooperation with China. 'The officers who came out with the Admiral were unanimous in speaking of his courage,

---

or the money: Whatever the truth, General Yee, as he was by the end of the war, went on to become a successful banker in Hong Kong and now has a major medical trust named after him.

fortitude and great powers of leadership,' wrote the military attaché, Brigadier Gordon Grimsdale. The ambassador put forward a strong recommendation that Chan be immediately awarded Britain's senior military order, the KCB (Knight Commander of the Bath). No Chinese had ever received such an award and it could give a badly needed boost to relations at a time when the British were coming in for a lot of criticism. General Wavell, Britain's Commander in Chief in India and the Far East, lent his support. Chan Chak had displayed 'great energy, leadership and disregard for personal safety under heavy fire', he wrote in a memo to the War Office, 'and it was entirely due to his organisation and personal authority that his party reached Free China safely.' The general also stressed the value of Chan's earlier activities against fifth columnists, saying they had contributed directly to a lengthening of Hong Kong's resistance.

Commander Montague, in his official report to the Admiralty, suggested that the actions of both the Admiral and Henry Hsu should be recognized and commended by Their Lordships: 'Throughout our trip His Excellency (Admiral Chan) was most attentive to our welfare and comfort, and in spite of his wound and ill health furnished us a most notable example of fortitude and cheerfulness. His instructions were zealously executed by his Aide-de-camp . . . whose character and ability we came to admire.' Montague also praised the hospitality of the villagers during the march, expressing the hope that they would suffer no reprisals from the Japanese. 'To this end,' he wrote, 'all members of the party have been instructed to regard details of our route and also the fact that officers of the Special Service were with us, as most secret.'

In due course, on 19 August 1942, Chan was made an Honorary Knight Commander of the Military Division of the Order of the British Empire.* At the same time, Hsu received the OBE (Order of the British Empire). According to Grimsdale, the Admiral's KBE was 'not at all the same thing' as the more prestigious KCB and it came 'so long after the event as to lose much of its value in Chinese eyes from the point of view of British prestige'. Once again, it seems,

---

Order of the British Empire: Chan was presented with his knighthood in Chungking on 4 November 1942 by the British Ambassador, Sir Horace Seymour, on behalf of His Majesty King George VI, for 'his services in assisting in the defence of Hong Kong and subsequent escape of a large party of high-ranking officials to Free China'.

London had its own eyes on other things—or simply had difficulty seeing clearly as far as the Far East.

Meanwhile, as soon as Chan Chak was well enough, the British embassy flew him to Calcutta to be fitted with a new artificial leg: a more lightweight and modern affair than the one left on the boat. After some difficulty, the ambassador succeeded in getting reimbursed for this expense, to the tune of 300 rupees (22 pounds, fourteen shillings and eight pence), by Whitehall. A Foreign Office mandarin wrote on his expenses claim, as only a Foreign Office mandarin could, 'Yes. Clearly we must stump up.'

Chan Chak himself, when asked later whether he had lost his leg in the war, had a neat line of his own. 'In the fake war I lost my real leg,' he said. 'In the real war, I lost my fake leg.'

On Christmas Day 1942—the first anniversary of the escape—Chan honoured the promise he made to Henry Hsu when they leaped into the water by getting baptized at the Union Church in Chungking. At the same time he adopted Christian names for himself (Andrew) and for his twin sons (Donald and Duncan).

Chiang Kai-shek kept Chan Chak under his eye in the capital for the next few years, to the disappointment of the Admiral's many admirers in Guangdong, who thought he was the one man who could get things done in the south. Rumours that he was about to become provincial governor came to nothing. But he continued to inspire the nation to keep up the fight against Japan, with typically stirring exhortations such as:

> An ancient saying, 'Doing our best till the hour of death', should be the firm conviction of those of us who are living in a grand age like this.

Later, the doughty one-legged admiral became the first postwar mayor of Canton. As such, he was able to give much-valued support to his old friend and fellow escapee, David MacDougall, who had been appointed to head the new civil administration in nearby Hong Kong and went on to become one of the most successful colonial secretaries in the territory's history.

28
Journey to the West

16 January . . .

Two days after the departure of Montague and the rest of the
Chungking group, the main naval party under Gandy began their long
overland journey from Kukong to Burma. They rose at 3.30 a.m. on
Friday 16 January and marched across town to the railway station,
where friends from the YMCA and the mission had gathered in the
predawn darkness to see them off. As an expression of gratitude for
looking after them so well, the sailors presented the mission members
with the White Ensign they had carried from Hong Kong, covered
with their signatures.*

Gandy's party that morning numbered exactly 50, comprising 10
naval officers, 4 merchant navy officers and 36 ratings. In addition,
a Dr Chiu and a Major Yu had been assigned to accompany them
for the first part of the journey, and an advance team consisting of
Ashby, Brewer and an interpreter had gone ahead three days earlier
to pave the way. No foreigner could travel anywhere in China without
various permits, and Ashby was carrying an elaborate *laissez-passer*
document signed by General Yu, authorizing him to travel as far as
Guangxi Province armed with two loaded revolvers.

To reach the start of the Burma Road—now the only land route
available out of China—they had first to travel some 1,400 miles to
Kunming, zigzagging across country by rail and then road. The first
600 miles, by rail, took five days. They began by going north on the
main Canton-Hankow line as far as Hengyang. Here, railway officials
had prepared the sort of welcome the party had grown used to in the
days when the Admiral was with them but hadn't expected to continue. The officers were led off to a twenty-course meal in a station
waiting room decorated with Allied flags painted on cardboard and

---

with their signatures: In her autobiography, *Daughter of China*, Jean Moore confessed that she later felt compelled to burn this valued gift when she and her
husband left the mission compound in June 1944, for fear their Chinese staff
would meet with reprisals from the Japanese.

an enormous placard reading: 'Welcome to our admirable comrades from the Great Britain'. The others dined equally well in the train's buffet car, where a more subtly worded banner said: 'Honoured be the British warriors, firm in disaster and courageous in danger'.

They then headed southwest in their own private train, each coach with its own 'boy' (in fact a grown man) who brought round pillows and blankets. Another boy brought meals from the dining car. Gandy was anxiously wondering how much to tip everyone, while also drafting speeches he might have to make at their next official reception. 'And to you who have been fighting the Japanese since 1937,' he wrote, 'we are proud now to join in the same fight, which we are determined to continue to its rightful end.'

Next day, as they approached Guilin, there was an air raid alert, obliging them to get out and take cover among the sugarloaf hills and limestone rocks. A solitary plane passed overhead. In peacetime the town was a tourist resort, and a truck was made available to take all the officers and some of the men on a sightseeing trip to the famous Seven Star Cave, regularly used as an air raid shelter by up to 50,000 Guilin residents at a time.

On the outskirts of Liuzhou, the train stopped, and they spent the next two days being shunted into different sidings. Brewer came to tell them Ashby was in bed with influenza at a local hotel. Dr Chiu was sent to attend to him, while Gandy and Major Yu took a horse-drawn carriage to the Fourth Army HQ to see the adjutant general, who had been asked to arrange onward transport. To pay for the hire of four lorries at the end of the railway line, he advanced them 80,000 Chinese dollars, which Gandy carefully tied up in another of his dirty towels. Still feverish with a temperature of 103°F, Ashby was declared fit to travel and joined them for the final 100-mile stretch of the train journey to the railhead town of Jinchengjiang.

The line was being extended to Guiyang, 200 miles away across the mountains, and hundreds of workers were building up embankments and blasting cuttings through the rock. Thanks to China's immense stock of human labour, it was hoped to have the new railway up and running within the year. But for the men of the Royal Navy, it was now back to the perils of the highway.

After a night spent in railhead sidings, they were up at dawn on 21 January, cramming their gear into the back of the four trucks and climbing in on top. There was then a three-hour wait for clearance papers and drivers' passes before the convoy finally moved off. When they stopped for a break at a small hotel, Ashby fainted in the toilet. Dr Chiu diagnosed typhoid and suggested taking him back to Liuzhou. But Gandy decided to press on to Guiyang, where they were to stay with the Chinese Red Cross. He proposed that the patient and doctor should travel slowly in the rear truck with a group consisting of himself, Yorath and the merchant navy officers, while the other three vehicles went on ahead with Collingwood in charge and Legge as interpreter.

At the boarding house where they stayed that night, the men had to sleep as many as four to a bed. Since the bed consisted only of planks, many decided to make do with the floor. Next day, at the ancient town of Dushan, Ashby said he couldn't go on. There was a better hotel here, run by the China Travel Service, so those in the rear truck stayed behind, and a telegraph was sent ahead to the Red Cross asking for an ambulance. That night Gandy sat at Ashby's bedside and tried to encourage him, saying he intended to recommend him for the Distinguished Service Cross for his part in the attack on the landing craft in Kowloon Bay. 'I believe that my remarks did a lot of good,' the commander commented later, pointing out that Ashby survived and received the medal in due course.

They had now entered China's undeveloped hinterland. The weather was raw and cold, the landscape forbidding and hostile. As the hills grew steeper and the mist came lower, the road twisted and turned endlessly. There was little or no other traffic apart from a few lorries and the occasional string of forty or fifty pack ponies, stumbling along with heavy loads and tinkling bells. Miao hill-tribe women near the roadside wore peaked caps and colourful, low-breasted smocks with pleated skirts like kilts—a far cry from the wide-brimmed hats and shiny black tunics they had seen in other provinces.

On 23 January, after a night's rain, the narrow, heavily rutted road had become treacherously muddy. One corner proved too much for Collingwood's truck, which skidded violently in the mud and overturned. Les Barker was one of the fifteen men inside:

> Before we knew what was happening, we toppled over, taking a complete turn and a half . . . If we had gone over once more there was a drop of 100 feet and we should have all been killed.

David Legge was also in the truck, looking out of the back between two 50-gallon petrol drums:

> I found myself sitting in the mud in the road with the truck on top of me. The truck had only iron hoops and a canvas cover and we would

all have been squashed had it not been for the fact that one of the gasoline drums fell on end with the end of the truck sitting on top of it. Some of those sitting right inside of the truck were thrown right past me out into the road.

Legge received a blow to the jaw and a cut to his head, which later required seven stitches. He and the other injured men were transferred onto the next truck and taken on to Guiyang. They were treated at the Red Cross hospital and their injuries were found to include a fractured collarbone, a dislocated shoulder and extensive lacerations, but nothing more serious. In the meantime, the overturned truck was righted and came on half an hour later. The driver had been seen weeping after the accident, and now drove more carefully. His vehicle was undamaged save for a missing hood, which gave those in the back a wretched 50-mile journey in the rain and cold.

The crash was officially blamed on defective brakes, but Gandy suspected the driver must have been coasting downhill to save petrol. He blamed Collingwood, who had been sitting in the front, for not keeping a closer eye on him. 'He should have made him use gears,' he insisted in a letter addressed to the Admiralty later that year. 'Thereafter I trusted nobody but myself in charge.' Collingwood had never felt Gandy should be leader of the flotilla anyway, and after their return to Britain accused his commanding officer of discrimination and favouritism. 'Who looked after the ratings when the CO was looking after his sick pal?' he complained bitterly, upon learning that Gandy was recommending Ashby for his DSC but not proposing any similar award for him.

By 7 p.m. all four lorries had arrived safely at Dr Robert Lim's hospital and camp, set in a fold of hills above the straggling city of Guiyang, some 4,000 feet above sea level. Dr Lim, an old friend and former golfing partner of Admiral Chan Chak's, was one of China's most remarkable men. An Edinburgh trained physiologist and a general in the Chinese army, he had served with British forces on the Western Front in the 1914–18 war. After Japan began its attacks on northern China in the 1930s, he had given up his professorship at the Peking Union Medical College to launch the national Red Cross movement, setting up its headquarters here in the interior, in the capital of one of China's poorest provinces, Guizhou.

Over cocktails, Dr Lim told the naval officers about the work being done to give the bare minimum of medical attention to the millions of Chinese under arms. He envisaged a future in which health and medical care would be the right of every Chinese. He was shortly sending several empty lorries down the road to Burma to bring back urgently needed medical supplies. The British party could travel in those, he suggested. In the meantime, a few days' stay at the camp should put Ashby on his feet again and also be good for the rest of them.

Dr Lim—known to all as Bobby—had married a Scotswoman, who had died some years before. He himself spoke English with a slight Scottish burr. Their fifteen-year-old daughter, Effie, wearing a kilt, acted as hostess for the evening, in the course of which the visitors finished her father's entire stock of Chungking gin—he apologized for the local brand, saying 'it's all I can get here'. After dinner, they picked their way back through the mud to the nearby army huts where hot baths, dry clothing, clean beds and even their own supply of cigarettes had been prepared for them.

David Legge was one of many who found their two-day stay with the Red Cross a highlight of the entire journey:

> We all bunked in a large dormitory, which had big stoves in the centre, heaven to us after the places we had been sleeping . . . They were very good to us and we were looked after like kings. There were one or two pretty ex-Shanghai girls there, with whom I spent most of my time the next few days, rather, I think, to the jealousy of other less fortunate officers.

The full programme Dr Lim had arranged for them included a trip to the nearby beauty spot of Huachi, where they visited the burial ground of a Miao king, climbed a hill known as 'Rhinoceros Rock' and went boating. Kennedy's photos show Legge and Gee—another sub-lieutenant with a Shanghai background—enjoying the company of Effie Lim and two of her slightly older friends, the Chen sisters, who were staying in Guiyang with their mother. Other diversions included a cinema show specially screened for them at the camp and a set of live sketches performed to apparently uproarious effect by members of the flotilla. The MTB football team also made another appearance, losing 6–1 to a fit side from the Red Cross training school.

After doing their best to spruce themselves up, the visitors were taken into the city to meet the provincial governor, who shook hands with every one of them and gave them the freedom of the city. He also gave them each a booklet of delicate woodcuts, stamped with his seal and signature. Among the pictures of local hill-tribe people, they recognized the costumes of the Miao peasants they had seen by the road the previous day. General Wu, a small, immaculate figure with white gloves, posed with them for a group photo in the courtyard and made a short speech, wishing them a safe return to their families. Gandy responded by saying that while they all looked forward to going home, their first duty was to 'prosecute the war' wherever they might be required. He ended by offering three cheers for their host and the Chinese nation.

'Lieut. Commander Yorath and I were now back on good terms, for he reassured me that my call for three cheers seemed not too theatrical,' Gandy wrote in his diary. (Collingwood was evidently not the only one who sometimes found him difficult.) But V2 admitted he had not done so well at a reception held for them at the Red Cross centre later that afternoon, when he had praised the Soviet Union as a heroic ally of Britain and China's. While this was no less than the truth, he had forgotten that since throwing out their own Russian advisers and launching 'bandit extermination' campaigns against Mao and his men, China's Kuomintang rulers had come to see all communists as highly subversive. In their eyes, he wrote on reflection, 'comrade Joe Stalin was no hero'.

Gandy's own politics were far from left-wing, as he made clear when describing his encounter at the same reception with some members of the International Brigade: 'Mid-Europeans I think; but I found it too delicate a subject to enquire how they came now to be established in China, my sympathies being with their opponent, general Franco.'

Also at the party was a visiting American army surgeon, Dr John Grindlay, who found Gandy a 'very thoughtless, demanding type'. But he got on well with the other, younger officers—particularly Parsons, who gave him a detailed account of the escape and the earlier battle for Hong Kong, which the young lieutenant called a 'huge British disaster'.

Among the members of a Friends Ambulance Unit staying at the camp was a Scottish Quaker called Braid who had brought his bagpipes with him to China. Kennedy asked if he could try them out, since his own set was now with the Japanese. The hut they were in was a small one and indignant protests soon forced the two of them outside, where as darkness fell, they continued playing 'Loch Duich' and other poignant Highland airs in a paddy field. 'We were totally absorbed,' Kennedy later recalled, 'and only when we stopped realised that a large crowd of children were watching us with awe from a safe distance with all the dogs in the neighbourhood howling sadly in the background.'

That night the Governor gave them a farewell dinner at which a large amount of potent rice wine was consumed. As the evening progressed, Chinese hosts and British guests alike burst into song. Many had retired to bed by the time it came to the national anthems, but one who had perhaps stayed too long was Chief Petty Officer Thums, sturdy coxswain of *MTB 10*, who was seen to 'stiffen like a ramrod during The King, although he was lying flat on his face on the floor'. Shortly afterwards even the normally upright Lieutenant Kennedy found his legs giving way as he headed back to his hut, and he had to be carried home by two fellow officers, Yorath and Pittendrigh.

The following day, 26 January, they clambered into their five Red Cross lorries and resumed their journey, heads throbbing with every bump in the road. Dust swirled through the open rear of the trucks as they headed west along a high plateau. Two ratings who had been injured in the crash—Kelly and Deakin—were left behind in hospital, to be sent on at the first opportunity. Another absentee was Bruce, their faithful spaniel. Effie Lim had fallen for him and had gladly agreed to keep him when offered the chance. On the plus side, Ashby was now well enough to travel; and in place of Dr Chiu and Major Yu they had a new Chinese escort in Dr Basil Wong of the Red Cross, who had done his medical training at Guy's Hospital in London and had practised in Hong Kong. He turned out to be an engaging personality and an excellent guide. He was also quick to dismiss their doubts about whether it was appropriate for healthy foreigners to be travelling under the protection of the Chinese Red Cross. It made no difference who or what was inside the vehicles, he said—the Japanese bombers went for the Red Cross in the same way they went for anyone else.

The 400-mile journey on to Kunming took four days. They found their new drivers more dependable than the previous, privately hired ones, and their convoy now made hourly stops to allow all five trucks to keep together. They were also getting more used to the routine of looking for billeting, food and water in places that had rarely if ever seen a non-Chinese before—let alone a group of fifty British sailors.

Their route took them past the Huangguoshou (Orange Tree) Waterfalls, the largest in Asia, and later through a deep gorge mentioned by Marco Polo, where a steel bridge across the river had been bombed by the Japanese just a fortnight before and swiftly replaced by a new pontoon bridge. One particularly steep hillside was traversed in a series of twenty-four spectacular hairpin bends. Finally, the road dipped through a valley, rising past woodland and glistening rice terraces to cross the border into Yunnan. The next afternoon brought them to the outskirts of the provincial capital, nestling beside a lake in the Wuliang Mountains. There, high over Kunming's multi-coloured gateways and curving tiled roofs, they saw their first friendly aircraft since the war began.

The fighter planes of the American Volunteer Group (AVG)—Colonel Claire Chennault's famous 'Flying Tigers'—had been in fierce action for the past month over Rangoon and the Burma Road, bringing down as many as a hundred Japanese fighters and bombers. Two squadrons of the AVG were based in Kunming. Over a whisky or two in their mess that evening, the young pilots told graphic tales of their successful dogfights, giving the newly arrived British sailors—already impressed by the Americans' racy leather jackets and pretty Chinese girlfriends—the first encouraging news they had heard for a long time. Even Gandy, who found them 'a rowdy lot', admitted they were 'certainly getting results'.

The British consul in Kunming had arranged for the naval party to put up at a military hostel a few miles outside the city. A group of British and Australian commandos were also staying there, on their way into China. They were members of the 204 Mission, recently set up to teach guerrilla warfare to Chiang Kai-shek's army and help harry Japanese supply lines. This first contingent of men were heavily laden with provisions—too heavily, by the Chinese standards the naval group had become used to—but were dressed as though for the tropics, having just come from a training course in the Burmese jungle. They cast envious eyes at the sailors' warm Chinese clothing and a round of brisk trading followed, with one side's khaki shirts and shorts being exchanged for the other's padded jackets and gauntlets.*

There was not only a British consul in Kunming but also a British shipping agent, as Kennedy, for one, well knew. For weeks, he had been half-dreading the opportunity that would present itself here to get news of Rachel's ship. He gritted his teeth and sought out the Jardines agent, a Mr Urquhart, who confirmed that the *Ulysses* had been bombed soon after leaving Hong Kong. As the young naval lieutenant's heart sank, the agent went on: 'But the amazing thing is that after being long overdue at Manila she turned up unexpectedly at

---

and gauntlets: It was perhaps no surprise, in view of how poorly prepared they were, that the 204 Mission folded later that year, with many of its members having fallen sick.

Singapore'. Still afraid to build up too much hope, Kennedy asked him eagerly whether he was sure. 'Yes, absolutely, although I haven't heard anything more about her since. Did you know someone on board?'

But the former captain of *MTB09* was no longer listening. A lot could have happened since then, but he now knew that the ship had at least survived that first day's attack. He wrote a long letter to his parents, telling them nothing about his own doings other than that he had a two-month beard and was 'somewhere in China', but plenty about his fiancée and his anxiety about her long and dangerous journey. 'I can only pray most deeply,' he wrote, 'that by the time you read this she will have got home and visited you.'*

Other members of the party also went to see Mr Urquhart. Four of the merchant servicemen who had previously worked for Jardines—Marchant, Christiansen, Brazel and Cox-Walker—decided to rejoin the firm here at its small regional office, which London was soon to appoint as Head Office in Free China. Kunming might not be Shanghai or Hong Kong (or even within 1,000 miles of the sea), but it was one of China's most attractive cities, with an excellent climate. It had also benefited from the evacuation of some of China's leading businesses and educational institutions from the east coast.

Meanwhile, a message had arrived from the ambassador in Chungking saying the embassy was seriously understaffed and asking Legge, Gee and Pittendrigh to report there to help with cipher work. All three had worked in China before and were happy to do so again, so they said their goodbyes and prepared to leave for the capital.

On the morning of February the first, the main party—now reduced to eleven officers and thirty-two men—left on the 600-mile journey to the Burmese frontier. The five Red Cross trucks had been given an overhaul during the three-day stop in Kunming and it was time to press on. Whatever the successes of the Americans in the air, Japanese ground forces had continued to advance through what the British had deemed to be impenetrable jungles and impassable mountain ranges between Thailand and southern Burma. Gandy said nothing to his men but was privately wondering if Rangoon was going to be the 'haven of rekitting and reorganization' he had hoped for.

The Burma Road had seemed such a faraway and almost fanciful objective when they left the coast at Mirs Bay that they could hardly

---

visited you: When the letter reached his parents almost three months later (on 24 April), they had still heard no news of Rachel.

believe they were now seeing it with their own eyes. China's famous lifeline carried a steady stream of American, Chinese and British trucks packed with the essentials of war: petrol, arms and ammunition, medical supplies and other stores. The road stretched 717 miles from Kunming to the railhead at Lashio, following an ancient trade route over the high mountains at the eastern end of the Himalayas that was traditionally little more than a rough path. Carved through some of the world's most difficult terrain, it was a magnificent feat of engineering, completed in 1939 after just two years of work by some 100,000 Chinese labourers.

The finishing touches were to be added with American help over the next few years, but for now the road was still in the most rudimentary of states for driving on. It was barely wide enough to allow an oncoming vehicle to pass, and since no tar was available anywhere in China, the uneven surface was coated with layers of dust or mud. This made for a tortuous and bone-shaking journey—and, with sheer drops of thousands of feet, a hair-raising one, even without the added threat of an air attack. The scenery, however, was breathtaking, as *MTB 07*'s Leading Stoker Charlie Evans told BBC Radio soon after his return:

> The Burma Road was the most wonderful sight I have ever seen, stretching out in a long white ribbon, trailing along for miles and miles through that amazing country. All along the road there were hundreds and hundreds of Chinese women carrying baskets of stones to fill up the many shell-holes and by the side of the road there was an endless number of lorries overturned by bombing or by accident on that very narrow road. It took us eight days travelling in those lorries down the Burma Road and almost every night we had to sleep in those lorries. In fact I don't think I ever want to see a lorry again.

The only alternative to sleeping in the trucks was to find rooms in one of the crowded boarding houses in small townships along the way. Typically these had no electricity or recognizable toilets and guests had to cross the courtyard warily to avoid being soaked by a basinful of dirty water pitched from an upper bedroom window. Some of the men slept on restaurant tables one night, while others bedded down outside in a field.

On 3 February they stopped for the day for repairs to one of the trucks and about twenty of them took the chance to visit the nearby mountain stronghold of Dali. The historic town lay beside a huge lake ringed by thousand-year-old white pagodas and snow-capped peaks. A bright sun shone on the cobbled main street, where tall, shaggy

Tibetans traded rings and leatherwear brought in by mule across the roof of the world. There was a distinct breath of Central Asia in the air, moving Gandy to write in his diary, in unusually poetic mode:

> Saw 3 Tibetan men, one long knife, one long gun, one long pipe between them; also selling charcoal and firewood a good-looking girl with silver bangles and a wonderful peach-like complexion. Was she Persian, or from a lost tribe of Israel? As tongue-tied strangers in a strange land we merely wondered.

Before leaving Dali, the group paid a visit to its tiny but well-attended church. An Englishwoman who had settled in the town in 1881 had saved up enough money to have it built after living there for more than thirty years. They were surprised to learn that the church was now part of the widely scattered diocese of the Bishop of Hong Kong, Ronald Owen Hall.* They had tea at Bishop Hall's cottage next door with a Mr McLelland, who taught at a theology college beside the lake.

The next day they came to the mighty, blue-green Mekong and on the day after that, on the other side of a wilderness known as the Dragon Hole, to the still more formidable Salween, at the bottom of a mile-deep gorge. Both rivers, emptying into different oceans thousands of miles apart, were crossed by suspension bridges that had been frequently attacked by Japanese bombers. But the men in the Red Cross lorries were preoccupied by more humdrum concerns such as the latest outburst from their commander, who was still fuming over the sharing out of a hundred hard-boiled eggs they had bought for their lunch. 'Delay over eggs and oranges,' wrote Kennedy in his diary, 'Gandy excelling himself!'

The last 50-mile stretch to the Burmese border was over level asphalt, a welcome change from the constant potholes of the past week. As they passed through two small Chinese Shan states, bamboo groves lined the way and warm tropical scents blew in on a gentle breeze. They were disappointed not to see a tiger—the commandos had told them in Kunming that they had seen one crossing the road here.

Ronald Owen Hall: RO Hall was Bishop of Hong Kong and South China from 1932–66. He was based in Hong Kong but was fortuitously attending a conference in the United States when the Japanese invaded. While his campaigning zeal made him a constant thorn in the government's side, he was probably Hong Kong's best-loved Anglican bishop.

At 6 p.m. on 6 February, they came to the frontier at Wanting, where the previous customs post had been burned down by local headhunters. As the convoy waited to cross the border, Chinese soldiers sang the national anthem and hauled down the flag to mark sunset. It was a moving moment, and the escape party reflected on the sense of national pride, stoicism and cheerfulness they had found throughout China, as well as the boundless hospitality, kindness and courtesy they had received at every level of society. All this, despite extreme poverty made worse by war. They left with some regret, according to Kennedy, for 'despite the failings of the Chinese, we felt that there was much to appreciate in their way of life'. At the same time, there was no disputing the fact that China still felt like a very strange world, and they looked forward to being back with their 'own folk', as Gandy put it.

They crossed over to the British lines of the Burma Frontier Force, whose men must have been more than a little surprised to see a contingent of the Royal Navy emerging from the Chinese interior. But they were soon made welcome with tinned salmon, biscuits and canned beer that 'tasted like nectar', and were invited to bed down in armchairs in the mess or wherever they could find space. The wireless news at 8.30 p.m. came direct from London and had a familiar, homely feel to it, even if its contents were as depressing as ever.

The most discouraging news of all was from Burma itself, where the Japanese had continued their lightning advance in the far south. As well as three airfields along the Tenasserim coast, they now held the key port of Moulmein, at the mouth of the Salween River—less than 100 miles from Rangoon. For the men of the Royal Navy, it seemed to be a case of 'out of the frying pan, into the fire'. After all the rigours of their momentous journey from Hong Kong, they were about to come face to face once again with the enemy.

29
Burma Shave

8 February . . .

Burma was to prove a shock. It was even more poorly prepared to deal with a Japanese attack than Hong Kong had been. Where Hong Kong had at least put up a good fight against the odds, Burma's defending forces were disorganized and demoralized before the battle had even begun.

Many of them were only half-trained, since the best troops available for the region had been sent to Malaya in a last-ditch effort to save Singapore. The British faced the additional disadvantage of an almost total lack of cooperation—and often active opposition—from the main indigenous group, the Burmans. They resented British rule, and they particularly disliked the Indians, who had come to dominate their country's economy as well as its armed forces.

Sandwiched between the subcontinents of India and China, Burma is often thought of as tiny, but is in fact bigger than France and Belgium combined. Rich in rice, oil, teak, silver and rubies, it also formed the Allies' only link with Free China, and should have been better protected than it was. The Japanese had started by capturing just the southeast corner in order to protect the western flank of their Malayan invasion, but they soon decided the whole country might make a useful addition to their much-vaunted East Asia Co-Prosperity Sphere.

The garrison strength in the north of Burma, where the escape group had arrived, had already been greatly reduced as troops were moved south in a desperate effort to hold the enemy on the banks of the Sittang, the last river barrier before Rangoon. A Chinese army was expected to cross over into northern Burma any day to help fill the gap by defending the Lashio end of the road to Kunming.

As the Red Cross lorries headed off to load stores for the return trip to Guiyang, the naval party covered the final 100 miles from the border to Lashio in four commandeered Dodge trucks belonging to Dodwell & Co, the trading company Ashby had worked for before the war. They had expected to find orders awaiting them in Lashio, but it turned out that even here, at the British terminus of the Burma Road, no one knew anything about their expected arrival. The eleven officers held a meeting to decide what to do next. There was a daily train leaving Lashio for Rangoon, and two of them—Warrant Officer Wright and Lieutenant Pethick—favoured going straight on. But the others thought it better to wait and rest. Gandy wired Rangoon for instructions, and in the meantime, they settled into an almost empty Royal Air Force camp on the edge of town, in beautiful, tree-covered surroundings. They heard nothing back for the next four days, and so took the chance to relax, do their laundry (or tip the camp's Indian bearers to do it) and mentally prepare themselves for whatever might come next.

The day after they reached Lashio, a small plane carrying Lieutenant General TJ Hutton, who had arrived the previous week to take over command in Burma, crashed in the jungle nearby. The general was not seriously hurt but his RAF pilot died from head injuries, and the MTB flotilla was called on to provide the firing party for his funeral. In steel helmets, white sweaters and trousers, ten of the sailors slow-marched to the haunting notes of a lament played by Indian army pipers. As one of those present reflected, 'it seemed a pitifully lonely ceremony for this man, unknown to any of the funeral party, who was to lie so far from home.'

The old hill station of Lashio, capital of the Northern Shan States of Burma, was set on a plateau in the monsoon clouds, amid gentle slopes and gardens full of exotic flowers. The war seemed far away, even though the whole area would be in Japanese hands within weeks. But there was also now a new town which had sprung up next to the old one with the building of the Burma Road—a boom city crammed with truck drivers, technicians and lend-lease officials, Chinese girls in tight dresses, Buddhist monks in orange robes and ragged child beggars smoking thick cheroots. British generals flew in and out from Calcutta on an air service for priority passengers only; ancient lorries and modern jeeps packed with goods bound for Chungking arrived daily from Rangoon; and hairy grey buffaloes plodded beside rickshaws and packhorses under streamers reading 'Welcome to our Gallant Chinese Troops'.

Members of the Royal Navy party were allowed to go into the new town by day, but it was declared out of bounds at night due to a case of bubonic plague. In the old town, there were milder pursuits such as darts and billiards to be enjoyed at the Lashio Club, along with colonial-style curries and whisky sodas. Pethick beat Kennedy on the green baize by 100 to 42 in spite of the older man's latest medical complaint—a hordeolum, or stye, for which Dr Wong had prescribed 'hot compress and aggyrol drops'. Pethick was soon joined on the sick list by Parsons, who was leading the way home after a long evening at the club when he fell into an air raid trench and broke his nose.

The rest of the men were now in remarkably good health, according to V2's diary—the only other exception being Petty Officer Prest, who had been diagnosed as having chronic alcoholic gastritis and told to abstain from spirits. As he prepared to hand over command to the Senior Naval Officer in Rangoon, Gandy was feeling proud of himself: he had led his men on a six-week journey of more than 2,500 miles and he considered they had done very well indeed 'in rather unusual circumstances for sailors'. His motto of 'so far so good' had been successfully borne out 'so far', he noted cautiously in his diary. 'I consider our party has kept together well and cheerfully and the behaviour of the RN ratings has been very good indeed and necessary in order to make a good impression on the Chinese.'

Having accepted an invitation from the District Commissioner, Mr Porter, to stay in his secluded, bougainvillea-draped bungalow, Gandy took advantage of the few days of peace and quiet to get his accounts done. Expenses as far as Kukong had been paid 'by charity of Chinese Admiral Chan Chak', he noted. Since then, it appeared that taking some fifty men across China to Lashio, including all food and accommodation for a month and all casual payments to individuals, had cost 73,131 Chinese dollars (less than £1,000 in total). In other words, £20 a head—an 'astonishingly cheap rate of transport', claimed Gandy.

On 10 February, the long-awaited Chinese troops reached Lashio, after being delayed by political problems and a lack of suitable camp facilities. Next day, a message arrived telling the naval party to proceed to Rangoon, where they would receive further instructions. They boarded the following night's train for the two-day trip south. It was several hours late in leaving, since rail services had been thrown into chaos by the mass of people trying to get away from Rangoon.

At 11 a.m. the next morning they got off the train at Maymyo, the last stop before the line left the hill country, to take up an invitation from the Army to visit its Bush Warfare School. Over a lively lunch, the sailors got to meet the latest intake of young commandos, one of whom stood on the tables amidst the beer bottles and plates of strawberries and cream and sang 'On the Road to Mandalay':

For the wind is in the palm-trees, and the temple-bells they say:
'Come you back, you British soldier; come you back to Mandalay!'

He was 'quite a good-looking chap with a slight cast in his eye and he'd got a good voice too,' noted Chris Meadows, wireless operator from *MTB 10*. He couldn't help wondering, though, if the emotional young singer would get through the war. The soldiers being brought in to defend Burma knew next to nothing of local conditions, but they would learn plenty over the next four months as they withdrew more than 1,000 miles back to India, finally emerging from the jungle 'gaunt and ragged as scarecrows' and riddled with dysentery and malaria, after the British Army's longest ever retreat.

Mandalay was just 45 miles away, and arrangements had been made for them to drive down to the plains by truck and catch up with their train there. They had no time to see anything of the fabled city—which was a pity, some reflected, as they were unlikely to pass that way again. But they did have a chance encounter on the platform with a French journalist, Eve Curie—daughter of the famous scientist, Marie Curie—who was able to tell them about Rangoon. There, she had smelled the same 'ghastly odour of defeat, of retreat, of fear' that she knew from the Fall of France and had seen refugees, 'like flocks of frightened animals', shivering with terror at the idea of being bombed again. Mademoiselle Curie was on a tour of battlefronts for a newspaper syndicate. Her brief account of her meeting with Gandy and his party appeared later that month in the *Daily Sketch*:

> Waiting for a train in the opposite direction was a naval officer in command of motor torpedo boats. He was travelling with 43 officers and men of his unit. All of them had escaped from Hong Kong across Japanese-occupied territory, getting constant help from Chinese guerrilla fighters and local Chinese inhabitants. They had fantastic stories to tell but told them reluctantly. They seemed to be solely interested in rushing south and getting hold of new motor-torpedo boats and fighting the Japanese again.

Having travelled a distance of some 3,100 miles overland since leaving Hong Kong on Christmas night, the group finally reached Rangoon on 14 February—Saint Valentine's Day. If truth be told, what most of them were really interested in now was getting out of Burma on the first available boat home. It turned out that a message had been sent to Lashio a week before but never received, and that had they arrived in Rangoon sooner, they would have been put straight on board a ship for Colombo. But General Wavell—based 2,000 miles away in Java—had now decided that their skills and experience could be put to good use, and that they should stay to help out in what had become a desperate situation.

The station was packed with hundreds of people pushing and clamouring to get on trains. Others sat forlornly on their bundles in the heat of the square outside. The bazaars beyond were eerily quiet, with shop windows barricaded and mounds of rotting fruit and filth lying on the roads. There was little sign of bomb damage—the recent raids had caused panic and chaos out of all proportion to the weight of the attacks. As they drove along deserted avenues between gardens of blue jacaranda and dark green papaya, one thing became obvious: Rangoon was already a lost city. The only signs of life came from scavenging pi-dogs and the occasional band of Burmans—the few that hadn't fled to monasteries—who were roaming the streets, armed with clubs and *dahs* (machetes), attacking Indian refugees and looting unprotected European houses.

The thirty-two ratings were billeted first at a mariners' club and later at the naval barracks. It was the first time they had seen the sea since 26 December 1941. They were to serve with the Burma RNVR, a local force composed of Burmese ratings with British and Burmese officers. Many of the force's original ratings and even some of its Burmese officers had deserted as soon as active war became a possibility, leaving barely enough men to crew the five motor launches and handful of auxiliary vessels that patrolled the coast and inland rivers.

The officers in the Hong Kong party, who were staying at the only hotel not yet closed, the Minto Mansions, were split up and given various different jobs. Gandy was told to go to the rice port of Bassein, 90 miles to the east, to plan its defence. He got there in time to see its airfield bombed and its ancient RAF planes destroyed, just as had happened in Hong Kong. 'A few bombs fell in the native town causing panic and a few fires,' he reported. 'I saw no ambulance, no regular fire engine, only a solitary old Burmese driving an iron-wheeled, steam driven, incredibly Victorian machine with a pump.'

Ashby was assigned to remain in Rangoon as senior officer of the Hong Kong party and head of naval motor transport, assisted by Brewer. Collingwood and Kennedy were taken on as personal assistants at Naval HQ by Commodore Cosmo Graham, who had just flown out from the Persian Gulf to take over the Burma Coast Command. Wright was to be sent about the country as engine examiner of requisitioned launches. The injured Parsons had been left behind in hospital in Lashio—as had Yorath, who had developed sinusitis. Both were later flown to India.

As with most of his colleagues, Kennedy's heart had sunk when he heard he was required to stay on in Burma till the bitter end. He was already deeply depressed at the continued lack of any news of Rachel. If the *Ulysses* was still intact, he expected her now to be in the Atlantic, where sinkings had risen sharply since America's entry into the war. He tried to send more cables, but the lines were blocked. To cheer himself up, he went along with some of the others to a local nightspot, where they found what was left of the colonial set enjoying a final, frenzied fling:

> The Silver Grill, the only restaurant still functioning, was a wild place that night, and although a hard-working orchestra played continuously the music was drowned in the general hubbub. A few European women, mostly from the nursing and cipher staffs not yet evacuated up country, attempted to dance jealously guarded by their partners, and in this Wild West atmosphere we celebrated our return to 'civilisation'.

Kennedy met a girl called Fleurette Pelly, who next day took him to the Kokine swimming club—an exclusive backwater where boys dispensed drinks to leisured members sunning themselves on the grassy banks. It was hard to reconcile any of this with the reality of the city outside. After all he had been through, he also felt distinctly awkward walking about in a pair of swimming trunks—especially with a beard, which made him feel 'top-heavy'. When he went to Fleurette's home the following evening, the offending item was promptly shaved off by her mother. 'Felt much better,' he wrote in his diary.

On the same day that they were told of their new jobs—Sunday, 15 February—came the shocking news of the capture of Singapore, complete with its 80,000 defenders. Never before had so many troops fighting under the British flag surrendered on a single occasion. It was already clear that Rangoon would be the next to go. A scorched earth policy was rapidly drawn up that would keep as many men and as much equipment as possible out of enemy hands. For the next three weeks, a haphazard process of evacuation and demolition was carried out in fits and starts, adding to the general air of uncertainty and frustration.

The battle of the Sittang bridgehead had been joined, but there was no news on whether the Japanese were being held. Between bouts of activity, the British naval officers sat in the torrid, unswept hall of the Minto Mansions, gloomily reading old newspapers. Most of the staff had already melted away, leaving guests to carry their own luggage and clean their own rooms. Eventually the hotel closed altogether, and the Hong Kong group moved into a private house that was being used as a naval mess.

The town centre, port, naval HQ and barracks were all a long way apart and there were no buses or taxis. But transport was one problem easily solved, for hundreds of jeeps and other vehicles lay in dumps near the abandoned docks, and members of the forces could simply help themselves. Collingwood commandeered a Buick to drive the Commodore around in. On 22 February, with military evacuation arrangements now complete, Naval HQ was transferred onto a requisitioned Danish merchantman, the *Heinrich Jessen*. Gandy and most of the others in the Hong Kong party moved on board along with the Commodore and his staff, ready to leave next day at the head of an evacuation convoy. Ashby, as gunnery officer, decided to set up two Lewis guns, six Brens and a Hotchkiss as the ship's anti-aircraft defences. The guns were manned by the MTB crews under Petty Officer Prest.

It had become obvious that Rangoon could not be held against seaborne attack, as by this time the Japanese Navy controlled the Indian Ocean and the Bay of Bengal. The last hope of driving back Japan's ground forces rested with the possible diversion of an Australian Division on its way from the Middle East to Java. However, Australia's Prime Minister, John Curtin, telegraphed Winston Churchill on 22 February, refusing to commit his forces to what he deemed an irrecoverable situation in Burma at a time when Australia itself was already threatened by the Japanese from several quarters. Early next morning, the British destroyed the vital Sittang Bridge, less than 90 miles east of Rangoon, even though two of their own brigades—comprising more than 5,000 men—were still on the far bank amidst the Japanese.

As they set sail on the *Jessen* at noon on 23 February, members of the naval party from Hong Kong were at last rejoicing at their good fortune. They watched with relief as the Burmese coast disappeared over the horizon. But their joy was short-lived. On the following morning, their ship was ordered to return to Rangoon. At first they thought there must be some mistake, and they put in at Diamond Island to have the signal confirmed. As they waited beside the island's palm-fringed beaches, famous for their giant turtles, Les Barker celebrated his twenty-second birthday—four years to the day since he joined the navy. But there was to be no reprieve—Churchill had insisted that Rangoon should be defended after all, and the entire convoy was being recalled.

Over the following days, as the situation worsened, the MTB men were employed in fighting fires, loading merchant ships, patrolling in motor launches, guarding the docks and placing depth charges under cranes on the wharves, ready for demolition. The city streets had become more dangerous than ever with the throwing open of prison doors and asylum gates at the start of the official evacuation. Fifth column activities were rampant and the corpses of rival looters lay in the streets. 'Officers are walking round shooting anyone who looks at anything,' Stoker Rann noted with wonder. 'Everyone seems to be going crazy.' 'Fires being lighted by the Burmans all over the city every night,' wrote Ashby in his log. 'Burmans cutting up Indians on every opportunity. Looting general—several good shoot-ups.' One night he and his men captured a Japanese officer and fifty Burmans trying to land in a sampan. According to Buddy Hide, they were all shot; other reports say the Japanese, at least, was taken prisoner.

On 1 March they received new orders to sail, and got as far as the mouth of the Rangoon River. But again, the evacuation was cancelled, and they returned to help unload a convoy containing fresh troops. The constant changes in policy were in part a result of constant changes in command. General Hutton was in the process of being replaced by General Sir Harold (later Field Marshal Lord) Alexander, who at first refused to abandon hope of saving the city. But he had failed to realize just how bad things were. The inadequately trained reinforcements proved to be a case of too little, too late, as had been the case in Hong Kong.

Late on 6 March, with the Japanese drawing ever closer, the new British commander decided the retention of Rangoon was no longer possible and the right course was to abandon the city and regroup his land forces further north. This time there was no going back. Ashby and his colleagues on the *Jessen* spent the next day and night setting off the charges they had laid and demolishing whatever else they could to deny the use of the port to the enemy. Jetties, wharves and warehouses were blown up, river craft scuttled and navigation equipment smashed or thrown into the river. The police headquarters, wireless and power stations and other key buildings were set ablaze and, most dramatically of all, the oil dumps and refineries dynamited, sending thick clouds of black smoke swirling high in the sky above the gleaming gold of the Shwe Dagon pagoda.

Having earlier escaped from both Hong Kong and Singapore, the *Heinrich Jessen* now became the last ship to leave Rangoon. On the morning of 8 March, with troops, refugees, port demolition parties and other 'last ditchers' packed on board, she headed downstream, bound for India. On the way out she passed incoming Japanese warships which ignored her, and at 10 a.m., just two hours after she set sail, the advance guard of the Japanese 215th Regiment entered Burma's stricken, empty capital without a shot being fired.

30
Glasgow Bound

8 March . . .

The column of smoke above Rangoon was still clearly visible 40 miles out at sea. But there was no sign of the expected enemy aircraft: the RAF and the Flying Tigers had taken a heavy toll of the Japanese air squadrons. As the *Jessen* headed northwest across the Bay of Bengal, tension slowly subsided and thoughts turned increasingly to the possibility that they might now, finally, be on their way home.

Those on board the Danish ship included most but not all of the surviving members of the MTB flotilla. Alick Kennedy had been sent in a Burmese minesweeper, the *Somagyi*, to the port of Akyab, halfway up the coast towards India. About a dozen of the men—including Alf Burrows, Ed Charlesen, Len Downey, Bill Dyer, Ken Holmes, Charles Moore, Len Rann, Al Rutter and Jack Thorpe—had also gone to Akyab, either in motor launches or on the *Somagyi*.

Tommy Brewer, itching for a fight as ever, had volunteered to stay behind in Rangoon to carry out some final demolition work. After setting off thousands of land mines he broke out through enemy roadblocks, cracking a rib when his jeep turned over, but escaping upcountry with a British army unit. Just a few months later he was killed—not by a Japanese bullet in the jungle, but in a motor accident on a main road in England at the start of his leave.

The *Jessen* reached Calcutta on 12 March, and the Hong Kong party put up at the Marine Club. They found it pleasant to be 'back in civilization', as one of them put it, but were also shocked at signs that India might be tainted with the same complacency that had been evident to some extent in Burma. The Great Eastern Hotel's pretentious dining room was still offering a choice of forty different dishes to patrons in full evening dress. Calcutta was apparently quite unaware that war existed anywhere, thought Ashby. Yet bomb attacks on the city were a real threat now that the Japanese were firmly established next door in Burma. The news on the radio was a grim recital of Allied defeats, the latest being the fall of Batavia (Jakarta) and Surabaya in the Dutch East Indies. An announcement by the British Foreign

Secretary confirming atrocities in Hong Kong put the final seal on any hopes that first reports had been exaggerated. They all knew people who had been left behind, but Anthony Eden's statement to the House of Commons—based partly on evidence brought out by Phyllis Harrop*—caused particular anxiety for those with immediate family still there, such as Gandy.

At last, on 24 March, came an order to 'proceed by train to Bombay en route to UK'. It was what they had all been waiting for, but just how many of them would actually be available to make the voyage home was hard to say, as the size of the party continued to shrink.

The oldest member of the group, Pethick, had found a job as master of an elderly steamer called the *Marylise Moller*. Like Pethick himself, she had spent most of her life on the China Coast (where she had been pirated the previous year), but she was currently on her way to the Middle East. Two more of the merchant mariners, Skinner and Halladay, also re-enlisted in the merchant service.

Two ratings from *MTB 09*, Able Seaman Les 'Lofty' Gurd and the coxswain, Bill Schillemore, were keen to stay on for a while in Calcutta. They volunteered to join the military's Medical Services department—a plan to which Gandy had no objection. One of their old shipmates, Ron 'Jez' Priestley, also remained behind after being admitted to the Barrackpore Hospital. Several of the men had come down with fever after their time in Burma.

John Collingwood and the flotilla's six telegraphists had returned on the *Jessen* to Burma soon after arriving in India, and were to be based for a spell at Akyab with Kennedy and the others. There was an airstrip near the port that was coming under heavy attack from high-level Japanese bombers. After the captain of an Indian Navy sloop absconded, Collingwood was put in command—he being the only officer who could speak Hindi, thanks to his family's history of service in the Indian Army.

Ron Ashby was sent back to Burma on a special mission with the Commodore in a Tiger Moth biplane. But unlike the others, he returned to India in time to join Gandy and his party of twenty-two remaining men on their train journey across the subcontinent. They

---

Phyllis Harrop: the former 'Lady Commissioner for Chinese Affairs' had avoided internment by agreeing to help the Japanese authorities set up licensed prostitution areas for their troops. She smuggled herself out of Hong Kong on a boat to Macao one month after the surrender, carrying secret information for SK Yee, whom she met in Chungking.

left from Calcutta's Howrah Station on 24 March and arrived at Bombay at 10 a.m. on the 26th to find a car and a truck waiting to take them on board the SS *Narkunda*. They set sail at 3.30 that afternoon (leaving 'no time to have clothes made', complained Ashby).

Twenty years earlier, the 16,000-ton *Narkunda* had been the pride of the P & O passenger fleet, but she was now a scruffy troop transport with poor food and frequent mechanical problems. Gandy was in charge of a naval draft of 200 men, for whom life below decks was far from luxurious, particularly in the heat of the tropics. But they were on their way home and no one was complaining. In the comfort of the first-class saloon, Gandy had a 'very unsatisfactory poker game with a "duchess" who couldn't play', and up on deck, he tried his hand at shooting flying fish with a .22 repeater. He didn't hit any but did see one being eaten by a dolphin. He also claimed he saw some albatrosses.

Their fellow passengers included survivors from HMS *Prince of Wales* and *Repulse*. As the different groups of sailors exchanged graphic accounts of their recent Far Eastern experiences, the war was rapidly spreading to the South Asian waters all around them. In early April, after heavy Japanese raids on Colombo and Trincomalee, the cruisers *Cornwall* and *Dorsetshire* and the aircraft carrier *Hermes* were sunk by air attack with the loss of many hundreds of lives. A simple and moving Easter Day church service was held on the *Narkunda*— attended, to Gandy's disappointment, by 'only nine' of his ratings.

They stopped on Thursday, 9 April, at Durban, where they picked up 657 Italian prisoners-of-war. There wasn't room for all of them in the ship's prison, so they were berthed out on deck, squashed together like sardines. The Hong Kong party were assigned to guard them, but got off to a bad start when fifteen of the men managed to escape from the ship while she was still tied up at the quay. From then on, the prisoners were kept firmly down below.

On 14 April the *Narkunda* arrived in Cape Town. Among the vessels tied up there, they found another troopship, the *Laconia*, a 20,000-ton Cunarder which turned out to be carrying Kennedy and nine of the MTB ratings who had been with him at Akyab.

Kennedy's group had left the Arakan coast on 24 March after they too received a signal with the magic words 'Proceed to UK'. They were again just one step ahead of the Japanese. Their ship, the *Ellenga*, sailed from Akyab with her decks crammed with refugees. After berthing at Calcutta they went straight to the station to catch the train to Bombay, where they stayed just long enough to do some shopping. They set sail on board the *Laconia* on 29 March—with Kennedy in charge of a total of just fifteen naval ratings on board the almost empty troopship—and made good progress across the Indian Ocean, overtaking Gandy and the others during their stopover in Durban, and arriving in Cape Town two days ahead of them.

After their surprise reunion in the dramatic setting of Cape Town harbour, Kennedy's group were ordered to transfer to the *Narkunda*, where they were warmly welcomed both as old shipmates and as extra hands to help guard the prisoners. With the Mediterranean closed, South Africa was getting plenty of practice at hosting British servicemen, and over the following week, the naval authorities offered their latest visitors a rich choice of entertainments and outings. By day, local residents took them for sunny drives to the botanical gardens and on cable car trips up Table Mountain; in the evenings, there were dinners at the Café Royal, drinks at the Blue Moon and parties where they were pleased to discover the Women's Auxiliary Air Force (WAAF) were also in town.

No one minded much when the *Narkunda* was forced to return with engine trouble soon after sailing from Cape Town on 18 April. Unfortunately, it was then discovered that they would be spending the next week anchored out in the bay and that there were no boats available to take them on shore leave. The ratings made the best of things by putting on their own concert, consisting of specially written songs and sketches that they had been rehearsing on board under the direction of the football captain, Stonell. Kennedy described the result in a single word: 'coarse'.

The young Scottish lieutenant had put on a lively show of his own a few days earlier, when at the end of a long night out in Cape Town, he had had trouble climbing up the ladder to the ship and had later been politely asked to stop playing the piano in the smoking room. He had gone back to his cabin and, as usual before going to bed, gazed at the photos of Rachel that he had been carrying with him ever since the day he waved goodbye to her ship at Lyemun Pass.

With the engine finally repaired, the *Narkunda* got under way on 28 April for the ten-day passage to Freetown, the only port of call on this final leg of the journey home. They stayed there for two days, and as they moved on up through the Atlantic, carried out frequent boat drills in preparation for an emergency. At each practice alarm, the hundreds of prisoners had to be brought up from two decks below and mustered at their boat stations. In contrast to the German prisoners-of-war that the ship had carried on an earlier trip, the remaining Italians turned out to be extremely docile and friendly.

The worst charge their sentries brought against them during the entire homeward run was that one of them had splashed water over the deck. He defended himself at an official hearing by saying he had done it 'for frolic'.

The British sailors had by now changed back into their winter uniforms, or 'blues', and with the temperature dropping further and the risk of attack growing, they were ordered to sleep in their clothes for the final few nights of the voyage. In the event, the *Narkunda* came through this trip unharmed, though both she and the *Laconia* were sunk before the year was out.

Until the last moment, it was unclear which British port they were being sent to. But as he looked out in the early hours of Friday, 22 May, and saw the misty rain sweeping in over the Firth of Clyde, Alick Kennedy, for one, knew that he was finally home. He walked round the deck one last time, picking out old haunts on the shoreline in the grey morning light, then sat impatiently in his cabin over Spam, biscuits and tea as the captain waited for the next tide to allow the ship to proceed further up the river into Glasgow.

The *Narkunda* finally tied up at 7 p.m. that evening at the King George V Dock. On board were twenty-four ratings and three officers from the original escape party that had left Hong Kong 148 days before.* They rode to Central Station on the back of luggage lorries piled high with kitbags before setting off by train to their various homes around the country to see wives, families and friends, many of whom thought they were dead.

Kennedy didn't have far to go to his own home, but soon discovered that his parents were out. The cook was mainly anxious to share details of her food rationing problems, but eventually told him they had gone to meet some people from Hong Kong called Smith. It was hard to believe, but after being completely out of touch for almost six months and travelling halfway around the world in different directions, he and Rachel had arrived back in their home country at the same port on the same day.

It turned out that the *Ulysses* had lived up to her name in her homeward wanderings, and that Ray and her father had had a journey almost as full of incident as his own. After surviving two days of dive-bombing attacks by Japanese planes in the South China Sea, they

---

148 days before: The flotilla's six telegraphists and the three others who had stayed on in the Burmese port of Akyab (Burrows, C Moore and Thorpe) sailed from Bombay on 14 April and reached Britain at the end of May.

had picked up three hundred women and children in Singapore and taken them to Australia, where the ship had undergone badly needed repairs. She had then sailed across the Pacific and through the Panama Canal, and was heading for Miami when she collided with another vessel. She limped on for a few more days, but on 11 April, off the coast of South Carolina, was hit by two German torpedoes and sank. The 300 passengers and crew were rescued from the sea by a US destroyer. Following several weeks of warm American hospitality, Hong Kong's former Colonial Secretary and his daughter left New York on board the SS *Myremidon* and, by extraordinary coincidence, sailed into Glasgow just a few hours ahead of the *Narkunda*.

After an emotional reunion, a long-delayed engagement was announced, and less than a month later, on Tuesday, 23 June 1942, Miss Rachel Lockhart Smith and Lieutenant Alexander Kennedy, RNVR, were married. The wedding hymn was 'O Perfect Love'.

Later . . .

RON ASHBY got back to England to find his wife Doreen—believing him dead—had found another man. He remarried in 1946, and he and Eileen celebrated their golden wedding shortly before he died. Ron spent the rest of the war as a flotilla leader, serving finally as Senior Officer, Coastal Forces, in the Arakan campaign to retake Rangoon. This earned him a Mention in Dispatches and a 'bar' to the DSC that he had won in the defence of Hong Kong. He retired from the navy after the war with the rank of commander and bought a boatbuilding and hiring company in Norfolk. For the next forty-one years, he and his family lived on a 72-foot motor torpedo boat, converted into a houseboat. According to his son, Vaughan—also a professional mariner—Ron remained 'the life and soul of any party' until his death at the age of eighty-seven in 1998.

LES BARKER married his prewar girlfriend, Ida, in 1943, and later that year took part in the invasion of Italy. After the war he found work as a mechanic in a sock factory. The job gave him the chance to move south from his mining town to the fresher, coastal air at Margate, where he brought up his two children. Les was a religious man, taught himself to play the piano and organ, and was an amateur painter. He looked after his wife, who died of cancer in 1992, and he lived on until 2002. It was his grandchildren to whom he told his war stories. Wanting to learn more after finding his wartime diary, his daughter Carol's eldest son, Russell, retraced the escape party's route in 2008 from Hong Kong to the China-Burma border.

TOMMY BREWER was Mentioned in Dispatches for services off the coast of Burma in May 1942 while serving as first officer on *HDML 1104*. After returning to England the following month, he transferred to the RNVR and was posted to HMS *Drake*, the Royal Naval shore establishment at Devonport, with the rank of temporary sub-lieutenant. Keen as ever for more excitement, he at once applied for transfer to the Fleet Air Arm, writing to his former commanding officer for a reference. Gandy gave him 5 out of 10 for professional ability, 5 for power of command, and 7 for zeal and energy. But his reply was returned unopened with a note giving the news of Brewer's death in a crash on the A1 on 28 July 1942. He was buried at Gillingham Cemetery in Kent.

EDMUND BRAZEL returned from his job at the Jardines office in Kunming to Wolverhampton in England, where he married Louie Hemingway at St Philip's Church on 12 July 1945. Soon afterwards the couple travelled out to Madras, where Eddie took up a job as a chartered electrical engineer, working for the local agents of English Electric (Stafford). They remained in India for more than twenty years, before returning to the UK to live at Fair Oak in Hampshire. Eddie died in June 2001 aged eighty-seven. His wife Louie passed away a few years before him.

CHAN CHAK worked closely with the Americans and British in the fight against the Japanese forces who continued to occupy much of China for the rest of the war. He was involved mainly in the exchange of intelligence and distribution of military hardware. In 1945 he became Mayor of Canton, but held the job for little more than a year. He was widely considered to be an incorrupt, capable and just official, and was, as ever, a clever strategist, but he continued to think of himself more as a military man than a politician. He was also out-weighed in power and influence by General Chang Fa Kuei, effective commander of South China. Admiral Sir Andrew Chan Chak died in Canton at the age of fifty-six on 1 September 1949, the day after hosting a large dinner party at which Leung Wingyuen was one of the guests. There was speculation that the Admiral might have been poisoned by an agent of Chiang Kai-shek, but his doctor blamed a recurrence of the stomach ulcer he had suffered during the escape, brought on by drink. He was buried with full military honours after a state funeral.

HOLGER CHRISTIANSEN gained a Mention in Dispatches for 'skilful and courageous services which enabled a party to make a daring escape from Hong Kong'. No further trace could be found of what befell the young Danish cadet in later life.

JOHN COLLINGWOOD returned home from India a few months after the rest of the flotilla, having stayed in Akyab until 18 April before making his way in late May from Calcutta to Ceylon. He was stationed at the Royal Navy base in Colombo from June to August, 1942.

He was Mentioned in Dispatches for distinguished service during the defence of Hong Kong. He married in 1943 and later in the war was based at Dover and Malta. Because of poor eyesight he retrained as an electrical officer. Then came a tour of duty in Istanbul, training Turkish officers. He retired from the navy after twenty-seven years' service and formed his own company specializing in the installation of electronic equipment on ships. He died in 2002. Seven years later, his widow Kay, at the age of eighty-nine, was the only first-generation member of HERO's visit to China.

LEN DOWNEY, *MTB 10*'s 'most reliable Able Seaman', had been advised by Kennedy in Burma to put in for advancement when he got home, but had replied: 'No, I'm quite happy, Sir, as a 3-badge A.B.' In the event, the two met up again in 1943 when Downey arrived at Fort William in Scotland as coxswain of one of the training motor launches. Len went on to serve on *ML 196* in the D-Day landings at Gold Beach, winning a Distinguished Service Medal after taking over the boat when his skipper was shot. According to his mother, he had suffered from nightmares ever since the Hong Kong escape and had begged her 'not to let the Navy send him to mental hospital.' He retired from the Royal Navy as a petty officer in 1948 and joined HM Customs, serving as a skipper of customs launches for twenty years before retiring to Totnes in Devon, where he died in 1979.

HORACE GANDY was Mentioned in Dispatches for 'daring and resource in Far Eastern waters' and for 'escaping as ordered'. He spent the rest of the war mostly at sea in Europe. He commanded HMS *Kingfisher* for two years, and led a squadron of landing craft in the relief of Holland. In 1946, Gandy was promoted to commander on the retired list. His wife, Dorothea, never fully recovered from the four years she spent in Stanley internment camp. The couple returned to Hong Kong, where Horace had worked before the war as a PWD land surveyor. For the next four years he was acting superintendent of Crown Lands and Surveys. In retirement, the Gandys lived in southeast England, Scotland and Holland. They finally settled in Devon, where 'Dolly' died in 1974 and 'Holly' thirteen years later at the age of ninety-one.

ARTHUR GEE stayed in Chungking doing cipher work at the embassy until June 1942, when he was seconded to the Army. On the way back to Britain, his ship was torpedoed in the Indian Ocean and he found himself adrift in a waterlogged raft, splashing the water to keep marauding sharks at bay. He was later commissioned into the Imperial RNVR and served as first officer on *ML 237*. He married in 1944, and after the war, went back to work at the *Hong Kong Mail* as night editor. Two years later, by now with two children, he moved to Canada and joined the Royal Canadian Air Force as a flight lieutenant ground crew. He developed his cipher skills and became an expert on nuclear defence. He returned to England in 1962 and worked for the Foreign Office as a cipher officer, but died three years later at the age of fifty-one.

ARTHUR GORING was promoted to lieutenant colonel in May 1942 after returning via Chungking to General Staff Branch in Delhi. He stayed on in India, where his brother Harold was also a general staff officer, and marked the first anniversary of the Christmas Day Escape by joining fellow officers Macmillan and Guest for a reunion meeting of what they christened the 'Aplichau Aquatic Club'. In August 1943, Goring was posted back to his old cavalry regiment, Probyn's Horse, which had recently become mechanized, and next year, was given command of a tank regiment in the Indian Armoured Corps. David MacDougall wanted to have him as his military adviser in the new administration in Hong Kong, but the appointment was turned down by Whitehall. Goring retired in the 1950s to a fruit farm in Devon.

FREDDIE GUEST and his friend Peter Macmillan carried out lecture tours for the Army in India, telling the story of their escape and giving tips on how to fight the Japanese. Freddie also gave instruction in the use of mules and packhorses to cadets bound for Burma. Towards the end of the war he rejoined his wife and young children in England. He was posted briefly to Germany after V-E Day but returned to civilian life in 1946, settling down with his family in Cheltenham, where he went to race meetings and played tennis, golf, snooker and bridge. His three books include one on a new variant of contract bridge. The idea for the game had come to him during his escape, he said, when he had kept a pack of cards in his pocket through thick and thin. The former Bengal Lancer, who by this time wore a monocle, also enjoyed going up to London to meet old friends for dinner at the Cavalry Club. He suffered a heart attack while driving his car in November 1962 and was dead before the ambulance reached hospital.

LES GURD, seen in photos of the escape with his nickname 'Lofty' on his helmet, stayed on in Calcutta, returning to join his wife and young son in Portsmouth after the war. His wife said later she was convinced 'he had met someone out East and had another family'. They later divorced. Les joined the Portsmouth City Fire Brigade and fought many local fires, some later in life with his son David by his side. In 1970, he was one of the first firefighters to board the blazing 3,000-ton Liberian supertanker *Pacific Glory*, which was carrying 70,000 gallons of crude oil when a collision off the Isle of Wight led to an explosion and a huge inferno. He never spoke about the war or his part in it, and had no inclination to travel abroad again, preferring to spend his retirement gardening, watching cricket and walking his dog. He died in 1999.

ROBERT HEMPENSTALL, who had spent some time in India in hospital with fever, returned home and joined HMS *Defiance* on 13 July 1942. He served in the Atlantic and later in support of the campaigns in France and Germany, qualifying for both the Atlantic and the France and Germany Stars. The cessation of hostilities in 1945 did not herald the end of Robert's service. He was then called upon to police the Mandate of Palestine. He was on the strength of HMS *St Angels*, which in October 1946 was being maintained, serviced and provisioned in the Palestine police security area at Haifa. Robert died there on 7 November 1946, at the age of twenty-seven, as a result of an explosion and not through enemy action. He was buried in the New War Cemetery at Haifa.

BUDDY HIDE married his longtime girlfriend eleven days after arriving back in England, and soon afterwards was sent back to sea. He was Mentioned in Dispatches for his role in Hong Kong, and in May 1945, was promoted to chief petty officer stoker mechanic. He remained in the navy until 1955. He then moved with his family to Tanganyika, working as a mechanical engineer in a diamond mine. On his return in 1958, he settled down to jobs in Hertfordshire, Essex and finally his home county of Sussex, where he worked in a water processing plant and enjoyed a quiet country life. He died in 1977 at the age of sixty-four. One of his three sons, Richard, runs the Hong Kong Escape website and became founding chairman of HERO. Another son, David, became the Australian representative on the committee.

JOHN HOLT, a former weaver at the Coronation Mill in the northern English town of Burnley, continued his naval service as an Able Seaman on many different ships and MTBs until the end of the Pacific War, when he was present on HMS *Teazer* at the surrender ceremony in Tokyo Bay. He returned to Burnley, met and married Edith, and they had two sons. John, known as Jack, worked for Marks and Spencer's department store and was active in the local Roman Catholic church. He died of a heart attack in 1963, when the boys, David and Stephen, were still very young. It was on the 60th anniversary of V-J Day in 2005 that they decided to find out what their father had done in the war. They learnt for the first time of the escape from his service records, and tracked down a local newspaper article from 6 January 1942 headlined 'Burnley Sailor in Hong Kong Escape'. After further enquiries they compiled a booklet about the escape in their father's memory, *John (Jack) Holt, A Biography 1941–46.*

HENRY HSU ended the war as captain of the Chinese Navy ship *Yung Ning.* He later began a successful business career in Hong Kong, becoming owner of the Hotel Fortuna Hong Kong. He also developed his earlier links with sporting and Christian communities. He was a member of the International Olympic Committee from 1970 to 1988, remaining an honorary member till 2009. He moved to Taiwan in 1982. As head of its Olympic Committee, he won recognition for Taiwan by the IOC under the name 'Chinese Taipei'. As well as developing his hotel business, he also served as a Member of Parliament and a presidential adviser. He attended the Beijing Olympics in 2008. Henry Hsu died in Taipei in February 2009, aged ninety-six, leaving a son and two daughters. He was given a state funeral, attended by Taiwan's President.

FW KENDALL was recommended by Britain's military attaché in China for a George Medal for his role in the escape, but he ended up getting nothing. He was forced to leave China in July 1942 because of political problems stemming from his communist contacts. There were also allegations from some of his senior British colleagues that his wife, Betty, who had joined him in Guangdong from occupied Hong Kong, was asking 'far too many indiscreet questions'. She was 'undoubtedly a nuisance and perhaps even a menace,' said one Foreign Office official. In one incident, Mike Kendall was alleged to have drawn a gun when his houseboat in Kukong was raided by police. He moved on to India, where he taught at the Force 136 Eastern Warfare School in Poona. He was then put in charge of an ambitious scheme to set out from Australia with a group of Canadian-Chinese he had trained as commandos and land by submarine on the South China coast. But the plan—Operation Oblivion—was cancelled after the Americans objected. In later years he worked in the airline business in Hong Kong, where he died in 1973. He was survived by Betty and their two children.

ALEXANDER KENNEDY served at the MTB training base at Fort William and the Naval College at Greenwich before joining the British Pacific Fleet to witness the Japanese surrender in Hong Kong. He took part in several small reunions of the escape party which took place soon afterwards in Hong Kong and Canton. He earned a Mention in Dispatches for his earlier role in the raid on Kowloon Bay. After the war, he returned to the family business and chaired many organizations associated with Glasgow or the laundry industry. Rachel died, tragically young, in 1956, after suffering stoically from asthma for many years. She left three sons, to be step-mothered two years later by Joy, a widow with three daughters, later joined by a half sister. Alexander's eldest son, Alick, says his father remained a popular 'pied piper' figure and enjoyed playing his bagpipes until his death in 1999.

DAVID LEGGE stayed on in China for most of the war, but soon found he hated living in the feverish atmosphere of Chungking and returned to Kunming, continuing to work in intelligence. After demobilization he returned to Shanghai, where his mother had remained, and married a medical secretary from Ireland. They moved in the 1950s to California, where he worked first for the coffee importer, Otis McAllister, and then, for seventeen years, for the airline, BOAC. David died in 2007. He spent his last years living in the home of his stepson, Steve, who described him as a 'sophisticated man-about-town who read voraciously and (when asked) loved to share his life's adventures'.

LEUNG WINGYUEN for a while became more powerful than ever following his official recognition by the Nationalists. But a split soon developed within his Mirs Bay group, and some members left to join the East River Column—taking with them weapons and stores from the MTBs. Leung was already at odds with other local guerrilla chiefs and had his first brush with the powerful communist group in October 1942. He was defeated and for a while switched allegiance to the East River band himself. But he was considered unreliable and the relationship ended in more conflict. He went his own way and soon disappeared from the area. In 1947, the British authorities in Hong Kong handed out monetary and other awards to various ex-guerrillas and ordinary fishermen and villagers for their 'gallant service in the Allied cause during 1941–45'. They included Leung Wingyuen, who received the King's Medal for Courage. Leung's son later worked for

Chan Chak's son Donald in Hong Kong, but the two families lost contact after the former guerrilla chief's death in the mid-1990s.

DAVID MACDOUGALL was posted soon after the escape to the United States, where he was reunited with his wife and daughter and worked to counteract American anti-colonial rhetoric. When Japan surrendered, he was rushed out to head Hong Kong's new civil administration, with the rank of brigadier and the task of feeding and rehabilitating the stricken colony. He also strove to reform aspects of prewar imperialism, such as 'whites only' areas, and to give the people a fuller share in government. In 1946 he became Colonial Secretary, a position in which he excelled. When he resigned in 1949, under the more conservative governorship of Sir Alexander Grantham, a petition was raised to keep him, but he wanted to return to Britain and try his hand at farming. He did, though, maintain a keen interest in Hong Kong. He had two more daughters by his second wife, Inez. David died in 1991 in Perthshire. His decorations included the CMG and, from China, the Order of the Brilliant Star.

PETER MACMILLAN stayed in India as a staff officer for almost two more years, lecturing and attending the staff course at Quetta. He returned to England and saw service with the Royal Artillery in northwest Europe, finishing up in Germany at the end of the war. By V-E Day he was at the Naval Staff College, where he met his wife and son off the SS *Cynthia* in the last convoy of the war. They had spent more than three years in prisoner-of-war camps at Baguio and Manila. Peter served briefly in the War Office before being given command of a Royal Artillery battery in Nigeria. At this point he left Viola and Robert—he and his wife were later divorced and both remarried. After postings to the Pentagon and the British Army of the Rhine, he formed a new RA unit in Edinburgh in 1956. He then served in Cyprus where he was badly wounded by a roadside bomb. He retired in 1965 as a colonel and died in Yorkshire in 1973 at the age of sixty.

COLIN MCEWAN remained in Guangdong Province for almost the entire war as a member of the BAAG. In his first letter home to his mother he said nothing about his escape—just that like all good gym teachers he had 'landed on his feet'. During a short spell in India in 1943, he helped sink a German ship in a sabotage operation in Goa—a story later turned into a Hollywood film, *The Sea Wolves*. For his war work in Hong Kong and China he received the MBE. After the war, and marriage to Elizabeth MacMillan, he returned to Hong Kong where he continued his career, becoming director of physical education. A keen proponent of outdoor activities, he introduced canoeing for young people. Ever the man of action, he chafed at promotion to a desk job and took early retirement to retrain as a chef in Scotland. Colin died in 1985.

CHRIS MEADOWS served in Gibraltar and on convoys to the Russian Arctic port of Murmansk. He met Doreen Bangay—a member of the WRNS whose brother had also been in the navy—at HMS *Mercury*, the naval shore establishment near Petersfield in Hampshire. The couple were married at Banham in Norfolk on 13 October 1944. They settled in Leicester, where Chris had been born. The former *MTB 10* telegraphist worked for the next twenty years as a carpenter, till his health deteriorated and he took up a new career as a clerk. He died in 1981 at the age of sixty-one. He is survived by two children—Ingrid and Christopher—and four grandchildren, one of whom married 'a gorgeous Japanese girl'.

HUGH MONTAGUE stayed only a short time in Rangoon after leaving Chungking, and in March 1942 served briefly as senior naval officer in Chittagong. He then returned to New Zealand, where he became boom defence officer. When an American naval party started to rig the anti-torpedo boom in Auckland Harbour, on 20 July 1942, he was moved to protest that 'while it is gratifying that the actual work should have been started, the feeble share borne hitherto by the R.N.Z. Naval Service is deplorable'. Commander Montague was made an OBE and was Mentioned in Dispatches 'for good services in charge of a party who made a daring escape by motor boat from Hong Kong'.

ALBERT 'PONY' MOORE, who had lifted spirits along the road to Waichow with his mouth organ, went back to his home town of Portsmouth to see his wife and two young daughters before returning to naval duty. He was soon seeing action in the Mediterranean, where he won a bravery award from the Greek government for his role in rescuing a merchant ship that had been hit by a German torpedo in rough seas. After the war, with an expanded family of four children, the Moores moved to North Wales, where Albert served as a lieutenant at the HMS *Conway* training school, teaching seamanship and signalling skills to cadets from the Royal and merchant navies. He retired to Leicester, where he joined the Corps of Commissionaires and worked in the front office of a printing firm. He remained fit, lively and 'fond of a lark', dying at the age of eighty-five 'of a broken heart', a fortnight after his wife, Bertha.

MAX OXFORD stayed on in Chungking till 1944 as Britain's assistant air attaché. While there he met and married Audrey Watson, an embassy secretary who had made her own hazardous journey to China from London, where she worked for the SOE. Max was promoted to wing commander and was later awarded the OBE. In October 1945, he returned to Hong Kong, becoming deputy director of civil aviation. In 1951 he became head of civil aviation in Malaya, staying on through the country's independence six years later. On retirement to Devon, he enjoyed music, brewing beer, gardening and family life with Audrey and their two daughters—one of whom, Emma, is on the committee of HERO. Max died in 1980 while out sailing his beloved boat.

TOMMY PARSONS, after recovering from his fall into a trench in upper Burma, flew to Calcutta, and then returned by boat to Britain. He was posted to HMS Hornet, a Coastal Forces base in Hampshire, where he saw active service in the English Channel, and in 1943 moved to another shore base, HMS Europa in Lowestoft. Later in the war he worked for naval intelligence in Ceylon. He was also involved in MI6 operations in southern China alongside the future Hong Kong Governor, Murray MacLehose. After the war he returned to Hong Kong, where, like his brother David, he worked for Jardine Matheson. He retired to England in 1969 but took up employment again for a few years with a shipping company in Cairo. He died in Tonbridge Wells in 1995.

DOUGLAS PETHICK was killed when his ship, the *Marilyse Moller*, was torpedoed and sunk northeast of Port Said on 6 July, 1942. The 786-ton steam merchant was on her way to Alexandria with a cargo of cased benzine, or petroleum ether. The master and 30 crew were lost. Four survivors were picked up by a passing ship.

ARTHUR PITTENDRIGH was Mentioned in Dispatches for 'skilful and courageous services which enabled a party to make a daring escape from Hong Kong'. By the end of the war, the former Chinese Maritime Customs officer had been promoted from temporary lieutenant to lieutenant colonel. He returned to Hong Kong after its liberation and joined MacDougall's new civil affairs administration, becoming commander of marine police. One of his first jobs was to bring the colony's more remote coasts and islands back under the rule of law and make them safe from pirates. He personally led a force to reoccupy the fishing ports of Tai O and Cheung Chau on 5 October 1945 at the request of villagers.

LEN RANN, the twenty-one-year-old stoker from *MTB 27*, spent the rest of the war on Atlantic duty. After being demobbed in 1945, he returned to the family home at Whippingham on the Isle of Wight, where he continued to live for the rest of his life. He started work at the Island Creameries, doing a daily milk round, and retired as area manager in 1983. He married in 1957, and he and his wife Sue had two sons, Ian and Keith. Len's main hobby after retirement was his large garden, and he also enjoyed walking and reading. He died in 2004. Seven years later, while looking for some old photos in the attic, Sue found an unknown diary that her husband had written during the escape.

WILLIAM ROBINSON returned to Calcutta but soon seized the chance to see more action. He flew to Lashio and took a train to Rangoon, but arrived just days before the evacuation. He went back to his old post in the Punjab, and from 1942 to 1949 was Superintendent of Police in Lahore and then Delhi. He received the Order of the British Empire in 1945 and the King's Police Medal in 1947. He and his wife, a member of the SOE, met and married in Lahore and returned in 1949 to Britain, where their daughter Philippa was born. In the 1950s Bill held senior police intelligence posts in Malaya and Cyprus. In the '60s he worked for the Commonwealth Relations Office, finding himself abroad again in 'interesting places at interesting times'. He retired to Dorset and died suddenly in 1972.

TED ROSS discovered that among his colleagues in his new position as transport manager for the British military mission was SK Yee. The two continued to meet for the rest of their lives. Ted's next job was with the British Political Warfare Mission in San Francisco, working alongside David MacDougall—with whom he also kept up a lifelong friendship, acting as best man at Mac's second wedding. In 1946, he accepted an offer to head up the Tokyo headquarters of Scott & English, a principal supplier to General Macarthur's administration in Japan. He later contracted tuberculosis and recuperated in Australia, there marrying June Kiel. Ted Ross returned to the Far East as head of the Hong Kong and Eastern Shipping Company Ltd and its Malayan mining affiliates. He held directorships of several other Hong Kong companies before retiring, with June and their two children, to their rural property in Australia in 1966. He died in 2005, aged ninety-three. His son Warwick is making a film of the escape.

CHARLES SKINNER, the merchant mariner from Sunderland with a taste for rice wine, returned to Hong Kong after the war and worked briefly for Swire shipping company as a 2nd/3rd officer. In December 1946, at the age of forty-six, he married a Miss Leung Loi-yee, daughter of Mr Leung Yung-ye of Aberdeen.

ROBERT STONELL, the stocky, bearded football captain and 'custodian of chow and cigarettes', received a Mention in Dispatches for his bravery and skill in taking over from *MTB 11*'s injured coxswain during the raid in Kowloon Bay. He went on to serve on HMS Theseus. His son, Christopher Theseus, was christened on board, using the ship's bell as a font. In later life Bob worked as a security man. His grand-daughter, Julie, remembers going into town on a Saturday 'to get his Baccy, his half bottle of whisky and to place a few bets on his favourite horse at the bookies'. Almost 40 years to the day after his dramatic escape, Robert Stonell died in December 1981 after falling out of an apple tree.

MONIA TALAN left China with Kendall in July 1942 and joined Force 136 in India. He was stationed in Calcutta as a general staff officer III and later as an assistant quarter master general. He returned to Hong Kong after the war, as Major Talan, MBE. He worked first as a member of the civil affairs section and later as an entrepreneur, with interests in both the travel and laundry businesses. He was often to be found playing tennis or bridge at the Jewish Recreation Club and became a director of Jimmy's Kitchen. His first marriage, to a glamorous English socialite, was a failure. The second, to an equally attractive East European called Tatiana, was very happy and resulted in two children. Monia's continued attempts to gain British citizenship met no success and he eventually moved to Australia. After Tatiana's premature death, he lived alone on an estate outside Melbourne where he kept his own horses—a lifelong interest. He died in 1999 aged eighty-six.

JACK THORPE was reported missing on war service on 19 January 1942, and his family feared the worst. More than four months later, his mother looked up from washing the dishes to see through the window, in his navy uniform, her only son opening the garden gate, smiling from ear to ear. After two weeks' leave, which saw the blossoming of a prewar romance with an Irish fisherman's daughter, Anne, Jack was posted to HMS *Defiance*, the naval training station at Devonport, Plymouth, where heavy German raids continued that summer. He then joined the destroyer, HMS *Mahratta*, based in northern waters off Scapa Flow. On leave in December 1942 he married Anne, but two months later, while escorting an Arctic convoy to Murmansk, his ship was hit by two torpedoes from a German U-boat. There were 17 survivors from a crew of 240. Of the newly married Jack Thorpe, there was no trace. His nephew, Jack Rosenthal, later wrote about the Hong Kong escape in a family history, *Letters from an Airfield*.

GILBERT THUMS got back to Plymouth at the end of May 1942 to find that not only was there a French sailor living with his wife, Hélène, but the couple had also had a baby. Now a commissioned bosun, Thums threw himself back into the war. In 1946, he was serving in a tug towing a 'battle practice target' when a shell intended for the target hit and sank the tug instead. He survived and was later Mentioned in Dispatches for distinguished service. He was divorced in 1947. After leaving the navy he returned to Nottingham, estranged from his children. He worked in the Royal Ordnance Depot, living in lodgings. He found it hard to adapt to his clerical job and to civilian life generally, and became increasingly isolated and depressed. His health deteriorated and he died in 1962, with his son living only a short distance away, unknown to either of them.

WILLIAM MORLEY WRIGHT was awarded the DSC for 'skilful and courageous services which enabled a party to make a daring escape from Hong Kong'. But there is no apparent record of what happened to him after he was sent upcountry from Rangoon soon after the escape party's arrival there on 14 February 1942. According to Gandy, 'all trace was lost'. However, the former Warrant Officer is known to have retired years later to a cottage on the banks of Loch Earn in Perthshire. Tommy Parsons' son Hugh recalls visiting him there as a schoolboy in the 1960s. "My father had said he ought to look after me well as he owed him a favour because he had fished him out of the water off Hong Kong. He seemed a very quiet old chap who spent his time gardening and listening to classical music on the radio." He died in 1981, at the age of 82.

YEUNG CHUEN continued living in China after the communists came to power in 1949. He owned a certain amount of land and leased his fields to peasants. Both his wives bore him children. His 'country' wife, in Longchuan, had two girls and a boy, but he left her soon after the end of the Japanese war. His 'town' wife had six sons, some of whom played with Chan Chak's sons in Canton in the late 1940s, flying kites together from the rooftops. The names of Yeung's sons, when put together, meant 'Chinese people be strong and steer the country towards the right route'. During the Cultural Revolution in the 1960s, Chan's former bodyguard suffered because of his background and lost his possessions to the Red Guards. But he was never seriously harmed, as no one would testify against him. He died in 1976 at the age of eighty. His 'country' wife continued to live in Longchuan until her death in 2011, and one of his seven sons is based in Nanao, where the MTBs were scuttled.

JOHN YORATH went on from Calcutta to Ceylon and from March 1942 was posted to HMS *Lanka*, the Royal Navy base in Colombo. In June 1943 he joined HMS *Highflyer*, the British naval base on the other side of the island at Trincomalee. At the end of that year he returned to the UK and from February 1944 until the end of the war was based in Cardiff as staff officer (Operations and Intelligence) to the flag officer in charge, HMS *Lucifer*. He died in 1980 in Surrey.

Notes

Page v
'balanced all the risks': James Bertram, *Shadow of a War*, London, 1947, p. 135.

Chapter 1 Last Ship Out

Page 3
Lyemun: now Lei Yue Mun.
Japanese attacks on junks: The National Archives (Public Record Office), Kew, London: ADM 213/1115 [National Archives/PRO referred to from here as Kew].

Page 4
'hysterical sieg heils': Alexander Kennedy, *Across Borders*; an unpublished personal account of his life and travels.

Page 5
'glamour boys' . . . hand signals: Arthur Gee, article in *Hong Kong Sunday Herald*, 9 Nov 1947.

Page 6
'Recent events should make': letter from Alexander Kennedy to his parents, 11 Nov 1941.
lieutenant's salary: Kennedy, letter to parents, 11 July 1941.
'downhomer' . . . ten shillings a month: Tim Carew, *The Fall of Hongkong*, 1960, p. 17.
'some Chinese girls . . . one doesn't need': Kennedy letter to parents, 5 Oct 1941.
'it gives men': Kennedy, letter to parents, 26 Oct 1941.

Page 7
birthday party: Kennedy, letter to parents, 10 Sep 1941.
'Nobody cared': Kennedy, *'Hong Kong' Full Circle 1939–45*, 1969, p. 17.
'when the balloon': Kennedy, *'Hong Kong' Full Circle 1939–45*, 1969, Foreword.

Page 8
'Would *you* want to share': Kennedy, *Across Borders*.
'She's a grand girl': Kennedy, letter to parents, 11 Mar 1942 (quoting his earlier letter, destroyed in bombing raid on 8 Dec 1941).
most expensive champagne . . . heartbreaking: letter from Rachel Smith to her mother (on Government House letterhead), 28 Nov 1941.

Page 9
'the most original': advertisement for ball, *South China Morning Post*, 4 Dec 1941, p. 2.
'Would all naval': quoted from firsthand memory by Michael Wright, former 2nd lieutenant gunner in the Hong Kong Volunteers (and later head of PWD), interview with author, London, 30 Jan 2008.

Page 10
'Read Ray's letter': diary of Alexander Kennedy, 1941–42, 7 Dec 1941.
torn between relief : Kennedy, *Full Circle*, p. 21.

Page 11
MTB movements, signals etc.: Ron Ashby, 'Fair Log' of *MTB 07*, 7–8 Dec 1941; John Collingwood, notes on battle; Kennedy diary, 7–8 Dec.
'underlying current': Kennedy, *Full Circle*, p. 22; and diary, 7 Dec.
more than forty warplanes: Donald Hill's RAF diary in Andro Linklater, *The Code of Love*, 2000.

Chapter 2 One-Legged Admiral

Page 12
'sampans and junks': David MacDougall, letter to his wife, Catherine MacDougall, 17 Jan 1942; Rhodes House, Oxford.
Chan's movements on 8 Dec: Chan Chak memoir, *Xiezhu Xianggang kang-zhan ji shuai Yingjun tuwei* (How I assisted in the war against Japan in Hong Kong and led British military men out of the encirclement), from the journal *Zhanggu Yuekan*, no. 4, Dec 1971, p. 16.

Page 13
'A tough little fellow': Morris 'Two-Gun' Cohen, quoted in *Life and Times of General Two-Gun Cohen*, by Charles Drage. New York, 1954, p. 282.
'Shoot first': interview with Duncan Chan, 22 Dec 2008, Hong Kong.
Chan's nickname: interview with Donald Chan, 1 June 2008, London. Chan Chak's original name was Chan Ming Tong. He later also became known as Chan Chau-shek ('clever and strong').
Chan's injury, operation and recovery: interviews with Donald Chan, and email 18 July 2010.

Page 14
'dark streaks of light': Freddie Guest, *Escape from the Bloodied Sun*, London, 1956, p. 18.

'If the Pacific War': Jen Yu-wen (Jian Youwen—or in Cantonese, Kan Yauman), *Ce Shu tuwei xiang ji* (A record of the escape of Uncle Chak), from the journal *Zhanggu Yuekan*, no. 4, Dec 1971, p. 22.

Page 15
calligraphy: Revd. James Smith and Revd. William Downes, *The Maryknoll Mission, Hong Kong 1941–46*. Journal of the Royal Asiatic Society Hong Kong Branch, Vol.19, 1979, p. 29.

Page 16
Maltby . . . in Battle Box . . . fighters: Tony Banham, *Not the Slightest Chance: The Defence of Hong Kong, 1941*. Hong Kong, 2003, p. 340.

Page 17
militarily mismanaged . . . 'willingness to fight': Maochun Yu, *The Dragon's War: Allied Operations and Fate of China 1937–1947*. Annapolis, Maryland, 2006, p. 60.

Page 18
kept a residence . . . and married: Carl Smith Collection, Hong Kong Public Record Office (images: 168983 and 761). The marriage ceremony was performed by Sun Yat-sen's son, Sun Foo, who was Mayor of Canton.
'gallantly . . . not equipped': Chan Chak, Chinese national radio broadcast on 'Youth and the Hong Kong Fighting', 20 Mar 1942; transcript in Kew, London: WO 208/381.
barefoot soldiers . . . banquets: Peter Moreira, *Hemingway on the China Front*. Washington DC, 2006, p. 96, 75.
Chungking's offers of army, etc.: Philip Snow, *The Fall of Hong Kong: Britain, China and the Japanese Occupation*. New Haven and London, 2004, p. 46.
'widespread delusion': report by Capt Charles Boxer, GSO III (Intelligence) on his visit to Japan, Sep 1939. Kew, London: FO 371/23573.
'so that British troops': Chan Chak broadcast, 20 Mar 1942. Kew, London: WO 208/381.

Page 19
'I created quite a stir': papers of Lt Col Harry Owen-Hughes, Imperial War Museum, Documents Section: 67/127/1. War Diary, 9 Dec 1941.

Chapter 3 Men from the Ministry

Page 21
'All well here': telegram to Catherine MacDougall, 11 Dec 1941.
'Get up': interview with David MacDougall conducted by Dr Stephen Tsang, 26 Feb 1987; transcript in Rhodes House, Oxford.
'pig-headed provincials . . . We cannot combat': letter to Catherine MacDougall, 27 Feb 1941.

Page 22
Meetings with Dai Li and Zhou Enlai: interview with David MacDougall conducted by Dr Stephen Tsang, 26 Feb 1987; transcript in Rhodes House, Oxford.
statues had been removed: Colonial Office papers, note by MacDougall, 27 May 1942. Kew: CO 129/591/20.
'I used a tin can': MacDougall, *Notes on the Siege*. Kew: CO 129/590/25.

Page 23
'The naval yard': CE Ross, letter to his mother written after arriving in Chungking, Jan 1942. Later published as 'Escape from Hong Kong' in *Maclean's magazine*, Canada, in three parts: 15 June, 1 July and 15 July 1942.
'cryptic': James Bertram, *Shadow of a War*. London, 1947, p. 109.
'The mainland . . . evacuated': *The Times*, London, 17 Dec 1941.
'They spotted . . .': Ross, letter to his mother.

Page 24
Chan's shadow government . . . vigilantes: Snow, pp. 59–61; Chan memoir, pp. 15–16.
'All the central government': MacDougall, *Notes on the Siege*.
'The Chungking representatives': Phyllis Harrop, Hong Kong Diary, 11 Dec. Kew: CO 129/590/23; and Harrop's book, *Hong Kong Incident*. London, 1944, pp. 71, 74.

Page 25
'wonderful . . . Arrests are being': Harrop, Hong Kong Diary, 12 Dec.
a hundred fifth columnists killed: interviews with Duncan and Donald Chan.
'SK Yee burst': Warwick Ross email, 28 May 2008.
'Internal order': MacDougall, *Notes on the Siege*.

Chapter 4 Battle Box

Page 27
'It felt so safe': Ross, letter to mother.

Page 28
'We're a bit in the dark': Alan Birch and Martin Cole, *Captive Christmas, the Battle of Hong Kong, December 1941*. Hong Kong, 1979, p. 160.
'psychological tomb': papers of Col. OJM Lindsay, IWM Documents Section: 65/124/1–9. Letter from Iain MacGregor, 28 Mar 1977.
'One rapidly became': Max Oxford, letter to his sister Margaret, written on the East River, 3 Jan 1942.
'most beautiful dug-out': Oxford, letter to Margaret.

Page 29
'Max Oxford had a . . . Everyone in Hong Kong': Emily Hahn, *China to Me*, 1944, p. 159.
'gentlemanly war . . . But the thought': Oxford, letter to Margaret.

Page 30

'It seemed a very long way': Arthur Goring, 'My Escape from Hongkong', *Wide World*, 'the magazine for men', Mar 1949, p. 295.

Goring's career: *Indian Army List*, Jan 1942.

'Suddenly a large number': George Wright-Nooth, *Prisoner of the Turnip Heads: Horror, Hunger and Humour in Hong Kong*. London, 1994, p. 37.

Robinson background: India Office Records, British Library (V/12/340–347).

Page 31

Robinson's careful handling . . . 'sullen and uncooperative': Colin Crisswell and Mike Watson, *The Royal Hong Kong Police, 1841–1945*. Hong Kong, 1982, p. 180. See also Snow, p. 68.

'Indian and Chinese families . . .': *War Diary of the Hong Kong Police*, 8–25 Dec 1941. Kew: CO 129/592.

'animated beehive': Lindsay papers, letter from MacGregor.

colourful scrapes: Freddie Guest, *Indian Cavalryman: Memoirs of a British Cavalry Officer in India*. London, 1959, pp. 48, 159.

Page 32

'we would not stand a chance': quoted by Anthony Hewitt in *To Freedom Through China*. Barnsley, 2004, p. 2. (Also published as *Bridge with Three Men*, London, 1986.)

'Freddie Guest came bursting in': Lindsay papers, letter from MacGregor.

flashing signals: Freddie Guest, *Escape from the Bloodied Sun*. London, 1956, p. 29.

'you're a tough beggar': Guest, p. 50.

Japanese cavalry: Lindsay papers, letter from MacGregor.

Page 33

'Robust, red-faced': Guest, p. 22.

Chapter 5 Cloak and Dagger Boys

Page 34

'took booby-traps': letter from Harry Owen-Hughes to Arthur Goring, 30 Dec 1942.

Page 35

'Canadian Bison': Col John Newnham, in a message from his POW camp in Hong Kong to the British Army Aid Group in China. BAAG archives, Ride Collection, the University of Hong Kong.

'Number One Guerrilla': Owen-Hughes papers, War Diary, 30 Dec 1941.

'quiet, soft-spoken': Dr Solomon Bard, email to author, 7 Feb 2009.

'Like all Mike's plans': Colin McEwan, *Tales from the City of Inexpensive Benevolence*, p. 16.

Page 36

Z Force's formation and role: see 'Introduction' by Dan Waters to *Colin McEwan's Diary: the Battle for Hong Kong and Escape into China*, Journal of the Royal Asiatic Society Hong Kong Branch, Vol. 45, 2005. Also papers written by Kendall (*Statement A*) and other members of Z Force (notably Maj. DR Holmes and Hugh Williamson), passed to Dr Waters by David Parsons, the last surviving member of the group, who died in 2006 without disclosing where he obtained them. Many of the papers are in the form of rough notes, with no indication of the date, or in some cases, the author. For the sake of convenience they are referred to here collectively as the 'Parsons papers'. NB: David was the younger brother of Lt Tom Parsons of *MTB 27*.

Madame Chiang Kai-shek and Free China passes: Hugh Williamson, *Statement on Z Force*, Parsons papers; see also Wright-Nooth, p. 39.

Kendall history: Anne Ozorio, *The Myth of Unpreparedness: The Origins of Anti-Japanese Resistance in Prewar Hong Kong*. RAS Vol.42, 2002; Marjorie Wong, *The Dragon and the Maple Leaf*, 1994; Kendall, *Statement A*, Parsons papers; SOE personnel files (PRO: HS 9/828/9).

Hainan agents . . . guerrillas: SOE Survey of global activities, Oriental Section, Oct 1941. Kew: HS7/221.

'pretty little piece': letter from Lt Col H Owen-Hughes to Col A Goring, 30 Dec 1942.

Page 37

visits to Flagstaff House: Lindsay papers, letter from MacGregor.

'Mike was endowed': Colin McEwan, letter to Bill Matheson, 20 Oct 1982.

$1000 a month: Daniel S. Levy, *Two-Gun Cohen: A Biography*. New York, 1997, p. 201.

Force 136, Singapore training: see papers of Maj. Gen. GE Grimsdale, IWM Documents Section: 8521; *Thunder in the East*, unpublished memoir, 1947.

Page 38

Minishant . . . 'Being a miserable': *Colin McEwan's Diary: The Battle for Hong Kong and Escape into China*, Dan Waters and Alison McEwan (eds.), Journal of the Royal Asiatic Society Hong Kong Branch, Vol. 45, 2005, 9 Dec 1941.

Page 39

'Out the platoon tumbled': McEwan diary, 9 Dec.

Page 40

'Some . . . threw hand grenades': Doi Teihichi diary, quoted in Oliver Lindsay, *The Lasting Honour*. London, 1978, p. 49.

'Aladdin's Lamps': Lane Crawford advertisement in *South China Morning Post*, 12 Dec 1941.

Chapter 6 Naval Light Brigade

Page 41
'windy buggers': papers of Lt Col JH Monro (10/16/1), IWM Documents Section.

Page 42
two small dry docks: The Lamont and Hope dry docks were built in 1868, when they were the only ones in Hong Kong. The No. 1 (Hope) dry dock was 428-feet long; No. 2 (Lamont) was 310 feet.

Thornycroft: The two old-style, 55-foot Thornycroft boats, with stepped hulls, had originally been ordered from Britain by China and were then reacquired from the Chinese by the Royal Navy for Hong Kong. They were not designed for extensive operations, being even smaller than the six Scott-Paine MTBs, produced by the British Power Boat Company, which made up the bulk of the flotilla.

'proceed into Kowloon Bay': John Collingwood, battle notes (unpublished, handwritten notes on the MTBs' role in the battle for Hong Kong; he also left a shorter, four-page account of the escape, also in note form).

'nothing remains': Ron Ashby, report to Admiralty on the 19 December raid. Kew: ADM 1/12382.

'the most daring adventure': Collingwood, battle notes.

'Our flotilla of MTBs': diary of Leslie Raymond Barker.

Page 43
'As we approached': papers of C Meadows, part 1. Imperial War Museum, Documents Section: 91/14/1.

Page 45
'Saw nothing': Ron Ashby, report to Admiralty.

Page 46
'slowest any of us': Arthur Gee, article in *Hong Kong Sunday Herald*, 9 Nov 1947.

'We went for': Collingwood, battle notes.

Page 47
'boring . . . Cantonese so-called seamen': David Legge, letter from China in January 1942 to his brother Brian, an RAF pilot. An edited version was published anonymously under the title 'With the MTBs, Escape from Hong Kong 1941' in the Hong Kong Defence Force journal, *The Volunteer*, Vol. 1, 1950.

'her motor mechanic': Gee, article in *Hong Kong Sunday Herald*, 9 Nov 1947.

Page 48
'They're not the only ones': Meadows papers, part 1.

'all ships in the harbour': papers of Capt AC Collinson RN, commodore in charge. IWM Documents and Sound Section: 66/361/1. *Commodore's*

Report on HK Operations, Admiralty, 1946. Enclosure C: *Events at Aberdeen*. Compiled by Commander HC Millett. 19 Dec. Also Kew: ADM 199/1286.
'Around us': Legge, letter to Brian.

Chapter 7 Exit Strategy

Page 51
'the power station': Ross, letter to mother.

Page 52
'The Japs don't love me': MacDougall, letter to Catherine MacDougall, 17 Jan 1942.
'certain duties': MacDougall, Tsang interview.
'I had good reason': MacDougall, letter to Lord Moyne, Secretary of State to the Colonies, from hospital in Chengdu, 3 Feb 1942. Kew: WO 208/733A.

Page 53
'Ross was keen': MacDougall, letter to Catherine.
Shaukiwan: (now spelt Shau Kei Wan). The fishing village near Lyemun had the biggest floating population in Hong Kong.
'Beyond that': Ross, letter to mother.

Page 54
'slow death': Guest, *Escape from the Bloodied Sun*, p. 58.
'What, planning your escape': Ted Ross, in one of a series of audio recordings of biographical interviews conducted and recorded by his son Warwick.

Page 55
Kendall meeting with Maltby: Marjorie Wong, *The Dragon and the Maple Leaf*, 1994, p. 120.
'so that Hong Kong information': Kendall, *Statement A*, p. 3.
'Chinese are still. . . . We cannot do': Colonial Office cable. Kew: CO 54058.

Page 56
'highest level': Wright-Nooth, p. 57.
'gentlemen's understanding. . . . He condemned himself': MacDougall, Tsang interview. NB: Ted Ross was more specific, saying in one of his recorded interviews with his son that 'the Governor guaranteed China Chan Chak's evacuation'.
'In general, the best chance': MacDougall, letter to Lord Moyne.

Page 57
'I was then given . . . The escape was': papers of Commander GH Gandy RN, Imperial War Museum, Documents and Sound Section: 66/42/1. Diary, 20 Dec 1941. NB: Gandy's various sets of notes are in rough form and often have no titles or page numbers, so it has been thought best to list them simply as 'diary' with the relevant date. All are to be found in the large box

of his papers in the documents section of the Imperial War Museum. He also sent some later, slightly different notes on the escape to the author, Oliver Lindsay, the original copy of which can be found in papers of Col OJM Lindsay, IWM Documents Section: 65/124/1–9.

Page 59
'feeding and argument': McEwan diary, 20 Dec.
'Her house': Harrop, *Hong Kong Incident*, p. 81; and diary, 20 Dec.
'since she looked': quoted in Ken Cuthbertson, *Nobody Said Not to Go: The Life, Loves and Adventures of Emily Hahn*. Boston, 1998.
'heaving our bedding': McEwan diary, 20 Dec.

Chapter 8 *Death of a Gunboat*

Page 60
Boxer injury . . . Forster, Price: Collinson papers, Appendix D, 21 Dec.
'all the British': Chan Chak memoir, p. 18.

Page 61
'There are indications': Major General CM Maltby, Despatch to the War Office: *Operations in Hong Kong from 8th to 25th December 1941*. Supplement to *The London Gazette*, 27 Jan 1948, par. 81.
'almost on a sixpence': quoted in Tim Carew, *The Fall of Hongkong*, 1960, p. 81.
'Oil fuel remaining': Collinson papers; report by Lt Cdr John Boldero on the last days of HMS *Cicala*.

Page 62
'Insolently': Bertram, *Shadow of a War*, p. 122.
'Stick after stick': Lieutenant Commander RB Goodwin, OBE, RNZNVR, *Hongkong Escape*. London, 1953, p. 6.

Page 63
'of great assistance': Gandy diary, 21 Dec.

Chapter 9 *Ducking and Diving*

Page 65
'The story of how': McEwan diary, 21 Dec.
'Here was the best . . . those heavenly twins': McEwan diary, 22 Dec.

Page 66
'They had been doing': Kennedy, *Full Circle*, p. 40.

Page 67
'authentic contact': Gandy diary, 21 Dec.
'Were we selfishly pleased!': Legge, letter to Brian, Jan 1942.
'shoot quick': Gandy papers, IWM: *Breaking from Encirclement: Unsensational Version*, 21 Dec.

Page 68
'liable to knock a man': Kennedy, *Full Circle*, p. 10.
'Flying Bedpan': Kennedy, *Full Circle*, p. 26.

Page 69
'while climbing out . . . that gallant sailor': McEwan diary, 24 Dec.

Page 70
Bush's Japanese wife: Lewis Bush, *The Road to Inamura*. Tokyo, 1972, p. 145.
'very worried': Gandy diary, 23 Dec.
'tough, bronzed': article in *South China Morning Post*, 17 Nov 1941.
'absolute chaos . . . the men were': Lt Col FW Kendall, *My Army and S.O.E. recollections*; sound recording of interview by Reginald H. Roy, 16 July 1968. Special Collections Library of the University of Victoria, British Columbia, Canada.

Page 71
'optimistic and encouraging': Gandy diary, 20 Dec.
'All of them': McEwan diary, 23 Dec.
'the Chungking people . . . nothing but intense anxiety': Harrop diary, 24 Dec.
Kendall in town: Richard Gough, *SOE Singapore 1941–42*. London, 1985, p. 63. NB: Gough acknowledges the help he received from FW Kendall in this account.

Page 72
'He left us with a': Benny Proulx, *Underground from Hong Kong*. New York: EP Dutton, 1943; quoted in Birch and Cole, *Captive Christmas*, p. 157.
'splendid rumour': Gandy diary, 24 Dec.
nearly adrift: *Note on Lt Parsons*, Gandy papers.
private letter: Gandy diary, 24 Dec. Gandy gave the commodore's letter to Montague in Kukong on January 14 and it was finally posted in Chungking.

Chapter 10 Surrender

Page 74
'the town was now helpless': Hong Kong Director of Public Works, quoted in Maltby Despatch, par. 116.
two of the civilians: Andrew Shields, an Executive Council member, and Major Charles Manners, a prominent businessman.
massacred: report to the British government on the fall of Hong Kong by Mrs Aloha Shields (the American wife of Peace Mission member, Andrew Shields). Kew: CO 129/590/25.

Page 75
'ruffians and Triad members': Wright-Nooth, *Prisoner of the Turnip Heads*, p. 56.
'What happened': MacDougall, *Notes on the Siege*, final paragraph.
'radical deterioration': Chan memoir, p. 18.

'imminent end of resistance': Jen Yu-wen, p. 23.
most disheartening Christmas Eve: Henry H. Hsu, *The 1941 Battle of Hong Kong*, unpublished report in English, p. 2.

Page 76

'break through . . . I then wrote on': Chan memoir, p. 19.
'I asked him if': Chan Chak broadcast, Mar 1942. Kew: WO 208/381.
the Governor invited: Henry Hsu, filmed interview with Donald and Duncan Chan, Hong Kong 2006.

Page 77

'Of course, but you've got': quoted by Ross, audio recording of family interview.
'coolie clothes': Ross, letter to mother.
only ones . . . asked to contact Chan: Guest, pp. 59–60.
Guest not a member: Lindsay papers, letter from MacGregor; GB Endacott, *Hong Kong Eclipse*. Hong Kong, 1978, p. 185.

Page 78

Guest destroying documents: Lindsay, *Lasting Honour*, p. 145; Banham, *Not the Slightest Chance*, p. 257.
'It's no earthly good': Charles Drage, *General of Fortune: The Story of One-Arm Sutton*. London, 1963, p. 256.
'thin, wan': John Stericker, *A Tear for the Dragon*, London, 1958, p. 43.
Robinson invitation: Wright-Nooth, p. 57.

Page 79

'I went into . . . "Sorry Iain"': Lindsay papers, letter from MacGregor.
'I told him again': Collinson papers, *Commodore's Report on HK Operations*, 25 Dec.
'Five minutes!' Goring, *My Escape from Hongkong*, p. 296.

Chapter 11 Waiting for the VIPs

Page 80

Aplichau: Ap Lei Chau, as it is now known, is today linked to Aberdeen by a bridge and boasts several high-rise estates, making it one of the three most densely populated islands in the world.
British battery: The battery's two four-inch guns pointed out to sea and had therefore been scarcely used throughout the battle.

Page 81

'received an Xmas . . . a good breakfast': Gandy diary, 25 Dec.
'Dinner consisted': diary of Leonard Rann, 25 Dec 1941.
'Except for a distant': Legge, letter to Brian.
Thums, Collingwood remarks: McEwan diary, 25 Dec.
'We returned from patrol': PO Stephen John Hide RN, *Sussex Express and County Herald*, Lewes edition, 5 June 1942.

Page 82
chicken . . . turkey: Gandy, who wasn't there, maintains in his diary that the Telegraph Bay group had turkey for their Christmas Day lunch—Kennedy, who was, says in *his* diary that they had chicken.
nuns . . . apple pie: John Robert Harris (Royal Engineers 1938–41), audio recording of Imperial War Museum interview, IWM Sound Section (22679/3).
'to swell their Xmas dinner table': Kennedy letter to parents, 5 Oct 1941.
'Go . . . Are you sure . . . We looked': Kennedy, *Full Circle*, p. 43.

Page 83
'unfit or unequal': Gandy papers, *Breaking from Encirclement*, 25 Dec.
'Propose go after dark': Lieutenant Commander Gerard Horace Gandy, official report to Admiralty, 8 Mar 1942: *Operations by the 2nd MTB Flotilla in Hongkong Waters December 8th 1941 to December 26th 1941*. Kew: CO 129 590/25 and ADM 267/131, 25 Dec.
'Go all boats': Gandy diary, 25 Dec.
'Ask Commissioner of Police': Gandy report, 25 Dec.

Page 84
'Should you be forced': Gandy report, 21 Dec.
'it was unheard of': Oliver Lindsay, *At the Going Down of the Sun, Hong Kong and South-East Asia 1941–45*. London, 1981, p. 7.
'Not only was I . . . come what may': Gandy diary, 25 Dec.

Chapter 12 Getaway Cars

Page 89
Japanese soldiers on Garden Road: Guest, *Escape from the Bloodied Sun*, p. 63.
plain-clothed agents: Chan memoir, p. 19.
'Christ, I wish we could go . . . Of course': Ross audio.

Page 90
hadn't the faintest idea: MacDougall, Tsang interview.
practice on stairs: Donald Chan, interview with author.
'Sino-British commander-in-chief': Ou Daxiong, *Dujiao Jiangjun Chen Ce chuan* (Biography of the One-Legged Admiral Chan Chak). Hainan, 1993, ch. 39.
'We go now': Guest, p. 64.

Page 91
craft along waterfront: Hewitt, *To Freedom Through China*, p. 1.
'Stop . . . MacDougall quickly . . . No, I'll take': Ross audio. Unlike One-Arm Sutton, Cohen survived prison camp, living till 1970. He made several visits to the People's Republic of China, first as a guest of Prime Minister Zhou Enlai and later as a consultant for various British defence firms.

Page 92
'For the local residents': Chan memoir, p. 19.
'I like the British': Sun Yat-sen, quoted in Drage, Cohen biography, p. 93.
ugly, gaping hole: Paul Tsui-ka Cheung, *My Life and My Encounters* (unpublished memoirs), ch.10.

Page 93
most intense shelling: Collinson Papers, *Events at Aberdeen*, Dec 25.

Page 94
'There were a lot of dead bodies': Henry Hsu, filmed interview by Donald and Duncan Chan, Hong Kong, 2006.
HMS *Robin*: Captain Douglas, *Weekly Intelligence Report no 122*, pages 8–11, 10 July 1942. Kew: ADM 267/131.

Chapter 13 Cornflower's Launch

Page 95
'most surprised': Commander Hugh Montague, report to Admiralty, *Proceedings of Party which Escaped from Hong Kong to China*. Kew: ADM 199/357, p. 7.
'The boats must . . . that's not much . . . if you can wait': Hsu, interview by the Chans; other details from Montague report and the various accounts by Ross and MacDougall.

Page 96
'Naval blokes are sly dogs': Guest, *Escape from the Bloodied Sun*, p. 67.
'continually passing': Guest, *Indian Cavalryman*, p. 182.
'we simply started': Guest, *Escape from the Bloodied Sun*, p. 65.
'We left it standing . . . Gosh': Ross, letter to mother.

Page 97
'getting quite worried': quoted by Goring, *My Escape from Hongkong*, p. 296.
'before a party of women': Guest, *Escape*, p. 67.

Page 98
'We set off': Goring, pp. 296–297.

Page 99
forty rifles: Goring, p. 297.
'thanks to the excellent': Chan memoir, p. 19.
through a blizzard . . . cool head: Hsu, *The 1941 Battle of Hong Kong*, p. 3.

Page 100
'that wonderful Damsgaard': Ross audio.
'it seemed every rifle': MacDougall, letter to Catherine.

abandon ship: Goring, letter to Harry Owen-Hughes, 20 Apr 1942.
Chan instructions: Poon Fook-wo, 'A Miraculous Charge' in *Young Companion Weekly*, Hong Kong, 17 Feb 1962; Chan memoir, p. 19.

Page 101
'harder than climbing to heaven': Henry Hsu, 'Xianggang Lunxian xing Chen Ce Jiangjun Tuwei', in *Huaxia Jibao*, No. 2, Aug 2005, p. 21.
'As a Christian': Hsu, *The 1941 Battle of Hong Kong*, p. 3.
become a convert: In a national broadcast a few weeks later, Chan, who was a Buddhist, thought it more expedient to attribute his survival to the miraculous powers of the Kuomintang than to God. He said he had been saved 'only by the Divine assistance of our National Father (i.e. the late Dr Sun Yat-sen) in the Heaven and the inspiration of the spirit of our leader (Generalissimo Chiang Kai-shek)'.
'surrender like a slave . . . Any more talk': Hsu, 'Xianggang Lunxian', p. 21.

Page 102
'The bullets were once again': Ross, letter to mother.

Chapter 14 The Island

Page 103
'It's just a small': Hsu, 'Xianggang Lunxian', p. 22.
'Although I was': Chan memoir, p. 19.
'sank like a stone': Goring, p. 297.

Page 104
'These horrible things': Guest, p. 70.
'I swam first . . . I reached': MacDougall, letter to Catherine, 17 Jan 1942.
'like someone putting in': Ross audio.

Page 105
'No sooner had I': Chan memoir, p. 19.

Page 106
'I tried to get over': Oxford, letter to his sister, Margaret, 3 Jan 1942.
'came across . . . parked behind a rock . . . run like a hare': Goring, p. 297.
'D.M. MacDougall, aged 37': MacDougall, letter to Catherine.

Page 107
'stupidity and futility . . . my feet soon became': Ross, letter to mother.

Page 108
'parley': McEwan diary, Dec 25.
'There's lots of chaps . . . lots of Japs': Christiansen as quoted by David Legge in his letter to his brother Brian the next month.
'quite a flap . . . Suddenly, over the top': Legge, letter to Brian.

Page 109
'Figures appeared': McEwan diary, Dec 25.
'It was extremely discouraging': Oxford, letter to Margaret.
'Grabbed by many hands': Gough, *SOE Singapore*, p. 64.

Page 110
'They might also think': Hsu, interview by the Chans.
'the mere thought': Guest, pp. 73–74.
very grateful: Oxford, letter to Margaret.
'Some angel': Goring, p. 297.
'dodged like water-rats': MacDougall, letter to Catherine.

Page 111
'it's okay' . . . beautiful and gratifying: Ross, letter to mother.
'a short, thick-set figure': MacDougall, letter to Catherine.

Chapter 15 *Finding the Admiral*

Page 112
'Call me Henry . . . hiding in a cave': Henry Hsu quoted in Gandy diary, 25 Dec.
'It was astonishing': Guest, p. 75.
'My wound was dressed': MacDougall, letter to Catherine.

Page 113
'apparently unarmed . . . kitless . . . unhealthy': Gandy diary, 25 Dec.
'still full of gunpowder smoke': Ou Daxiong, ch. 40.

Page 114
'Merry Christmas': Interview with Donald Chan, 30 Mar 2011.
'The admiral was': Yorath, quoted in Lindsay, *At the Going Down of the Sun*, p. 9.
'Thank God': unpublished 21-page account by William Robinson, beginning *'Here is a story for what it is worth'*, p. 12a.
Chinese versions: e.g. Ou Daxiong, ch. 40; Jen Yu-wen, p. 24.
ovation: Hsu, *The 1941 Battle of Hong Kong*, p. 4.

Page 115
'I no mind': Guest, p. 76.
'cheerfulness, pluck': Gandy diary, 25 Dec.
presenting it to him: Kennedy talk to HMS *Pioneer*, 10 Sep 1945.
'great pang of despair': Kennedy, p. 44.

Page 116
'meet west of Aberdeen': Gandy diary, 25 Dec.
'Out we came': McEwan diary (full original version), 25 Dec.

Chapter 16 Night Voyage

Page 119
'all this damned regatta stuff': Guest, p. 79.
'comfortable distribution': Gandy diary, 25 Dec.

Page 120
'If they get hold of': quoted by Wright-Nooth, p. 60.
'into the silence': Goodwin, pp. 19–20.

Page 121
'everyone on our floor': Harrop diary, 25 Dec.
'Signal by flashing . . . Sorry, Impossible': Meadows papers, 25 Dec.

Page 123
last sight of Hong Kong: Collingwood, escape notes.

Chapter 17 Shore Party

Page 124
'Although he was lying . . . spearhead': Hsu, *The 1941 Battle of Hong Kong*, p. 5.

Page 125
A biographer of Chan Chak: Ou Daxiong, *The Empty City strategy*, ch. 40. Henry Hsu in his later interview with Chan's sons says it was not in fact the Admiral who gave the advice but he himself. Since Chan was down in the cabin and Henry was standing on the bridge next to Gandy, this does seem a more likely scenario.
A young, tough Volunteer: Ross audio. Who this was we don't know—very possibly, William Morley Wright, the HKRNVR Warrant Officer.
no order given: Collingwood, escape notes.
'an escaping enemy': Kaigun ichihan shiryō, Dai ni kenshi kantai senshi nisshi sentō shōhō (Wartime Diary of HQ, Second China Fleet), 25 Dec 1941.
Ping Chau: the name literally means 'Flat Island'. The island in Mirs Bay is sometimes called Tung (East) Ping Chau to distinguish it from an island of the same name near Lantau.

Page 126
'Make for Ping Chau': quoted in Gandy/Lindsay papers, 25 Dec.
'We were all armed': Goring, p. 298.

Page 127
'We had 8 Lewis': Ted Ross, *Diary 1* (written in a notebook in the form of a letter, beginning 'Dear Folks').
'Anyone there?': this and the following passage are based on material in Hsu interview; Jen Yu-wen, p. 25; Ou Daxiong, ch. 40; McEwan diary; and interviews with the Chans and residents of Ping Chau.

Page 131
£25,000 MTBs: Goring, p. 298.

Chapter 18 Guerrillas

Page 135
'He smelt': Gandy diary, 26 Dec.
'Train the Lewis guns': Gandy diary, 26 Dec.
'A-hoy there': Goring, p. 298.

Page 136
false teeth: Kennedy, p. 47.
'most plausible individual': According to Gandy's diary for 30 Jan 1942, the British Consul in Kunming made out an official letter that day authorizing the police further along the escape party's route to take Skinner into custody if requested by the flotilla commander. Gandy added that he could never work out how Skinner got hold of the wine as he had 'stopped his money' long before.
'drunk while scuttling': Gandy diary, 26 Dec. In a letter the following year, Gandy wrote: 'The bottle of gin put out in the forecastle for the soaked and confused refugee party of military staff officers and Chinese crowding on board my boat must have been partaken of by others for it was a lachrymose coxswain who assisted me in scuttling the boat he'd spent 3 years in. He was admonished next day.' (Gandy papers, Nov 1942, IWM.)
'Not finding': Montague report, p. 8. By 7 p.m. MTBs *10* and *27* would have just moved round the headland to the southwest of Aplichau. The torpedo boats seen by Montague before sunset on the northwest corner of the island near Magazine Island must have been *MTB 10* giving *11* its tow start en route to Telegraph Bay.

Page 137
as long as ten minutes . . . 10.30 p.m.: Edmund Brazel, letter to his brother Bill, 16 Mar 1942.
'we were greatly alarmed': Montague report, p. 8.

Page 138
'We're Chinese and British': Hsu quoted by MacDougall in Tsang interview.
expecting a Japanese . . . trained their guns: recollections of villagers in Nanao, 27 Dec 2009.
'the commander's here': Hsu, interview by the Chans.
'They're anti-Japanese': Ross, *Diary 1*.
set up a 'market': Gough, p. 65.
launch . . . escorts . . . chests: Jen Yu-wen, p. 25; Donald Chan interview.

Page 139
'keen to fight': Chan memoir, p. 20.

Page 140
'During this period': McEwan diary, 25 Dec.
'With a hatchet': Kennedy, p. 47.

Page 141
'We had still to': Goring, p. 298.
'We have a hundred . . . without turning': Robinson, p. 13.

Page 142
'An interesting crowd': Guest, p. 85.

Chapter 19 Ready to March

Page 143
Kowtit: is today under a reservoir. The map used the Wade-Giles romanization of the Cantonese versions of place names. In Mandarin, using the modern pinyin system, the name would be written alphabetically as Gaotie.
map: War Office Map of HK & Canton, 1927 (names revised 1938); scale 1/250,00 (1 inch = 3.95 miles); British Library: 60875.

Page 144
'Excluding Admiral Chan Chak . . . The officer': Gandy diary, 26 Dec.
'Knowing that': Guest, p. 84.

Page 145
'Mr. Kendall of the Special Service': Montague report, p. 8.
'After we had landed': Arthur Goring, letter to Lt Col Colin Mackenzie, General Staff, India, 2 Jan 1943.
'Canadian with a various past': Hugh Williamson, *Statement on Formation of Z Force*, Parsons papers. Williamson was an early member of Kendall's SOE unit.
'continually obstructive': S/Ldr Russell. G.S.I.(e), G.H.Q. India, *Report on M.I.9, China* (PRO WO 208/3260), Appendix.
'totally unreliable': Lindsay Ride, letter to British embassy, Chungking, June 1942; BAAG Series Vol. 3, Ride Collection, the University of Hong Kong.
'a complete failure': Gordon Grimsdale, British Military Attaché, Chungking. Grimsdale papers, *Thunder in the East*.
'brave and tough': PA Macmillan, letter to Lt Col Colin Mackenzie, General Staff, India, 6 Jan 1943. Kew: HS 9/828/9.
'there are opportunities': A Goring, letter to Mackenzie, General Staff, India, 2 Jan 1943. Kew: HS 9/828/9.

Page 146
an 'army': Goring, *My Escape* magazine article, p. 298.
'we could not help': McEwan diary, 27 Dec.
'Our Tommies': McEwan, *Discourse on Guerrillas and Cakeshops*, unpublished essay.

'They're experts': Gandy diary, 26 Dec.
'Mostly they were . . . The average guerrilla': MacDougall, newspaper article, 'Japs Dread Guerrillas', *The Standard*, Montreal, 21 Feb 1942.

Page 147
'a devil of a lot of rice': Guest, p. 90.
'dreaded hum': Guest, p. 87.

Page 148
'Ready to march! . . . You'll need': Kennedy, p. 49.
muttered the staff officers: Guest and Macmillan, quoted by Guest, p. 87.
explosives . . . fish: recollections of Nanao villagers, 27 Dec 2009.
'It's yours, old boy': Kennedy, pp. 48–49.

Page 149
'In all, the pack': Legge, letter to Brian.
'From Albion Point': Gandy diary, 26 Dec.

Page 150
'But Brucie's': based on information from Collingwood's widow, Kay, son Nigel and daughter Pippa.
'Shells from': Bush, *The Road to Inamura*, p. 139.
'most tiresome mongrel': Goring, p. 298.

Page 151
hard to sleep on: Kennedy diary, 26 Dec.
'matey places . . . most penetrating': Gandy diary, 26 Dec.

Chapter 20 Through Japanese Lines

Page 153
'like a team of . . . However': Kennedy, p. 50. Montague and Pethick may have seemed old to the others, but official records show them to have been only fifty-three and fifty-two respectively.
'Our following train': McEwan diary, 27 Dec.

Page 154
'The rarefied air': Guest, p. 91.
threw away their rifles: Ross audio.
'This march . . . But willpower': Gandy diary, 27 Dec.
'The only thing': BBC Radio talk recorded in July 1942 by *MTB 07*'s leading stoker, Charlie Evans. BBC Sound Archives/4889. IWM Sound Section (acc. no. 2556).
Dafengkeng: Taifunghang in Gandy's diary. Now Lowutian reservoir, just east of the town of Kuichong.
'in a meadow for tiffin': Gandy diary, 27 Dec.
smugglers' route: this section of the old stone path, over a wooded hill between Lo Wu Tian and Shitouhe reservoirs, still survives today.

Page 155
'The guerrillas knew': Ross, letter to mother.
'masterly scouting': Montague report, p. 8.
'Those guerrillas': Legge, letter to Brian.
little devils: Chan Sui-jeung, *East River Column: Hong Kong Guerrillas in the Second World War and After*. Hong Kong, 2009, p. 50.
Tangpu: or Tong Po, as McEwan has it in his diary, using the Cantonese version. The village and duck pond remain but are now next to a large hydro-electric complex.
Heshuxia: Hoshueha in Gandy's diary, again using the Cantonese. The name literally means 'down the river and under the tree'.

Page 156
Wang Jingwei: was a Nationalist Party rival of Chiang Kai-shek's who ran a Japanese-supported collaborationist government in Nanjing.
'pro-enemy agencies . . . I organized': Chan memoir, p. 21.
'The guerrillas went': Ross audio (1974).
'The guerrillas . . . What a mix-up': Gandy diary, 27 Dec.

Page 157
'prepared to put up': Barker diary, 28 Dec.
'It was again': Kennedy, p. 51.
'we all crashed': Goring, p. 299.
'However, our guerrilla escort': Ross, letter to mother.
'You could almost reach out': Ross audio.

Page 158
'Ready to march . . . the road stretched': Kennedy, p. 52.
'Once again we were free': Edmund Brazel, letter to brother Bill, 16 Mar 1942.
'My heart would pound': Guest, p. 95.

Page 159
'To our astonishment': Goring, p. 299.
'negotiating . . . sumptuous gifts': Jen Yu-wen, p. 25.
McEwan said: statement to Sub-Lt DF Davies, HKRNVR, of Lindsay Ride's escape group, Jan 1942. Kew: CO 129/590/23.
second river: the Xishu—another branch of the earlier one, the Danshui River.
Sishui: what was then a lychee orchard is now the site of the Palm Island Golf Resort, with a course designed by Jack Nicklaus Junior, aimed at today's weekend escapers from Hong Kong.
'Apparently acting'. . . 31 miles: Gandy diary, 27 Dec. Kennedy put the total for the day at 25 miles. As the crow flies the distance is more like 16 miles, but that does not allow for the twisty paths and circuitous route.

Page 160
'the moon for a blanket': Barker diary, 28 Dec.

Chapter 21 Into Free China

Page 162
'Just a rough track': Barker diary, 28 Dec.
'Ready to fall over': Evans, BBC talk.
'I belong to the New China': Gandy diary, 28 Dec.

Page 163
pro-Nationalist guerrilla group: MacDougall, *Japs Dread Guerrillas*.
Yenan: Yan'an, Shaanxi Province—now a communist shrine.
East River Column links: Chan Sui-jeung, p. 27.
Zeng Deping: interview with author, 27 Dec 2009.
'was sighted . . . I took aim . . . Puff!': Gandy diary, 28 Dec.

Page 164
Spandau machine guns: German-made MG 42's.
'Here we were': Montague report, p. 8.
'smart, pleasant-looking': McEwan diary, 28 Dec.
'cooks of messes . . . now that the eyes . . . I made the mistake': Gandy diary, 28 Dec.

Page 165
$1 oranges: Ashby log, 28 Dec.
'great fresh duck eggs': McEwan diary, 28 Dec.
military post: David Bosanquet, *Escape through China*. London, 1983, p. 135.
Dashanxia: Taisanha in Kennedy's diary—literally, 'below the big mountain'. The half-ruined walled village was still there in 2011, with the Chinese characters for 'Kill Japanese' scrawled on one wall.

Page 166
reinforcements . . . What a pity: Chan memoir, p. 20.
One story has it: Jen Yu-wen, p. 26; Snow, p. 76.
'Really good Chinese food': Ashby log, 28 Dec.
'Dinner was': McEwan diary, 28 Dec.

Page 167
'extremely comfortable': Goring, p. 299.
'My recollection': Gandy diary, 28 Dec.

Chapter 22 Welcome to Waichow

Page 168
'My particular host': Goring, p. 300.

Page 169
'I was worried': Ross audio.
'No hardship': quoted in Gandy diary, 29 Dec.
six men: Kennedy diary, 29 Dec.
Fenghuang Gang: listed by Kennedy as Fung Wong Kung. Teahouse, temple and duck pond were all still there seventy years later.
'At about 1200': Barker diary.

Page 171
'A host of dogs': Kennedy, p. 54.
'I felt an irresistible': McEwan diary, 29 Dec.

Page 172
'milling conglomerate': Bosanquet, p. 145.
'a most delightful place': Goodwin, *Hongkong Escape*, p. 137.

Page 173
Stars and Stripes: Tsui, ch. 14.
'the Chinese nurses': Barker, 30 Dec.
'a great treat': Kennedy, p. 54.
'by some form of': McEwan diary, 29 Dec.
3,000 people: Hsu, *The 1941 Battle*, p. 5.
twenty courses . . . 'unlimited delicacies': Kennedy diary, 29 Dec.
week's meat ration: Goring, p. 300.

Page 174
He thought fondly: Kennedy, p. 54.
'None of us sailors': Barker diary, 31 Dec.
small china spoon: Lindsay, *At the Going Down of the Sun*, p. 14.
toasts: Ashby log, 29 Dec.
'very keen': Collingwood, escape notes.
'I don't remember': Gandy diary, 29 Dec.

Chapter 23 Photos and Shopping

Page 175
'close-packed organization': Gandy diary, 28 Dec.
'It did seem a pity': McEwan, 30 Dec.

Page 176
'had not made a sound': Collingwood's family, interviews.
'as spick and span': Gandy diary, 30 Dec.
'I shall always keep': Barker, quoted in his local paper, *The Hucknall Dispatch*, 10 July 1942.

Page 177
'It was a warm': Goring, p. 300.

'very agitated': Kennedy, p. 55.
Canton Bay: present-day Zhanjiang.
cosy agreement . . . generals' concern: Gough, p. 66.

Page 178
'A good meal': Gandy diary, 30 Dec.
'dear old Chinese dame' . . . wash up: Goring, p. 300.
'Up rose the Major': McEwan diary, 30 Dec.

Page 179
'our memories . . . for the honour . . . No point': Gandy diary, 30 Dec.

Page 180
'How many are you': Owen-Hughes papers, message sent via Maj. Gen. Chu Lai Chuen, 29 Dec.
'surgical aid . . . virtually a guerrilla': Gandy diary, 30 Dec.

Page 181
'fantastic' prices: Ashby log, 30 Dec.
'My camera': Legge, letter to Brian.
'took out a great': Ross audio.

Page 182
'It was very new': MacDougall, Tsang interview.
'One could speak': Kennedy, p. 56.

Chapter 24 River Boats

Page 186
'for some purpose . . . unnecessary . . . it didn't take' Gandy diary, 31 Dec.
'usual fee': Kendall, *Statement A*, Parsons papers.
Shuihu Juan: also published in English under various other titles, including *Men of the Marshes* and *All Men Are Brothers*.

Page 187
'I see 108': Ou Daxiong, ch. 41.

Page 188
'A grander trio': Robinson, p. 15.
Waichow hogmanay: McEwan diary, 31 Dec.
'b. cold' . . . 'v. unpleasant': Kennedy diary, 31 Dec.
'open fore and aft': Ashby log, 31 Dec.
'the wind whistled': Legge, letter to Brian.

Page 189
'pretty gorge': Collingwood, escape notes.
'They'd all look': Russell Joyce, told to author, Jan 2010.
'The scenery': Barker diary, 1 Jan 1942.

Page 190
'Old Pethick . . . Our boat': Gandy papers, *V2's Diary*, 1 Jan.
'much overcrowded': Oxford, letter to sister Margaret, written on the East River on 3 Jan 1942.
'take the damned': Guest, *Escape from Bloodied Sun*, p. 102.
'To think that': Guest, *Indian Cavalryman*, p. 188.
$300 . . . police: Gandy diary, 1–2 Jan.

Page 191
1.5 million people: Graham Peck, *Two Kinds of Time*. Boston, 1950; Beijing, 2004, p. 24.
getting enough to eat: Kennedy, *Hong Kong: Full Circle, 1939–45*, p. 57.
buns and oranges: Ross audio.
dispute over bully beef: Guest, *Escape*, p. 103.
chickens: Guest, p. 109.
Guanyinge (Guonyumkok): Ross, *Diary 2* (day-by-day notes), 2 Jan.
warmer and pleasanter: Ashby log, 2 Jan.
'very little room': Goring, p. 301.
Gandy shouting: Ashby log; Kennedy diary, 3 Jan.
'I got considerable': Gandy, 2 Jan.

Page 192
Heyuan: Kennedy diary, 3 Jan. (Mr Deng's is one of several original name cards included in the *Escape From Hong Kong* exhibition.)
'Under way again': Barker diary, 3 Jan.
'barbel-like fish': Gandy, 3 Jan.

Chapter 25 'Bow, You Buggers, Bow'

Page 193
'where the hell': Owen-Hughes papers, *Report from Kwangtung Province—December 1941/January 1942*, 18 Feb 1942.

Page 194
'We had to': Legge, letter to Brian.
'excellent preparations': Owen-Hughes papers, War Diary, 3 Jan.
'for our comfort': Barker diary, 4 Jan.

Page 195
'went down . . . perforce': Owen-Hughes, War Diary, 4 Jan.
'you heroes . . . you heels': Collingwood, escape notes; Kennedy, p. 59.
'a deep shade of pink': Guest, p. 112.
'British Party': Kennedy, p. 59.
'Ship's Company': Goring, p. 302.
'Come on': Guest, p. 112.
'Never before': Goring, p. 302.

Page 196
'Where his troops ate' . . . long chat: Owen-Hughes, War Diary, 4 Jan.
'the inevitable result': Oxford, letter to Margaret.
'It did seem . . . The personnel': Owen-Hughes papers, Report on Mission to China.
'excuses of one sort . . . A study of': Owen-Hughes papers, Mission to China.

Page 197
clear evidence . . . 'carved up with knives': Capt PA Macmillan, *Reported Japanese Atrocities during the Siege of Hong Kong*, Kew: CAB 106/11.
'The latter': Owen-Hughes, War Diary, 5 Jan.

Page 198
'Our Chinese hosts': Kennedy, p. 60.
'As these came': Goring, p. 302.
'excellent' coffee: Brazel, letter to Bill.

Page 199
'pleasant little town . . . in two long lines': Kennedy, p. 60.
10,000 troops: Ashby log, 6 Jan.
'looked as if': MacDougall, Tsang interview.

Page 200
'one some 1,200 years': Ashby log, 6 Jan.
'I do not imagine': Owen-Hughes, War Diary, 6 Jan.

Chapter 26 Kukong Comforts

Page 201
'choir of maidens': Goring, p. 303.

Page 202
parade . . . 'good public parks': Gandy diary, 6 Jan.
Hankow: On the north bank of the Yangtze in central China, Hankow was one of three adjoining cities which merged to form present-day Wuhan.
attack by thirteen planes: Owen-Hughes, War Diary, 31 Dec 1941.
a hundred people: memorial plaque in today's central Shaoguan.

Page 203
'rather primitive': Gandy diary, 6 Jan.
'English pictures': Guest, p. 116.
Minsheng Street ('People's Life' Street): now called Dong Di Yi Lu.

Page 204
drinking contest: Moreira, *Hemingway on the China Front*, p. 75.
black patch: Gandy diary, 6 Jan.
fat and prosperous: Kennedy, p. 62.

high circles: Legge, letter to Brian.
share the room . . . Owen-Hughes, War Diary, 6 Jan.
first bath: MacDougall, letter to Catherine, 17 Jan.

Page 205
'Welcome . . . Smash': Ashby log, Kennedy diary, 7 Jan.
'Democracies . . . Hail': Ross, *Diary 2*, 7 Jan.
speeches: Barker diary, 7 Jan.
'spouts like a': Owen-Hughes, *Report from Kwangtung* and War Diary, 7 Jan.
'No fancy': Gandy diary, 7 Jan.
Japanese plane: Goring, letter to Owen-Hughes, 26 July 1942.

Page 206
dependable hospital: Tsui, ch. 12. The mission hospital is now the Yuebei People's Hospital, the largest in the region. One of the old houses in the compound where the foreign doctors lived has been turned into a charming museum.
'very short . . . the peanut butter': Jean Moore, 'Bend in the River', in *Daughter of China*, edited by Margaret Moore, privately published, 1992, p. 5.
Colin MacDonald: Ross, audio.
'first direct contact': *The Times*, London, 8 Jan 1942.

Page 207
discovery of a jacket: Guest, p. 99.
one member of the party: Brazel, letter to Bill, p. 3.

Page 208
air raid alarms: Ross, *Diary 2*, 12 Jan; Kennedy, p. 64.
'feverish buying': Ashby log, 8 Jan.
'the ministration of the barber': Owen-Hughes papers, *Statement of expenses incurred by party which escaped from Hong Kong with Admiral Chan Chak*, 22 Jan 1942.
'iniquity of': Gandy diary, 8 Jan.
'Shopping is difficult': Oxford, letter to Margaret.

Page 209
'very homey . . . piles of tea': Papers of Major EB Teesdale, IWM Documents Section: 90/6/1, diary, 20 Feb 1942.
'custodian of chow': Gandy papers, summary of later stages of journey: *2nd MTB Flotilla Party ex-Hongkong crosses China to Burma*, Jan–Feb 1942, p. 13.
'ground too small': Gandy diary, 9 Jan.
'small football': Ashby log, 9 Jan.
to play in goal: Kennedy diary, 9 Jan.
Christiansen . . . Pethick: Owen-Hughes, War Diary, 8 Jan.

Page 210
'must have been': Moore, p. 6.
IXL an Australian company that began making jams in 1898.
Chan's operation: Jen Yu-wen, p. 26; Ou Daxiong, ch. 41; Moore, p. 6;
Owen-Hughes war diary, 8 Jan. Having almost fainted when he learned for
the first time that the bullet was still inside him, the Admiral later had the
offending item mounted in gold and wore it on the end of a chain for the rest
of his life.
Peredur Jones: letter from the missionary's brother, G Whittington Jones, to
A Kennedy, July 1942; Moore, p. 6.
'bereft of paint': Moore, p. 7. The British Army Aid Group later paid to have
the stairs repainted.

Chapter 27 *Parting of the Ways*

Page 211
'bold and patriotic': Jen Yu-wen, p. 26.
Leung appointment: Ou Daxiong, ch. 41.
'typical Cantonese officer': J Arthur Duff, 'Escape from Hong Kong to Free
China, January and February 1942', *South China Morning Post*, Hong Kong,
p. 29.
'In the evening . . . It is the business': Duff, p. 29.
Yeung mission: interview with his sons, Yeung Yu-kwok and Yeung Yu-zhong,
Hong Kong, 28 Oct 2009; email from his granddaughter Ellen Sin, 15 July
2009.

Page 212
Chan family escape: interviews with Anita, Donald and Duncan Chan.
'flatly despised': Peck, p. 417.
hadn't even fought . . . military HQ visit: Owen-Hughes, War Diary, 20/10 Jan.
'concrete and . . .': Major A Goring, *Some notes on Japanese methods used in
their invasion of Hong Kong.* 1942. Kew: CAB 106/11.
'fanatical bravery': Capt PA Macmillan, *Notes on strength, organization
and tactics of Japanese troops employed against Hong Kong.* 1942. Kew: CAB
106/11.

Page 213
'raging fever' . . . left for Chungking: Goring, p. 303.
'I had come': Guest, *Escape from the Bloodied Sun*, p. 116.
'great relief . . . own people': Guest, *Indian Cavalryman*, p. 188.
'flew by the seat': Ross audio.
'My gosh': Ross, letter to mother.

Page 214
'charming and intelligent': Wladimir Petro, *Triple Commission*, London,
1968, p. 190.

Page 215

'Here I am': MacDougall, letter to Catherine, 17 Jan 1942.

'rather unsatisfactory': letter to Sir Archibald Clark Kerr from EC Wilford, Chief Surgeon, West China Canadian Mission Hospital in Chengdu, after examination of MacDougall's wound, 31 Jan 1942. Kew: WO 208/733A.

'the East': Guest, *Indian Cavalryman*, p. 189.

'to talk about Hong Kong': Owen-Hughes, War Diary, 19 Jan.

Page 216

'fit and cheerful': letter from David MacDougall to Alexander Kennedy's mother, 26 March 1942.

rags and a monocle: Dr Douglas Scriven, who joined the Red Cross after his escape and remained in southern China.

Page 217

birth of the BAAG: Elizabeth Ride, email to author, 15 Jan 2010; Edwin Ride: *BAAG, Hong Kong Resistance 1942–1945*, 1981, p. 49; and Owen-Hughes, War Diary, 30 Jan.

'09 still had': Colin McEwan, letter to Alexander Kennedy, 17 May 1970.

'made to pay hell': Gandy diary, 14 Jan (quoting news from Chinese military HQ).

Page 218

'doing some practice . . . During their terrible': letter from Suyamu, 3 Mar 1942. Kew: ADM 199/1287.

Page 219

Harbour Mission Church: *South China Morning Post*, 28 Dec 1945.

Henry's Bible: Hsu, interview by Chans.

SK arrest: Owen-Hughes, War Diary and personal diary, IWM, 5–8 Feb; Kendall, *Statement A*; Ross, audio; McEwan, *Tales*, ch.1.

Page 220

'Unhappily, by this time': Report on Mission to China.

'He is a very loyal': War Diary, 30 Jan.

'foster and return': Owen-Hughes papers, report from Kwangtung Province.

'In appreciation': Owen-Hughes papers, letter to Major General Chu Lai Chuen, 6 Feb 1942.

'The officers who': GE Grimsdale, cable to War Office from Chungking, 31 Mar 1942. Kew: WO 208/301.

Page 221

'great energy': General Archibald Percival Wavell, cable to War Office from Delhi, 19 Apr 1942. Kew: WO 208/301.

'Throughout our trip . . . To this end': Montague report, final page.

Page 222
'stump up': handwritten note on letter to Colonial Office from Sir Horace Seymour, July 1943; Kew: FO 371/35862.
'In the fake war': Jen Yu-wen, p. 26. Chan pays the British the compliment of favourably comparing the defence of Hong Kong with that of Canton three years before.
'An ancient saying': broadcast on national Chinese radio, 20 Mar 1942.

Chapter 28 Journey to the West

Page 224
'And to you': Gandy diary, 16 Jan.
$80,000: Gandy summary (of last part of journey), p. 2.

Page 225
'I believe that': Gandy, quoted in Lindsay, *At the Going Down of the Sun*, p. 17.
'Before we knew': Barker diary, 23 Jan.
'I found myself': Legge, letter to Brian.

Page 226
'He should have . . . capable of . . . not on results': Gandy papers, letter addressed to the Admiralty, Dec 1942.
'Who looked after': Collingwood, letter to Gandy, Nov 1942; Gandy papers.

Page 227
'all I can get': Kennedy, p. 73.
finished . . . entire stock: Dr John Grindlay diary, Manuscripts Division, University of Minnesota library.
cigarettes: Barker, *Hucknall Dispatch*, 10 July 1942.
'We all bunked': Legge, letter to Brian.

Page 228
'prosecute the war . . . Lieut. Commander Yorath': Gandy diary, 24 Jan.
'very thoughtless . . . huge British': Grindlay diary.
'We were totally': Kennedy, p. 76.

Page 229
'stiffen like a': Kennedy, p. 77.

Page 230
'a rowdy lot': Gandy summary, p. 7.
'But the amazing . . . Yes, absolutely': Kennedy, p. 80.

Page 231
'I can only pray': Kennedy letter, 31 Jan 1942.
'haven of rekitting': Gandy summary, p. 8.

Page 232
'The Burma Road': Evans, BBC talk, July 1942.
twenty to Dali: Ashby log, 3 Feb.

Page 233
'Saw 3 Tibetan': Gandy diary, 3 Feb.
Dali church: Kennedy diary, 3 Feb. Fifty years after Lt Kennedy was there, his granddaughter Liza visited the church, and it was she who found out from local people the story of how it was built.
'Delay over eggs': Kennedy diary, 5 Feb.

Page 234
'despite the failings': Kennedy, p. 85.
'own folk': Gandy, summary, p. 11.
'tasted like nectar': Kennedy, p. 86.

Chapter 29 Burma Shave

Page 235
Burmans: or Bamar, as Burma's dominant ethnic group are now known.
commandeered Dodwell trucks: Ashby log, 7 Feb 1942.

Page 236
'it seemed a': Kennedy, p. 86.
billiard score: Kennedy diary, 10 Feb.

Page 237
'hot compress': Gandy papers, medical report from Dr Wong, 9 Feb.
'in rather . . . so far . . . I consider': Gandy summary, pp. 12–13.
an 'astonishingly cheap': Gandy papers, Itinerary and Expense Accounts.

Page 238
'For the wind': Kipling's poem *Mandalay* was first published in 1892 in the collection *Barrack Room Ballads*. It was adapted for the song 'On the Road to Mandalay' by Oley Speaks and recorded by Peter Dawson in 1939.
'quite a good-looking': Meadows papers, 13 Feb.
'gaunt and ragged': Field Marshal Sir William Slim's famous description of the state of his British, Indian and Gurkha soldiers after their initial withdrawal, before they regrouped and eventually retook Burma by the end of the war.
some reflected: Kennedy, p. 87.
'ghastly odour . . . like flocks': Eve Curie, *Journey among Warriors*, 1943, p. 316.
'Waiting for a train': *Daily Sketch*, 27 Feb 1942.

Page 239
'A few bombs': Gandy, quoted in Lindsay, *At the Going Down of the Sun*, p. 18.

Page 240
'The Silver Grill': Kennedy, p. 89.
Fleurette Pelly . . . 'much better': Kennedy diary, 15–17 Feb.

Page 241
Jessen gun plan: Ashby papers.

Page 242
'Officers are walking': Rann diary, 3 March 1942.
'Fires being lighted': Ashby log, 26 Feb.
all shot: Hide, quoted in *Sussex Express and County Herald*, 5 June 1942.
other reports: e.g. Kennedy, p. 94; Ashby log, 4 Mar.

Chapter 30 Glasgow Bound

Page 244
'back in civilization' . . . Calcutta unaware: Ashby log, 12 Mar 1942.
forty different dishes: Curie, p. 306.

Page 245
Gurd, Schillemore, Priestley: Gandy papers, list of individual appointments and destinations.

Page 246
'no time': Ashby log, 26 Mar.
'very unsatisfactory poker': Gandy diary, 2 Apr.

Page 247
'coarse': Kennedy diary, 23 Apr.

Page 248
'for frolic': Kennedy, p. 108.

Chinese names

Aplichau (Apleichau) 鴨脷洲
Bias Bay (Daya Bay) 大亞灣
Bijia Shan 筆架山
Chan, Anita 陳琼芬
Chan Chak (Chen Ce) 陳策
Chan Chi (Chen Ji) 陳籍
Chan, Donald 陳安國
Chan, Duncan 陳安邦
Chen Jitang 陳濟堂
Chen Qi 陳琦
Dafengkeng 大鳳坑
Dai Li 戴笠
Danshui 淡水
Dapeng 大鵬
Dashanxia 大山下
Deng Yingyuan 鄧應元
Dushan 獨山
Fenghuang Gang 鳳凰崗
Guanyinge 觀音閣
Heshuxia 河樹下
Heyuan 河源
Hosai 河西
Hsu, Henry (Heng) 徐亨
Jen Yu-wen 簡又文
Jiang Guangnai 蔣光鼐
Jinchengjiang 金城江
Kowtit (Gaotie) 高鐵
Kuichong 葵涌
Kukong (Qujiang) 曲江
Leung Shuichi 梁少芝
Leung Wingyuen 梁永元
Lianping 連平
Liao Chengzhi 廖承志
Li Hanhun 李漢魂

Lim, Robert (Kho seng) 林可勝
Longchuan 龍川
Longxian 龍仙
Luowutian 羅屋田
Lyemun (Lei Yue Mun) 鯉魚門
Mirs Bay 大鵬灣
Nanao 南澳
Nanhua 南華
Nanxiong 南雄
Ou Daxiong 歐大雄
Paiya Shan 排牙山
Ping Chau 平洲
Shaoguan 韶關
Shayuchong 鯊魚涌
Shitouhe 石頭河
Sin, Ellen (Yuk-ping) 冼玉萍
Sishui 四水
Tangpu 塘橫
Tiantou Shan 天頭山
Tsui, Paul (Ka-cheung) 徐家祥
Waichow (Huizhou) 惠州
Wai On 惠安
Wang Dafu 王達夫
Wangmu 王母
Wuliting 五里亭
Wu River 武江
Wutong Shan 梧桐山 (五洞山)
Xinxu 新墟
Yee SK 余兆祺
Yeung Chuen 楊全
Yeung Yu-kwok 楊汝國
Yeung Yu-zhong 楊汝中
Yi He 義和
Yu Hanmou 余漢謀

Zau Sinmay (Shao Xunmei) 邵洵美
Zeng Deping 曾德平
Zeng Sheng 曾生
Zhangshu Pu 樟樹埔
Zheng Jiemin 鄭介民
Zhenlong 鎮隆
Zhen River 滇江
Zhong Shan 中山

Bibliography

Correspondence, diaries and interviews

Ashby, Ronald. 'Fair Log' of *MTB 07*, 1941/2 and other papers. Family collection.

—— Report to Admiralty on 19 December raid. Kew: ADM 1/12382.

Ashby, Vaughan. Interviews and correspondence with author.

Barclay, Jane (MacDougall). Interviews and correspondence with author.

Bard, Solomon. Correspondence with author.

Barker, Leslie Raymond. Diary. Family collection.

Beardsley, Eric and John (Thums). Interviews and correspondence with author.

Brazel, Arthur. Email to author, 10 Mar 2011.

Brazel, Edmund H. Letter to brother, Bill, 16 Mar 1942. Family collection.

Calthrop, Supt LHC (ed). *War Diary of the Hong Kong Police*, 8–25 Dec 1941. Kew: CO 129/592.

Chan Chak. Diary and papers. Family collection.

—— *Youth and the Hong Kong Fighting*, Radio broadcast to China's youth, 20 Mar 1942. Central News Agency transcript in English. Kew: WO 208/381.

Chan, Anita. Interview with author, 21 Dec 2009.

Chan, Donald. Interviews and correspondence with author.

Chan, Duncan. Interview with author, 22 Dec 2008.

Cochrane, Ingrid (Meadows). Telephone interview, 17 Mar 2011.

Collingwood, John. Notes on battle and escape. Family collection.

Collingwood, Kay, Nigel and Pippa. Interviews with author.

Collinson, AC. *Commodore's Report on Hong Kong Operations*. Admiralty, SW1, 1946. Papers of Captain AC Collinson RN, IWM Documents Section: 66/36/1.

Evans, Charlie. Radio talk, recorded July 1942. BBC Sound Archives/4889. IWM Sound Section: acc. no. 2556.

Forster, Michael. Correspondence with author.

Forsyth, Penny (Gee). Email to author, 7 Mar 2011.

Gandy, Horace. Diary and other manuscripts. Papers of Commander GH Gandy RN, IWM Documents Section (66/42/1); see also Papers of Colonel OJM Lindsay, IWM Documents Section: 65/124/1–9.

Giles, Julie (Stonell). Emails to author, Mar 2013.

Goring, Arthur. Correspondence with Harry Owen-Hughes, 1942–4. Owen-Hughes family collection.

Grimsdale, Gordon. *Thunder in the East*, unpublished memoir, 1947. Papers of Major General GE Grimsdale, IWM Documents Section: 8521.

Grindlay, Dr John. Diary. Manuscripts Division, University of Minnesota library.

Guest, Fred. Interview with author, 5 June 2010, and email 4 Mar 2011.

Harris, John Robert. Audio recording of interview, IWM Sound Section: 22679/3.

Harrop, Phyllis. Hong Kong Diary. Kew: CO 129/590/23.

Hide, Richard. Interviews and correspondence with author.

Holroyd, Max. *A Good War*. Unpublished account of his father Maxwell Holroyd's escape, Jan 1942. Family collection.

Holmes, Major DR. *East River Guerrilla area*. Kew: HIS/171

——— Statement 'B'. *Statement by Hon R. Holmes, Force Z.* Parsons papers, Waters Collection.

Holt, Stephen. Interview 11 Mar 2010 and correspondence with author.

Hooper, Philippa (Robinson). Interviews with author, 2013.

Hsu, Angela. Correspondence with author.

Hsu, Henry H. *The 1941 Battle of Hong Kong*, 5-page unpublished report in English. Family collection.

——— Filmed interview with Donald and Duncan Chan, Hong Kong, 2006.

Hunt, Alf. Interview with author, 25 Sep 2008.

Hyatt, Lucy and Helen (Owen-Hughes). Interviews and correspondence with author.

Joyce, Carol (Barker). Interviews with author.

Joyce, Russell (Barker). Interviews and correspondence with author.

Kaigun ichihan shiryō (KIS). *Dai ni kenshi kantai senshi nisshi sentō shōhō* (Wartime Diary of HQ, Second China Fleet), 1-31 Dec 1941. NDI, JACAR, Ref: C08030033500.

Kendall, FW. *Statement A*, 6-page handwritten account of his role in the Hong Kong battle, the escape and SOE actions in China. Parsons Papers, Waters Collection.

——— *My Army and S.O.E. recollections*, sound recording of interview by Reginald H. Roy, 16 July 1968. Special Collections library of the University of Victoria, British Columbia: Record ID 00000225.

Kennedy, Alexander. Correspondence, diaries, scripts of talks, articles. Family collection.

——— *Across Borders*. Unpublished personal account of life and travels. Family collection.

Kennedy, Alick. Interviews and correspondence with author.

Kennedy, Liza. Diary of China trip, 1992.

Klein Bog-Kruize, Nel (Gandy). Interview on 1 Aug 2009 and correspondence with author.

Legge, David. Letter to his brother, Brian, Jan 1942. Family collection.

Lindsay, Oliver. Correspondence and manuscripts. Papers of Colonel OJM Lindsay, IWM Documents Section: 65/124/1–9.

MacDougall, David. Correspondence and papers. Rhodes House, Bodleian Libraries, Oxford.

—— Interview by Dr Stephen Tsang, 26 Feb 1987. Transcript in Rhodes House. Tape in family collection.

—— *Notes on the Siege* and other reports and official letters. Kew: CO 129/590/25.

—— Telegrams, personal letters. Family collection.

MacGregor, Iain. Letter to Oliver Lindsay, 28 Mar 1977. Lindsay papers, IWM.

Macmillan, Capt PA and Goring, Maj A. *Notes to War Office and Cabinet Office on Japanese invasion of Hong Kong*, 1942. Kew: CAB 106/11.

Macmillan, Robert. Interviews and correspondence with author.

Madden, Margaret (Hempenstall). Emails to author, Mar 2011.

Maplesden, Sheila (Gurd). Emails to author, 22, 24 Feb 2011.

Mathews, Steve (Legge). Emails to author, Apr 2008.

McEwan, Colin. Correspondence and war diary (full original—see also Published Works). Family collection.

—— *Tales from the City of Inexpensive Benevolence*, unpublished personal account of war years with the BAAG in Yanping, Guangdong. Family collection.

—— *Discourse on Guerrillas and Cakeshops*, unpublished essay. Family collection.

Meadows, Christopher. Diary. Papers of C Meadows, IWM Documents Section: 91/14/1.

Monro, John. Diary. Papers of Lieutenant Colonel JH Monro, IWM Documents Section: 10/16/1.

Montague, Commander Hugh. Report to Admiralty: *Proceedings of Party which Escaped from Hong Kong to China*. Kew: ADM 199/357.

Moore, Ted. Telephone interviews, Feb 2009, 13 Mar 2011.

Owen-Hughes, Harry. Diaries and reports. Papers of Lieutenant Colonel H Owen-Hughes, IWM Documents Section: 67/127/1.

—— Correspondence with Arthur Goring, 1942–4. Family collection (Owen-Hughes).

Oxford, Emma. Interviews and correspondence with author.

Oxford, Max. Letter to his sister Margaret in Cape Town, 3 Jan 1942 ('on the East River'). Family collection.

Parsons, David. *The Recce Unit HKVDC*, 8 Aug 1995. Parsons papers, Waters Collection.

Partridge, Ann (MacDougall). Interviews and correspondence with author.

Rann, Leonard. Diary. Family collection.

Rann, Sue. Correspondence with author.

Recaldin, Sheena (MacDougall). Interviews and correspondence with author.

Ride, Elizabeth. Correspondence with author.

Robinson, William. 21-page story of escape. Family collection.

Rosenthal, Jack (Thorpe). Correspondence and interviews with author.

Ross, C. E. (Ted). Letter to his mother, Jan 1942. (Edited version published later that year in *Maclean's* magazine as '*Escape from Hong Kong*'.)

——— Diaries, 1 and 2, 1941–2. © C.E. Ross 1985. Family collection.

——— Audio recordings of interviews with his son Warwick Ross and other family members, 1970s and 80s. © C.E. Ross 1985.

Ross, Warwick. Interviews and correspondence with author.

Scott, Susan (Legge). Interviews and correspondence with author.

Sin, Ellen (Yeung). Correspondence with author.

Smith, Rachel. Letters to her mother and fiancé. Kennedy papers.

Storr, Christian (Downey). Emails to author, 14, 15 Apr 2009.

Teesdale, Eddie. Diary. Papers of Major EB Teesdale, IWM Documents Section: 90/6/1.

Titchen, Roy and Jacqueline (Thums). Interview, 16 Aug 2009 and correspondence with author.

Williamson, Hugh. *Statement on Z Force*. Parsons papers, Waters Collection.

Wright, Michael. Interviews with author, 2008–10.

Yeung Yu-kwok and Yeung Yu-zhong. Interview with author, 28 Oct 2009.

Zeng Deping. Interview with author, Dec 27, 2009.

Archives

Bodleian Libraries, University of Oxford.

British Library, India Office and East Asian collections.

Hong Kong Public Record Office, Carl Smith Collection.

Hong Kong University, Ride Collection.

Imperial War Museum, Documents and Sound Section.

National Archives (Public Record Office), Kew, London.

University of Victoria, British Columbia, Special Collections Library.

Published Works

Allen, Louis. *Burma: The Longest War 1941–1945*. London: Dent, 1984; Phoenix, 2000.

Banham, Tony. *Not the Slightest Chance: The Defence of Hong Kong, 1941*. Hong Kong: Hong Kong University Press, 2003.

Bertram, James. *Shadow of a War*. London: Victor Gollancz, 1947.

Birch, Alan. Articles on the SOE, the escape and the BAAG. *South China Morning Post*, 12 and 13 Oct 1973, and 29 Jan 1978.

—— and Martin Cole. *Captive Christmas: The Battle of Hong Kong, December 1941*. Hong Kong: Heinemann Asia, 1979.

Bonavia, David. *China's Warlords*. Hong Kong; Oxford: Oxford University Press, 1995.

Booth, Martin. *The Dragon Syndicates: The Global Phenomenon of the Triads*. London: Doubleday, 1999.

Bosanquet, David. *Escape through China*. London: Robert Hale Limited, 1983.

Bush, Lewis. *The Road to Inamura*. Tokyo: Charles E. Tuttle Company, 1972.

Carew, Tim. *The Fall of Hongkong*. London: Anthony Blond, 1960.

Chan Chak. Memoir: *Xiezhu Xianggang kangzhan ji shuai Yingjun tuwei*, in *Zhanggu Yuekan*, no. 4, Dec 1971, pp. 14–21.

Chan, Sui-jeung. *East River Column: Hong Kong Guerrillas in the Second World War and After*. Hong Kong: Hong Kong University Press, 2009.

Chapman, F. Spencer. *The Jungle is Neutral*. London: Chatto & Windus, 1948.

Cooper, Bryan. *[P.T. boats] The Buccaneers*. London: MacDonald & Co., 1970.

Crisswell, Colin and Watson, Mike. *The Royal Hong Kong Police, 1841–1945*. Hong Kong: Macmillan, 1982.

Crow, Carl (Ed: Paul French). *The Long Road Back to China: Along the Burma Road to China's Wartime Capital in 1939*. Hong Kong: Earnshaw Books, 2009.

Cruickshank, Charles. *SOE in the Far East*. Oxford and New York: Oxford University Press, 1983.

Curie, Eve. *Journey among Warriors*. London: Heinemann, 1943.

Cuthbertson, Ken. *Nobody Said Not to Go: The life, Loves and Adventures of Emily Hahn*. Boston; London: Faber & Faber, 1999.

Drage, Charles. *General of Fortune: The Story of One-Arm Sutton*. London: William Heinemann, 1963.

—— *Life and Times of General Two-Gun Cohen*. New York: Funk & Wagnalls, 1954.

Duff, J. Arthur. *Escape from Hong Kong to Free China, January and February 1942*. Hong Kong: printed by South China Morning Post, undated.

Endacott, GB. *Hong Kong Eclipse*. Hong Kong: Oxford University Press, 1978.

Field, Ellen. *Twilight in Hong Kong*. London: Frederick Muller, 1960.

Fragrant Harbour magazine, Hong Kong. June, July/Aug issues, 2004.

French, Paul. *Carl Crow: A Tough Old China Hand*. Hong Kong: Hong Kong University Press, 2006.

Gandt, Robert L. *Season of Storms: The Siege of Hongkong 1941*. Hong Kong: South China Morning Post Ltd, 1982.

Gee, Arthur. Articles in *Hong Kong Sunday Herald*, 9–13 Nov 1947; *China Mail*, 5 Feb 1948.

Goodwin, Lt-Com RB. *Hongkong Escape*. London: Arthur Barker Ltd, 1953.

Goring, Lt-Colonel Arthur. 'My Escape from Hongkong', *Wide World* magazine, Mar 1949, pp. 295–305.

Gough, Richard. *SOE Singapore 1941–42*. London: William Kimber, 1985.

Guest, Captain Freddie. *Escape from the Bloodied Sun*. London: Jarrolds, 1956.

——— *Indian Cavalryman: Memoirs of a British Cavalry Officer in India*. London: Jarrolds, 1959.

Hahn, Emily. *China to Me*. Philadelphia: Blakiston, 1944.

Harland, Kathleen. *The Royal Navy in Hong Kong since 1841*. Liskeard: Maritime Books, 1985.

Harrop, Phyllis. *Hong Kong Incident*. London: Eyre & Spottiswoode, 1944.

Hemingway, Ernest. *For Whom the Bell Tolls*. New York: Charles Scribner's Sons, 1940.

Hewitt, Anthony. *To Freedom Through China*. Barnsley, UK: Pen and Sword, 2004 (also published as *Bridge with Three Men: Across China to the Western Heaven in 1942*, London: Jonathan Cape, 1986).

Hide, PO Stephen. Article in *Sussex Express and County Herald*, 5 June 1942.

Hsiao Ch'ien. *Harp with a Thousand Strings*. London: Pilot Press, 1944.

Hsu, Dr Henry H. *Xianggang Lunxian xing Chen Ce Jiangjun Tuwei*, Taiwan. Reprinted in the Hong Kong magazine, *Huaxia Jibao*, No. 2, Aug 2005, pp. 17–24.

Jen Yu-wen. *Ce Shu tuwei xiang ji*, in *Zhangu Yuekan*, no. 4, Dec 1971, pp. 22–27.

Jung Chang and Halliday, Jon. *Mao: The Unknown Story*. London: Jonathan Cape, 2005.

Kennedy, Lt. Alexander. *'Hong Kong' Full Circle 1939–45*. London: privately published, 1969.

Ko Tim Keung and Wordie, Jason. *Ruins of War: A Guide to Hong Kong's Battlefields and Wartime Sites*. Hong Kong: Joint Publishing (HK) Co., 1996.

Konstam, Angus. *British Motor Torpedo Boat, 1939–45*. Oxford: Osprey, 2003.

Levy, Daniel S. *Two-Gun Cohen: A Biography*. New York: St Martin's Press, 1997.

Li Shu-fan. *Hong Kong Surgeon*. London: Victor Gollancz, 1964.

Lindsay, Oliver. *The Lasting Honour*. London: Hamish Hamilton, 1978.

——— *At the Going down of the Sun*. London: Hamish Hamilton, 1981.

Linklater, Andro. *The Code of Love*. London: Weidenfeld & Nicholson, 2000.

MacDougall, David. Article headlined 'Japs Dread Guerrillas' in *The Standard*, Montreal, 21 Feb 1942.

Maltby, Major-General CM. Report to the War Office, *Operations in Hong Kong from 8th to 25th December 1941*. Supplement to *The London Gazette*, 27 Jan 1948.

Marsman, Jan Henrik. Article on the Battle for the Repulse Bay Hotel. *Saturday Evening Post*, 6 Jun 1942; *Sunday Express*, 9 Aug 1942.

Matthews, Clifford and Cheung, Oswald (eds). *Dispersal and Renewal: Hong Kong University during the War Years*. Hong Kong: Hong Kong University Press, 1998.

Moore, Jean (Ed: Moore, Margaret). *Daughter of China*. Privately published, 1992.

Moreira, Peter. *Hemingway on the China Front*. Washington, DC: Potomac Books, 2006.

North, Denise. *John (Jack) Holt: A Biography 1941–46*, compiled by David and Stephen Holt. Scarborough: Farthings Publishing, 2010.

Ou Daxiong, *Dujiao Jiangjun Chen Ce chuan* (Biography of the One-Legged Admiral Chan Chak). Hainan Publishing Company, 1993.

Ozorio, Anne. The Myth of Unpreparedness: The Origins of Anti-Japanese Resistance in Prewar Hong Kong. *Journal of the Royal Asiatic Society Hong Kong Branch*, Vol. 42, 2002.

Peck, Graham. *Two Kinds of Time*. Boston: Houghton Mifflin Company, 1950; Beijing: Foreign Languages Press, 2004.

Petro, Wladimir. *Triple Commission: An Autobiography*. London: John Murray, 1968.

Poon Fook-wo. 'A Miraculous Charge' in *Young Companion Weekly*, Hong Kong, 17 Feb 1962.

Priestwood, Gwen. *Through Japanese Barbed Wire*. London: Harrap & Co., 1944.

Reynolds, LC and Cooper, HF. *Mediterranean MTBs at War*. Stroud: Sutton in association with the Imperial War Museum, 1999.

Ride, Edwin. *BAAG: Hong Kong Resistance 1942–1945*. Hong Kong: Oxford University Press, 1981.

Rosenthal, Jack. *Letters from an Airfield*. Gloucestershire: The History Press, 2009.

Ross, C. E. (Ted). *Escape from Hong Kong*. Article published in Maclean's magazine, Canada, in three parts: June 15, July 1 and July 15, 1942.

Ryan, Thomas F. *Jesuits under Fire in the siege of Hong Kong, 1941*. London & Dublin: Burns Oates & Co., 1944.

Slim, Field Marshal Sir William. *Defeat into Victory*. London: Cassell, 1956.

Smith, James and Downes, William. The Maryknoll Mission, Hong Kong 1941–46. *Journal of the Royal Asiatic Society Hong Kong Branch*, Vol. 19, 1979.

Snow, Philip. *The Fall of Hong Kong: Britain, China and the Japanese Occupation*. New Haven and London: Yale University Press, 2004.

Stericker, John. *A Tear for the Dragon*. London: Arthur Barker Ltd, 1958.

Stewart, Major Evan. *A Record of the Actions of the Hong Kong Volunteer Defence Corps*. Hong Kong: Ye Olde Printerie, Ltd., 1953. (Republished as *Hong Kong Volunteers in Battle*, Blacksmith Books, 2004.)

Tan, Pei-ying. *The Building of the Burma Road*. New York, London: McGraw-Hill, 1945.

Tsang, Steve Yui-Sang. *Democracy Shelved*. With a foreword by David M. MacDougall. Hong Kong: Oxford: Oxford University Press, 1987.

———— *A Modern History of Hong Kong*. London; New York: IB Tauris, 2004.

Wakeman, Frederic, Jr. *Spymaster: Dai Li and the Chinese Secret Service*. Berkeley: University of California Press, 2003.

Ward, Iain. *Sui Geng: The Hong Kong Marine Police 1841–1950*. Hong Kong: Hong Kong University Press, 1991.

Waters, Dan and McEwan, Alison (eds). Colin McEwan's Diary: The Battle for Hong Kong and Escape into China. *Journal of the Royal Asiatic Society Hong Kong Branch*, Vol. 45, 2005.

Whitehead, John S. and Bennett, George B. *Escape to Fight On With 204 Military Mission in China*. London: Robert Hale, 1990.

Wong, Marjorie. *The Dragon and the Maple Leaf: Chinese Canadians in World War II*. London Ontario: Pirie, 1994.

Woodburn Kirby, S. *The War Against Japan*, Vol. 1. London: HMSO, 1957.

Wright-Nooth, George. *Prisoner of the Turnip Heads: Horror, Hunger and Humour in Hong Kong*. London: Leo Cooper, 1994.

Yu Maochun. *The Dragon's War: Allied Operations and Fate of China 1937–1947*. Annapolis, Maryland: Naval Institute Press, 2006.

Websites

Tony Banham, *Hong Kong War Diary*. http://www.hongkongwardiary.com/

Richard Hide, *Hong Kong Escape*. http://www.hongkongescape.org/Escape_09.htm

Emma Oxford, *Destination Chungking*. http://destinationchongqing.blogspot.com

Paul Tsui Ka-cheung, *My Life and My Encounters*. http://www.galaxylink.net/~john/paul/paul.html

World War Two Unit Histories http://www.unithistories.com/

Index

*Note: Page references in **bold** indicate illustrations. Where appropriate, sub-headings are in chronological order rather than alphabetical order.*

2009 Waichow Re-enactment. Fifteen families represented: Chan, Ross, MacDougall, Hide, Oxford, Thums, Barker, McEwan, Collingwood, Kennedy, Legge, Owen-Hughes, Macmillan, Thorpe, Yeung.